Hedging the
China Threat

Hedging the China Threat

US-Taiwan Security Relations Since 1949

Shao-cheng Sun

LYNNE
RIENNER
PUBLISHERS

BOULDER
LONDON

Published in the United States of America in 2024 by
Lynne Rienner Publishers, Inc.
1800 30th Street, Suite 314, Boulder, Colorado 80301
www.rienner.com

and in the United Kingdom by
Lynne Rienner Publishers, Inc.
1 Bedford Row, London WC1R 4BU
www.eurospanbookstore.com/rienner

© 2024 by Lynne Rienner Publishers, Inc. All rights reserved

Library of Congress Cataloging-in-Publication Data
Names: Sun, Shao-cheng, 1966– author.
Title: Hedging the China threat : US-Taiwan security relations since 1949
   / Shao-cheng Sun.
Description: Boulder, Colorado : Lynne Rienner Publishers, Inc., 2024. |
   Includes bibliographical references and index. | Summary: "Explores the
   history of US commitments to Taiwan (the Republic of China) and the
   evolution of the complicated US-Taiwan-China relationship since the
   presidency of Harry S. Truman"— Provided by publisher.
Identifiers: LCCN 2024005336 (print) | LCCN 2024005337 (ebook) | ISBN
   9781685859961 (hardcover) | ISBN 9781962551151 (ebook)
Subjects: LCSH: United States—Foreign relations—Taiwan. | Taiwan—Foreign
   relations—United States. | United States—Foreign relations—China. |
   China—Foreign relations—United States. | Taiwan Strait—Strategic
   aspects.
Classification: LCC E183.8.T3 S86 2024 (print) | LCC E183.8.T3 (ebook) |
   DDC 327.73051249—dc23/eng/20240313
LC record available at https://lccn.loc.gov/2024005336
LC ebook record available at https://lccn.loc.gov/2024005337

British Cataloguing in Publication Data
A Cataloguing in Publication record for this book
is available from the British Library.

Printed and bound in the United States of America

 The paper used in this publication meets the requirements
of the American National Standard for Permanence of
Paper for Printed Library Materials Z39.48-1992.

5 4 3 2 1

Contents

1	China, Taiwan, and the United States	1
2	Early Commitments to Taiwan: The Truman Administration	25
3	The Offshore Islands Crises: The Eisenhower Administration	41
4	Maintaining the Status Quo: The Kennedy Administration	63
5	The PRC Nuclear Test and the Vietnam War: The Johnson Administration	85
6	The Opening of China: The Nixon Administration	105
7	Moving Slowly Toward Normalization: The Ford Administration	125
8	Establishing Diplomatic Relations with China: The Carter Administration	143
9	Arms Sales Disputes and Reassurances: The Reagan Administration	171
10	Dealing with the Tiananmen Square Crisis: The George H. W. Bush Administration	193
11	The 1995–1996 Taiwan Strait Crisis: The Clinton Administration	215
12	From Strategic Competitor to Strategic Partner: The George W. Bush Administration	237

vi   *Contents*

13 Seeking a Rebalanced Policy: The Obama Administration   257

14 Confronting a More Assertive China: 277
       The Trump Administration

15 The Taiwan Strait Crisis of 2022–2023:   299
       The Biden Administration

16 The Future of US-China-Taiwan Relations   323

List of Acronyms   341
Bibliography   345
Index   367
About the Book   373

1

China, Taiwan, and the United States

THE RELATIONSHIP BETWEEN CHINA AND TAIWAN, KNOWN AS "CROSS-STRAIT relations," is one of the most highly controversial and important topics in world politics today. It is also the central flash point in US-China relations. In May 2021, *The Economist* labeled Taiwan "the most dangerous place on Earth." If China were to attack Taiwan, it is expected that the United States would intervene in the cross-strait military conflict. It is likely that such an intervention would result in a major war between the two superpowers.[1] Because of US alliances with other powerful countries, it is easy to imagine that such a conflict could conceivably escalate into a world war.

American philosopher George Santayana said, "Those who cannot remember the past are condemned to repeat it."[2] An in-depth study of the security relations between the United States and Taiwan (formally known as the Republic of China, or ROC) would be in vain without a close examination of their historical background. China (formally known as the People's Republic of China, or PRC)[3] has never dropped its claim that it has the right to use force against Taiwan in realizing its goal of reunification. Because of China's continued threats, Taiwan has modernized its military capability and enhanced its security relations with the United States

The goals of this book are twofold. First, it describes the inside story of the US security relationship with Taiwan, a country under China's threat since the Harry S. Truman administration. By reviewing the most important events and crises involving these three countries, the book explains how the US government has assisted Taiwan in responding to this threat since 1949. Second, the book systemically examines the US government's security policy toward Taiwan from the Harry S. Truman to the Joe Biden administration across three levels of analysis. The individual level examines the

2 Hedging the China Threat

beliefs, philosophies, and worldviews of different US presidents in determining cross-strait policy. The state level introduces cross-strait policy decisions and changes by the US National Security Council, the US State Department, and the US military. The international level looks at the impact of the changing international politics and security concerns on US cross-strait policy.

China and Taiwan: A Brief History

When I was in middle school and high school in Taiwan during the 1980s, the media, politicians, and history teachers taught us that cross-strait relations were like "siblings" and that "blood is thicker than water." At the time, most Taiwanese students were proud of being Chinese because we had 5,000 years of history and culture as well as the world's largest population. Taiwanese were told that "Taiwan is a part of China." Today, however, most youth are taught that "Taiwan has nothing to do with China." As I explored this subject more deeply, I discovered that cross-strait relations were far more complicated than I had imagined.

To understand the current cross-strait tensions, it is important to begin with a broad overview of their history. As early as the seventh century, Chinese merchants and fishermen visited Taiwan; however, most historians who study Taiwan and China relations begin with the seventeenth century.

Before 1949: Exploring Taiwan

Prior to 1949, Taiwan experienced many influences from both Western powers and Chinese governments. In the early seventeenth century, the Dutch East India Company established a trading base in Taiwan. In the early 1660s, fleeing from the Qing conquest of the Ming dynasty (1368–1644 CE), Ming loyalists led by Zheng Cheng-gong drove out the Dutch from Taiwan.[4] With a labor force of both Chinese immigrants and Indigenous people, Taiwan gradually became an important trading center. Merging trade with military capability, Zheng's regime was able to rule Taiwan for two decades.[5] Zheng was highly regarded and even viewed as a deity in Taiwan. Several temples, as well as the National Cheng Kung University, were built to remember his contributions.

In 1683, the Qing dynasty (1644–1912 CE) launched a naval invasion against Zheng's regime and reestablished control of Taiwan. After the conquest, the emperor of Qing was unconvinced of Taiwan's strategic value. But Admiral Shi Lang, who had directed the invasion, argued that due to its geostrategic location and natural resources, China should maintain control.[6] He recognized that if Taiwan was occupied by foreign powers, it would pose a grave threat to China's security. Shi's advice prevailed. In 1684, Taiwan was formally included within the territory of the Qing dynasty.

In the first Opium War of 1839, British forces attacked China and ushered in the "Century of Humiliation" for the Chinese people. The Opium War marked the beginning of a century of military defeats, unequal treaties, and territorial concessions for the Chinese. After the end of that terrible century, China resolved that it must never let history repeat itself.[7] Taiwan was also affected by the Opium War. The treaty signed by the defeated Qing government and the victorious British Empire required Taiwan to open its harbors to British opium dealers. The United States and Russia also demanded the opening of ports to trade and foreign residents. As Taiwan's economic importance increased, the Japanese Empire began to covet Taiwan. The threat to China's sovereignty pushed the Qing government to launch the Self-Strengthening Movement (1865–1895) in Taiwan by developing basic infrastructure, agriculture, industry, commerce, and education. Several leaders spearheaded the movement, the most renowned of which was Liu Mingchuan. Liu advocated modernization strategies, including the revival of modern coal mining, and the establishment of a railway line, cable, and telegraphic infrastructure.[8] His contribution to the Taiwanese people was profound. In commemoration of his achievements, Mingchuan University in Taipei, Taiwan's capital, was named after him.

When Japanese imperial forces defeated the Qing military in 1895, the Qing government ceded the islands of Taiwan and Penghu to Japan in the Shimonoseki Treaty.[9] Chinese elites viewed the loss of Taiwan as a national humiliation. A local resistance movement in Taiwan rose to fight against Japanese rule. Despite their brave armed resistance, the Qing forces were defeated. After the Japanese takeover, Japan exploited Taiwan's natural resources and agricultural output.[10] The imperial Japanese ruled Taiwan with an iron fist and treated the Taiwanese people as second-class citizens.

After Japan's defeat in World War II, Taiwan was returned to the Republic of China. While the ROC forces fought against Chinese Communists during the Chinese Civil War (from 1945 to 1949), the ROC government was not able to control mainlanders who arrived in Taiwan. Because some mainlanders thought they were superior to the Taiwanese, tensions emerged. The conflict erupted on February 28, 1947, when a quarrel between a cigarette vendor and a government official ignited a widespread riot. The ROC government sent forces from China to put down the uprising.[11] The impact of this incident had far-reaching effects. Relations were so bad that intermarriage between mainlanders and Taiwanese was discouraged by some Taiwanese parents.

4   Hedging the China Threat

Chiang Kai-shek Administration (1950–1975):
The Military Confrontation

From 1943 to 1948, Chiang Kai-shek was chairman of the National Government of China, based in mainland China. In 1949, when his defeated forces were forced to retreat from mainland China to Taiwan, Chiang Kai-shek established an authoritarian government there and vowed to retake China. When I was in elementary school, we learned to sing patriotic songs like "Retaking Mainland China." Patriotic education was common in all sectors of Taiwan's society. Chiang Kai-shek was determined to retake China to rebuild his tarnished image after his loss of mainland China.

During the Cold War, hostility across the Taiwan Strait became a flash point throughout East Asia. In the 1950s, when the ROC government recognized that it had lost control of mainland China, it deployed troops to the offshore islands. This caused cross-strait tensions that led to military conflict. The ROC leaders viewed these islands as a launching pad for their forces to retake China.[12] In 1951, the US military began to equip and train the ROC military.[13] In 1954, the United States and Taiwan signed a Mutual Defense Treaty. The People's Republic of China viewed this treaty as collusion between the United States and Taiwan and a threat to its national security. The Mutual Defense Treaty precipitated what came to be called the "First Taiwan Strait Crisis." The PRC began to bombard the island of Quemoy, and soon expanded its targets to the Matsu Islands and the Dachen Islands. The Chinese bombardment aimed to stop the defense treaty as Beijing worried about the separation between China and Taiwan. To assert its support of Taiwan, in January 1955 the US Congress passed the Formosa Resolution, which gave the US president authority to defend Taiwan and the offshore islands. In exchange for a private promise from the United States to defend Quemoy and Matsu, Chiang Kai-shek agreed to withdraw his troops from the Dachens.[14] To avoid the offshore islands crisis from escalating, both Washington and Beijing felt a need to maintain communication. The crisis introduced ambassadorial talks in 1955. The dialogues, however, made little progress on the issues of Taiwan.[15]

The Chinese People's Liberation Army (PLA) artillery assault against Quemoy in 1958 was a continuation of the First Taiwan Strait Crisis. Throughout the crisis, Mao Tse-tung was concerned not by the presence of ROC troops on Quemoy, but by the aggressive attitudes of the US government. The PRC Central Military Commission (CMC) forbade combat forces from engaging the US military. Even when US destroyers escorted the ROC's logistical ships, Mao ordered his troops to "only attack Chiang's ships, not U.S. vessels." The United States proposed resuming ambassadorial talks at Warsaw in 1955. The PRC leaders agreed, deciding to shift their policy from a military confrontation to a diplomatic approach and, through the Warsaw talks, to create a wedge between Taipei and Washington.[16]

The 1958 Quemoy Crisis prompted US leaders to reassess Quemoy's military value and put pressure on Chiang Kai-shek's administration to reduce the ROC forces stationed on the islands. This resulted in tension between Taipei and Washington. Later, the PRC and ROC came to an arrangement in which they shelled each other's garrisons on alternate days. This continued for twenty years until the PRC and the United States normalized relations in 1979.[17]

Chiang Ching-kuo Administration (1972–1988): Thawing Relations

President Chiang Ching-kuo, the son of Chiang Kai-shek, was the driving force behind Taiwan's modernization and democracy. He initiated the "Ten Major Construction Projects" that led to over 10 percent economic growth for Taiwan and the world's second-largest foreign exchange reserves. Under his leadership, Taiwan's successful economic performance was labeled the "Taiwan Miracle." By 1971, Taiwan's economic edge could compete against China on the international front even after Taiwan was expelled from the United Nations and replaced by the PRC. However, when China's top leader, Deng Xiaoping, launched "reform and opening up" in 1978, Chiang Ching-kuo decided to move toward becoming a democratic country to confront China's authoritarian regime.[18] Chiang Ching-kuo understood that if Taiwan moved toward democracy, it would garner US support.[19]

Mao's policy toward Taiwan sought to achieve unification by force; whereas Deng changed the PRC's Taiwan policy in the hope that it would bring about a peaceful unification. When the United States shifted diplomatic recognition from Taiwan to China in 1979, Deng felt confident that his government had an advantage in convincing Taiwan to engage in dialogue. On January 1, 1979, the National People's Congress (NPC) of the PRC called for a peaceful unification with Taiwan. In 1981, Ye Jianying, chairman of the NPC, proposed several initiatives: party-to-party talks, postal communication, commercial exchanges, and maritime shipping with Taiwan.[20] In 1982, Beijing introduced the "One Country, Two Systems" policy for Hong Kong and Macau, with the suggestion that this could also be applied to Taiwan under peaceful reunification.[21] Chiang Ching-kuo responded with "Three No's": no contact, no negotiation, and no compromise.

In 1986, the China Airlines incident, however, "untied the knot" of the cross-strait stalemate. When a Taiwanese pilot hijacked a cargo airplane and landed in China, Chiang Ching-kuo's administration had no choice but to engage in dialogue with its counterparts. Consequently, officially appointed representatives from both sides met in Hong Kong.[22] Having been away from mainland China for almost forty years, many China-born veterans in Taiwan pressed Chiang Ching-kuo's government to allow family reunions. Consequently, the president began to soften his China policy

6 Hedging the China Threat

and decided to open links with the PRC, allowing Taiwanese citizens to visit relatives on the mainland.[23] My father was one of them. When he returned to his hometown, my father was warmly welcomed by his family members, relatives, and even local officials. It was a momentous period for thawing relations. The Chinese government also highlighted the family reunions as proof of the saying that "blood is thicker than water." This has been a common strategy in its propaganda to promote unification.

Lee Teng-hui Administration: Rising Tension

Taiwanese president Lee Teng-hui proposed "One Country, Two Governments" (or "one Chinese culture, two independent governments") and pursued pragmatic diplomacy. On one hand, Lee's administration recognized the division of China and renounced the use of force against China. On the other hand, Lee actively sought opportunities to join international organizations. Beijing was suspicious of Lee's intentions. To send an olive branch to China, President Lee established a National Unification Council in 1990 and announced the Guidelines for National Unification, which proposed three phases that were intended to lead to eventual reunification: a short-term phase of exchanges and reciprocity, a medium-term phase of mutual trust and cooperation, and a long-term phase of consultation and unification.[24] Negotiations were held between Taiwan's Straits Exchange Foundation (SEF) and its Chinese counterpart, the Association for Relations Across the Taiwan Strait (ARATS).

The 1992 Consensus was an agreement by negotiators who found a way to sidestep Beijing's long-standing precondition that, before talks could begin, both sides had to declare that there is only one China. These negotiators decided to agree to disagree, in that each side had a different interpretation of what "China" was: for the Taiwan delegates "China" meant the Republic of China, but the Chinese delegates had in their minds that "China" was clearly the People's Republic of China.[25] For the PRC, the two sides belonged to one China and needed to work together to seek national reunification. For the ROC, "One China" had a different interpretation with the ROC representing One China. Thanks to the 1992 Consensus, representatives of China and Taiwan later had a productive meeting in Singapore. In 1995, President Lee accepted an invitation to speak at his alma mater, Cornell University. At first, the US State Department refused to issue Lee a visa because of Taiwan's unofficial relationship with the United States. The US Congress, however, passed a resolution and pushed the State Department to give a green light to Lee's visit. Beijing believed that President Lee had no interest in unification talks, but was attempting to lead Taiwan into becoming an independent country.[26] In March 1996, Taiwan conducted its first presidential election. As a result, the PLA launched military exercises and missile tests in the Taiwan Strait. The Chinese unification strategy had shifted from emphasizing a peaceful stimulus to using a carrot-and-stick strategy. In response, the Bill Clinton administration sent two carrier battle groups to the waters near Taiwan to deter the crisis from further escalating.[27]

In July 1999, President Lee defined *cross-strait relations* as "two countries." Lee also noted that there was no need for Taiwan to declare independence again since the ROC had established an independent country in 1912.[28] After Lee's announcement of the "two states" theory, the PRC government issued a white paper titled "The One China Principle and the Taiwan Issue." The white paper said that the ROC's position as the sole legal government was terminated in 1949, and the PRC assumed that role, giving it the right to exercise sovereignty over all of China, including Taiwan.[29]

Chen Shui-bian Administration: A Tumultuous Period

In the 1990s, China's cross-strait policy focused on economically integrating Taiwan, internationally isolating Taiwan, and blocking the movement toward Taiwan's bid for formal independence. Since 2000, China's definition of the "One China" policy regarding Taiwan had become flexible with a trend of moving toward equality. For example, the interpretation of "one China" had moved from "Taiwan is a part of China" to "both Taiwan and the mainland are a part of China." Beijing was attempting to make it easier for Taiwanese to accept the One China principle.[30]

When Chen Shui-bian won Taiwan's presidential election in 2000, China was concerned about Chen's stance on Taiwan's independence.[31] The PRC assumed that Chen would basically continue Lee's separatist policy and, although Chen's China policy would be neither reunification nor independence, Chen would deviate from the ROC government's long-term goal of ultimate reunification with China. Eventually, the independence movement would gradually erase the bilateral cultural ties. PRC president Jiang Zemin responded that Chen was welcome to come to China for dialogues and vice versa, but Chen must first recognize the "One China principle." In his inauguration speech, Chen announced the "Five Nots"; namely, not to declare independence, not to change the national title, not to push for the inclusion of the "two states" description in the constitution, not to promote a referendum to change the status quo on the question of independence or unification, and not to abolish the National Unification Council and the Guidelines for National Unification.[32]

In 2001, President Chen authorized three "mini-links" between Quemoy and Matsu and mainland China. His intention was to express goodwill to Beijing and pave the way for future economic cooperation; nevertheless, Beijing did not respond positively to Chen's initiatives. Beijing refused to

8   Hedging the China Threat

return to the negotiating table until Taipei accepted the One China principle. To encourage Taiwan to acknowledge One China, PRC vice premier Qian Qichen proposed a new One China position. He reiterated that both the mainland and Taiwan belong to one China. Qian argued that this position was more pragmatic and inclusive than previous formulations, but Taipei dismissed the statements as nothing new.[33]

In 2004, the reelection of Chen encouraged supporters of Taiwan's independence. They thought it was time for Taiwan to move toward independence. Chinese leaders perceived that the rising Taiwan identity was causing a threat to its national security. In March 2005, the National People's Congress of the PRC passed the Anti-Secession Law. In this new law, Article 8 stated that the PRC would use nonpeaceful means against the separation of Taiwan from China. The law aimed to coerce the Taiwan independence movement by threatening the use of force, if the PRC deemed Taiwan had crossed the redline. The Chen administration strongly condemned the PRC's aggressive stance.

I served as an intelligence analyst in the ROC Ministry of National Defense from 1998 to 2008, during which time President Lee and President Chen were in office. I found that whenever China increased its military activities, such as when warplanes crossed the middle line of the Taiwan Strait, these actions were usually directly related to political issues. The Chinese government was using military pressure to send a signal to Taiwan and the United States that it would not hesitate to use military force if Taiwan drifted away from the One China policy.

Ma Ying-jeou Administration: A Period of Reconciliation

After eight tumultuous years of the Chen administration, tensions diminished during the next administration. During the 2008 presidential election campaign, candidate Ma Ying-jeou stated that he would abide by a Three No's approach (no unification with the PRC, no declaration of indipendence, and no use of force) with China.[34] After he was elected, under the 1992 Consensus negotiations between the Straits Exchange Foundation and the Association for Relations Across the Taiwan Strait resumed. The two semiofficial organizations agreed to focus on the economy first, and to set politics aside. They produced agreements on a wide range of functional and economic issues.[35]

Normalization with China became a top priority for President Ma. His administration believed that improved cross-strait relations not only would strengthen Taiwan's security, but also would increase economic trade with China.[36] Ma's goodwill gesture received a positive response from his Chinese counterpart, Hu Jintao. President Hu stated that China was willing to resume a dialogue with Taiwan under the 1992 Consensus.[37] Ma's policy generated economic benefits for both sides. As of 2024, Taiwan has now become China's largest trading partner and more than 1 million Taiwan compatriots live and work in mainland China. Ma's China policy also has unleashed a surge of commerce and tourism.[38]

The Ma administration has sought to integrate Taiwan into a global economic system through closer economic engagement with China. A key example is the signing of the Cross-Strait Economic Cooperation Framework Agreement in 2010.[39] Ma, however, did face pressure from the Taiwanese people, who strongly disapproved of his cooperation with Beijing. This opposition culminated in the 2014 Sunflower Movement when student activists occupied the Legislative Yuan (Congress) in protest of a free service trade agreement.[40]

In 2015, a summit took place in Singapore between Ma Ying-jeou and Xi Jinping, to develop further peaceful relations and economic cooperation. During the summit, Ma expressed the following concerns with Xi: the needs to resolve disputes peacefully, to diminish China's growing military threat, and to participate in regional economic integration. Xi responded to each of Ma's requests in noncommittal ways. The only practical result of the meeting was a commitment to establish a hotline between the two governments.[41]

The Ma administration adopted policies that would capitalize on opportunities for cooperation with China. First, Taiwan would help to stabilize cross-strait relations by expanding economic engagement with China, including an expansion of Taiwan's bilateral and multilateral free-trade agreements (FTAs). Second, Taipei would continue accommodating Beijing as part of its hedging strategy. The Ma administration moderated its diplomatic activities in compliance with Beijing's One China principle, despite criticism from the opposition.[42] Some Taiwanese people accused Ma of going too far with his policies and were afraid that China would perceive Ma as being a weak leader. This perception could develop into military action to invade Taiwan.

Tense Current Relations Between China and Taiwan

After winning Taiwan's 2016 presidential election, Democratic Progressive Party (DPP) candidate Tsai Ing-wen refused to accept the 1992 Consensus. Public opinion in Taiwan seems to be moving in her direction. Since 2020, Chinese leaders have appeared to believe that increasing its military threats is the most effective means of preventing Taiwan from moving toward independence. I believe that there are several reasons for their aggressiveness. First, with Hong Kong and Macau handed over to China, Taiwan is China's last lost territory that must be subdued to recreate a unified nation. Second, the relationship of Taiwan and the United States poses a serious threat to Chinese security. Tsai's administration has greatly improved its relations with the United States, clearly evident by increased visits of high-ranking

10   Hedging the China Threat

US officials, arms sales, and military cooperation. Third, the PLA's capability has greatly improved. The rapid military buildup and modernization have boosted China's confidence. China feels that it is in a good strategic position to take Taiwan by force and to resist US intervention.[43]

China's coercive responses. President Xi has been taking increasingly aggressive actions in response to the rise of the Taiwan independence movement, and deteriorating US-China relations. According to the PRC Anti-Secession Law, China is justified in the use of force if Taiwan were to declare its independence or if it were to indefinitely delay cross-strait dialogue on unification.[44]

On September 21, 2020, after PLA warplanes flew over the Taiwan Strait, PRC Foreign Ministry spokesman Wang Wenbin denied the existence of a median line in the Taiwan Strait, claiming that there is no such thing as a "median line" in the Taiwan Strait. The PLA ramped up this rhetoric when Defense Ministry spokesman Ren Guoqiang told reporters that, regarding the Taiwan issue, "Those who play with fire are bound to get burned."[45]

Since 2020, China has been conducting a show of force in the Taiwan Strait with increased air patrols around Taiwan. It is obvious that the purpose of these exercises has been to test Taiwan's response time in preparation for a future military invasion.[46] According to the US Department of Defense 2020 report *Military and Security Developments Involving the People's Republic of China,* the PLA could initiate the following options at any time: an air and maritime blockade, a limited force of coercive options, an air and missile campaign, or a military invasion of Taiwan.[47]

It is likely that if China were to attack Taiwan, it would be a full invasion. China's state broadcaster, CCTV, warned that "the first battle would be the last battle." Prior to a military invasion, the PLA would likely utilize cyber and electronic forces to target Taiwan's key infrastructure. Airstrikes would target Taiwan's top leaders in a decapitation attack, and an invasion would follow with PLA warships and submarines traversing the Taiwan Strait.[48]

In the face of the mounting threat from China, the ROC military has said its armed forces have the right to self-defense and counterattack amid "harassment and threats." Taiwan originally vowed to follow a guideline of no escalation of conflict and no triggering incidents,[49] but recently Taiwan has been taking steps to prepare for future military conflict. It will enhance its electronic warfare, shore-based mobile missiles, fast minelaying, minesweeping, and drones.[50]

In August 2022, House Speaker Nancy Pelosi visited Taipei, enraging Chinese leaders who viewed the move as a violation of China's internal affairs. As a result, China conducted serval large-scale military exercises, which ushered in the 2022 Taiwan Strait Crisis.[51] In response, President

Biden sent a clear message to Beijing that the United States would defend Taiwan should the PLA attempt an invasion.

In late March and early April 2023, enroute to a state visit in South America, President Tsai transited through the United States and met with House Speaker Kevin McCarthy. From April 8 to 10, China conducted military drills in response. Beijing stated that the exercises were a serious warning to the Taiwan independence separatist forces and external conspirators.[52]

Reasons for the rising tensions. According to China's Taiwan Affairs Office, the reason for the rise in tensions was Tsai's refusal to accept the One China principle and her continuing collusion with the US government.[53]

China has observed that the ROC government has moved toward de-Sinicization (a process of reducing Chinese culture identity) by removing Chinese history from Taiwanese textbooks and portraying the PRC as an enemy. It thinks that if the trend does not cease, the Tsai administration will eventually move toward de jure independence. The Chinese media also have accused her administration of promoting de-Sinicization, claiming that Taiwan has moved toward the path of separatism by severing its connection with China and allying itself with the United States.

The percentage of ROC citizens who identify as Taiwanese is on the rise, according to a 2023 survey conducted by the National Chengchi University. Only 2.7 percent of participants said they self-identified as Chinese, compared to 60.8 percent as Taiwanese, and 30.5 percent identified as both Chinese and Taiwanese.[54] Because mainlanders who arrived in Taiwan in the late 1940s have passed away and the DPP government has promoted Taiwanese identity, PRC authorities have become frustrated by the trend of a rising Taiwanese identity and a continuing drift away from the Chinese identity.

The PRC has increased its diplomatic pressure on Taiwan, discouraging Taiwan's efforts to participate in any intergovernmental organizations.[55] In 2024, only twelve countries recognized Taiwan as a sovereign state, due to the rise of China's international influence and its buying of Taiwan diplomatic allies. Most of the intergovernmental organizations bar Taiwan's participation at China's behest. Taiwan is seeking strategies to reverse this problem. During the coronavirus pandemic, Taiwan donated millions of masks and medical supplies to its thirteen diplomatic allies and to other friendly countries around the world, including the United States. Both Taiwan's medical diplomacy and its exemplary handling of Covid-19 garnered positive coverage in the international press. In contrast, China's international image has suffered due to its intervention in Hong Kong, its culpability in the spread of coronavirus worldwide, and its aggressive territorial expansion in the South China Sea.[56] Taiwan's active pursuit of international recognition has been criticized by the Chinese government as an attempt to disrupt the status quo of cross-strait relations.

12 Hedging the China Threat

Beijing has perceived Taiwan's de-Sinicization, international recognition seeking, and US support as threats to its fundamental goals. Beijing has employed a host of methods in response, including coercive rhetoric, aggressive diplomacy, and belligerent military posturing against the Tsai administration.

US Security Relations with Taiwan

Over the past seven decades, the US government has played a crucial role in hedging China's threat in the Taiwan Strait. Without US assistance, Taiwan already would have been occupied by a PRC military invasion. A key element of US security commitments to Taiwan has been the prevention of any Chinese military invasion. To understand US obligations in a peaceful resolution of the Taiwan issue is to consider how those interests might be harmed if China attacked Taiwan. The impact on US interests would include the following: first, a cross-strait military conflict would draw the United States into an armed confrontation with China. Second, US trade interests in East Asia would be greatly affected.[57]

During the Cold War

Most observers expected Chiang Kai-shek's government to eventually fall in response to a Communist invasion of Taiwan, and the United States initially showed no interest in supporting him in his final stand. Things changed with the onset of the Korean War in June 1950. At this point, allowing a total Communist victory over Chiang Kai-shek became politically unacceptable for the United States, and President Truman ordered the Seventh Fleet into the Taiwan Strait to prevent the ROC and PRC from attacking each other.[58]

The PRC attempted to achieve its political objectives through military aggression during the Cold War. In response, US intervention, either by diplomatic or military means, successfully de-escalated the tensions. At the time, the United States and Taiwan security relationship was robust because both countries were allies, grounded on the 1954 US-ROC Mutual Defense Treaty. From the time of the outbreak of the Korean War in 1950 until the late 1960s, the United States considered Taiwan to be an important link in the strategy to contain Chinese Communists. However, the relative importance of Taiwan to the United States declined throughout the 1970s and 1980s as the United States attached higher priority to a better relationship with China to counter the rising threat of the Soviet Union.

The perceptions of the US top leaders on the balance of power in Asia and the cross-strait relations played a central role in determining their Taiwan policy. After Richard Nixon assumed the presidency, he and his national security advisor, Henry Kissinger, sought a rapprochement with China because of US-Soviet tension. In 1978, the worsening crises in Afghanistan made Washington and Beijing more flexible on the terms under which normal relations would be established.[59] In 1979, the Jimmy Carter administration established diplomatic relations with the PRC, ended formal diplomatic recognition of the ROC, and terminated the Mutual Defense Treaty. From the perception of US national interests, it is easy to understand why Kissinger said, "America has no permanent friends or enemies, only interests."

In 1979, the US government enacted the Taiwan Relations Act (TRA), which has become the US foreign policy guide for its unofficial relations with the Taiwanese government. The TRA states that the United States would maintain the capability to resist any force or action that would imperil the security of Taiwan.[60]

During the period to 1992, which included the Ronald Reagan and George H. W. Bush administrations, the United States sought to preserve its interests through a balanced "dual track" policy of maintaining friendly official ties with China and friendly unofficial ties with Taiwan. During the latter half of the 1980s, internal developments in China and Taiwan and changes in the international system began to have a negative impact on US interests in Taiwan. The Tiananmen Square incident in 1989 was a major setback to US-China relations. The United States condemned the brutality of the Beijing regime and imposed an arms embargo on China. After the incident, the United States developed a closer relationship with Taiwan.

After the Cold War

At the end of the Cold War, China lost its strategic value to the United States. However, since 1990 the "China threat theory" has become a popular topic in academic circles, as China's economic growth at the end of the twentieth century was unprecedented. China's emergence as an economic and military power has been interpreted by some as a threat to the United States on issues such as Taiwan.[61] In this study, however, I focus on the security threat posed by China against Taiwan. In response to China's growing security threat, the United States has been more willing to provide military assistance to Taiwan than previously. The US security assistance to Taiwan has given the United States an advantage and a bargaining chip in its dealings with both Taiwan and China.

Cross-strait relations have also played an important role in influencing the US security commitment to Taiwan.[62] Prior to the 1990s, Taiwan had been committed to eventual unification with China, based on the ROC constitution and patriotic education. In 1990, President Lee promoted Taiwan's identity to

14   Hedging the China Threat

achieve international recognition. Consequently, Taiwan shifted away from its commitment to the One China policy toward a separate political identity for Taiwan. The impact of Lee's 1995 visit to the United States and the United States' dispatch of naval forces to the Taiwan area led to a low ebb in US-China relations. The United States' intervention in the 1995–1996 Taiwan Strait Crisis succeeded in deterring China's military aggression.

The pillar of US policy in cross-strait relations is China's nonuse of force and Taiwan's not declaring its independence. However, the PLA is preparing for war against Taiwan by acquiring advanced weapon systems and performing frequent military exercises. The United States opposes any changes in the status quo in the Taiwan Strait made by either side. The United States has been bolstering its military capability in East Asia. If China were to launch an assault, the United States would likely respond with strong political rhetoric, economic sanctions, diplomatic mediation, and military intervention to deter China. Consequently, since 2020, the relations between the United States and China have become tense. The US government has taken a more assertive approach to dissuade China's coercion.

Strategic Ambiguity or Strategic Clarity?

It is currently unclear as to whether the United States would defend Taiwan in case of an attack by China. Since the Carter administration terminated the defense treaty with Taiwan in 1980, Washington has intentionally abided by a policy of strategic ambiguity to govern its cross-strait relations. US strategic planners believe that ambiguity can confine any unilateral decisions by either China or Taiwan. First, it can prevent a declaration of independence from Taiwan on the assumption that the United States will come to defend the island if China attacks. Second, it allows the United States to conceal its intention of whether it will come to defend Taiwan or not. Thus, Beijing will be reluctant to use force against Taiwan because it does not know how the United States will respond to a cross-strait crisis. This strategy acts as a deterrence, restricting China and Taiwan from escalating the tension.[63]

However, the downside of strategic ambiguity is that Washington is not able to send a clear and consistent message of deterrence to leaders in Beijing. Most Chinese people think that if a military conflict were to occur across the Taiwan Strait, the chances that the United States would deploy military forces to defend Taiwan are slim. This perception has encouraged Beijing to become more aggressive. Thus, some US scholars and strategists have advocated for a change of its current policy to one of strategic clarity. These advocates believe that Washington should send a clear message of US military support for Taiwan against any Chinese military action. Richard Haass, former president of the Council on Foreign Relations, supports the advocates of the strategic clarity policy. He has argued that the United States should unequivocally state that it would intervene to deter China to reassure US allies. Commander of the Indo-Pacific Command, Admiral Phil Davidson, stated that "more than 40 years of the strategic ambiguity has helped keep Taiwan in its current status," but that "these things should be reconsidered routinely."[64] After Joe Biden became president, he publicly stated several times that he would defend Taiwan. Biden believes in "peace through strength" and moves toward strategic clarity on Taiwan's defense.

To prevent China from launching a military invasion, the ROC government, in recent years, has encouraged the United States to adopt a policy of strategic clarity, which would go a long way toward making China think twice before launching any military attacks against Taiwan.

Why Taiwan Matters to the United States

With a population of 24 million people, Taiwan is one of the world's most vibrant and democratic countries. The ROC and the United States have had a long and close relationship dating back to World War II. After the defeated nationalist forces retreated to Taiwan, the United States continued to recognize the ROC as the sole legitimate government of China.[65] Sending US aid to the ROC in the 1950s and 1960s helped Taiwan to develop its economy.[66] Although official diplomatic relations ended with the ROC, the United States maintained unofficial, but robust, ties with Taiwan. I was a briefing officer when the US delegations visited the ROC Ministry of Defense from 2000 to 2008. Our Taiwan delegation always emphasized that the ROC government shared many core values with the United States, particularly its mutual dedication to democracy and a market economy. Taiwan is also an important trading and security partner with the United States. The two countries enjoy a multidimensional relationship that serves both of their interests.

Democratic values. With the end of the Cold War, the ROC government underwent a transition, evolving from an authoritarian to a democratic regime. Taiwan's transition to democracy has augmented the US-Taiwan relationship from one based primarily on shared security and financial interests to one based on shared values. Taiwan's successful democratic and economic transformation is an inspiration for other countries in Asia that are still under the rule of authoritarian regimes. As a beacon of democracy, Taiwan serves as a role model for future democracy throughout all of China.[67]

Economic interests. Since 1979, the United States and Taiwan have maintained robust economic ties. In 2020, bilateral trade reached $83.1 billion. Taiwan's imports from the United States amounted to $32.6 billion. Most of the imported products included electronics, precision instruments, information and communication products, and transportation equipment. Taiwan was the United States' ninth-largest trading partner, ahead of much bigger countries like Brazil and India. The United States is Taiwan's second-largest trading partner.[68] Taiwan has been the seventh-largest source of international students in the United States. During the 2021–2022 school year, more than 20,487 students from Taiwan studied at higher education institutions in the United States, contributing over $706 million to the US economy.[69]

Strategic interests. Taiwan is located in the middle of the First Island Chain, which is composed of the Kuril Islands, the Japanese archipelago, the Ryukyu Islands, Taiwan, and the Philippines. During the Cold War, the First Island Chain served as an important frontier to prevent communist expansion. Taiwan's location is critical to Japan and the United States in East Asia.[70] With the end of the Cold War, the United States has insisted on the peaceful resolution of cross-strait differences, opposed unilateral changes to the status quo by either side, and encouraged both sides to engage in constructive dialogue.[71] Since 2013, China has become aggressive in the South China Sea by constructing long-range sensor arrays, port facilities, runways, and reinforced bunkers. The PLA has also increased its military exercises and patrols.[72] Taiwan occupies the biggest island, Taiping Island (known as Itu Aba) in the region. In the face of China's growing military threat in the South China Sea, the US government has enhanced its military cooperation with Taiwan. In March 2021, both governments signed a Coast Guard Cooperation Memorandum of Understanding (MoU) that would create a working group to build cooperation and share information. Taiwan's military has also ramped up training of troops and added defensive weaponry on Taiping Island.[73]

Science and technology cooperation. Taiwan has made efforts to become Asia's "Silicon Valley," and it has achieved a certain degree of success. Some of the most advanced technologies have been developed and manufactured by Taiwanese engineers. Yahoo and YouTube have Taiwanese-born founders. Semiconductor manufacturing companies in Taiwan are responsible for more than half of the global production.[74] Taiwan has advanced up the value chain in manufacturing as an innovator and producer of information technology. The science and technology cooperation between Taiwan and the United States includes areas of high-level research such as nuclear energy, environmental conservation, space science, and biomedical engineering. As of June 2019, there have been over 260 bilateral collaborative agreements and MoUs signed to promote science and technology.[75] In 2023, the Taiwan Semiconductor Manufacturing Company (TSMC) produced 90 percent of the world's most advanced processor chips.[76]

Taiwan matters to the United States because of the countries' shared interests and values. Besides the previously mentioned interests, Taiwan is a longtime friend and loyal democratic ally of the United States. Taiwan stands as a beacon for US policy in East Asia.[77] Taiwan needs the US security umbrella, whereas the United States needs Taiwan to contain China's expansion and access to Taiwan's microchip technology.

Levels of Analysis

When we study international conflicts, we must ask what is happening and why did an event occur.[78] If political scientists can find out what elements influence foreign security policy, it will help us to better understand the decisionmaking process during international crises.[79] Kenneth Waltz categorized the causes of international conflict into three "images." Known as levels of analysis, his categorization distinguishes between international influences, state influences, and individual influences for explaining the causes of conflicts.[80] At the international level are structural features of the international system. At the state level are domestic influences. At the individual level are the characteristics of national leaders. All three levels influence decisions. Overall, the United States' hedging of China's threat was influenced by changes of the international system, policymaking of key political institutions, and decisions of US presidents. This study adopts three levels of analysis to dissect the United States and Taiwan's security relations.

The chaotic nature of the international system is the most important factor at the international level. A country's behavior is shaped by its traditions, common goals, and shared norms.[81] The international level focuses on the states' interactions, states' relative power positions in the international system, and the interactions between them.[82] The distribution of power in the system (e.g., unipolar, bipolar, multipolar) and the nature of order (e.g., balance of power and collective security) are also important factors.[83] From the realists' point of view, international conflict is caused by the clash of interests between states and the absence of an effective international agency for resolving disputes.[84]

The state level concerns the groups of individuals within nations that influence actions of the top leaders. The term *state* refers to the key political institutions responsible for making and implementing important policies in a country.[85] The objective of national security is to sustain freedom from foreign dominance.[86] National security is equal to military security. The aim of a nation's security policy is to enhance the national safety against threats arising from other states.[87] In defense of its national survival, the predominant duty of a nation is to prevent the loss of anything that would threaten its fundamental values.[88] This level concerns those political organizations

18   Hedging the China Threat

and government agencies influencing the US security policy regarding Taiwan. Standard operating procedures (SOPs) in an organization are major determinants of foreign policy behavior. Organizations employ SOPs to respond to a range of events. Bureaucratic politics suggest that agencies compete with one another for control over resources and policy. The result of this competition creates the policy.[89]

The individual level concerns the perceptions, choices, and actions of individuals.[90] When we study international conflict at the microscopic level, human beings are the primary cause of war. Many people believe that war may be anticipated as a natural and recurrent inevitability. War not only has its roots in the hearts and minds of people, but these roots cannot be eradicated.[91] Most leaders are rational and choose a policy that maximizes benefits and minimizes costs, but other factors such as beliefs, personality, and perceptions also influence decisionmaking.[92] Rational leaders are able to differentiate between all of their options, and usually select the higher valued options.[93] This study focuses on how top leaders influence the course of history. The protection of a nation from all types of external aggression, espionage, hostile reconnaissance, sabotage, and subversion is the duty of a nation's leader.[94] Without neglecting the international and state levels of analysis, this study pays special attention to individual-level explanations in the decisionmaking process; specifically, how the presidents perceived the crisis, and how they made their decisions.

The three levels of analysis provide multiple explanations of the triangular relations between the United States, China, and Taiwan. For example, many possible explanations exist as to why the United States and China established diplomatic relations in 1979. At the international level, the relations between the United States and China improved in the 1970s. By working together, both countries could more strongly confront their threatening rival, the Soviet Union. At the state level, key security leaders of the Carter administration such as Secretary of State Cyrus Vance and National Security Advisor Zbigniew Brzezinski wanted to establish diplomatic relations with China. For China, after the devastation of the Cultural Revolution from 1966 to 1976, normalizing relations with the United States could improve China's image in the world. At the individual level, President Carter calculated that improving relations with China could help his poor domestic approval rating. Chinese leaders believed that the establishment of relations with the United States would consolidate their newly established political power.

Organization of the Book

Few publications have touched on US-Taiwan security relations since 1949 when the ROC government retreated to Taiwan.[95] As a result, readers have not been able to grasp the entire background and overall picture of bilateral military relations. This is the main purpose of this book, which is based on historical analysis. Furthermore, I would like to clarify the fact that US security commitments to Taiwan for a peaceful settlement have been backed by every administration since President Truman and that the principal reason the United States has assisted Taiwan in its drive for defense self-sufficiency is that the policy serves many US interests.

The book begins in 1949 because that is when Chiang Kai-shek retreated to Taiwan. From there, we study each US administration to the present. Each chapter is divided into similar sections to allow for comparative study. The historical events section introduces the administration and its policies, and is followed by analysis at the individual, state, and international levels. Chapter 2 ushers in the beginning of US security commitments to Taiwan with the Harry S. Truman administration (1945–1953). Chapter 3 explores the importance of the US-ROC Mutual Defense Treaty to Taiwan's national security during the Dwight Eisenhower administration (1953–1961). Chapter 4 assesses why President John F. Kennedy (1961–1963) thought that any change in the China policy would have been a disaster for his new administration. Chapter 5 explains how PRC nuclear testing and the Vietnam War influenced Taiwan policy during the Lyndon Johnson administration (1963–1969).

Chapter 6, the Richard Nixon administration (1969–1974) and Chapter 7, the Gerald Ford administration (1974–1977), examine the reasons for détente with China and the move toward normalization of the relations, leading to the Jimmy Carter administration (1977–1981) establishing diplomatic relations with China as discussed in Chapter 8. Chapter 9, which covers the Ronald Reagan administration (1981–1989), explains the US arms sales policy and security assurances to Taiwan before looking at how the 1989 Tiananmen Square incident affected US-China relations under the George H. W. Bush administration (1989–1993) in Chapter 10. Under Bill Clinton (1993–2001), the US government dispatched carriers to the Taiwan Strait and the administration focused on the Taiwan missile crisis (Chapter 11). Under the George W. Bush administration (2001–2009), the government moved from a strategic competitor to a strategic partner with China as explained in Chapter 12. Notably, the Barack Obama administration (2009–2017) sought a rebalanced policy toward Asia. Chapter 13 looks at its impact on China policy. A more assertive China then led to rising confrontation during the Donald Trump administration (2017–2021), as discussed in Chapter 14. The Joe Biden administration (2021–) had to deal with the Taiwan Strait Crises of 2022–2023 as discussed in Chapter 15. Chapter 16 concludes the book with a look at the future of US-China-Taiwan relations and suggestions for curbing the cross-strait conflicts.

Notes

1. "The Most Dangerous Place on Earth," *The Economist*, May 1, 2021.
2. George Santayana, *Life of Reason: Introduction and Reason in Common Sense* (New York: Charles Scribner's Sons, 1905), p. 284.
3. Having been born and raised in Taiwan, I use the PRC, China, mainland China, and Beijing interchangeably; I do the same for the ROC, Taiwan, and Taipei.
4. "History," Government of Portal the Republic of China (Taiwan), https://www.taiwan.gov.tw.
5. Emma J. Teng, "Taiwan and Modern China," *Oxford Research Encyclopedias,* May 23, 2019, https://oxfordre.com.
6. Ibid.
7. Michael Zhou, "For China, the History that Matters Is Still the Century of Humiliation," *South China Morning Post,* September 28, 2021.
8. Teng, "Taiwan and Modern China."
9. "History."
10. Teng, "Taiwan and Modern China."
11. Ibid.
12. "The Taiwan Straits Crises: 1954–55 and 1958," US Department of State, https://history.state.gov.
13. Alden Whitman, "The Life of Chiang Kai-shek: A Leader Who Was Thrust Aside by Revolution," *New York Times*, April 6, 1975.
14. "The Taiwan Straits Crises: 1954–55 and 1958."
15. Yafeng Xia, "The Cold War and Chinese Foreign Policy," E-International Relations, July 16, 2008, https://www.e-ir.info.
16. Melvin Gurtov, "The Taiwan Strait Crisis Revisited: Politics and Foreign Policy in Chinese Motives," *Modern China* 2, no. 1 (January 1976): 49–103.
17. "The Taiwan Straits Crises: 1954–55 and 1958."
18. Hengjun Yang, "Chiang Ching-kuo, China's Democratic Pioneer," *The Diplomat,* December 10, 2014.
19. Robert D. Blackwill and Philip Zelikow, *The United States, China, and Taiwan: A Strategy to Prevent War* Council Special Report (Washington, DC: Council on Foreign Relations, 2021), p. 23.
20. Baogang Guo and Chung-Chian Teng, eds., *Taiwan and the Rise of China: Cross-Strait Relations in the Twenty-first Century* (Lanham, MD: Lexington Books, 2012), p. 3.
21. Teng, "Taiwan and Modern China."
22. Guo and Teng, *Taiwan and the Rise of China,* p. 11.
23. Blackwill and Zelikow, *The United States, China, and Taiwan,* p. 23.
24. Gang Lin, "The Changing Relations Across the Taiwan Strait," in *Interpreting U.S.-China-Taiwan Relations: China in the Post–Cold War Era,* edited by Xiaobing Li, Xiabo Hu, and Yang Zhong (Lanham, MD: University Press of America, 2008), p. 135.
25. Dalei Jie, "The Rise and Fall of the Taiwan Independence Policy: Power Shift, Domestic Constraints, and Sovereignty Assertiveness (1988–2010)" (Philadelphia: University of Pennsylvania Dissertations, 2012), p. 7.
26. Weixing Hu, "Chapter 7 Beijing's Military Exercises and the Changing Cross-Strait Relationship," in *Interpreting U.S.-China-Taiwan Relations: China in the Post–Cold War Era,* edited by Xiaobing Li, Xiabo Hu, and Yang Zhong (Lanham, MD: University Press of America, 2008), p. 155.
27. Ibid, p. 158.

28. Sheng Lijun, *China and Taiwan: Cross-Strait Relations Under Chen Shui-bian* (Singapore: Institute of Southeast Asian Studies (ISEAS), 2002), pp. 11−39.

29. Sheng Lijun, "Chen Shui-bian and Cross-Strait Relations," *Contemporary Southeast Asia: A Journal of International and Strategic Affairs* 23, no. 1 (April 2001): 122.

30. Ibid.

31. "What's Behind the China-Taiwan Divide?" BBC, May 26, 2021.

32. Lijun, "Chen Shui-bian and Cross-Strait Relations."

33. Dennis Van Vranken Hickey and Yitan Li, "Cross-Strait Relations in the Aftermath of the Election of Chen Shui-bian," *Asian Affairs: An American Review* 28, no, 4 (2002): 201−216.

34. Dennis Van Vranken Hickey, "Parallel Progress: US-Taiwan Relations During an Era of Cross-Strait Rapprochement," *Journal of Chinese Political Science* 20, no. 4 (December 2015), p. 373.

35. Ibid.

36. "Full Text of President Ma's Inaugural Address," *China Post*, May 21, 2008.

37. "Hu Jinto: The Cross-Strait Resume Dialogue Under the 1992 Consensus," Xinhua, March 26, 2008.

38. Van Vranken Hickey, "Parallel Progress," p. 373.

39. Tse-Kang Leng and Nien-chung Chang Liao, "Hedging, Strategic Partnership, and Taiwan's Relations with Japan Under the Ma Ying-jeou Administration," *Pacific Focus* 31, no. 3 (December 2016): 362.

40. Blackwill and Zelikow, *The United States, China, and Taiwan,* p. 23.

41. Richard Bush, "Order from Chaos: What the Historic Ma-Xi Meeting Could Mean for Cross-Strait Relations," Brookings Institution, November 9, 2015, https://www.brookings.edu.

42. Leng and Liao, "Hedging, Strategic Partnership, and Taiwan's Relations with Japan," p. 362.

43. Gerry Shih, "China Launches Combat Drills in Taiwan Strait, Warns U.S. Not to 'Play with Fire,'" *Washington Post,* September 18, 2020.

44. Office of the Secretary of Defense, *Annual Report to Congress: Military and Security Developments Involving the People's Republic of China 2020* (Washington, DC: Office of the Secretary of Defense, 2020), p. 112.

45. Michael Schuman. "Keep an Eye on Taiwan," *The Atlantic*, October 10, 2020.

46. Office of the Secretary of Defense, *Annual Report to Congress,* p. 70.

47. Ibid., pp. 113−114.

48. Samson Ellis, "Here's What Could Happen if China Invaded Taiwan," *Japan Times,* October 8, 2020.

49. Yimou Lee, "Taiwan Military Says It Has Right to Counterattack Amid China Threats," Reuters, September 21, 2020.

50. Office of the Secretary of Defense, *Annual Report to Congress,* pp. 119−120.

51. Christopher P. Twomey, "The Fourth Taiwan Strait Crisis Is Just Starting," War on the Rocks, August 22, 2022.

52. "China Begins Three Days of Military Drills in Taiwan Strait," Al Jazeera, April 8, 2023.

53. Ibid.

54. "Taiwanese/Chinese Identity (1992/06~2022/12)," Election Study Center of the National Chengchi University, January 13, 2023, https://esc.nccu.edu.tw.

55. Schuman, "Keep an Eye on Taiwan."

56. Jared Ward, "Taiwan's Medical Diplomacy in the Caribbean: A Final Stand Against Beijing?" *The Diplomat,* May 11, 2020.

57. Martin Lasater, *U.S. Interests in the New Taiwan* (Boulder: Westview, 1993), pp. 208–209.

58. "The Taiwan Straits Crises: 1954–55 and 1958."

59. Harold C. Hinton, *The Republic of China on Taiwan Since 1949 in America and Island China* (New York: University Press of America, 1989), p. 13.

60. "Taiwan Relations Act." American Institute in Taiwan, January 1, 1979, https://www.ait.org.tw.

61. Dennis Van Vranken Hickey, *United States–Taiwan Security Ties: From Cold War to Beyond Containment* (Westport, CT: Praeger, 1994), pp. 41–55. Emma Broomfield, "Perceptions of Danger: The China Threat Theory," *Journal of Contemporary China* 12, no. 5 (2003): 265–266.

62. Derek Grossman, "Is the '1992 Consensus' Fading Away in the Taiwan Strait?" RAND, June 3, 2020.

63. Ibid.

64. Therese Shaheen, "Why Taiwan Matters," *National Review,* July 15, 2021.

65. "Taiwan-U.S. Relations," Taipei Economic and Cultural Representative Office in the United States, March 18, 2021, https://www.roc-taiwan.org.

66. "U.S. Relations with Taiwan," US Department of State, August 31, 2018, https://www.state.gov.

67. *Why Taiwan Matters: Hearing Before the House Committee on Foreign Affairs,* 112th Congress, Serial No. 112-42, June 16, 2011, https://www.govinfo.gov.

68. Ibid.

69. "Taiwan Education and Training Services Industry Snapshot," International Trade Administration, March 24, 2023, https://www.trade.gov.

70. *Why Taiwan Matters.*

71. "U.S. Relations with Taiwan."

72. Steven Stashwick, "China's South China Sea Militarization Has Peaked," *Foreign Policy,* August 19, 2019.

73. Ralph Jennings, "Wary of Beijing, Taiwan Doubles Down on South China Sea Island," Voice of America, March 29, 2021.

74. Therese Shaheen, "Why Taiwan Matters."

75. "Taiwan-U.S. Relations."

76. David Sacks and Chris Miller, "The War over the World's Most Critical Technology: A Conversation with Chris Miller," Council on the Foreign Relations, January 3, 2023, https://www.cfr.org.

77. *Why Taiwan Matters.*

78. Shannon L. Blanton and Charles W. Kegley, *World Politics: Trend and Transformation* (Boston: Cengage, 2020), p. 15.

79. Steven L. Lamy, John S. Masker, and John Baylis, *Introduction to Global Politics* (New York: Oxford University Press, 2019), p. 144.

80. Blanton and Kegley, *World Politics,* p. 14.

81. Lamy, Masker, and Baylis, *Introduction to Global Politics,* p. 147.

82. Jon Pevehouse and Joshua Goldstein, *International Relations* (London: Pearson, 2020), p. 15.

83. Lamy, Masker, and Baylis, *Introduction to Global Politics,* p. 147.

84. J. David Singer, "Review: International Conflict: Three Levels of Analysis," *World Politics* 12, no. 3 (April 1960): 459.

85. Mark Kesselman, Joel Krieger, and William A. Joseph, *Introduction to Comparative Politics: Political Challenges and Changing Agendas* (Boston: Cengage, 2019), p. 9.

86. Joseph Romm, *Defining National Security: The Nonmilitary Aspects* (New York: Council of Foreign Affairs, 1993), p. 85.

87. Samuel P. Huntington, *Political Order in Changing Societies* (New Haven: Yale University Press, 1968), p. 1.

88. Amos A. Jordan, William J. Taylor Jr., and Lawrence J. Korb, *American National Security: Policy and Process* (Baltimore: Johns Hopkins University Press, 1989), p. 3.

89. Lamy, Masker, and Baylis, *Introduction to Global Politics,* p. 146.

90. Blanton and Kegley, *World Politics,* p. 15.

91. Singer, "Review: International Conflict," p. 454.

92. Lamy, Masker, and Baylis, *Introduction to Global Politics,* p. 145.

93. Ibid., p. 146.

94. Douglas J. Murray and Paul R. Viotti, *The Defense of Policies of Nations: A Comparative Study* (Baltimore: Johns Hopkins University Press, 1994), p. 593.

95. See, for example, *United States and Taiwan Security Ties*, an introductory study of the complex security relationship that exists between the United States and the ROC. Ian Easton, *The Chinese Invasion Threat: Taiwan's Defense and American Strategy in Asia* (Arlington, VA: Project 2049 Institute, 2017), an exploration of the secret world of war planning and strategy, espionage, and national security; Brendan Taylor, *Dangerous Decade* (London: International Institute for Strategic Studies, 2019), which primarily looks at current tension between China and Taiwan; Richard Bush, *Uncharted Strait: The Future of China-Taiwan Relations* (Washington, DC: Brookings Institution Press, 2013), which states that tensions between China and Taiwan have eased since 2008; and Shelley Rigger, *Why Taiwan Matters: Small Island, Global Powerhouse* (Lanham, MD: Rowman & Littlefield, 2013), which offers a comprehensive and engaging introduction to a country that exercises a role in the world far greater than its tiny size would indicate.

2

Early Commitments to Taiwan: The Truman Administration

THE UNITED STATES HAS A TRADITION OF MISSIONARY ZEAL AND IDEOLOGICAL commitment to its foreign policy. One of the most complicated issues facing US policy in East Asia involves its relations with both China and Taiwan. US foreign policy naturally requires the country to act in its national interest.[1] US policies are not built on abstractions, but on the result of practical considerations of national interests.[2] Since World War II, the United States has acted as the leader of democratic countries and provided security assistance to noncommunist countries to counter communist aggression. The US humanitarian, religious, and cultural involvement in China vanished as the Chinese Communist Party (CCP) took over mainland China. The Harry S. Truman administration was ready to abandon the Republic of China (ROC). The Korean War, however, altered US policy. Concerned that the Korean War might spread beyond East Asia, President Truman sent the Seventh Fleet to the Taiwan Strait. After the People's Liberation Army (PLA) entered the Korean War, US military aid to Taiwan increased significantly.[3]

Historical Events:
The Founding of the People's Republic of China

In 1912, the ROC was established as the first republic in Asia, ending 2,000 years of imperial rule. After founding the new republic, mainland China soon became fragmented and controlled by different warlords across the nation. In 1921, several intellectuals, inspired by Marxism and the Bolshevik Revolution, created the CCP. In 1931, when Japan invaded mainland China, Chiang Kai-shek's military fought against Japanese forces.[4] During Japan's invasion, the CCP expanded its influence in rural areas, recruiting many farmers to join the Red Army. After Japan surrendered in 1945, a civil war between Chiang Kai-shek and Mao Tse-tung ensued. Since the CCP had strong grassroots support and sufficient weapons from the Soviet Union, it eventually occupied mainland China.

After Japan surrendered in 1945, the Tuman administration hoped that the ROC could become a democratic country. To support building the ROC into a major power, the United States continued to supply military aid to Chiang Kai-shek's government. Mao's forces, however, controlled the areas they had recovered from Japan. When the CCP sought to expand, their conflicts with Chiang Kai-shek's forces turned into a civil war. When the war intensified, Truman sent Secretary of State George Marshall to China for mediation. Arriving in China in December 1945, Marshall encouraged both sides to reach a cease-fire and a political settlement. Eventually, Marshall's mission failed. The Chinese Communists received Japanese arms, which were captured by the Soviet forces in Manchuria. By possessing more advanced weaponry, the CCP gained an upper hand in its battles with the ROC forces.[5] In 1948, the State Department undertook a study of China. The report concluded that the outcome of the Chinese Civil War was being decided by forces far beyond the control of the United States.[6]

In January 1949, Truman replaced Secretary of State Marshall with Dean Acheson. Acheson was eager to disengage the United States from involvement in China. He recommended that the US government should: (1) continue to recognize the ROC government until the situation was clarified; (2) maintain official contact with all the elements in China; and (3) seize the chance to exploit any rifts between Beijing and Moscow. The National Security Council (NSC) accepted Acheson's recommendations and forwarded them to Truman in March 1949.[7]

Since the Truman administration believed that Chiang Kai-shek was doomed to lose, the US government had no reason to provide military assistance to his forces. The Truman administration's idea to end military aid to Chiang Kai-shek, however, encountered opposition from the US Congress. Republican congressmen asked Truman to appoint a commission to survey the situation in China. Acheson responded, "When a great tree falls in the forest, one cannot see the extent of the damage until the dust settles."[8]

In 1949, the ROC government was forced to retreat from mainland China to Taiwan. Early in the year, the Communist forces won a series of military campaigns across northern and central China. After the Red Army crossed the Yangtze River in April, the major cities in mainland China fell under the control of the Communist forces. Chiang's forces were collapsing. Southeastern China's harbors were filled with ships ferrying ROC officials and troops to Taiwan.[9] On October 1, Mao declared the founding of the People's Republic of China (PRC). Two months later, Chiang Kai-shek and the remnants of the ROC government fled to Taiwan.

Because of the Chinese Communist takeover of mainland China, a debate broke out in the United States over who was at fault. The State Department blamed the loss on inefficiency within the ROC government. On August 5, 1949, Acheson released the China white paper. It stated that the ominous result of the Chinese Civil War was beyond US control. Nothing that the US government could have done would have changed that result.[10] Acheson sought to impress upon the public that the defeat of the ROC, which he believed stemmed from inherent military, political, and social weaknesses, was beyond the United States' ability to remedy.[11]

In the face of catastrophe in mainland China, Truman believed that it would be in the best interests of the United States to wait until the dust settled. His administration wanted to formulate a new policy by establishing diplomatic relations with Beijing at an appropriate time. The PRC's ill treatment of US diplomats and the outbreak of the Korean War caused the Truman administration to drop this idea.[12]

The Individual Level:
Truman's Reluctance to Become Involved

The decision on whether to defend the ROC government or not was a difficult decision for President Truman. In a cabinet meeting on March 7, 1947, Truman said that he thought Chiang Kai-shek was not fit to be the ROC leader, and that giving him money would be pouring sand in a rat hole. When Chiang Kai-shek's forces retreated to Taiwan, the Central Intelligence Agency (CIA) assessed that directly supporting Taiwan was the only way to defend the island from a PRC invasion, but doing so could precipitate World War III.[13]

Truman was in no mood to defend Taiwan after Chiang Kai-shek's defeat in the civil war. On January 5, 1950, he announced that the United States would not establish military bases in Taiwan. The US government would not offer any military aid or advice to the Nationalist forces.[14] Following Truman's statement, on January 12 Acheson delivered a speech at the National Press Club in which Korea, Indochina, and Taiwan were excluded from the US defense perimeter in the Western Pacific. Acheson announced that "the perimeter ran along the Aleutians to Japan, then to the Ryukyu Islands, then to the Philippines."[15] At the time, Truman expected a quick defeat of the ROC government. The United States would then consider normalizing diplomatic relations with the PRC. Before Mao proclaimed the establishment of the PRC, US ambassador John Leighton Stuart met with Communist leaders to discuss US recognition of the PRC.

28   Hedging the China Threat

Those talks failed when Mao announced his intention to lean toward the side of the Soviet Union.[16]

President Truman faced criticism from Republicans, who claimed he had lost China. They criticized him for not providing enough aid to the ROC government. Truman also faced internal criticism regarding his commitment to anticommunism at home. Republican senator Joseph McCarthy had begun his hunt for communists within the US government. Under increased domestic pressure, Truman did not want to appear soft on communism abroad, so he pledged to defend Taiwan from attack, but he had no wish to provoke a war with the Soviets.[17]

After the outbreak of the Korean War in 1950, Truman argued that communism had passed beyond the use of subversion to conquer independent nations. He believed the attack by North Korea had been part of a larger plan by Communist China and the Soviet Union and that the invasion was a scheme encouraged by the Soviet Union. "If we don't put up a fight now," Truman observed to his staff, there was "no telling what they'll do."[18] Although the United States took the lead in the Korean action, it did so under the UN framework. Truman made it clear that his actions fell within the guidelines recommended by the United Nations.[19]

The deployment of the Seventh Fleet to neutralize Taiwan was considered the beginning of the US policy to defend Taiwan from China. Truman was concerned about the increased threat of World War III if the United States did not respond. He saw the situation in Taiwan and Korea as similar to that of the early Nazi invasions of Germany's surrounding countries, and he wanted to avoid appeasement.[20] The decision for intervention, however, did not entail long-term military assistance to the defense of Taiwan or a revitalized political commitment to the ROC. Truman made it clear that the US naval presence in the Taiwan Strait was temporary and did not represent a fundamental change in his China policy. The intervention of US forces would localize the Korean conflict and prevent it from evolving into a general Far Eastern war. Truman emphasized that once the Korean conflict ended, the fleet would be withdrawn.[21] Its mission as a buffer, between Taipei and Beijing, was only temporary.

In the early days of the Korean War, Truman's military assistance to Taiwan was defensive in nature and not meant to reinforce the ROC military forces in retaking mainland China.[22] ROC and US relations, however, improved steadily during the Korean War. The United States continued to recognize the ROC as the de jure government of China and increased efforts to safeguard the ROC's seat in the UN. Truman's only concern with Taiwan was not to let it fall into unfriendly hands because an enemy's control of Taiwan could sabotage US war efforts in Korea. There was no consideration at this time of Taiwan's political future at all.[23]

The State Level: From the "Hands-off" to "Neutralize the Taiwan Strait" Policy

During the Truman administration, the National Security Council played an important role in formulating US foreign policy. Created in 1947, Truman used the NSC to form options for him to finalize his security policy. Before the creation of a national security advisor (NSA), Truman authorized Secretary of State Acheson to run the NSC and determine recommendations for decisionmaking. Acheson was not in favor of the defense of Taiwan. He detested Chiang Kai-shek and thought that before the US government would support Taiwan, he had to be removed.[24]

US military leaders had different perspectives than the State Department regarding Taiwanese issues. Secretary of Defense Louis Johnson wanted to provide aid for Taiwan's defense, as did the chairman of the Joint Chiefs of Staff (JCS), General Omar Bradley. General Douglas MacArthur also supported the defense of Taiwan due to its strategic value. These military leaders, however, could not convince Acheson to recommend this course of action to Truman.[25]

The State Department's Disdain for Chiang Kai-shek's Administration

In late 1948, the Truman administration began to pay more attention to the Taiwan problem. It recognized the importance of preventing Taiwan from falling into the hands of the Communist regime. The Truman administration, however, agreed that no military assistance should be committed to the defense of Taiwan. Diplomatic and economic measures would be used instead.[26] The NSC prepared an assessment of the strategic implications to US security should Taiwan come under the CCP's control. State Department officials did not recommend that the United States support Chiang Kai-shek's regime. They suggested that the United States should wait until they better understood what governing groups they would have to deal with in Taiwan.[27]

On February 3, 1949, the policy statement (NSC 37/2) adopted by the NSC, and later approved by Truman, was based on State Department proposals. While recognizing the importance of Taiwan to the United States, the NSC rejected establishing a US military presence in Taiwan.[28] This major policy focused on two points. First, the US government had no desire to see chaos on mainland China spread to Taiwan. Second, US support for the governing authorities of Taiwan would depend in a large measure on the effectiveness of its regime and its ability to meet the needs of the people.[29]

In a memorandum to the NSC on August 4, 1949, the State Department emphasized that if the control of Taiwan's destiny was in the hands of the

30 Hedging the China Threat

same incompetent rulers who had squandered US aid, there could be no assurance that US efforts would keep Taiwan out of Communist hands.[30] On October 6, the State Department again expressed the fear that if the United States furnished economic aid to Chiang Kai-shek's regime, Taiwan would end up in Communist hands. It concluded that the current policy should be continued. Additional US aid should be made dependent on the reform of the ROC government, but an enlarged program of aid was rejected at that time.[31] The State Department, under the leadership of Acheson, would be open only to options that would oppose any suggestions by the Pentagon and the Joint Chiefs of Staff to provide military support for Chiang Kai-shek's government.

Conflicts Between the State Department and the Military

The Department of State and the Department of Defense had major differences in dealing with Taiwan's issues, particularly with providing military aid. After Chiang Kai-shek lost mainland China, the State Department viewed his administration as corrupt. If the United States continued to support his regime, it would waste US resources. The US military leaders, however, believed that Taiwan had important strategic value. If the CCP controlled Taiwan, it would pose a serious threat to US allies and seriously damage US interests in East Asia.

In December 1949, Secretary of Defense Johnson asked Acheson for a larger budget to defend Taiwan. Acheson objected because he had already given "the China area" money to Korea, Indochina, and the Philippines. Johnson was furious and replied that the JCS agreed with him. Johnson requested the budget be diverted to Taiwan, but it was futile. On December 23, chairman of the JCS, General Bradley, sent a proposal to the NSC for a new military policy for Taiwan. This was to include a modest military training and advisor program for the Taiwanese military. The State Department also turned it down. On December 29, Bradley argued that he was in favor of the military program because it would prevent a PLA invasion. Acheson responded that the military would fail. Johnson, fed up with Acheson, stormed out of the room in anger.[32]

On January 5, 1950, Truman's declaration that the United States would not defend or provide military aid to Taiwan caused controversy in Congress. The Truman administration explained its decision to the US Congress. Acheson responded that General Bradley did not consider Taiwan a "vital interest" to the United States. In fact, Acheson was misrepresenting and distorting Bradley's assessment. Bradley said that he could not make Taiwan a vital interest due to a lack of troops. On February 9, Senator McCarthy alleged that there were Communist agents in the State Department, and specifically in the Far East Section, which was why the United

States had surrendered Taiwan. McCarthy's charge put pressure on Truman and Acheson.[33] Acheson shared a similar mentality with Truman regarding Chiang Kai-shek's poor leadership. When US military leaders asked for more military support for him, Acheson simply turned it down. He believed that Truman would be on his side. Acheson's opposing stance on Taiwan collided with the military leaders because most of the top brass acknowledged that Taiwan had an important geostrategic value to the United States.

Neutralize the Taiwan Strait

After the North Korean military launched a surprise attack on South Korea on June 25, 1950, Truman asked Acheson to hold a series of NSC meetings to deal with the crisis. On the same day, Truman met with leaders from the State Department and the Defense Department. Chairman of the JCS, General Bradley, presented a memorandum prepared by General Douglas MacArthur. This memorandum emphasized the importance of denying Taiwan to the Communists.[34]

After hearing the memorandum from MacArthur, Acheson suggested that Truman should order the Seventh Fleet to proceed to Taiwan and prevent an attack on Taiwan from mainland China. Operations from Taiwan against mainland China should be prevented. He emphasized that the United States should not partner with Chiang Kai-shek, as the future status of Taiwan might be determined by the United Nations. Truman agreed. The deployment of the Seventh Fleet could monitor both mainland China and Taiwan. Chief of naval operations, Admiral Forrest Sherman, agreed, as did General Bradley.[35] The JCS suggested that the United States should continue to deny Taiwan to the Communists by furnishing supplies for the ROC government. Other requirements should be determined through a survey conducted by the Far East Command (FECOM).[36] The JCS recommendations were discussed by the NSC on July 27, 1950. Truman approved them in principle.[37] Truman's hands-off policy on Taiwan lasted until the outbreak of the Korean War. The deployment of the Seventh Fleet placed Taiwan under US protection.[38]

The Rift Between Truman and MacArthur

In August 1950, the rift between Truman and MacArthur started to surface in connection with Taiwan when Truman announced that the Seventh Fleet would be sent into the Taiwan Strait. The JCS directive to MacArthur had made him responsible for defending Taiwan. Truman, however, had not yet authorized a military aid program for Chiang Kai-shek's government.[39]

MacArthur's trip to Taiwan on July 31 was to have damaging consequences, marking the beginning of the breach between him and Truman.

32 Hedging the China Threat

MacArthur was sent to Taipei to assess ROC military capabilities in confronting the PLA. He said that plans had been made to coordinate steps by Taipei and Washington to meet any attack that a hostile force might launch against Taiwan. It was his responsibility to defend Taiwan from a Communist invasion. Some criticized MacArthur's statements as rejecting Truman's policy of neutralizing Taiwan. MacArthur denied any disagreement between his headquarters and Washington.[40]

MacArthur sent a message to the Department of the Army. He intended to transfer three squadrons of F-80C fighters to Taiwan in case Taiwan was to come under attack. The State Department representative in Taiwan reported that the transfer of fighters had already been decided by MacArthur. The State Department's concern was expressed to the JCS. The JCS then warned MacArthur that any such action should not be undertaken. This decision had to be considered at the "highest levels" in Washington. MacArthur replied that there was no intention to transfer any aircraft to Taiwan except in case of an attack.[41]

Secretary Johnson hoped that the JCS recommendation to allow Chiang Kai-shek greater latitude in operations against China would be approved at the NSC meeting on August 3, 1950. The JCS drafted a message that would grant MacArthur authority to permit the ROC to attack China when intelligence indicated that a PLA attack was imminent. Truman rejected Johnson's recommendations and instructed him to send MacArthur a reminder to stop the ROC forces' plan to attack on China. Truman reminded MacArthur that only the president has the authority to order such a preventive action.[42]

In a further effort to eliminate misunderstanding, the JCS, at the direction of Truman, sent MacArthur a message on August 14, 1950, clarifying the directive of June 27. The president's intention had been to limit the US defense of Taiwan to operations that could be carried out without committing any forces to Taiwan itself. MacArthur was therefore to make no commitment to the ROC government to place fighter squadrons in Taiwan in case of an attack.[43]

Improved Relations Between the United States and Taiwan

At the same time that the US and the PRC military confrontation during the Korean War intensified, US military support to the ROC government improved. This included military and economic aid, establishing the Military Assistance Advisory Group, and intelligence sharing between the two governments. Previously, in April 1948, the US Congress had approved an emergency package, which the Nationalists spent on military hardware and supplies. However, the United States, frustrated by the Chiang Kai-shek government's failure in mainland China, cut off aid until the beginning of the Korean War.[44] In 1951, the Truman administration resumed a program of military and economic assistance to Taiwan.[45]

The US advisory experience with the ROC began in World War II as the ROC forces fought against the Japanese. The US mission withdrew after the war, but returned in 1948 when the ROC fought against the Communists. In September 1948, the advisory groups merged into the Joint US Military Advisory Group to the Republic of China (JUSMAG ROC). It provided technical assistance and training guidance. Its operations were suspended in March 1949.[46] As a result of the PRC's fighting against the US forces in Korea, US attitudes once again shifted. In May 1951, Major General William Chase, leading his Military Assistance Advisory Group, arrived in Taiwan to reorganize, train, and equip ROC forces. The group was also responsible for coordinating the military aid program, making recommendations, and filing reports on the progress of the ROC forces.[47]

Even the State Department had improved its relations with the ROC government during the Korean War. On May 18, Dean Rusk, assistant secretary of state for Far Eastern affairs and the right-hand man of Acheson, emphasized the changing US policy toward the ROC. This happened because the CCP had already become a Soviet satellite. Rusk said, "We recognize the Nationalist Government of China. Although the territory under its control has been greatly reduced, we believe that it truly represents the ideals of the great Chinese people, especially in its historical demand to be free from foreign control. The Nationalist government will continue to receive our aid and support."[48]

Keeping Taiwan from falling into Communist hands aligned with US strategic interests.[49] The US military assistance to Taiwan, from the outbreak of the Korean War up to the end of the Truman presidency, included, at least the following: (1) deploying the Seventh Fleet to the Taiwan Strait; (2) resuming economic and military aid; (3) sending military personnel to assess the needs of the ROC's armed forces; and (4) providing Taipei with important intelligence information about PRC ground forces. The US military and economic aid contributed to military buildup, economic stability, and social order after the ROC government retreated to Taiwan.

The International Level: The Rise of Containment Policy

During the Truman administration, the international distribution of power was bipolarity between the United States and the Soviet Union. After the founding of the new Chinese regime, the ability of the PRC and the United States to find common ground was hampered because Mao proclaimed that the CCP could work with Soviet Russia on major world issues. The world balance of power tipped in favor of the Communist bloc. This section

34 Hedging the China Threat

examines the containment policy adopted by the Truman administration, mainly looking at the Truman Doctrine, his containment policy, NSC-68 (US Objectives and Programs for National Security), and China's entry into the Korean War.

The Truman Doctrine

At the dawn of the Cold War, Truman stated that the United States would help all democratic nations under threat from authoritarian forces. This principle became the Truman Doctrine. This doctrine reoriented US foreign policy away from its usual stance of withdrawal from regional conflicts to that of intervention in international crises.[50]

The Truman Doctrine originated from having to cope with the rise of aggression from the Soviet Union. In 1946, Moscow's interference in the domestic affairs of other countries prohibited any chance of achieving a post–World War II rapprochement between Washington and Moscow. These interferences included: (1) the Soviets failed to withdraw their troops from northern Iran; (2) Moscow attempted to force the Turkish government into granting it base and transit rights through the Turkish Straits; and (3) the Soviet Union supported the Greek Communist war effort.[51]

The Truman Doctrine arose from a speech delivered by Truman to Congress on March 12, 1947. The cause for the speech was an announcement by the British government that, as of March 31, it would no longer provide aid to the Greek government in its civil war against the Greek Communist Party. Truman asked Congress to support the Greek government against the Communists. Truman requested that Congress provide $400 million worth of aid to both the Greek and Turkish governments.[52]

The Truman Doctrine signaled to the world that the US policy supported free people who were resisting attempted subjugation. The United States would no longer accept the expansion of Soviet totalitarianism into free nations. The doctrine committed the United States to offering assistance to preserve the political integrity of democratic nations. This proposal was approved by Congress, becoming the first fundamental step taken by the United States to check Soviet aggression.[53]

US Objectives and Programs for National Security

The US Policy of Containment was first stated publicly in an article in *Foreign Affairs* in 1947 and signed simply "X." It was written by George Kennan, US deputy head of the mission in Moscow at the time. Under this policy, the democratic countries were to join together to stop the encroachment of Soviet Communism. Kennan's article reflected the US policy during the Truman administration. In March 1947, Secretary Marshall implemented the containment policy by promising aid to European nations for rehabilitation. This policy was instituted for the defense of the European countries against communism.[54]

In January 1950, a warning was raised by a CIA report that the Soviet Union would be able to launch an atomic attack on the United States. This report also forecast that the Soviets would possess 120 to 200 atomic bombs by 1954. Acheson was alarmed by the CIA's estimates. He agreed with the CIA's suggestion that a comparable US military buildup was critical to US security. On January 31, 1950, Truman directed Acheson and Johnson to embark on a reexamination of the Soviet threat and the US military response. [55]

Acheson asked the policy planning staff to conduct a comprehensive review of the US national security strategy. Paul H. Nitze, newly appointed director of policy planning, supported the CIA's assessment of the Soviet intentions. Nitze emphasized that the ideological system of the Soviet Union, combined with its military capability, would pose a "permanent threat" to US national security. It thus was vital for the United States to make military buildup its top priority. Nitze's belief was shared by the majority of his colleagues in the State Department, which was to become the foundation for the contents of NSC-68.[56]

NSC-68 was a top secret report completed on April 7, 1950, that recommended heavy increases in military funding to help contain the Soviets.[57] This report is among the most influential documents composed by the US government during the Cold War. Its authors argued that one of the most pressing threats confronting the United States was the "hostile design" of the Soviet Union. The Soviet threat would be augmented by increasing production of weapons, including nuclear weapons. Thus, the best approach was to respond with a massive buildup of the US military by enhancing the technical superiority and increasing the defense budget.[58]

Several US officials opposed NSC-68's recommendations. Critics, such as Secretary Johnson and former director of policy planning Kennan argued that the United States already had a substantial military advantage over the Soviet Union. Kennan disagreed with the report's assertion that the Soviet Union was bent on achieving domination through force of arms. Kennan argued that the United States could contain the Soviet Union through political and economic measures rather than purely military ones. At the time, Congress, however, strongly criticized the Truman administration for being soft on communism, thus settling matters in favor of the report's recommendations. From 1950 to 1953, the administration increased its defense spending of the gross domestic product (GDP) from 5.0 to 14.2 percent.[59]

After the release of the NSC-68 report, the Far Eastern Bureau, under Dean Rusk, began to revise the military strategy that was beyond Acheson's defensive perimeter. The Taiwan policy of the State Department was subject

36   Hedging the China Threat

to more intense debates. In May 1950, Republican State Department consultant John Foster Dulles (who later became secretary of state during the Dwight Eisenhower administration) sent a memorandum to Acheson emphasizing Taiwan's strategic importance for US security interests and urging stronger support for Chiang Kai-shek's regime.[60]

China Entered the Korean War

At the end of World War II, the United States and the Soviet Union had agreed to divide Korea along the 38th parallel. In 1946, Kim Il Sung organized a Communist government, the Democratic People's Republic of Korea (DPRK) in the North. Shortly after, Syngman Rhee established a rival government, the Republic of Korea (ROK), in the South. The Korean Peninsula was thus divided between a Soviet-backed government in the North and a US-backed government in the South. When the Korean War broke out, Truman committed US forces to a combined UN military effort and named General Douglas MacArthur as commander of the UN forces. Fifteen other nations also sent troops under the UN command.[61]

The Korean War determined the Truman administration's reversal of its position from abandonment to enhancing the security of Taiwan.[62] Truman announced that he had dispatched the Seventh Fleet to neutralize the Taiwan Strait. This move deterred the PRC from invading Taiwan. Meanwhile, the Truman administration requested the ROC government to cease military operations against mainland China.[63] The Korean War not only pushed the United States into military conflict with the PRC, but also led to a complete turnabout of US policy toward the ROC.

MacArthur's Inchon landing led to the retreat of North Korean forces. The next decision by the United States was whether or not its troops should cross the 38th parallel. The Truman administration had determined what Beijing's probable responses would be if US troops crossed the 38th parallel. The JCS requested MacArthur to assess if the PRC planned to enter the war. He felt confident that there was no present indication of a PLA entry into North Korea. MacArthur was authorized to cross the 38th parallel.[64]

When South Korean troops crossed the 38th parallel on October 1, 1950, Mao met with the CCP Central Committee Secretariat. Most participants did not support dispatching forces. On October 3, Premier Zhou Enlai met with Indian ambassador K. M. Panikkar and asked him to send an urgent message to the Truman administration. The message emphasized that if the South Korean troops crossed the 38th parallel, the PLA would not intervene because it was its internal affair. However, if US troops crossed the parallel, China would send troops into North Korea. When the State Department received the message, officials at the China Desk argued that Zhou was bluffing. They did not believe that the PRC would intervene.

Acheson agreed.[65] In the CIA's estimate, if the PRC had intended to help North Korea, it would have done it earlier, but that time had passed. Truman concluded that Communist China would not intervene in North Korea. When the United States launched its offensive into North Korea on October 7, Mao informed Kim Il Sung and Joseph Stalin of the PRC's decision to send troops to Korea.[66]

Conclusion

After Mao took over in 1949, President Truman believed Chiang Kai-shek was unfit to lead. If he provided aid to Chiang Kai-shek's government, Truman feared that it would eventually end up in the hands of Chinese Communists. The State Department, led by Acheson, was opposed to defending Taiwan because Acheson despised Chiang Kai-shek. However, the majority of US military leaders supported Taiwan's survival because of its strategic importance. After Mao declared that the PRC would support the Soviet Union in major international affairs, the world balance of power shifted in favor of the Soviet Union.

From the outbreak of the Korean War until the end of Truman's presidency, the United States' main policy outcomes toward Taiwan were as follows: to begin, the US military sent the Seventh Fleet to the Taiwan Strait to prevent China from invading Taiwan. Second, the Truman administration resumed aid to Taiwan, dispatched military personnel to assess the ROC's military needs, and provided Taiwan with critical intelligence about China's military activities.

In analyzing the US-China relationship at an individual level, following Chiang Kai-shek's loss of mainland China, Truman was in no mood to defend Taiwan and was in favor of ending relations with the ROC government. However, the outbreak of the Korean War shifted Truman's hands-off policy toward assisting Taiwan. At the state level, the State Department under Acheson shared a similar opinion to Truman's regarding Chiang Kai-shek's poor leadership. Acheson's opposing stance on Taiwan often collided with the military leaders because most of the top brass acknowledged that Taiwan had an important geostrategic value to the United States. At the international level, after the Korean War began, Truman believed North Korea's attack was part of a larger plan devised by Communist China and the Soviet Union. Truman believed that sending the Seventh Fleet into the Taiwan Strait not only would prevent an invasion by the PLA, but also would prevent Chiang Kai-shek's forces from attacking the mainland. If the Korean War had not broken out, the United States probably would have recognized the Beijing regime sooner. Significant changes in international conditions prompted Truman to initiate fundamental changes in the US-Taiwan relationship.

38 *Hedging the China Threat*

Notes

1. Charles O. Lerche, *Foreign Policy of the American People* (Englewood Cliffs, NJ: Prentice Hall, 1967), p. 20.

2. David W. Clinton, *The Two Facts of National Interest* (Baton Rouge: Louisiana State University, 1994), p. 119.

3. Victoria Marie Kraft, *The U.S. Constitution and Foreign Policy: Terminating the Taiwan Treaty* (New York: Green Press, 1991), pp. 16–17.

4. "The Chinese Revolution of 1949," Office of the Historian, https://history.state.gov.

5. Kenneth W. Condit, *The Joint Chiefs of Staff and National Policy,* vol. 2: *1947–1949* (Washington, DC: Office of the Chairman of the Joint Chiefs of Staff, 1996), pp. 235–236.

6. Ibid., p. 248.

7. Ibid., p. 249.

8. Ibid., p. 255.

9. Ian Easton, "The Korean War Saved Taiwan from the Clutches of Chairman Mao," *The National Interest*, April 10, 2020.

10. "Dean Acheson: United States Position on China," USC US-China Institute, August 5, 1949, https://china.usc.edu.

11. Condit, *Joint Chiefs of Staff,* p. 256.

12. "The Chinese Revolution of 1949."

13. Eric P. Swanson, "Seventh Fleet Standoff: A Two-Cut Analysis of the Decision to Neutralize Taiwan in June 1950," *Concept,* no. 38 (2015). https://concept.journals.villanova.edu/article/view/1861/1741.

14. Harry S. Truman, "Statement on Formosa, January 5, 1950," February 25, 2014, USC US-China Institute, https://china.usc.edu.

15. Dean Acheson, "Dean Acheson's 'Perimeter Speech' on Asia," Alpha History, 1950, https://alphahistory.com/coldwar/dean-acheson-perimeter-speech-asia-1950/.

16. US Department of State, "United States Relations with China: Boxer Uprising to Cold War (1900-1949)," US Department of State Archive, https://2001-2009.state.gov; "United States Relations with China: Boxer Uprising to Cold War (1900-1949)," US Department of State Archive, January 20, 2001, to January 20, 2009, https://2001-2009.state.gov/r/pa/ho/pubs/fs/90689.htm.

17. "US Enters the Korean Conflict," National Archives, https://www.archives.gov.

18. Ibid.

19. Ibid.

20. Swanson, "Seventh Fleet Standoff."

21. Martin Lasater*, Policy in Evolution: The US Role in China's Reunification* (Boulder: Westview, 1989), p. 27.

22. Dennis Van Vranken Hickey, *United States–Taiwan Security Ties: From Cold War to Beyond Containment* (Westport, CT: Praeger, 1994), p. 20.

23. Karal Rankin, *China Assignment* (Seattle: University of Washington Press, 1964), p. 29.

24. Swanson, "Seventh Fleet Standoff."

25. Ibid.

26. James F. Schnabel and Robert J. Watson, *The Joint Chiefs of Staff and National Policy,* vol. 3: *1950–1951 The Korean War Part One* (Washington, DC: Office of the Chairman of the Joint Chiefs of Staff, 1998), p. 14.

27. Condit, *Joint Chiefs of Staff,* p. 257.

28. Ibid., p. 258.

29. US Department of State. "Note by the Executive Secretary of the National Security Council (Souers) to the Council, February 3, 1949," US Department of State, https://history.state.gov.

30. Condit, *Joint Chiefs of Staff,* p. 259.

31. Ibid., p. 260.

32. Swanson, "Seventh Fleet Standoff."

33. Ibid.

34. "Memorandum on Formosa, by General of the Army Douglas MacArthur, Commander in Chief, Far East, and Supreme Commander, Allied Powers, Japan, June 14, 1950." Office of the Historian, https://history.state.gov.

35. US Department of State. "Memorandum of Conversation, by the Ambassador at Large (Jessup), June 25, 1950," *FRUS,* 1950, vol. 7, *Korea.* https://history.state.gov.

36. Swanson, "Seventh Fleet Standoff"; Schnabel and Watson, *The Joint Chiefs of Staff and National Policy,* p. 17.

37. Schnabel and Watson, *Joint Chiefs of Staff,* p. 232.

38. Condit, *Joint Chiefs of Staff,* p. 262.

39. Schnabel and Watson, *Joint Chiefs of Staff,* p. 17.

40. Ibid., p. 233.

41. Ibid., p. 234.

42. Ibid.

43. Ibid., p. 235.

44. Nathaniel R. Weber, "United States Military Advisory Assistance During the Cold War, 1945–1965" (PhD diss., Texas A&M University, 2016), pp. 130–131.

45. George Bernard Noble and E. Taylor Parks, *American Foreign Policy, 1950–1955: Basic Documents* (Washington, DC: US Government Printing Office, 1957), pp. 2470–2471.

46. Nathaniel R. Weber, "United States Military Advisory Assistance During the Cold War," p. 132.

47. Don Wiggins, "History of U.S. Military Assistance to Taiwan—1950–1959, Part 1," *US Taiwan Defense Command Blog*, September 20, 2010, http://ustdc.blogspot.com.

48. "Korea and China, Volume VII, Part 2, *1951*," *Foreign Relations of the United States,* https://history.state.gov.

49. Rough N. Clough, *Island China* (Cambridge: Harvard University Press, 1978), p. 1.

50. US State Department, "1945–1952: The Truman Doctrine, 1947," *Milestones in the History of U.S. Foreign Relations: 1945–1952,* https://history.state.gov.

51. Ibid.

52. Ibid.

53. "Policy of Containment and Policy of Liberation," *Taiwan Today,* June 1, 1953.

54. Ibid.

55. Simei Qing, "The US-China Confrontation in Korea: Assessment of Intentions in Time of Crisis," in *Northeast Asia and the Legacy of Harry S. Truman: Japan, China, and the Two Koreas,* edited by James Irving Matray (Kirksville, MO: Truman State University Press, 2012), pp. 95–96.

56. Ibid., p. 96.

57. "US Enters the Korean Conflict."

58. US State Department, "1945–1952: NSC-68, 1950," *Milestones in the History of U.S. Foreign Relations: 1945–1952,* https://history.state.gov.

59. Ibid.

60. Qing, "US-China Confrontation in Korea," pp. 96–97.

61. "US Enters the Korean Conflict."

62. George Tsai, "The Taiwan Strait Crises: Analysis of China, Taiwan and United States Relationship" (PhD diss., Northern Arizona University, 1985), p. 68.

63. Hungdah Chiu, ed. *China and the Taiwan Issue* (New York: Taylor and Francis, 1979), p. 116.

64. Qing, "The US-China Confrontation in Korea," pp. 98–99.

65. Ibid., p. 107.

66. Ibid., pp. 108–109.

3

The Offshore Islands Crises:
The Eisenhower Administration

DURING THE 1950S, THE OFFSHORE ISLANDS CONTROLLED BY THE REPUBLIC OF China (ROC) had become an important issue for the leaders of Taiwan, China, and the United States. Chairman Mao Tse-tung thought his national unification was incomplete without controlling Taiwan and that the seizure of these islands was an essential step for realizing his goal of reuniting mainland China with Taiwan.[1] After the ROC government retreated to Taiwan in 1949, it deployed a large number of troops on the offshore islands of Quemoy, Matsu, and the Dachens, as a launching pad for retaking mainland China. In the 1950s, there were two crises over these islands. The US government was deeply involved in both.[2]

Historical Events: Offshore Islands Crises in the 1950s

On December 2, 1954, the United States and the ROC signed the US-ROC Mutual Defense Treaty. In return, Mao invaded the Yijiangshan and Dachen Islands.[3] Secretary of State John Foster Dulles recommended to President Dwight Eisenhower that the United States transfer the Dachens's defenders to Quemoy and Matsu in exchange for US help defending the two islands.[4] Chiang Kai-shek consented. In January 1955, Congress passed the Formosa Resolution, giving President Eisenhower the authority to defend Taiwan and the offshore islands.[5] The defense treaty and the Formosa Resolution did not deter the aggression of the People's Republic of China (PRC). Fearing the PLA could occupy Quemoy and Matsu, which would be disastrous for Taiwan, the United States threatened the use of nuclear weapons if a war was to break out in the Taiwan Strait.[6] In return, the PRC sought a relaxation of its relations with the United States. By the end of

42   Hedging the China Threat

May 1955, an unofficial cease-fire had taken hold.[7] On August 23, 1958, the PRC resumed bombardment of the offshore islands. The Eisenhower administration resupplied the ROC garrisons on Quemoy and Matsu, and later publicly stated that it would defend them.[8]

The US-ROC Mutual Defense Treaty

After the end of the Korean War in 1953, the Chiang Kai-shek administration urged the United States to sign a defense treaty with the ROC. In 1954, the Eisenhower administration considered the feasibility of signing a defense pact with Taiwan. The PRC viewed it as a national security threat.[9] For Mao's regime, this treaty not only was a containment strategy of the United States, but also a reflection of the ROC's security strategy against China. With a formal US security commitment, the ROC felt more secure against the PRC's invasion. Without the consent of the United States, the ROC would not be able to take offensive action against the PRC.[10]

Secretary Dulles supported the idea of building an alliance in Asia, but he turned down the ROC's request for a treaty because many Americans had become disillusioned with Chiang Kai-shek's "return to the mainland" slogan. However, the signing of the US-South Korean Security Treaty at the end of the Korean War in 1953 rekindled Chiang Kai-shek's hope. In a meeting with the US ambassador to the ROC, Karl Rankin, he expressed his desire to have a similar treaty. To remove the US concern about his unilateral decision to attack mainland China, he promised that his government would obtain US permission before taking any military action.[11]

In August 1954, PRC premier Zhou Enlai claimed that Taiwan should be liberated. In response, on August 18 the National Security Council (NSC) held a meeting on the crisis. The participants concluded that these islands were not essential to Taiwan's defense, but that the political and psychological effects of their loss would be harmful to the US strategic position. On September 3, the People's Liberation Army (PLA) launched an artillery attack against Quemoy. The bombing provided Chiang Kai-shek with justification to push the United States for a treaty. Most of the Joint Chiefs of Staff (JCS) believed that Quemoy could be defended with US military assistance. Dulles suggested that the islands could be neutralized under a UN declaration. Eisenhower agreed.[12]

On October 12, Assistant Secretary of State for Far Eastern Affairs Walter Robertson arrived in Taiwan to explore the possibility of a treaty with Chiang Kai-shek. They first discussed the Oracle Operation to be presented by New Zealand at the UN. The Oracle suggested that the PRC end hostilities in exchange for the United States' recognition of the PRC. Chiang Kai-shek, however, firmly opposed it. Robertson proposed that Oracle, combined with a defense treaty, would improve the ROC's position. Chiang

Kai-shek replied that if implementing Oracle was inevitable, negotiating a treaty should precede New Zealand's move.[13]

On October 28, Dulles presented his views on the treaty at the NSC meeting. He emphasized that the United States intended to defend its national interests without inciting a war. He proposed several recommendations: first, the United States should conclude a defense treaty with the ROC, covering Taiwan and the Pescadores, but not the offshore islands. Second, this treaty should be defensive in nature. Third, the immediate threat to the offshore islands should be referred to the UN. Dulles's emphasis on the defensive nature of the treaty aroused the concern of the JCS. Despite their opposition, Eisenhower approved Dulles's recommendations.[14]

ROC foreign minister George Yeh arrived in Washington on November 2 to discuss the treaty with his US counterparts. During the negotiations, three things triggered the differences between Dulles and Yeh. The first was the territorial scope of the US security commitments. Yeh avoided specifying only Taiwan and the Pescadores. Dulles responded that the treaty would extend protection only to Taiwan and the Pescadores, but not the offshore islands.[15] The second was the limitation of ROC military operations. The United States insisted that, without mutual consent, the ROC would not take any offensive military action. The third was that the United States should have a voice in the ROC military deployment. In the end, a compromise was reached when Chiang Kai-shek accepted all the United States' requests.[16]

The US government believed that the US-ROC Mutual Defense Treaty could deter the PRC from attacking Taiwan and discourage Chiang Kai-shek from invading China. Chiang Kai-shek viewed the treaty as his greatest diplomatic achievement after losing China.[17] The PRC charged that the defense pact was "a treaty of naked aggression."[18]

The Beginning of the First Taiwan Strait Crisis

On February 2, 1953, Eisenhower announced in his State of the Union Address, that his new government would abandon the previous policy of "neutralizing" Taiwan. The Seventh Fleet would no longer prevent the ROC's military activities against the PRC.[19] After his so-called unleashing Chiang, the Chiang forces began dropping supplies to the guerrillas from raids and flights over mainland China. The unleashing policy caused the cross-strait tension to escalate. The JCS thus issued orders to Admiral Arthur Radford, commander in chief, Pacific (CINCPAC), instructing him to secure a commitment that the ROC forces would not engage in offensive operations that were not in the United States' interests.[20]

In early 1954, Mao approved the plan of the East China Military Command to take the Dachens. In July, the Politburo decided that the PLA must

44   Hedging the China Threat

liberate Taiwan to prevent a US-ROC alliance. The Central Military Commission (CMC) gave an order to the PLA to take Yijiangshan first, to get within artillery range of the Dachens. PRC leaders adopted the plan "from small to large, one island at a time, from north to south, and from weak to strong."[21] The PLA shelled Quemoy in early September, but by September 5 the US military had assembled three carriers, one cruiser, and a three-destroyer division near Quemoy. The Eisenhower administration permitted the ROC air and naval attacks on Chinese installations. The majority of the JCS recommended that the United States defend the islands. However, Dulles reasoned that a war over the offshore islands would alienate world opinion.[22]

When the NSC met on September 12, Eisenhower opposed making too many commitments worldwide. Dulles stated that most of the countries would condemn the United States for a war with the PRC over insignificant islands. Dulles offered an alternative: to take the case to the United Nations to forestall the PRC's use of force to overturn the status quo. The NSC authorized Dulles to explore the UN option.[23]

The 1955 Formosa Resolution

On January 10, 1955, PLA bombers attacked the Dachens. The ROC proposed to attack China in retaliation. The NSC decided that the United States should not agree to the ROC offensive actions, except under circumstances approved by President Eisenhower. On January 18, the PLA invaded Yijiangshan, an islet close to the Dachens.[24] Dulles suggested to Eisenhower that the United States should encourage the ROC to evacuate from the Dachens and assist them in doing so. Eisenhower agreed.[25] On January 24, Eisenhower asked Congress for authority to use US forces against the PLA over the offshore islands. The House and the Senate approved the Formosa Resolution.[26] It committed the United States to defend Taiwan, the Pescadores, and other closely related localities (likely referring to Quemoy and Matsu). This would happen when the president would recognize an attack on them as preliminary to an assault on Taiwan.[27]

On January 31, Dulles directed the US ambassador to Taiwan, Karl Rankin, to inform Chiang Kai-shek of the US intention to defend Quemoy and Matsu in exchange for his agreement to withdraw his forces from the Dachens.[28] Despite his compliance, Chiang Kai-shek was furious with the United States. His understanding, based on Dulles's talk with Foreign Minister George Yeh, had been that the United States would make public its commitment to Quemoy and Matsu. Even though Dulles and Robertson had informed the ROC of the United States' decision not to make its commitment public, Chiang Kai-shek insisted that Washington live up to its promise or his forces would not withdraw from the Dachens.[29] After Eisenhower delivered the Formosa Resolution, the PRC reacted harshly. Premier Zhou Enlai charged that "Eisenhower's statement was a war message. . . . China was not afraid of the threat of war."[30]

The initiative that ended the crisis came from the PRC. On April 23, Zhou announced at the Bandung Conference that China wanted no war with the United States. He was willing to negotiate with the United States for the reduction of tensions. On April 26, Dulles indicated that the United States would talk with Beijing about a cease-fire.[31] On May 17, Zhou stated that the PRC would seek the liberation of Taiwan by peaceful means. Dulles concluded that the crisis had eased.[32]

The 1958 Quemoy Crisis

The Quemoy Crisis was an extension of the previous crisis. Once the PLA occupied Yijiangshan and the Dachens, its successful military campaign convinced it that it was capable of conquering Quemoy and Matsu. The crisis had four stages: the preparation period (from July to August 23), the blockade period (from August 23 to September 4), the convoy period (from September 4 to 24), and the bargaining period (September 24 to October 25).[33]

The PLA military preparation period. When the United States deployed a large force in Lebanon in 1958, Beijing assessed that the US leaders were preoccupied with the Middle East turmoil and might not be able to deal with the Taiwan issues concurrently. In April, the commander, Han Xianchu, and political commissar, Ye Fei, of the Fuzhou Military Region presented the operational plan to attack Quemoy to Mao. Mao agreed to their proposal.[34] When the PLA increased its military preparations in July, Taiwan put its forces on alert. The US forces also conducted naval and air force patrols near Taiwan.[35] In mid-August, Mao commanded the PLA to get prepared to shell Quemoy.

In the face of mounting tensions in Quemoy, Chiang Kai-shek promulgated the Quemoy Operational Guidelines, based on the Taibai Plan (the ROC force operational plan during the crisis). The forces were to conduct a self-defense plan to annihilate the invading PLA. They were also to demonstrate their determination to fight so as to win US support for the joint operation.[36] By mid-July, ROC officials started to express their concern to the United States that a crisis was developing and requested assistance. Meanwhile, the ROC leaders flew to Quemoy and Matsu to review military preparations of stationed forces, and to boost morale.[37]

The artillery blockade period. On August 23, the PLA artillery forces in Fujian heavily bombed Quemoy. This attack took place when the Quemoy headquarters was holding a welcoming ceremony for ROC defense minister

46   *Hedging the China Threat*

Yu Ta-wei's visit, which wounded Yu and killed three vice commanders of the Quemoy Command. At a Politburo Standing Committee meeting on August 25, Mao stated that the bombardment was only a "probe" to explore the US attitude. Mao was not concerned about the ROC troops. Even though the United States had signed a defense treaty with Taiwan, that treaty did not clearly indicate whether its defense perimeter included Quemoy and Matsu. The PRC could test the US resolve to defend these islands by firing artillery shells.[38] During the meeting, PRC defense minister Peng Dehuai explained that their purpose was to expel Quemoy's defenders, obtain air supremacy in the Taiwan Strait, and understand the United States' bottom line.[39]

The convoy period. The United States deployed a large force in the Taiwan Strait in early September 1958 and proposed resuming ambassadorial talks in Warsaw. Because the United States had increased its military presence in the Taiwan Strait, the PRC began to moderate its bombardment. The PLA declared a three-day cease-fire on September 4.[40] On September 7, the US fleet began to conduct convoy missions with the ROC logistical vessels en route to Quemoy.[41] The PRC leaders forbade their forces from engaging the US military. Even when the United States convoyed the ROC's ships, Mao ordered his troops to "only attack Chiang's ships, not the American vessels." The US convoy fleet observed a three-mile limit to Quemoy.[42]

The bargaining period. By mid-September 1958, Washington and Beijing had resumed ambassadorial talks in Warsaw. In October, Mao held a series of Politburo Standing Committee meetings discussing responses of the United States and the ROC to their artillery blockade of Quemoy. The Chinese leaders began to alter their policy by imposing a cease-fire and attempted to drive a wedge between Taipei and Washington.[43] On October 6, PRC defense minister Peng issued a "Message to the Compatriots in Taiwan." He called for a peaceful solution to the Taiwan issues so that all Chinese might unite in opposition to the "American plot" to divide China. Peng also stated that their artillery forces should not fire a single shell during the next two days.[44]

As the PLA relaxed its siege of Quemoy, the crisis gradually diminished. On October 25, the PRC announced the "Second Message to the Compatriots in Taiwan." It stated that they would suspend firing on even days against airfields, beaches, and wharves, conditional on there being no US escorts. The message also called for cross-strait negotiations and stressed the common interest in avoiding a Two Chinas policy.[45]

After the establishment of the PRC, the Harry S. Truman administration refused to recognize the country. As more nations, including India, the United Kingdom, and Poland, established diplomatic relations with the PRC, this trend began to change. These nations urged the United States to adopt a Two Chinas policy. Chiang Kai-shek, on the other hand, vowed to recapture China and achieve reunification, whereas Mao asserted that Beijing was the only legitimate government. China attempted to divide Taipei and Washington by proposing that both China and Taiwan should oppose the Two Chinas policy.

At the beginning of November, the on-again, off-again firing pattern settled down, with firing only on the odd days. With these actions, the 1958 Quemoy Crisis came to an end.

The Individual Level: Eisenhower's Dilemma

Eisenhower was an astute political leader who advanced his purposes by playing down the political side of his leadership and playing up his role as a head of state.[46] Eisenhower made operational decisions in informal meetings with small groups of advisors in the Oval Office. He entered the presidency with extensive experience in the realm of national security policy.[47] Eisenhower had a rich military experience. He was able to govern and did not spend a lot of effort on convincing the other branches of the government to do his bidding. Eisenhower was a supporter of Taiwan, but he prevented having any military conflict with China.[48] From late 1954, the cross-strait situation deteriorated, prompting Eisenhower to respond. The 1955 Formosa Resolution gave the president authority to defend Taiwan and the offshore islands.[49] His administration considered several options, ranging from convincing Chiang Kai-shek to give up the islands, to employing nuclear weapons against the PRC. By the end of March 1955, Eisenhower felt that the United States should not be committed to the defense of these islands.[50]

Eisenhower's Predicament

The US commitment came under debate during the crisis. When the PLA attacked the Dachens in mid-January 1955, the ROC proposed retaliation. Eisenhower had reserved for himself the power to sanction retaliatory strikes by the ROC.[51] During the January 21 NSC meeting, Eisenhower stated that he avoided being pinned down to a defense of Quemoy and Matsu. However, he would not abandon them as long as the PRC menaced the islands. The United States might change its policy in the future after tensions eased but, at present, the United States had to help hold the islands. Eisenhower said that if there were an emergency during this crisis, he would do whatever had to be done to protect the US interests, even if his actions should be interpreted as acts of war. Eisenhower said he "would rather be impeached than fail to do his duty."[52]

48   *Hedging the China Threat*

Even the withdrawal of ROC troops from the Dachens did little to resolve the crisis. The PRC continued its military preparation, while Chiang Kai-shek determined to hold Quemoy and Matsu.[53] Eisenhower called his advisors on March 11 to discuss the ways in which to defend Taiwan. Eisenhower said that the United States should do whatever it could to help the ROC defend itself. If US intervention was inevitable, it should first use only conventional weapons.[54] On March 16, when Eisenhower was asked whether the United States would use nuclear weapons, he replied: "Where these things are used on strictly military purposes, I see no reason why they shouldn't be used, just as exactly as you would use a bullet or anything else." [55] He hoped that his statement would convince the Chinese of the determination of the United States.

At a White House meeting on April 1, Eisenhower suggested that the United States should get Chiang Kai-shek to withdraw voluntarily. In return, the United States would accelerate programs for strengthening the ROC forces and station additional US air, marine, and antiaircraft units in Taiwan.[56] The United States might seek to convince Chiang Kai-shek to reduce his forces on the offshore islands; to recognize them as "outposts, not citadels."[57] On April 5, Eisenhower urged Dulles to come up with a specific course of action. Dulles and his group had concluded that Eisenhower's path was self-defeating. The position paper that Dulles showed Eisenhower said, "Unless the PRC renounce their purpose to take Taiwan by force, the U.S. and the ROC will institute a naval interdiction along the China coast from, and including, Swatow in the south to Wenchow in the north." The blockade would aim at stopping the Communists from building up their supplies and facilities for an attack against Taiwan. Dulles also proposed stationing nuclear weapons on Taiwan to demonstrate US resolve. Eisenhower approved Dulles's plan. At Eisenhower's direction, on April 20 Admiral Radford and Assistant Secretary of State Robertson left for Taipei to present the downsizing forces plan to Chiang Kai-shek.[58] Eisenhower hoped that the ROC forces could improve their situation by withdrawing from the offshore islands. They suggested that Quemoy and Matsu garrisons be cut back to "outpost" strength.[59] Chiang Kai-shek refused to accept any idea of reducing his forces on the islands, let alone abandoning them to the PRC. Radford and Robertson tried to press him by telling him the United States was withdrawing its secret January 31 pledge to join in the defense of Quemoy and Matsu. Chiang Kai-shek still would not budge.[60]

Eisenhower's Objectives in Resolving the 1958 Crisis

After the PLA began a heavy bombardment of Quemoy, the ROC resupply ships en route to the offshore islands came under attack on August 25, 1958. Eisenhower met with his senior advisors, and said he did not wish to put the United States on the line with a full commitment: "The Orientals can be very devious."[61] Eisenhower considered that Quemoy was not worth American lives. He used military measures to decrease the conflicts while favoring the diplomatic approach. Eisenhower was dissatisfied with Chiang Kai-shek stationing a large force on the offshore islands in preparation for retaking China. He criticized Chiang Kai-shek for making ROC soldiers "figuratively hostages" on the islands. Eisenhower's objectives in resolving the crisis were to avoid conflicts with China, to prevent the crisis from escalation, and to maintain the US status as a world leader.

First, he avoided military conflicts with the PRC. At a White House meeting in mid-August, the chairman of the JCS, General Nathan F. Twining, expressed that US forces should be used to help the ROC resist a PLA blockade. With the belief that the offshore islands had no strategic value, and his desire to avoid war, Eisenhower emphasized that a hasty response to PLA action might spread hostilities. When the ROC requested a public statement of US support for the defense of Quemoy, Eisenhower was unwilling to do so. Eisenhower stated he was quite prepared to see the abandonment of Quemoy, but could not state that publicly.[62]

Second, he wanted to prevent the crisis from escalating. Eisenhower believed that if the crisis heated up, it might result not only in a military conflict with China, but also one with Russia.[63] His administration tried to manage the crisis by requesting that the ROC exercise self-restraint and to encourage the PRC to carry out a cease-fire. Throughout the crisis, Eisenhower put pressure on Chiang Kai-shek to take no retaliatory action against PLA facilities, to counter battery fire.[64] The United States sought a diplomatic approach through the UN or by a direct dialogue with China. Eisenhower's position was first to arrange a cease-fire, and then to conclude with an agreement renouncing the use of force.[65]

Third, Eisenhower desired to maintain the US status as a world leader. The United States believed that if Quemoy fell into the hands of Communists due to US inaction, it would tarnish the international image of the United States. Eisenhower explained, at a press conference, the necessity to defend Quemoy under the Formosa Resolution. He added that his administration viewed these islands as having more strategic importance. The United States would not desert its responsibilities.[66] In spite of an unwillingness to commit militarily, Eisenhower did state publicly that these islands had become more important. This was a common political cliché of US crisis management. Eisenhower did not want to show weakness as a world leader.

The State Level: The Threat of a Nuclear Attack

The Dachens, Quemoy, and Matsu were used for intelligence collection and launching raids against mainland China. In 1952, the US government encouraged the Chiang Kai-shek administration to defend these islands. As

50 Hedging the China Threat

a result, he desired that the United States extend its protection to these islands. On August 18, 1954, the NSC held a meeting on how the United States would respond if these islands were under attack. Most of the NSC members urged the United States to help the ROC prevent the loss of the outposts. However, General Matthew Ridgway, Army chief of staff, opposed this idea. He thought those islands were unimportant to the United States.[67] After the PLA's shelling of Quemoy in fall 1954, Acting Secretary of Defense Robert Anderson alerted Eisenhower that the attack could be an overture to an all-out war.[68]

Divisions over the Offshore Islands Defense, September 1954 to January 1955

From September 1954, the Eisenhower administration held divergent views in dealing with the conflict. First, General Ridgway differed from the perspectives of the JCS that US forces be employed in the defense of these islands. Chairman of the JCS, Admiral Radford, speaking for most of his colleagues, advocated a defense of the islands and the use of atomic weapons if the PLA launched a major assault.[69] Second, the majority of the NSC was reluctant to have another war with China. Secretary of Defense Charles Wilson feared that the US involvement would cause the United States to be trapped in the cross-strait conflict.[70]

Eisenhower agreed with Secretary Dulles and JCS chairman Radford that Quemoy and Matsu could not be held without US interposition. At the January 20 NSC meeting, Dulles stated that the PRC seemed to believe that the United States would not fight for any of the offshore islands. He suggested that, while seeking a cease-fire through the UN, the Eisenhower administration should ask Congress to grant the president the power to commit US forces to the defense of Taiwan, the Pescadores, Quemoy, and Matsu.[71] Dulles believed that leaving the US position unclear would create a greater risk. National Security Advisor (NSA) Robert Cutler, Treasury Secretary George Humphrey, and Defense Secretary Charles Wilson all disagreed with Dulles's view. They believed that the United States would be drawn into a war with China over these islands. Wilson said that the United States should hold Taiwan and the Pescadores, and let the others go. Eisenhower endorsed Dulles's proposal.[72]

Preparations for Nuclear War, February–March 1955

Since the PRC seemed to be ready for its military invasion of Quemoy and Matsu, following the fall of the Dachens, the Eisenhower administration decided to prepare for a nuclear war to deter the PLA from further invasion. As the Dachens were being evacuated in mid-February 1955, Eisenhower told the NSC that the surrender of Quemoy and Matsu could accelerate the collapse of the ROC. On March 6, Dulles suggested to Eisenhower that, to prevent the PLA from taking Quemoy and Matsu, the use of nuclear weapons might be necessary. The president agreed.[73] On March 9, Dulles expressed these feelings to Senator Walter George.[74] At the March 10 NSC meeting, Dulles stated that the United States had to prepare for the use of nuclear weapons in the defense of the offshore islands to make up for the deficiency in conventional forces. Admiral Radford endorsed Dulles's position.[75] The rest of the NSC members were quiet. Dulles informed the NSC that it was at the president's direction that he had included the reference to tactical nuclear weapons in his recent speech. After the meeting, Eisenhower and NSA Robert Cutler reviewed top secret policy papers on nuclear warfare. Cutler recommended, and Eisenhower agreed, "In the event of hostilities, the U.S. will consider nuclear weapons as available for use as other munitions."[76]

Starting in March, the Eisenhower administration began to use media to express the potential use of nuclear weapons. Eisenhower directed Dulles on March 8 in his TV address to explain that the government considered atomic weapons interchangeable with conventional weapons. Dulles spoke of powerful weapons of precision, which can destroy military targets.[77] At a March 15 press conference, Dulles said that "the likelihood of using city-destroying bombs in a war went down as the availability of smaller atomic weapons went up." At a news conference on March 16, Eisenhower said he saw no reason "why they shouldn't be used exactly as you would use a bullet, or anything else." The next day, Vice President Richard Nixon made it clear that should a war break out over the offshore islands, the United States would be forced to use nuclear weapons.[78] They hoped that these statements would have an effect in persuading the Chinese of the strength of the United States' determination.

After the political leaders' statements on using nuclear weapons, the military also prepared its nuclear mobilization. On March 25, Admiral Robert Carney, chief of naval operations, leaked to the press that the United States had plans to conduct an attack on China. He revealed that the military was planning nuclear attacks. On March 31, Radford briefed the NSC on the contingency plans in case of war with China. Precision atomic weapons would be used. On the same day, General Curtis LeMay, commander of the Strategic Air Command, confirmed that plans for B-36 strikes on Chinese targets were ready. The Eisenhower administration authorized the delivery of nuclear bombs to US bases in Okinawa.[79] On April 1, eighteen US warplanes flew over Chinese territory. The PRC condemned the flights as provocations.[80] On April 23, Premier Zhou announced that China did not want to have a war with the United States. China was ready for a dialogue with the United States to make peace across the Taiwan Strait. After Zhou's statement, the shelling of Quemoy and Matsu soon diminished.[81]

52   *Hedging the China Threat*

Admiral Radford, the principal JCS advocate of a more militant policy, was able to carry most of his colleagues with him in recommending that the United States defend Quemoy and Matsu. On this issue, General Ridgway stood in opposition to his colleagues. He found a powerful ally in Dulles, whose counsel of restraint was heeded by the NSC.[82] US policymakers did not want to be drawn into the conflict, but wanted the ROC to maintain control of the islands.[83] At the time, public opinion in the United States supported a tough stand against China. A Gallup Poll showed that 55 percent of those polled supported the use of atomic weapons in a war with China.[84] The Eisenhower administration hoped that the threat of using nuclear weapons would have a deterrent effect in persuading the PRC to de-escalate the crisis.

Decisionmaking Alternatives

During the 1958 Quemoy Crisis, Eisenhower did not want to have a direct military conflict with the PRC; neither would he tolerate Taiwan falling into the hands of an adversary. Under this thinking, the US alternatives for crisis management included showing US military might, offering security commitments to Taiwan, calling for the PRC cease-fire, and requesting the ROC's reduction of Quemoy forces.

Showing the US military might. At an August 14, 1958, NSC meeting, the chairman of the JCS, General Nathan Twining, stated that US forces should be used to assist the ROC in defending against a major PRC assault.[85] After discussion with military and political leaders, they agreed that the following actions should be taken: (1) one carrier should be added to the Seventh Fleet and three carriers should be kept in the Taiwan Strait; (2) a joint fleet exercise should be conducted; (3) the United States should increase its fighters on Taiwan; (4) there should be an increase in the flow of supplies to the offshore islands; and (5) there should be a US-ROC joint air defense exercise.[86]

Offering a security commitment. During the crisis, the ROC officials requested that the United States, especially Eisenhower, offer a security commitment to the defense of the offshore islands. Eisenhower refused to offer such a statement. As the crisis continued to develop, the NSC determined that without the Eisenhower statement, the PRC would intensify its aggression. Dulles, after consulting with the State Department and the JCS, was convinced that it was about time to state the US position in deterring the PLA invasion. On September 4, Dulles gave Eisenhower a memorandum. Dulles and Eisenhower started to edit it so that the statement might be made by the president. After consideration, Eisenhower decided to have it put out as a statement by Dulles.[87]

Calling for a PRC cease-fire. Seeking a diplomatic approach through the UN, or having a dialogue with the PRC, was the major thinking of Eisenhower on how to end the crisis.[88] The US position was first to arrange a cease-fire, and then to conclude an agreement renouncing the use of force. Following Zhou Enlai's public statement on September 6 urging a reopening of US-PRC talks, the United States reaffirmed its willingness to resume the talks at an ambassadorial level.[89]

Implementation of Crisis Management

After the PLA imposed shelling against Quemoy, the United States feared that it was a prelude to invasion. At the White House meeting on August 25, 1958, Eisenhower commented that US involvement would be for one reason, which was to sustain the defenders' morale. He decided to augment the Seventh Fleet, expedite aid to the ROC, and prepare for an escort of ROC ships to deter China's aggression.[90] After the meeting, the JCS instructed the Pacific Command to reinforce US air defense forces on Taiwan, to prepare to escort ROC supply ships to offshore islands, and to expedite the delivery of modern equipment to Quemoy. They cautioned that only conventional weapons would be authorized, but they were also instructed to be prepared to make atomic strikes deep into China.[91] The United States implemented its choices during the crisis as follows.

Requesting the ROC to exercise self-restraint. Soon after the attack, Ambassador Drumright and Vice Admiral Roland Smoot called on Chiang Kai-shek. They emphasized that Eisenhower expected the ROC to consult with the United States concerning any use of force, unless an attack was required in an emergency action. Chiang Kai-shek promised his government would inform the United States before attacking China.[92]

Convoying ROC supply ships to Quemoy, but observing a three-mile limit. On August 28, the officials from the State Department, Pentagon, and Central Intelligence Agency (CIA) discussed the convoy mission to Quemoy. Deputy Secretary of Defense Donald Quarles recommended the convoy assistance. Admiral Burke presented a paper outlining courses of action. These actions proposed to escort ROC convoys to the offshore islands, and the United States to assume responsibility for the air defense of Taiwan and the Pescadores.[93] At a White House meeting on August 29, Eisenhower wanted to find ways of avoiding close-in escorts. The participants suggested

54 Hedging the China Threat

that the United States could define the area of escort activities as "within international waters." Eisenhower acquiesced.[94]

Offering the security commitment to the defense of the offshore islands. In a meeting with Eisenhower, Dulles gave the president a memorandum regarding the offshore islands issue. A statement would be given by Dulles as an authorization of the president.[95] The emphasis of the memorandum stressed that if the PRC believed the United States would intervene, perhaps using nuclear weapons, it was probable there would be no attempt to take Quemoy by assault, and the situation might quiet down, as in 1955.[96] The White House press release was stated by Dulles, which emphasized that the United States was bound by a treaty to help defend Taiwan from armed attack. The president was authorized by Congress to employ US forces for the securing of related positions such as Quemoy and Matsu.[97] Dulles concluded by expressing US interest in a peaceful end to the crisis. The "war and peace" strategy was used by the US government to discourage enemy military hostility.

Urging the reduction of forces in the offshore islands. On October 6, the PRC announced the suspension of the bombardment. After the PRC's ceasefire statement, the US State Department and Department of Defense suggested that the US Navy should suspend convoy activities for as long as the PLA suspended bombardment.[98] Later, Eisenhower wrote to Dulles that he believed Chiang Kai-shek might be persuaded to accept the proposal to reduce ROC forces from Quemoy because it would be in a better military position to carry out the "return policy" in the event of internal disorder on the mainland. To help the ROC accomplish this objective, the United States would assist in providing an adequate amphibious lift capability.[99] Thereafter, the United States started to push the ROC government to reduce forces in the offshore islands.

Eisenhower and Dulles were the two most important players who directed the US decisionmaking in the Quemoy Crisis. Both leaders were determined to deal with the military conflict through a diplomatic approach with limited military intervention. They also requested their officials to urge the ROC leaders to exercise restraint.

The International Level:
The US Allies Push for US-PRC Dialogues

Eisenhower believed that the 1950s offshore islands crises had triggered a split between the United States and its allies. During the 1950s, US allies were concerned that the two crises might further trigger a major war between the United States and the PRC, eventually leading to a world war. Therefore, they proposed several solutions to diminish the crisis.

New Zealand Call for a Cease-Fire

During the First Taiwan Strait Crisis, the United Kingdom and the United States pushed New Zealand to act as a front for the reference to the United Nations. On January 28, 1955, New Zealand introduced a resolution in the Security Council calling for a cease-fire in the Taiwan Strait. The Security Council invited the PRC to participate in a discussion on the resolution. The PRC refused to participate in any meeting that would include the ROC on an equal basis. Instead, the PRC proposed direct negotiations with the United States. Premier Zhou told the Swedish representative in Beijing that they would not accept the New Zealand resolution as it placed the ROC and the PRC on an equal footing.[100]

The US Allies Urge Dialogue

The United Kingdom, Australia, Canada, and NATO all urged Dulles to talk to the PRC. British prime minister Winston Churchill recommended the evacuation of Quemoy and Matsu, while defending Taiwan and the Pescadores islands. Australian prime minister Robert Menzies made it clear that the Australian people would not support war over these islands. Canadian foreign minister Lester Pearson ruled out Canada's support for the United States in the dispute. General Alfred Gruenther, Supreme Allied Commander, Europe, wrote to Eisenhower that the United States faced a handicap in terms of public relations: only the ROC and South Korea supported the US defense of these islands. The rest of the Far East reacted with "uneasiness to outright condemnation of the U.S. stand."[101] At a NATO ministerial meeting in May 1955, Belgian foreign minister Paul-Henri Spaak raised concerns about the US support to the ROC. He argued that recognition of the PRC was inevitable.[102]

The Geneva Talks

The Bandung Conference, a meeting of twenty-nine African and Asian nations in April 1955, invited the PRC, and not the ROC, to represent China. At the conference, Premier Zhou announced the PRC's desire to initiate dialogue with the United States.[103] In response, US officials requested the UK to convey their interest in engaging with China.[104] The State Department intended to bring back the American civilians detained in China and facilitate the peaceful settlement of Taiwan's issues through dialogue. At the end of July, the PRC released eleven Americans.[105] The ambassadorial talks, held

56   Hedging the China Threat

in Geneva, began on August 1, 1955, by the US ambassador to Czechoslovakia, Alexis Johnson, and the PRC ambassador to Poland, Wang Ping-nan. During the following rounds of meetings, Wang highlighted China's sovereignty over Taiwan, and urged the US forces to leave Taiwan.[106]

International Responses During the 1958 Quemoy Crisis

In spite of an unwillingness to commit militarily, Eisenhower did state publicly that the offshore islands had become more important, and that the United States would defend them. Eisenhower and Dulles adopted diplomatic and military measures to decrease the tensions simultaneously and favored the diplomatic approach.

Resuming the US and PRC ambassador talks. The ambassadorial talks, held in Geneva, began on August 1, 1955, by US ambassador to Czechoslovakia Alexis Johnson and PRC ambassador to Poland Wang Ping-nan.[107] Johnson later was transferred from Czechoslovakia to Thailand. Dulles assigned a representative of nonambassadorial rank to continue the dialogue. The PRC rejected this proposal, and the meetings were suspended at the end of 1957. To restart the dialogue, in June 1958 the State Department named US ambassador to Poland Jacob Beam as the representative. The PRC demanded the talks should resume within fifteen days.[108] In return, Dulles declared that the United States did not intend to be bound by the ultimatum. A letter proposing the resumption of talks in Warsaw was sent to Ambassador Wang. Wang referred the matter to Beijing.[109] At the time, Mao had decided to launch a military assault on Quemoy. They ignored the response.

The PRC decided to inform the United States of its desire to resume dialogue with the intent to observe the US and ROC's intentions regarding the crisis. Word reached Washington on September 6 of the Zhou statement offering to reopen the ambassadorial talks. Eisenhower held a meeting with officials from the State Department, CIA, and military. After the meeting, a statement was issued expressing the United States' willingness to resume the talks.[110]

The Warsaw Talks. On September 12, Ambassador Wang arrived in Warsaw after stopping in Moscow on the way from Beijing. Ambassador Beam received his instructions for the first meeting. The first objective was the cessation of hostilities. If this were secured, it would then turn into a discussion of renunciation of the use of force. On September 13 and 14, Dulles cabled Beam stating that world opinion demanded measures to reduce the tension. Beam referred to the long record of frustrating meetings previously held in Geneva. One thing that could not be entertained was the turning over of the offshore islands to the PRC.[111] Beam and Wang renewed the talks on September 15. Beam urged a cease-fire and stated that once this had been accomplished, they would turn to questions of terminating provocative activities. Wang pressed him for more details, but Beam insisted that a cease-fire was a prerequisite to other discussions. Wang declared that Taiwan and the coastal islands were Chinese territories, and their liberation was an internal affair. Beam replied that the ROC was a sovereign state and trusted ally. The US forces in the area were for defensive purposes in fulfillment of treaty obligations.[112] Most State Department officials were supportive of using the Warsaw talks to end the crisis. When the negotiations began, both parties explored their rivals' intent. After the PRC declared the cease-fire, the United States responded with the suspension of escort missions. In retrospect, the Geneva and Warsaw talks did play some role in ending the crisis.

Before the end of the First Taiwan Strait Crisis, Beijing feared that the United States might launch a general war with the possibility of using nuclear weapons against them. The PRC decided to propose negotiations with the US government.[113] The American mastermind of the Warsaw talks was Dulles. There was one basic rule guiding Dulles's negotiations: initiatives for settlement of conflicts must not be undertaken when the adversary appears to be dealing from a position of strength. Dulles was convinced that minor concessions would be interpreted by the Communists as a sign of weakness. This would make them less likely to make concessions.[114]

In 1958, the Beijing leaders had made up their minds to launch an artillery bombardment. In light of the bombardments not achieving their goal, and the United States increasing its military assistance to Taiwan, the PRC decided to reopen the Warsaw talks. During the talks, the United States adopted the incremental approach to push the PRC for a cease-fire, and not give up its Taiwan stance. The Beijing strategy was to state the standard line repeatedly, to lure the United States to withdraw its forces from Taiwan. The Warsaw talks did contribute to ending the crisis.

Conclusion

During the 1954–1955 Offshore Islands Crisis, President Eisenhower believed that these islands were not worth the lives of US soldiers. He preferred diplomatic approaches to military conflict resolution. As China escalated the crisis, the National Security Council and US military hoped that the threat of nuclear retaliation would persuade the PRC to de-escalate. The Eisenhower administration's goals in dealing with the 1958 Quemoy Crisis were not only to keep Quemoy from falling, but also to avoid a direct conflict with China. Most US allies urged the Eisenhower administration to engage in negotiations with China to alleviate the crisis.

58   Hedging the China Threat

The primary US policy outcomes of the 1954–1955 Offshore Islands Crisis were the decision to assist in the evacuation of ROC military and civilian personnel from the Dachen Islands and to deter the PLA from continuing the PRC invasion by threatening China with nuclear war. Three years later, during the 1958 Quemoy Crisis, the US government urged the Chiang Kai-shek administration to exercise restraint. US military vessels convoyed ROC supply ships to Quemoy, while strictly adhering to a three-mile limit.

Eisenhower's goals in resolving both crises were to avoid military conflicts with the PRC, to prevent the crises from escalating, and to maintain the United States as a world leader. During the 1954–1955 Offshore Island Crisis, Eisenhower was unwilling to commit to sending US troops to intervene in the conflict, but he did threaten China with the use of nuclear weapons to defend these islands. During the 1958 Quemoy Crisis, however, Eisenhower became more cautious because he suspected Chiang Kai-shek was intending to use the crisis to draw the United States into his ultimate plan: to retake mainland China. Eisenhower's perspective strongly influenced the State Department, the NSC, and the military leaders. Relations between the United States and its allies were becoming strained because of allies' concerns that the crises could conceivably escalate into a world war.

Consequently, the US leaders began to oppose Chiang Kai-shek's retaking of mainland China and support the former proposal of Two Chinas. The John F. Kennedy administration continued to deal with this issue.

Notes

1. Kenneth W. Condit, *History of the Joint Chiefs of Staff,* vol. 6: *The Joint Chiefs of Staff and National Policy, 1955–1956* (Washington, DC: Office of the Chairman of the Joint Chiefs of Staff, 1998), pp. 193–194.

2. US Department of State, "1953–1960: The Taiwan Straits Crises: 1954–55 and 1958," *Milestones in the History of U.S. Foreign Relations: 1953–1960,* https://history.state.gov/milestones/1953-1960/taiwan-strait-crises.

3. Shin Chu and Yong Wang "The Beginning and End of the Three Taiwan Strait Crises," *Literary Circles of CPC History, vol. 3* (Nanchang: Party History Research Office of Jiangxi Provincial Committee, 1997), p. 44.

4. Dwight D. Eisenhower, *The White House Years: Mandate for Change, 1953–1956* (Garden City, NY: Doubleday, 1963), pp. 461–463, 469–470.

5. US Department of State, "1953–1960: The Taiwan Straits Crises."

6. Gordon H. Chang, "To the Nuclear Brink: Eisenhower, Dulles, and the Quemoy-Matsu Crisis," *International Security* 12, no. 4 (Spring 1988): 106.

7. Bennett C. Rushkoff, "Eisenhower, Dulles and the Quemoy-Matsu Crisis, 1954–1955," *Political Science Quarterly* 96, no. 3 (Autumn 1981): 479.

8. US Department of State, "1953–1960: The Taiwan Straits Crises."

9. Robert J. Watson, *History of the Joint Chiefs of Staff,* vol. 5: *The Joint Chiefs of Staff and National Policy, 1953–1954* (Washington, DC: Office of the Chairman of the Joint Chiefs of Staff, 1998), p. 261.

The Offshore Islands Crises   59

10. Hsiao-ting Lin, "U.S.-Taiwan Military Diplomacy Revisited: Chiang Kai-shek, Baituan, and the 1954 Mutual Defense Pact," *Diplomatic History* 37, no. 5 (November 2013): 972.

11. Ibid., p. 983.

12. Watson, *History of the Joint Chiefs,* pp. 261–262.

13. Lin, "U.S.-Taiwan Military Diplomacy Revisited," p. 985.

14. Watson, *History of the Joint Chiefs,* p. 263.

15. US Department of State, "Memorandum of Conversation, by the Director of the Office of Chinese Affairs (McConaughy)," *FRUS, 1952–1954,* vol. 14, part 1, *China and Japan,* https://history.state.gov.

16. Lin, "U.S.-Taiwan Military," p. 988.

17. Ibid., p. 989.

18. Watson, *History of the Joint Chiefs,* p. 263.

19. Harry Harding, "The Legacy of the Decade for Later Years: An American Perspective," in *Sino-American Relations 1945–1955: A Joint Reassessment of a Critical Decade,* edited by Harry Harding and Yuan Ming (Washington, DC: Scholarly Resources, 1989), p. 321.

20. Kuttan A. Soman, "A Rash and Quixotic Policy: The Taiwan Strait Crisis of 1954–1955," in *Double-Edged Sword: Nuclear Diplomacy in Unequal Conflicts— The United States and China, 1950–1958* (Westport, CT: Greenwood, 2000), pp. 118–121.

21. Ibid., p. 122.

22. Ibid., pp. 125–126.

23. Ibid., pp. 126–127.

24. Watson, *History of the Joint Chiefs,* pp. 265–266.

25. Soman, "Rash and Quixotic Policy," p. 129.

26. Watson, *History of the Joint Chiefs,* p. 266.

27. Soman, "Rash and Quixotic Policy," pp. 130–131.

28. Chang, "To the Nuclear Brink," p. 104.

29. Ibid.

30. Soman, "Rash and Quixotic Policy," p. 131.

31. Chang, "To the Nuclear Brink," p. 117.

32. Condit, *History of the Joint Chiefs,* p. 208.

33. Charles A. McClelland, "Action Structures and Communication in Two International Crises: Quemoy and Berlin," *Background* 7, no. 4 (February 1964): 201–215.

34. Huai-chi Han, *Contemporary Chinese Army's Military Work* (Beijing: China Social Sciences, 1989), p. 386.

35. Kenneth W. Allen, "The PLA Air Force: 1949-2002, Overview and Lessons Learned," in *The Lessons of History: The Chinese People's Liberation's Army at 75,* edited by Laurie Burkitt, Andrew Scobell, and Larry M. Wortzel (Beijing: Strategic Studies Institute, 2003), p. 113.

36. Military Affair Bureau of the Ministry of National Defense, *August 23 Taiwan Strait Battle* (Taipei: Military Affair Bureau of the Ministry of National Defense, 1998), p. 29.

37. "Artillery Combat of the August 23 Quemoy Bombardment," Republic of China (ROC) Ministry of National Defense, CD, no. 000267140001003 (Top Secret).

38. Dinglie Wang et al., *Contemporary Chinese Air Force* (Beijing: Chinese Social Science Press, 1989), pp. 334–336.

39. Niu Jun, "A Further Discussion of Decision-making in the 1958 Shelling of Jinmen," *Journal of Modern Chinese History* 3, no. 2 (2009).

60   Hedging the China Threat

40. Han, *Contemporary Chinese Army's Military Work,* pp. 386–400.

41. Military Affair Bureau of the Ministry of National Defense, *August 23 Taiwan Strait Battle,* pp. 198–204.

42. Bing-Nan Wang, *Memoirs of Nine Years' Sino-US Ambassador Talks* (Beijing: World Knowledge Press, 1985), p. 75.

43. "Mao Zedong, 2 October 1958," in Mao Zedong, *Selected Works of Mao Zedong on Diplomacy* (Beijing: Central Historical Literature Press and World Knowledge Press, 1994), p. 356.

44. Jun, "Further Discussion."

45. Mao Zedong, "Mao Zedong on Chen Geng's Report, December 18, 1957," *A Collection of Mao Zedong's Military Papers* (Beijing: Military Science Press, 1993), p. 373.

46. Charles W. Ostrom Jr., and Brian L. Job, "The President and the Political Use of Force," *American Political Science Review* 80, no. 2 (June 1986): 541–566.

47. Fred I. Greenstein and Richard H. Immerman, "Effective National Security Advising: Recovering the Eisenhower Legacy," Political Science Quarterly, vol. 115, no. 3. (Autumn, 2000), pp. 335–345.

48. Watson, *History of the Joint Chiefs,* p. 256.

49. US Department of State, "1953–1960: The Taiwan Straits Crises."

50. Soman, "Rash and Quixotic Policy," p. 149.

51. Condit, *History of the Joint Chiefs,* p. 195.

52. Chang, "To the Nuclear Brink," p. 103.

53. Condit, *History of the Joint Chiefs,* pp. 202–203.

54. Soman, "Rash and Quixotic Policy," p. 149.

55. Ibid., p. 137.

56. Ibid., p. 142.

57. US Department of State, "188. Memorandum of a Conversation Between the President and the Secretary of State, Washington," April 4, 1955, *FRUS, 1955–1957,* vol. 2, *China,* https://history.state.gov.

58. Chang, "To the Nuclear Brink," pp. 113–115.

59. Condit, *History of the Joint Chiefs,* p. 206.

60. Chang, "To the Nuclear Brink," p. 116.

61. Byron R. Fairchild and Walter S. Poole, *History of the Joint Chiefs of Staff,* vol. 7: *The Joint Chiefs of Staff and National Policy, 1957–1960* (Washington, DC: Office of the Chairman of the Joint Chiefs of Staff, 2000), p. 210.

62. US Department of State, "Memorandum of Meeting, Subject: Summary of the Meeting at the White House on the Taiwan Strait Situation," August 29, 1958, *FRUS, 1958–1960,* no. 52, pp. 96–99.

63. Vladislav Zubok and Constantine Pleshakov, *Inside the Kremlin's Cold War: From Stalin to Khrushchev* (Cambridge: Harvard University Press, 1996), pp. 217–229.

64. Leonard H. D. Gordon, "United States Opposition to Use of Force in the Taiwan Strait, 1954–1962," *Journal of American History* 72, no. 3 (December 1985): 637–660.

65. Wang, *Memoirs,* pp. 72–73.

66. M. H. Halperin, *The 1958 Taiwan Strait Crisis: A Documented History* (Santa Monica: RAND, 1966), pp. 187–188.

67. Watson, *History of the Joint Chiefs,* pp. 261–262.

68. Soman, "Rash and Quixotic Policy," p. 115.

69. Condit, *History of the Joint Chiefs,* p. 194.

70. Chang, "To the Nuclear Brink," p. 100.

The Offshore Islands Crises   61

71. Ibid., pp. 101–102.
72. Ibid., p. 104.
73. Ibid., pp. 105–106.
74. Soman, "Rash and Quixotic Policy," p. 134.
75. Chang, "To the Nuclear Brink," p. 107.
76. Gregory Kulacki, "Nuclear Weapons in the Taiwan Strait Part I," *Journal for Peace and Nuclear Disarmament* 3, no. 2 (October 2020): pp. 310–341.
77. Ibid.
78. Chang, "To the Nuclear Brink," p. 108.
79. Kulacki, "Nuclear Weapons."
80. Chang, "To the Nuclear Brink," p. 112.
81. Ibid., p. 117.
82. Watson, *History of the Joint Chiefs,* p. 279.
83. US Department of State, "1953–1960: The Taiwan Straits Crises."
84. Soman, "Rash and Quixotic Policy," p. 140.
85. US Department of State, "Memorandum for the Record, No. 33, August 14, 1958," *FRUS,* pp. 52–53.
86. US Department of State, "Memorandum from Acting Secretary of State Herter to the Secretary of State Dulles, Subject: Summary Recommended Warning to Peiping Against Attacking the Offshore Islands," August 15, 1958, *FRUS,* no. 34, pp. 56–57.
87. US Department of State, "Memorandum of Conference with President Eisenhower," September 4, 1958, *FRUS,* no. 66, pp. 130–131.
88. US Department of State, "Memorandum Conference with President Eisenhower: Newport, Rhode Island," White House press release, Subject: Statement by the Secretary of State, September 4, 1958, *FRUS,* no. 68, pp. 131–136.
89. Wang, *Memoirs,* pp. 72–73.
90. US Department of State, "Memorandum of Meeting: Summary Meeting at the White House on Taiwan Straits Situation," August 25, 1958, *FRUS,* vol. 19, no. 43, *China* (Washington, DC: Government Printing Office, 1996), pp. 73–76.
91. Jacob Van Straaveren, *Air Operation in the Taiwan Crisis of 1958* (USAF Historical Division Liaison Office, 1962), pp. 17–18.
92. US Department of State, "Telegram from the Embassy in the Republic of China to the Department of State," August 24, 1958, *FRUS, 1958–1960,* vol. 19, no. 42, *China,* p. 70.
93. US Department of State, "Memorandum of Conversion: Meeting in Pentagon on Offshore Islands Situation," August 28, 1958, *FRUS,* no. 51, pp. 89–95.
94. US Department of State, "Memorandum of Meeting, Subject: Summary of Meeting at the White House on the Taiwan Strait Situation," August 29, 1958," *FRUS,* no. 52, p. 99.
95. US Department of State, "Memorandum of Conference with President Eisenhower," September 4, 1958," *FRUS,* no. 66, pp. 130–131.
96. US Department of State, "Memorandum Prepared by Secretary of State Dulles," September 4, 1958, *FRUS,* no. 77, pp. 131–134.
97. US Department of State, "White House Press Release, Newport, Rhode Island, Statement by the Secretary of State," September 4, 1958, *FRUS,* no. 68, pp. 134–136.
98. US Department of State, "Memorandum of Conversation, Suspension of US Convoy Escorting during Chicom Ceasefire," October 7, 1958, *FRUS,* no. 156, p. 329.
99. US Department of State, "Memorandum from President Eisenhower to the Secretary of State," October 7, 1958, *FRUS,* no. 166, p. 347.

62 Hedging the China Threat

100. Soman, "Rash and Quixotic Policy," p. 132.

101. Ibid., p. 140.

102. Kulacki, "Nuclear Weapons."

103. Rushkoff, "Eisenhower," p. 479.

104. Baijia Zhang and Qingguo Jia, "Steering Wheel, Shock Absorber, and Diplomatic Probe in Confrontation Sino-American Ambassadorial Talks Seen from the Chinese Perspective," in *Re-examining the Cold War: U.S.-China Diplomacy, 1954–1973,* edited by Robert S. Ross and Changbin Jiang (Cambridge: Harvard University Asia Center, 2001), pp. 173–199.

105. Ta-Jen Liu, *A History of Sino-American Diplomatic Relations, 1840–1974* (Taipei: China Academy, 1978), p. 350.

106. T. N. Schroth, et al., *China and U.S. Far East Policy, 1945–1967,* Congressional Quarterly Series, (Washington, DC: 1967), pp. 74–75.

107. Ibid.

108. "Statement by the Chinese Government on China-US Ambassadorial Meeting, June 30, 1958," *Compilation of Documents in China-US Relations,* vol. 2 (Beijing: World Knowledge Press), pp. 2626–2628.

109. US Department of State, "State Department Telegram to Warsaw," July 21, 1958, *FRUS,* no. 73.

110. Halperin, *1958 Taiwan Strait Crisis,* pp. 441–442.

111. US Department of State, "Telegram from the Secretary of State John Dulles to the Embassy in Poland," September 14, 1958, *FRUS,* no. 89, pp. 186–187.

112. US Department of State, "Telegram from the State Department to the Embassy in Poland," September 15, 1958, *FRUS,* no. 91, pp. 191–193.

113. Bennett C. Rushkoff, "Eisenhower," p. 479.

114. Ole Holsti, "The Operational Code Approach to the Study of Political Leaders: John Foster Dulles' Philosophical and Instrumental Beliefs," *Canadian Journal of Political Science* 3, no. 1 (March 1970), pp. 123–157.

4

Maintaining the Status Quo: The Kennedy Administration

WHEN IN OFFICE, JOHN F. KENNEDY WAS THE MOVER OF POLICY, BUT HE WORKED closely with his senior advisors such as Secretary of Defense Robert McNamara, Secretary of State Dean Rusk, and National Security Advisor (NSA) McGeorge Bundy. Kennedy was at the center of foreign policy and made it clear that decisions were his to make.[1] Several of his foreign policy advisors suggested that Dwight Eisenhower's policy of containment and isolation of the People's Republic of China (PRC) should be reconsidered. Before his presidency, Kennedy thought that the US policy toward the PRC was too rigid. He felt that it was time for the US government to reevaluate its China policy by promoting a more flexible approach. Kennedy said, "We should indicate our willingness to talk to them when they desire to do so." Nevertheless, after Kennedy was elected president, he believed that any change in the China policy would have been a disaster for his new administration.[2]

Historical Events: Two Chinas, Retaking Mainland China, and the 1962 Taiwan Strait Crisis

Due to his slim election victory, Kennedy was unwilling to take any significant risk of the US government shifting its China policy. During the Kennedy administration, there were three major events regarding China: a reevaluation of the Two Chinas policy, controversy over the ROC's retaking mainland China policy, and the 1962 Taiwan Strait Crisis.

The Two Chinas Policy

After its founding in 1949, recognition of the PRC was withheld by the Harry S. Truman administration, but the United States did not close the

64 Hedging the China Threat

door on future recognition. When Mao Tse-tung sent the People's Liberation Army (PLA) to fight in the Korean War, the United States decided to continue to recognize the Republic of China (ROC) government as the only legitimate Chinese government in the United Nations. As more and more countries such as India, the United Kingdom, and Poland established diplomatic relations with the PRC at the start of the Kennedy administration in January 1961, anticipation for change in the China policy increased. Kennedy's secretary of state, Dean Rusk, advocated a Two Chinas policy. Rusk asked Kennedy if he wanted the State Department to study potential changes in China policy, and the two drew up possible alternatives: recognize both Chinas, the so-called Two Chinas approach; work behind the scenes to reconcile Beijing and Taipei; and wait for further developments. Kennedy, however, was not prepared to alter existing policies.[3] In the early 1960s, public opinion endorsing a Two Chinas policy remained slim because most Americans continued to support the ROC as the only legitimate China.[4] In 1961, newly elected President Kennedy sent a letter to President Chiang Kai-shek, stating that his government would continue to work closely with and support the ROC government.[5]

The Kennedy administration's refusal to recognize the PRC was driven by domestic politics in the United States. To begin with, both the House of Representatives and the Senate were opposed to changes in US policy toward China. The majority of high-ranking Kennedy administration advisors, particularly those in the Department of Defense, were hesitant to pursue a policy that would appear soft on the PRC. Second, the powerful China lobby, comprised of advocacy groups urging for US support for the ROC, was staunchly opposed to any shift in China policy. Third, evidence of increased PRC activity in Southeast Asia, particularly in Vietnam, made a change of course unwise. Changing China's policy was a risky option for the new administration.[6]

The PRC insisted that the United States leave Taiwan before any normalization between the two countries could be possible. Premier Zhou Enlai stated in January 1961 that the PRC would refuse to join any international organization if the ROC was a member. He urged any country that wished to establish diplomatic relations with the PRC to sever ties with the ROC. The PRC would not take part in any international activities where Two Chinas would be acknowledged. In response, the United States stated unequivocally that it would maintain diplomatic recognition of the ROC, honor defense treaty commitments, and continue to support UN membership for the ROC.[7]

Despite the above unfavorable factors, there were different voices in the State Department advocating for a change in China policy. Adlai Stevenson, UN ambassador, W. Averell Harriman, under secretary of state for Far Eastern affairs, and Chester A. Bowles, under secretary of state, were all supporters of a more flexible China policy. They advised the United States to pursue flexible US-China relations while reducing mutual hostility.[8]

Others emphasized the risks of increasing contact with the PRC, predicting that the risks posed by the PRC would rise rather than fall in the coming years. To deter the PRC's military aggression, the United States needed to maintain a strong military posture in East Asia. The idea of accommodating the PRC was also rejected by Walter P. McConaughy, assistant secretary of Far Eastern affairs. He argued in favor of nonrecognition, claiming that the disadvantages of recognition outweighed the benefits.[9]

In July 1962, the State Department sent Kennedy a draft paper titled "Basic National Security Policy," which advocated a carrot-and-stick approach to the PRC. The following key measures were outlined in the paper: (1) the United States should leave the door open to expanding commercial and cultural ties with the PRC; (2) it should accept a Two Chinas policy with two separate Chinese governments; (3) it should gradually withdraw military support for the offshore islands; (4) it should refrain from participating in ROC operations against China; and (5) it should deter PRC aggression while also promoting the possibility of improved relations.[10]

Retaking Mainland China

Since the ROC government retreated to Taiwan in 1949, President Chiang Kai-shek vowed to "retake mainland China" and garrisoned large elite forces in the offshore islands as a strategic platform to reclaim China. The ROC government could not persuade the Kennedy administration to support the recovery of their lost territory.[11] Instead, US policymakers became concerned about ROC's constant statements to "retake mainland China" as provocative, as this could create armed conflict across the Taiwan Strait, including the United States' involvement.

Chiang Kai-shek's opportunity for reclaiming mainland China increased in the early 1960s, when China experienced a severe famine, killing an estimated 30 million people. Chiang Kai-shek also hoped to use the deterioration of the situation in Vietnam to open a new front against the PRC. While Pentagon officials sought to use ROC forces in the Vietnam War, senior State Department officials disagreed, warning that the presence of ROC troops would invite PRC intervention.[12]

President Chiang Kai-shek put pressure on the Kennedy administration in February 1962 to allow the United States and Taiwan to take joint military action to reclaim mainland China. He was dead set on launching an invasion that year, but the ROC lacked the capability for sealift, air cover, and supply. The ROC government requested in March that the United

66 Hedging the China Threat

States provide Taiwan with military transport aircraft to drop paratroopers. Kennedy agreed to send two C-123 aircraft to Taiwan, but he asked the chief of the CIA station in Taiwan, Ray Cline, to persuade Chiang Kai-shek to refrain from publicly declaring that he would use force to retake China.[13]

On May 17, 1962, Cline briefed Kennedy on the China situation at the White House. Cline said that Chinese refugees had arrived by the thousands on the Hong Kong border. This tended to confirm Chian Kai-shek's belief that the time was ripe for establishing a beachhead in South China. Chiang Kai-shek wanted Kennedy to consider the following points: first, any operations against the mainland, whether clandestine or open military operations, must be jointly decided on by the United States and the ROC. Second, Chiang Kai-shek promised to take no action until October 1, but it would be very difficult to postpone beyond this date. Third, the United States should provide C-123s, B-57s, and LSTs for amphibious forces.[14]

According to the memorandum from the director of the Bureau of Intelligence and Research, Roger Hilsman, to the Secretary of State, Dean Rusk, in May 1962, the ROC sought increased US material support and eventual US involvement in an attempt to regain control of China. The US estimates showed that the ROC plan was not going to work, based on three reasons: (1) there was no chance that a mainland uprising would extend beyond a single province; (2) it was unlikely that such an uprising would guarantee ROC leadership; and (3) even if an ROC-sponsored uprising threatened the PRC, Russian intervention would be forthcoming.[15]

On June 5, 1962, the director of the Central Intelligence Agency (CIA), John McCone, visited Taipei for talks with Chiang Kai-shek. Chiang Kai-shek stated that the initial military operations against the PRC were originally scheduled to take place in April–May 1962, but he had been persuaded by the United States to postpone them. His forces would have to be prepared to act in October. Chiang Kai-shek stated that he would not undertake any "formal military operations" without consultation with the United States. McCone questioned him on the meaning of "formal military operations," asking whether dropping teams of 200 or 300 troops constituted a formal military action. Chiang Kai-shek responded that such drops would not fall under the definition of formal action and, therefore, would not require US consent. Large-scale amphibious operations would constitute a formal military action and would require concurrence. McCone stated that a 200-troop drop was a sizable operation. Any such operation must be agreed on between both governments. Chiang Kai-shek finally agreed.[16]

In discussing the question of US support for ROC efforts to recover the mainland, McCone advised Chiang Kai-shek that two C-123 aircraft were being prepared and that the ROC request for three additional C-123s was under consideration. McCone said that no decision had been reached concerning the provision of B-57 bombers and Landing Ship, Tanks (LSTs) for the ROC.[17]

The 1962 Taiwan Strait Crisis

In June 1962, cross-strait military tension escalated. PRC troop movements in mid-June led State Department officials to take a serious view of PRC intentions. Their assessment was that the PRC decided to exploit the troop movements politically by creating a new Offshore Islands Crisis. The State Department, nonetheless, did not think a sudden attack was either imminent or likely.[18] On June 23, PRC ambassador to Poland Wang Ping-nan, summoned his US counterpart, John Cabot, and warned that the United States would bear the responsibility if Chiang Kai-shek's forces invaded China. On June 27, Kennedy declared that the United States opposed the use of force in the Taiwan Strait.[19]

After meeting with Chiang Kai-shek in July, the newly appointed US ambassador to Taiwan, Alan Kirk, proposed that the United States provide him with bombers and landing craft in exchange for the United States being able to oversee ROC military planning. On August 8, Assistant Secretary of State for Far Eastern Affairs Harriman sent a telegram to Kirk. Regarding the ROC request for bombers and landing craft, the United States would not agree to supply the requested items under present circumstances. Only two C-123s would be brought to Taiwan in support of the small drop program.[20]

After the crisis subsided, Chiang Kai-shek's forces continued to launch intelligence-gathering operations, using fishing boats to land infiltration on mainland China. The State Department was concerned that these operations would lead to drawing the United States into ROC plans for an invasion. In February 1963, Ambassador Kirk noticed that the ROC military was building landing craft, training soldiers in a new airborne division, and stating that the time was right for retaking the mainland.[21]

Realizing that Chiang Kai-shek might be preparing to invade mainland China, in May 1963 Kennedy reiterated his statement regarding the United States' position that the Mutual Defense Treaty prevented Taipei from taking unilateral action and that Washington did not support it.[22] On September 11, 1963, Kennedy met with Defense Minister Chiang Ching-Kuo. When the minister proposed that the United States and the ROC take advantage of the situation in China, Kennedy responded that the United States did not wish to become involved in cross-strait military operations.[23]

In the wake of the 1962 Cuban Missile Crisis, Kennedy, when dealing with an international crisis, shifted from a potential military confrontation to mutual negotiations. Although Kennedy was assassinated in November 1963, Roger Hilsman, who was assistant secretary of state for

68 *Hedging the China Threat*

Far Eastern affairs, later stated that Kennedy had approved adding flexibility to its policy toward the PRC.[24]

The Individual Level:
Maintaining the Status Quo with Kennedy

Throughout the 1950s, then-senator Kennedy viewed Communist China as an aggressor. In a 1957 article in *Foreign Affairs,* Kennedy wrote that the Eisenhower administration's China policy was "probably too rigid." He suggested a policy reassessment and stressed that the United States needed to show its willingness to negotiate with China. Through dialogues, it might pave the way for mutual recognition and the release of American prisoners.[25] During the 1960 presidential campaign against Richard Nixon, Kennedy suggested that the US commitment to the ROC should not extend to a defense of the Quemoy and Matsu Islands. Kennedy argued that these islands were indefensible and a vehicle for Chiang Kai-shek to draw the United States into war with China.[26] Nixon responded that abandoning these islands would appease the PRC's aggression.[27]

Kennedy's desire for China's policy flexibility waned after assuming the presidency. Because of China's turbulent power struggle and promotion of Communist expansion, he saw the PRC as a serious threat. In his first State of the Union Address on January 30, 1961, he referred to the threat of PRC expansion. In May, Rusk asked Kennedy if he wanted the State Department to explore possible changes in China's policy. Kennedy felt that any change would garner strong domestic resistance. Fearing the issue might divide the nation, Kennedy was unwilling to risk a political confrontation at home. He told Rusk, "I don't want to read in the *Washington Post* or the *New York Times* that the State Department is thinking about a change in our China policy!"[28]

Withholding Official Recognition of the PRC

The US government adopted a nonrecognition policy toward the Mao Tse-tung regime. In July 1961, a Senate resolution opposed both the PRC's admission to the United Nations and the diplomatic recognition of the PRC by a vote of 76 to 0. The same resolution was approved in the House of Representatives by a vote of 395 to 0. Kennedy would not run political risks to introduce flexibility toward the PRC.[29] While Kennedy withheld official recognition of the PRC, the decision was beyond his control. Not only did both the Senate and House oppose changes to existing China policy, but many high-ranking policy advisers did as well.

The PRC's adamant stance also made it difficult to propose US recognition of the PRC. The PRC insisted on US withdrawal from Taiwan prior to any US-PRC normalization. Premier Zhou stated on January 31, 1961, that his government would refuse to participate in any international organization if the ROC were a member. The PRC insisted that any country seeking diplomatic relations with the PRC must sever diplomatic ties with the ROC.[30]

When the challenge to the ROC's status in the UN increased in the 1960s, Kennedy pledged his support to maintain the ROC membership in the UN and to keep the PRC out. Nonetheless, support for Taiwan eroded, as newly independent countries in Africa were sympathetic to the PRC.[31] The Kennedy administration sought an annual suspension of any consideration of the PRC's entry into the UN. The result of this tactic was to keep the question of the PRC's entrance off the agenda. However, there was concern that the United States might suffer a diplomatic defeat soon if it did not alter this obstructionist tactic.

In May 1961, the State Department prepared a proposal outlining the policy of "successor states." It called for the UN General Assembly to recognize that the ROC and the PRC held authority in mainland China. The UN would affirm the continuing membership of the ROC, but also would provide for the concurrent membership of the PRC. Kennedy thought the successor states plan was an option, but he saw the recognition of the PRC as "political dynamite." Kennedy asked the US ambassador to the UN, Adlai Stevenson, if he favored PRC's entrance into the UN. Stevenson replied that he did not. Eventually, the successor states plan did not materialize.[32]

Outer Mongolia's Admission to UN

The PRC representation issue in the UN became complicated when Outer Mongolia applied for admission into the UN. Since the early twentieth century, Outer Mongolia had been under the ROC's control. Chiang Kai-shek insisted that Outer Mongolia was a part of ROC's territory and could therefore not be admitted on its own. As a permanent member of the Security Council, the ROC was threatening to veto Outer Mongolia's admission.[33] Kennedy feared that an ROC veto could lead to a communist bloc push for Taiwan's ouster from the UN. Kennedy warned Chiang Kai-shek that the United States might not be able to rally majority support for continued ROC representation in the UN if the ROC vetoed Outer Mongolia's application. Chiang Kai-shek, however, refused to back down.[34]

Kennedy faced difficulty in changing Chiang's position in the UN. By the end of July 1961, the Kennedy administration shifted toward another approach. It considered having the UN designate PRC's entrance as an "important question," and all important questions required a two-thirds vote for approval.[35] Kennedy struck a deal with Chiang Kai-shek by pledging that the United States would exercise its veto to block the PRC's admission should the General Assembly vote to oust Taiwan and admit the PRC. The

70 Hedging the China Threat

United States also agreed not to vote for Outer Mongolia's entrance into the UN, in exchange for Chiang Kai-shek's promise not to veto Mongolia's admission. Chiang Kai-shek finally agreed. Outer Mongolia was voted into the UN, with the United States and the ROC abstaining.[36] The United States also persuaded the General Assembly to declare, by a vote of 61 to 34, that the question of China's entrance into the UN was an important question.[37]

The PRC's Nuclear Development

During the Korean War, US nuclear threats against the PRC convinced Beijing leaders that the PRC needed to develop a nuclear weapons program. In 1955, Mao authorized a full-scale effort to build an atomic bomb.[38] In January 1961, Kennedy became aware that the PRC was developing nuclear weapons. US intelligence estimated that the PRC's first testing of an atomic bomb would occur in the next several years.[39] Kennedy regarded the PRC's possession of nuclear weapons to likely be the worst event of the 1960s. Kennedy and his advisors not only discussed, but also pursued, the possibility of taking military action with the Soviet Union against the PRC's nuclear installations. In January 1961, the commander in chief of US Pacific Command, Admiral Harry Felt, advised the Pentagon that the PRC might test an atomic device by the end of 1962, and would be capable of constructing a small arsenal of nuclear weapons by 1965. Such a prospect chilled Kennedy.[40]

Kennedy had deep concerns about a Mao regime armed with nuclear weapons because of its irrationality. By negotiating an international test ban treaty, Kennedy hoped to prevent the Beijing regime from developing nuclear weapons.[41] As the Soviet-PRC rift widened, US leaders hoped to exploit the opportunity. The test ban treaty initiative would drive a further wedge between the Soviets and the Chinese. Kennedy explained to his advisors that he was willing to accept some Soviet cheating within the treaty system, if it meant that the PRC's bomb program could be stopped. Much to Washington's surprise, the Soviets responded positively to a proposal for test ban negotiations in June 1963. Under Secretary of State for Political Affairs Averill Harriman arrived in Moscow on July 14 to negotiate a test ban treaty. Kennedy instructed Harriman that he should try to elicit Nikita Khrushchev's view of limiting or preventing PRC nuclear development. Harriman responded that Moscow wanted a treaty to isolate Beijing, but was not willing to take more radical steps.[42]

The Offshore Islands Tension

On June 20, 1962, Kennedy held a meeting concerning the possibility of a PLA attack on the offshore islands. The meeting began with CIA director

McCone briefing the NSC members on PRC military intentions. He stated that the PRC had moved seven army divisions, with possibly five more on the way, across the strait from Taiwan. McCone concluded that the movements were either defensive, designed to put pressure on the offshore islands, or intended for a surprise attack on Quemoy. Secretary of Defense McNamara said there were an additional 300 motorized junks and 1,300 sailing vessels in China's ports. The chairman of the JCS, General Lyman Lemnitzer, said there were other possible scenarios: to attack Taiwan, or to get the United States out of Southeast Asia. The military leaders recommended the following approaches: deployment of carriers closer to Taiwan and reconnaissance efforts by F-101s.[43]

On June 27, 1962, Kennedy told a news conference that the United States would take any PRC move against Taiwan or Quemoy and Matsu very seriously.[44] Kennedy stated that in the event of the PLA's aggressive action against Quemoy and Matsu, the US government would abide by the 1955 Formosa Resolution. The United States would take whatever action was necessary to assure the defense of Taiwan and the Pescadores. At a June 28 meeting with John McCone, Kennedy commented on his press conference statement and explained that he was restating US policy and emphasizing the defensive nature of the United States' treaty commitment. He simply wanted to prevent a conflict.[45]

On July 5, 1962, the CIA and US intelligence organizations produced an estimate to assess the PLA buildup in the Foochow Military Region facing the Taiwan Strait. According to the estimate, the PLA had moved into the military region in large numbers on June 20. PRC propaganda then began to attack the ROC and the United States, accusing them of a concerted intention to invade mainland China. On June 23, PRC ambassador Wang sought out US ambassador Henry Cabot Lodge Jr. in Warsaw to ascertain the United States' intentions. He was told that the United States would not support a ROC attack on mainland China. A press conference remark by Kennedy reaffirmed earlier declarations of the US policy on the issues involved. After the Kennedy statement, the offshore islands tension began to decline.[46]

In summary, Kennedy advised Rusk not to consider any changes to US policy toward China. Kennedy felt constrained for several reasons, two of which were: his marginal victory and domestic political pressures prevented him from pursuing a flexible China policy; and a March 1963 poll that found that 47 percent of respondents thought the PRC posed a greater threat to world peace than the Soviet Union.[47] Kennedy maintained several characteristics of the policies he inherited, including preventing PRC expansion and practicing diplomatic containment. Kennedy remained convinced that Mao's regime was a disrupter of international order. If his government did not contain the PRC, it would likely become a destabilizing factor in Asia.[48] However, those within the administration

72   Hedging the China Threat

who perceived a positive revision of China's policy pushed for accommodation with the PRC.

The State Level:
The Disputes Between Security Organizations

Through the 1950s, China became more critical of US policy, causing Kennedy's foreign policy team on Asia (including Adlai Stevenson, Walt Rostow, and Chester Bowles) to begin focusing on the rising importance of Asia to the United States. When Kennedy was in office, Stevenson served as US ambassador to the UN. In late 1961, he worked as the President's special advisor on Asian, African, and Latin American affairs. Rostow began as deputy national security advisor and, in November 1961, shifted to the State Department as chairman of the Policy Planning Council.[49] These advisors recommended that the United States should reconsider its China policy. Robert Komer, a member of the National Security Council (NSC) staff, also recommended to NSA McGeorge Bundy that the State Department reexamine China's relationships. Some of Kennedy's foreign policy makers (including Stevenson, Averell Harriman, and Bowles) suggested that the United States work toward an accommodation approach with the PRC.[50]

Despite the rising voices of a flexible US foreign policy toward the PRC, most of Kennedy's advisors in the State Department, the CIA, and the Pentagon believed that the PRC was a grave threat that had to be contained. For example, Dean Rusk exhibited tactical flexibility, but viewed the PRC as a threat and saw little hope for a rapprochement. Under Secretary of State Bowles was a strong advocate for breaking new ground in US-PRC relations.[51] Although they suggested that the United States needed to be more flexible in dealing with the PRC, their desire for flexibility seldom sought major revisions in China's policy.[52]

The State Department

By 1961, after investigations by Senator Joseph McCarthy, which targeted suspected communists, the State Department had been staffed with anti-communists who favored containment of the PRC. After taking office, Kennedy recruited new blood into the State Department. For example, he assigned Averell Harriman as assistant secretary of state for Far Eastern affairs. Under Harriman's leadership, his bureau started to reevaluate its policy toward China.[53]

Bureaucratic changes. As he took the lead in the Bureau of Far Eastern Affairs, Harriman began to elevate the importance of a revised PRC policy. Until 1962, a single China Desk dealt with the affairs of the ROC and the PRC. Harriman established two separate desks: a PRC affairs desk and an ROC affairs desk. This reorganization created more room for new ideas in formulating PRC policy. Staffers of the bureau (including Roger Hilsman, Edward Rice, and Robert Barnett) contended that it was time to propose a realistic China policy.[54] Deputy Assistant Secretary of State for Far Eastern Affairs Edward Rice and Deputy Assistant Secretary of State for Far Eastern Economic Affairs Robert Barnett favored new approaches to the PRC.[55] They expected the United States to support the ROC while also being willing to negotiate with the PRC.

Reevaluation of China policy. In January 1961, with the beginning of the Kennedy administration, hope for change in China's policy was felt both inside and outside government circles.[56] In the 1960s, there was growing pressure in the UN concerning ROC membership as the challenge to ROC's status in the UN increased. Director of the Policy Planning Council Walt Rostow suggested that the United States expand commercial and cultural contacts with the PRC.[57] In the fall of 1961, the council recommended that the United States pursue a more satisfactory bilateral relationship, while trying to subdue mutual hostilities. Harriman supported a new orientation, but he endorsed the objective of keeping the Mao regime out of the UN and maintaining the policy of nonrecognition of the PRC. James Thomson, special assistant to Bowles, asserted that the United States should endeavor to assume a more conciliatory attitude toward the PRC.[58]

Nonetheless, many policymakers in the State Department expressed concerns about the dangers of increasing contact with the PRC. At the end of March 1961, J. Graham Parsons left his position as assistant secretary of state for Far Eastern affairs (1959–1961). Parsons cautioned that the dangers created by the PRC were expected to increase. He urged the need to remain cautious regarding the PRC due to the possibility of its increased hostility. It was essential for the United States to maintain a strong military posture in East Asia, and he urged caution in future contact with the PRC. Parsons's successor, Walter McConaughy, also rejected the idea of accommodating the PRC. McConaughy feared that recognition by the United States would cause a chain reaction of PRC recognition among the East Asian countries.[59]

Warsaw talks. Since the Quemoy Crisis in 1958, the Warsaw talks had served as a channel of communication between the United States and the PRC. During the Kennedy administration, the US ambassador, first Jacob Beam and then Henry Cabot Lodge Jr., engaged in dialogues with the PRC representative, Ambassador Wang, in Warsaw. The PRC government expected through this platform to be informed of any new US initiatives.

Wang, however, repeated the official refrains: (1) US forces must leave Taiwan; (2) if the United States ended its ties with the ROC, Beijing and Taipei would make a peaceful settlement; and (3) US-PRC relations would not improve if the United States remained tied to the ROC.[60] For example, on April 5, 1962, Wang attacked US policies, emphasizing that the US occupation of Taiwan was the primary source of strained relations.[61]

During the Wang-Lodge meeting on June 29, Wang stated that the ROC government was preparing to invade China, and that the US government supported this military operation. Wang warned that the United States was playing with fire. Cabot responded that the Kennedy administration had no intention of supporting any ROC attack on China under existing circumstances. He emphasized that the United States had discovered a PRC military buildup opposite Taiwan. He said the United States had a defense treaty obligation with the ROC.[62] The Warsaw talks did not produce any breakthrough for improving US-China relations, but they did serve as a valuable means of direct communication. The State Department instructed Beam and Lodge to inform Wang that the United States desired to identify areas of possible cooperation. Wang, however, constantly stated his previous clichés. The United States suspected that the PRC was trying to drive a wedge between Washington and Taipei.[63] The Warsaw talks, in addition to providing a channel of communication to observe US-PRC intentions, prevented a cross-strait conflict from further escalating.

The Pentagon Position

The threat haunting US military leaders was a nuclear-armed PRC. In December 1960, then chairman of the Joint Chiefs of Staff (JCS), Lyman Lemnitzer, reminded the service chiefs that the PRC might test a nuclear device soon. He requested different services to assess the impact of the PRC's nuclear capability. After completing the assessment, the JCS sent it to Secretary of Defense McNamara on June 26, 1961. They concluded that the PRC might test a nuclear device sometime between 1962 and 1964.[64]

General Maxwell Taylor toured the Far East in September 1962, just before becoming chairman of the JCS. General Taylor commented that he sensed the need to deter the PRC in a way much like how the United States deterred the Soviet Union. He described President Chiang's most pressing problem as acquiring advanced air defenses. Secretary McNamara responded to Taylor's report by assigning two tasks to the JCS. First, study how early use of nuclear weapons against large-scale PRC aggression would affect US and allied force requirements. Second, prepare a plan for coping with the growing threat of PRC airpower. In response to McNamara's request, the JCS recommended steps that included: continuing to put primary reliance on nuclear deterrence, increasing deployments of US fighters, and stationing

Polaris submarines in the Pacific. McNamara agreed that sole reliance on conventional capabilities would be unwise, but opposed putting primary dependence on nuclear deterrence because that would be ineffective against insurgency and subversion. He agreed about deploying Polaris submarines, but questioned whether increased air deployments were necessary.[65]

In November 1962, Rusk requested an analysis of the impact of the PRC's nuclear development from the military. The JCS produced a draft regarding the United States' posture before and after a PRC detonation. The draft stated that the United States ought to be "calm and assured." The JCS emphasized that US nuclear power far exceeded the PRC's nuclear capability. In a crisis, the United States needed to demonstrate its ability to respond appropriately against any PRC military aggression, but the JCS "calm and assured" approach was not shared with the administration.[66]

The CIA Approach

The CIA station chief in Taiwan, Ray Cline, was a close friend of President Chiang Kai-shek's son, Defense Minister Chiang Ching-Kuo. Therefore, Cline became a back channel to Kennedy. For example, on April 14, 1962, Cline sent a message to NSA Bundy. Cline stated that President Chiang Kai-shek agreed to postpone the target date for a military attack against mainland China from June until October.[67] During the 1962 Taiwan Strait Crisis, CIA director McCone briefed former president Eisenhower on the intelligence of a PRC military buildup in Fukien Province. Eisenhower recollected that he had asked Chiang Kai-shek to evacuate civilians from Quemoy and Matsu. McCone observed that Quemoy had been a fortress for ROC forces and was of considerable psychological importance to Chiang Kai-shek.[68]

Disputes Between the CIA, the Pentagon, and the State Department

During the Offshore Islands Crisis, there was much infighting and competition between the CIA, the Pentagon, and the State Department. At the June 20, 1962, NSC meeting on the crisis, the participants included NSC members and State Department officials. The meeting opened with McCone briefing them on China's military intentions. The briefing concluded that the PLA movements were defensive, designed to put pressure on the offshore islands, or intended for a surprise attack on Quemoy. Defense Secretary McNamara thought this briefing was "for the birds." This put the CIA in a terrible position. McNamara "jumped all over him." The chairman of the JCS, Lemnitzer, also downgraded the presentation. McNamara claimed that "we gotta have intelligence." He implied that the CIA was doing an abysmal job.[69]

76   Hedging the China Threat

On June 6, the JCS had written a memorandum to McNamara on US policy toward the ROC. The memorandum emphasized that the ROC-held offshore islands were closely bound to the defense of Taiwan, which formed an important link in the defensive chain extending from the Aleutians to Australia. These islands were of significant strategic, military, political, and psychological importance to the United States.[70]

On June 21, Assistant Secretary of Defense for International Security Affairs Paul Nitze wrote a letter on the Offshore Islands Crisis to Under Secretary of State for Political Affairs George McGhee. Nitze expressed the view of the JCS's June 6 memorandum to McNamara. The JCS recommended that the United States seek to preserve the status quo of the offshore islands by providing ROC forces with equipment and training to assist them in defending the islands. This letter went further by expressing that "the U.S. supports the ROC in defense of the islands with U.S. forces, to the extent required to ensure the defense of Formosa and the Pescadores."[71] Deputy Under Secretary for Political Affairs U. Alexis Johnson commented in a memorandum: "I find it surprising that Defense now feels there is not a policy of seeking the withdrawal of the ROC from the offshore islands. I thought this had been a consistent policy since 1955, even though this administration may not have formally reaffirmed it."[72] On June 25, McNamara wrote a memorandum to Kennedy stating that the islands could be effectively defended with full US support without tactical nuclear weapons.[73]

The International Level:
The Global Responses to Rising Threats from the PRC

As the United States and the Soviet Union worked toward détente, both sides sought to avoid confrontation. Most US officials during the Kennedy administration believed that leaders in Moscow and Beijing were ideologically divided. The Cuban Missile Crisis and the China-India War at the end of 1962 strained Soviet-PRC relations even further. Kennedy hoped that US-Soviet cooperation would result in the ability to postpone the PRC nuclear program. During the first half of the 1960s, the Kennedy administration developed a view of the PRC as a more radical adversary than Moscow.[74]

The Soviet-PRC Rift

When war broke out in the Korean Peninsula in 1950, Joseph Stalin was unwilling to risk a direct military confrontation with the United States. He requested Mao to intervene. Mao agreed, and demanded that Stalin provide military aid and air cover for his troops. Stalin agreed to send military equipment to China, but he insisted that China take the lead in the fighting.

Stalin, however, failed to fulfill his promise to send warplanes to Korea. Mao was disappointed by Stalin's inaction. The experience of the Korean War cast a shadow over Soviet-PRC relations.

When Stalin's successor, Nikita Khrushchev, denounced Stalin's cult in 1956, Mao regarded Khrushchev as a revisionist. Since Mao became "Stalin" in China, he enjoyed absolute control. When Khrushchev said Stalin was wrong and proposed a "peaceful coexistence" with the West, Mao strongly denounced it. In 1958, Mao unleashed the Great Leap Forward, an ambitious project to transform industrialization. It was fueled by a drive to rid the PRC's dependency on the Soviet Union. The movement was a disaster and resulted in a famine that cost the lives of 30 million people. Khrushchev openly criticized Mao, and later Khrushchev withdrew all the Soviet experts and aid from China.

The deepening Soviet-PRC dispute influenced the Kennedy administration's view of the PRC. In 1956, Khrushchev decided to seek peaceful coexistence with the United States. Mao insisted on the "inevitability of war" in the revolutionary struggle and condemned Soviet "revisionism." Mao's regime challenged the Soviet position of communist ideology.[75] In April 1961, the CIA assessed that the conflict between Russia and China was deep and would not be quickly healed. They feared that as the split widened, the PRC could become more threatening.[76]

The Soviet-PRC rift did appear to be widening. In mid-January 1963, the CIA issued a memorandum discussing the status of the Soviet-PRC tension. It concluded that the conflict had become so fundamental that a split had occurred. Although the breakup seemed to hold significant advantages for the West, the immediate concern for the United States was the role that the PRC would assume in East Asia. In May 1963, a National Intelligence Estimate confirmed that differences stemming from fundamental issues of conflicting national interests precluded the reconciliation between the Soviet Union and the PRC. Director McCone argued that the differences between the Soviet Union and the PRC were significant. A final break between the two Communist powers, however, appeared to be unlikely.[77]

The India-PRC Conflict

The PRC and India established diplomatic relations in 1950. After the Bandung Conference in 1955, there was a power struggle between these two Asian giants because both wanted to become the leader of the non-Western world. When Tibet was on the verge of rebellion in 1959, Mao sent the PLA to crack down on Tibet's independence movement. As a result, Tibet's spiritual leader, the Dalai Lama, fled to India and was granted political asylum. The issue of Tibet ripped bilateral relations apart. By 1962, a bitter border war broke out.

78   *Hedging the China Threat*

The Tibetan objection to the PRC reached a boiling point in 1959. In March, a rumor claimed that Beijing's authorities planned to abduct the Dalai Lama to Beijing. Hundreds of thousands of Tibetans protested and surrounded his palace to protect him. The PLA responded with its crackdown on Lhasa and quickly took back the capital. Since India had a long historical connection with Tibet, Indian public opinion was sympathetic to Tibet. When the Jawaharlal Nehru administration granted the Dalia Lama asylum, Mao was furious and claimed that Prime Minister Nehru was behind the rebellion. Their differences triggered their border dispute.

The PRC had two contested borders with India, Aksai Chin in the west and Arunachal Pradesh in the east. In August 1959, along the McMahon Line in Arunachal Pradesh, a clash broke out between their border garrisons. Both forces opened fire at Kongka Pass in Aksai Chin. Premier Zhou visited New Delhi to diminish the crisis and suggested to China that, if India gave Aksai Chin to the PRC, which Nehru rejected, it would stay behind the western McMahon Line. In 1962, the PLA artillery units inflicted devastating hits on the Indian troops at the eastern and western borders. While the fighting was ongoing, the PRC appealed to India again and restated its previous claim over the territory. Nehru again refused and rallied another 30,000 troops to launch a counterstrike. The PLA almost wiped out the Indian forces.

During the 1962 India-PRC border conflict, Kennedy responded to Nehru's request for assistance by providing firearms, light artillery, and transport planes. Kennedy dispatched a special mission headed by Harriman to evaluate Indian requests for assistance. Just as the Harriman mission was about to depart, the PRC declared a cease-fire. According to estimates of the PRC's actions, done by the State Department, the reports emphasized that the PRC was seeking to improve its geostrategic position in the contested India-PRC border areas.[78]

The International Responses to the Offshore Islands Crisis

On June 21, 1962, the State Department provided an analysis of the Offshore Islands Crisis. It concluded that there were disadvantages in making any firm decisions on US defense of the offshore islands under present circumstances. A decision to defend the islands risked ROC efforts to involve the United States even more deeply in its counterattack actions, and a tightening of the Soviet-PRC alliance.[79] On the same day, Acting Secretary of State George Ball suggested to Kennedy that he use diplomatic action regarding the PRC threat to the offshore islands. Ball suggested the following approaches: requesting information from the Soviet ambassador to the United States, approaching the PRC through the Warsaw talks, and consulting US allies.[80] The international responses to the Offshore Islands Crisis of 1962 are listed below.

The Soviet Union. During the Vienna meeting between Kennedy and Khrushchev on June 3, 1961, both leaders had differences on issues with Taiwan. Khrushchev said that he was glad that there were voices in the United States asking for a change in US policy toward the PRC. He believed the relations between Chiang Kai-chek and Mao were China's internal affair, and neither the United States nor the Soviet Union should interfere. Kennedy replied that the situation should be viewed in light of the PRC's hostility. If the United States were to withdraw from Taiwan, the US strategic position in Asia would be impaired. Khrushchev stated that the PRC could not reconcile with the United States while its bases were still in Taiwan. Kennedy said the United States would not leave Taiwan. Khrushchev replied that the best thing for the United States would be to recognize the PRC and settle its differences with it.[81]

The United Kingdom. On June 24, 1962, Rusk visited the United Kingdom and met with Prime Minister Harold Macmillan. Rusk assured the British that the United States would not allow a ROC attack on China. Macmillan replied vehemently that he did not understand the US policy on China, as the United States did not even admit that the PRC existed, while the Beijing regime controlled all of China. He claimed that the United States had "a fellow from Taiwan" sitting in China's seat in the UN. Macmillan admitted that the United States and the United Kingdom had come out of the last session of the UN well, but only because they had "bullied all the South Americans into voting for us."[82]

The United Nations. At the June 26, 1962, NSC meeting, US ambassador to the UN, Adlai Stevenson, presented the problems confronting the US delegation to the UN. Stevenson stated that if the PRC continued its aggressive attitude toward India, the PRC representation problem would be less of an issue than in recent years. However, if Chiang Kai-shek's provocative statements concerning returning to the mainland were repeated, they would cause problems for the United States in the UN. Stevenson stated that he, like others, wished that Chiang Kai-shek would be out of the islands and, therefore, the problem would be removed.[83]

Conclusion

President Kennedy maintained the status quo regarding cross-strait policy. Despite the rising voices in favor of a flexible US foreign policy toward the PRC in the State Department, most of Kennedy's senior advisors believed that the Chinese Communists were a grave threat to the United States and its allies and had to be contained. During the 1962 Offshore

Islands Crisis, there was much infighting about cross-strait policy between the CIA, the Pentagon, and the State Department. As the US and the Soviet Union governments worked toward détente, leaders of both countries wanted to avoid conflicts. Particularly, the intensifying Soviet-PRC dispute negatively affected the Kennedy administration's perception of the PRC.

The Kennedy administration produced the following cross-strait policies: first, Kennedy pledged his support to maintain the ROC's status in the UN as the legitimate government of China. Second, the US government hoped to thwart Beijing's nuclear weapons development. Third, during the 1962 Offshore Islands Crisis, Kennedy stated that his administration would take military measures, if necessary, to defend Taiwan and the Pescadores.

At the individual level of analysis, Kennedy believed that any change in US policy toward China would face stiff domestic opposition. Not only did both Houses of Congress oppose changes to the existing US policy toward China, but so did many high-ranking advisors. Kennedy felt constrained by his marginal victory in the election, and domestic political pressures kept him from pursuing a flexible China policy.

At the state level of analysis, with the beginning of the Kennedy administration, hope for change in policy was felt both inside and outside governmental and academic circles. The United States also faced growing pressure in the United Nations concerning the Taipei government as the challenge to the ROC's status in the UN increased. Nevertheless, many policymakers in the State Department, the CIA, and the Pentagon expressed concerns about the dangers of increasing contact with the PRC.

At the international level, Khrushchev decided to seek peaceful coexistence with the United States. Mao condemned Khrushchev's "revisionism." During the 1962 PRC-India border conflict, Kennedy responded to Nehru's request for military assistance to India by confronting India's military conflicts with the PRC. The Kennedy administration was convinced that Mao's regime was a disrupter of international order and, if the United States did not contain the Chinese Communists, it would become a destabilizing factor throughout Asia.

US policy developed from President Kennedy's belief that the PRC was an expansionist and threatening power. Communist China's aggressiveness, exhibited during the Taiwan Strait Crisis and the Sino-India border conflict, further confirmed Kennedy's view of China's expansionist intentions. Kennedy's fear of domestic political reprisals, however, prevented him from introducing new elements into his US-China policy. For the above reasons, Kennedy chose to maintain the China policy in the rigid pattern he had inherited from the Eisenhower administration. The challenge of enacting new initiatives toward the PRC, which governed the lives of one-fifth of the world's population, was left to John F. Kennedy's successors.[84]

Notes

1. William W. Newmann, "Kennedy, Johnson, and Policy Toward China: Testing the Importance of the President in Foreign Policy Decision Making," *Presidential Studies Quarterly* 44, no. 4 (December 2014): 649.

2. Jean S. Kang, "Firmness and Flexibility: Initiations for Change in U.S. Policy, Toward Communist China, 1961–1963," *American Asian Review* 21, no. 1 (Spring 2003): 114–117.

3. US Department of State, "24. Editorial Note," August 8, 1962, *FRUS, 1961–1963,* vol. 22, *Northeast Asia,* https://history.state.gov.

4. Kang, "Firmness and Flexibility," p. 120.

5. Alex Herkert, "U.S. Intelligence and Cross-Strait Relations: Intelligence Failures and U.S. Policy Toward the Two Chinas," *American Intelligence Journal* 34, no. 1 (January 2017): 103.

6. Kang, "Firmness and Flexibility," p. 123.

7. Ibid., pp. 123–125.

8. Ibid., pp. 123–128.

9. Ibid., pp. 128–130.

10. Ibid., pp. 130–131.

11. David Shambaugh, *Tangled Titans: The United States and China* (Lanham, MD: Rowman and Littlefield, 2012), p. 33.

12. Charles J. Pellegrin, "There Are Bigger Issues at Stake: The Administration of John F. Kennedy and United States–Republic of China Relations, 1961–63," in *John F. Kennedy History, Memory, Legacy: An Interdisciplinary Inquiry,* edited by John Delane Williams, Robert G. Waite, and Gregory S. Gordon (Grand Forks: University of North Dakota, 2010), pp. 108–109.

13. Ibid., pp. 109–110.

14. US Department of State, "110. Memorandum for the Record: White House Briefing on China," May 17, 1962, Central Intelligence Agency, DCI (McCone) Files, Job 80-B01285A.

15. US Department of State, "113. Memorandum from the Director of the Bureau of Intelligence and Research (Hilsman) to Secretary of State Rusk," May 29, 1962, *FRUS, 1961–1963,* vol. 22, *Northeast Asia,* https://history.state.gov.

16. US Department of State, "116. Telegram from the Central Intelligence Agency Station in Saigon to Director of Central Intelligence McCone, Saigon," June 7, 1962, *FRUS, 1961–1963,* vol. 22, *Northeast Asia,* https://history.state.gov.

17. Ibid.

18. US Department of State, "119. Memorandum from the Director of the Bureau of Intelligence and Research (Hilsman) to Secretary of State Rusk," June 18, 1962, *FRUS, 1961–1963,* vol. 22, *Northeast Asia,* https://history.state.gov.

19. Allen S. Whiting, "China's Use of Force, 1950–96, and Taiwan," *International Security* 26, no. 2 (Fall 2001): 111–112.

20. US Department of State, "148. Message from the Assistant Secretary of State for Far Eastern Affairs (Harriman) to the Ambassador to the Republic of China (Kirk)," August 8, 1962, *FRUS, 1961–1963,* vol. 22, *Northeast Asia,* https://history.state.gov.

21. Pellegrin, "There Are Bigger Issues," p. 111.

22. Charles D. Pasquale, "Pivotal Deterrence and United States Security Policy in the Taiwan Strait," Norfolk, VA: Old Dominion University Dissertation, 2007, p. 178.

23. Pellegrin, "There Are Bigger Issues," p. 112.

82 Hedging the China Threat

24. Pasquale, "Pivotal Deterrence and United States Security Policy in the Taiwan Strait," p. 180.

25. Noam Kochavi, *A Conflict Perpetuated: China Policy During the Kennedy Years* (Westport, CT: Greenwood, 2002), pp. 39–40.

26. Ibid., p. 42.

27. James Fetzer, "Clinging to Containment: China Policy," in *Kennedy's Quest for Victory,* edited by Thomas G. Paterson (Oxford: Oxford University Press, 1989), p. 179.

28. US Department of State, "24. Editorial Note."

29. Fetzer, "Clinging to Containment," p. 184.

30. Kang, "Firmness and Flexibility," pp. 125–126.

31. Pellegrin, "There Are Bigger Issues," p. 105.

32. Fetzer, "Clinging to Containment," pp. 185–186.

33. Ibid., p. 186.

34. Pellegrin, "There Are Bigger Issues," pp. 106–107.

35. Fetzer, "Clinging to Containment," p. 187.

36. Pellegrin, "There Are Bigger Issues," p. 108.

37. Fetzer, "Clinging to Containment," p. 187.

38. Lyle J. Goldstein, "When China Was a 'Rogue State': The Impact of China's Nuclear Weapons Program on US–China Relations During the 1960s," *Journal of Contemporary China* 12, no. 37 (November 2003): 740.

39. Kang, "Firmness and Flexibility," p. 119.

40. Gordon H. Chang, "JFK, China, and the Bomb," *Journal of American History* 74, no. 4 (March 1988): 1287–1288.

41. Evelyn Goh, *Constructing the U.S. Rapprochement with China, 1961–1974: From "Red Menace" to "Tacit Ally"* (Cambridge: Cambridge University Press, 2004), p. 27.

42. Goldstein, "When China Was a 'Rogue State,'" p, 743.

43. US Department of State, "122. Record of Meeting," June 20, 1962, *FRUS, 1961–1963,* vol. 22, *Northeast Asia,* https://history.state.gov.

44. US Department of State, "118. Memorandum for the Record," June 18, 1962, *FRUS, 1961–1963,* vol. 22, *Northeast Asia,* https://history.state.gov.

45. US Department of State, "137. Editorial Note," June 27, 1962, *FRUS, 1961–1963,* vol. 22, *Northeast Asia,* https://history.state.gov.

46. US Department of State, "141. Special National Intelligence Estimate," July 5, 1962, *FRUS, 1961–1963,* vol. 22, *Northeast Asia,* https://history.state.gov.

47. Goh, *Constructing the U.S. Rapprochement,* pp. 29–30.

48. Fetzer, "Clinging to Containment," pp. 179–180.

49. Kochavi, *Conflict Perpetuated,* p. 26.

50. Pellegrin, "There Are Bigger Issues," pp. 101–102.

51. Fetzer, "Clinging to Containment," p. 185.

52. Ibid., pp. 180–181.

53. Pellegrin, "There Are Bigger Issues," p. 102.

54. Ibid., pp. 113–114.

55. Fetzer, "Clinging to Containment," p. 191.

56. Kang, "Firmness and Flexibility," p. 118.

57. Pellegrin, "There Are Bigger Issues," pp. 105–112.

58. Kang, "Firmness and Flexibility," pp. 126–128.

59. Ibid, pp. 128–130.

60. Ibid., p. 187.

61. US Department of State, "101. Telegram from the Embassy in Poland to the Department of State," April 5, 1962, *FRUS, 1961–1963,* vol. 22, *Northeast Asia.*

62. US Department of State, "131. Telegram from the Embassy in Poland to the Department of State," June 23, 1962, *FRUS, 1961–1963,* vol. 22, *Northeast Asia,* https://history.state.gov.

63. Fetzer, "Clinging to Containment," pp. 187–188.

64. Walter S. Poole, *The Joint Chiefs of Staff and National Policy,* vol. 8: *1961–1964* (Washington, DC: Office of the Chairman of the Joint Chiefs of Staff, 2011), p. 282.

65. Ibid., pp. 280–281.

66. Ibid., pp. 282–283.

67. US Department of State, "105. Message from the President's Special Assistant for National Security Affairs (Bundy) to the Chief of the Central Intelligence Agency Station in Taipei (Cline)," April 17, 1962, *FRUS, 1961–1963,* vol. 22, *Northeast Asia,* https://history.state.gov.

68. US Department of State, "123. Memorandum for the Record, Gettysburg," June 21, 1962, *FRUS, 1961–1963,* vol. 22, *Northeast Asia,* https://history.state.gov.

69. US Department of State, "122. Record of Meeting."

70. US Department of State, "Memorandum from the Joint Chiefs of Staff to Secretary of Defense McNamara," June 6, 1962, JCSM-429-62, Washington, https://1997-2001.state.gov.

71. US Department of State, "126. Letter from the Assistant Secretary of Defense for International Security Affairs (Nitze) to the Under Secretary of State for Political Affairs (McGhee)," June 21, 1962, Department of State, Central Files, 611.93/6-2162, Secret, *FRUS, 1961–1963,* vol. 22, *Northeast Asia,* https://history.state.gov.

72. Ibid.

73. US Department of State, "134. Memorandum from Secretary of Defense McNamara to President Kennedy," June 25, 1962, *FRUS, 1961–1963,* vol. 22, *Northeast Asia,* https://history.state.gov.

74. Goh, *Constructing the U.S. Rapprochement,* pp. 35–36.

75. Ibid., p. 34.

76. Fetzer, "Clinging to Containment," pp. 182–183.

77. Kang, "Firmness and Flexibility," pp. 138–139.

78. Fetzer, "Clinging to Containment," p. 193.

79. US Department of State, "125. Memorandum from the Director of the Bureau of Intelligence and Research (Hilsman) to the Assistant Secretary of State for Far Eastern Affairs (Harriman)," June 21, 1962, FE Files: Lot 64 D 25, Communist China, Secret.

80. US Department of State, "124. Memorandum from Acting Secretary of State George W. Ball to President Kennedy," June 21, 1962, *FRUS, 1961–1963,* vol. 22, *Northeast Asia,* https://history.state.gov.

81. US Department of State, "29. Editorial Note," *FRUS, 1961–1963,* vol. 22, *Northeast Asia,* https://history.state.gov.

82. US Department of State, "132. Memorandum of Conversation," June 24, 1962, *FRUS, 1961–1963,* vol. 22, *Northeast Asia,* https://history.state.gov.

83. US Department of State, "135. Memorandum for the Record," June 26, 1962, *FRUS, 1961–1963,* vol. 22, *Northeast Asia,* https://history.state.gov.

84. Fetzer, "Clinging to Containment," p. 197.

5

The PRC Nuclear Test and the Vietnam War: The Johnson Administration

THE LYNDON JOHNSON ADMINISTRATION'S POLICY TOWARD CHINA AND TAIWAN remained similar to that of the John F. Kennedy and Dwight Eisenhower administrations. President Johnson's cross-strait policy was nonrecognition of the People's Republic of China (PRC), support for the Republic of China (ROC), and support for the ROC's holding of the Chinese seat in the United Nations. Johnson did not make major changes in US policy because his administration was preoccupied with the Vietnam War. The Cultural Revolution launched by Mao Tse-tung in 1966 also had lessened pressure on the Johnson administration for policy changes toward the PRC.[1]

Historical Events: The US-ROC Relations Under the PRC Nuclear Weapon Threat

When the PRC successfully tested a nuclear bomb on October 16, 1964, the US containment strategy against the PRC became less effective. When the US Joint Chiefs of Staff (JCS) and Central Intelligence Agency (CIA) proposed launching a preemptive strike against China's nuclear facilities, the top leaders of the Johnson administration opposed the option because of the PRC's possible retaliation. In September 1965, when ROC Defense Minister Chiang Ching-kuo visited the United States, he presented Secretary of Defense Robert McNamara with a plan to reclaim China's five Southwest provinces. McNamara rejected the idea. Johnson was interested in the political and social turmoil in China caused by the Cultural Revolution in 1966 because chaos in China could reduce support for the Communists in Vietnam.[2] The following historical events introduce the US-ROC relations under the PRC nuclear threat.

86   Hedging the China Threat

The PRC Becoming a Member of the Nuclear Club

After the PRC tested the atomic bomb, Johnson and McNamara met with the bipartisan congressional leadership on October 19, 1964. During the meeting, McNamara explained that half a dozen countries would seek to arm themselves with nuclear weapons because of China's nuclear test.[3] In late October, Ray Cline, CIA deputy director for intelligence, discussed the PRC nuclear threat with ROC officials, who feared that three nuclear bombs could destroy the cities of Keelung, Taipei, and Kaohsiung in Taiwan. Chiang Kai-shek complained to Cline that US assurances for the defense of Taiwan were inadequate to calm fears.[4] The US military conducted analyses of the PRC's nuclear development, and believed that the PRC's nuclear capability had not affected the balance of power between the United States and the PRC.[5] The US intelligence community assessed that the PRC was developing a medium-range ballistic missile (MRBM), and had given top priority to its nuclear weapons and missile programs.[6] On November 3, 1966, the US intelligence community reported that the PRC had launched a guided missile, which could carry a nuclear warhead.[7]

US-PRC Relations

During the US involvement in the Vietnam War, policymakers advocated a containment policy against the PRC. In the meantime, a Cultural Revolution occurred in mainland China. US leaders were interested in what might happen to China's foreign policy, particularly in Vietnam. Both countries still engaged in ambassadorial communication via the Warsaw talks in Poland, to probe each other's intentions.

The Warsaw talks. During the Warsaw talks, representatives of the PRC (Wang Ping-nan until April 1964, and then Wang Guoquan) complained to the US representatives (John Cabot until late 1965, and then John Gronouski) that no progress would be made until the United States withdrew its forces from Taiwan. Since the Johnson administration regarded the Taiwan issue as non-negotiable, US-PRC relations did not make any progress.[8] The Johnson administration sought to use the talks to assure Beijing that the United States did not want to confront the PRC, while conveying US firmness concerning Vietnam.[9] US officials also viewed the talks as a communication channel. The PRC leaders, such as Zhou Enlai and Chen Yi publicly stated how the Warsaw talks contributed to reducing tension and lessening the threat of war.[10] Both countries agreed that the talks served as a channel of communication and a tool for probing each other's intentions.

Initiatives on travel to China. During the Johnson administration, several policymakers developed proposals for a flexible China policy. In 1965,

Assistant Secretary of State for Far Eastern Affairs William Bundy proposed permitting travel to China by scholars and representatives of humanitarian organizations.[11] On June 16, Bundy suggested to Secretary Dean Rusk that the United States could broaden the categories to include scholars and graduate students to visit China.[12] Rusk did not agree with this proposal, but endorsed an initiative to permit travel to China by doctors and public health specialists because they were unlikely to request extensive access. Johnson initially rejected the idea, but authorized it later.[13] On September 26, ROC defense minister Chiang Ching-kuo visited the United States and met with Assistant Secretary Bundy. Bundy informed him that the United States would announce a change in its passport policy soon, which would permit doctors and public health workers to be issued passports with no restrictions to travel to China.[14]

US-ROC Relations

The Johnson administration supported the ROC in the international community, upheld the ROC's possession of China's seat in the UN, and continued the bilateral military relations.

Military relations. During Johnson's years in the White House, the US-ROC military relationship was robust. President Chiang Kai-shek asked the US government to sell advanced weaponry to Taiwan, especially after the PRC's successful atomic bomb detonation.

On March 20, 1965, President Chiang Kai-shek held a special meeting to discuss the Military Aid Program (MAP) with the US political and military leaders in Taiwan. He stated that all intelligence indications showed that the PRC's second atomic blast would happen soon. This time, it would be delivered from the air. He requested ground-to-air missiles to counter the PRC's nuclear threat.[15]

In a previous meeting with President Chiang Kai-shek, Ambassador Jerauld Wright stated that President Chiang Kai-shek had expressed grave concern over the capabilities of the ROC's air defense. This was because the PRC's fourteen TU4s (Soviet strategic bombers) could be used to conduct an atomic attack on Taiwan. On April 9, Wright met with the minister of defense, Chiang Ching-kuo, to discuss military matters regarding US nuclear deterrence. Wright said that the US defensive alliance with the ROC, and the entire retaliatory capability of US nuclear forces, would be equally effective in deterring an attack against Taiwan.[16]

On June 16, Secretary McNamara wrote a letter to Minister Chiang Ching-kuo, revealing that there was no evidence to the ROC's claim that the PRC planned to attack Taiwan. However, McNamara claimed that the US temporary deployments of fighters to Taiwan could respond promptly with adequate force if necessary. The United States would replace ROC

88   *Hedging the China Threat*

force F-86F with F-5 aircraft. The US cumulative Military Assistance Program to Taiwan, for the period FY 1951 through FY 1966, amounted to more than $2.4 billion, making the ROC the second-largest recipient worldwide of US military assistance. Congress also authorized the loan of a destroyer and destroyer escort to the ROC. [17]

Five Southwest provinces. Chiang Kai-shek had been pressing for US support for ROC operations on the mainland since 1962. The Kennedy administration had agreed to small-scale raids, but rejected larger-scale operations. At the beginning of the Johnson administration, the United States continued this policy. As US forces became involved in the Vietnam War and Mao launched the Cultural Revolution, Chiang Kai-shek thought that this might be his last opportunity to reclaim China.

When Rusk visited Taiwan in April 1964, President Chiang Kai-shek again suggested considering operations against the mainland. Rusk told him that the ROC could not establish itself on the mainland without large-scale assistance from the United States.[18] On August 5, 1965, Ray Cline visited Taiwan, and Chiang Kai-shek informed him that his government was ready to provide troops to Vietnam if the United States wanted them. Chiang Kai-shek insisted that it was time for an amphibious ROC landing on the South China coast to cut PRC's supply lines to Vietnam and retake the mainland.[19]

On September 22, Minister Chiang Ching-kuo met Secretary McNamara and stated that the five Southwest provinces were the most important from a strategic viewpoint. McNamara asked what evidence the ROC had that the people would rise up. Minister Chiang Ching-kuo replied that in the five Southwest provinces, resistance to the PRC was strongest, PLA deployments were weakest, and the popularity of Chiang Kai-shek was the greatest.[20] On December 29, the chairman of the JCS, General Earle Wheeler, called on President Chiang Kai-shek. Chiang Kai-shek restated that the United States should consider ways to use ROC forces in the Vietnam War. The best way to win the Vietnam War was assisting the ROC forces to seize the five Southwest provinces.[21]

On January 24, 1966, the United States rejected an ROC request to consider a contingency plan for large-scale landings in South China with US logistic assistance.[22] The State Department thought that the concept of seizing five Southwest provinces appeared to be impractical. After the United States rejected Chiang Kai-shek's request, Cline found the state of morale in the upper echelons of the ROC very low. President Chiang Kai-shek was dispirited and discouraged.[23]

In 1967, with the Cultural Revolution at its height, President Chiang Kai-shek renewed his request for support in retaking mainland China. He sent a message to Johnson urging that the Beijing-Moscow split, and mainland social unrest, created an excellent opportunity to rid China of the Mao regime, destroy the PRC nuclear threat, and end the Vietnam War. He would need only US approval and logistic support. President Johnson opposed such action.[24]

The Individual Level: Johnson's Inflexible China Policy

The Johnson leadership style was described as delegation to key advisors and domination by the president. His foreign policy making process was defined as the elevation of the State Department and the de-emphasis of the National Security Council (NSC). He finalized foreign policy decisions in large part based on Rusk's advice because they had a close working relationship.[25] Rusk and Johnson could bond as the Southerners who were surrounded by Yankees, and Rusk could thrive under a president who wanted more information and analysis.[26]

On July 12, 1966, Johnson delivered an address to the American Alumni Council regarding problems with China. He emphasized that the United States had left an invitation for the PRC, and they needed to accept it. His administration proposed travel exchanges with the PRC, but Beijing directly rejected the US proposals.[27] Thus, US-PRC relations during the Johnson administration made no progress and remained tense.

The Chinese Representation

After becoming president when John F. Kennedy was assassinated on November 22, 1963, Johnson acknowledged that the economic embargo against the PRC did not work effectively. This was because of increased trade between the PRC and US allies such as Japan, Canada, Australia, and Britain. On December 14, 1963, PRC premier Zhou Enlai and foreign minister Chen Yi started a two-month tour of Africa. As a result, fourteen African countries recognized Beijing.[28] Speaking with Senator Richard Russell Jr. in early 1964, Johnson did confide that eventually the United States would have to recognize the PRC. Johnson was under pressure to allow PRC entry into the UN, while preserving the ROC's seat.[29]

The Chinese representation created differences in US politics and among US allies such as Canada. At a White House meeting on November 18, 1964, Johnson and his national security team laid out their foreign policy. National Security Advisor (NSA) McGeorge Bundy and US ambassador to the UN Adlai Stevenson agreed that the Chinese representation policy had reached its limits.[30] Stevenson told Johnson that the best solution to deal with the representation issue was to shift toward a Two China policy. Rusk responded that if the United States wavered before Beijing, it would boost its aggression. Stevenson argued that other foreign policy makers felt that the PRC could be included in the UN. Johnson responded that he did

90 *Hedging the China Threat*

not pay the foreigners at the UN to advise him on foreign policy, but he did pay Rusk and was inclined to listen to him.[31]

By 1965, the vote on Chinese representation in the UN was closer than ever before. There was a tie vote on a resolution to admit the PRC and expel the ROC. US representatives at the UN were concerned that the US strategy of requiring a two-thirds majority for a change in Chinese representation might not work in the future.[32]

On April 30, Arthur Goldberg, who was Stevenson's successor, proposed to Johnson that the United States could push the Canadians to propose a "successor state" position on the Chinese representative issue, recognizing both Beijing and Taipei as UN members at the next General Assembly.[33] Rusk informed Johnson on May 14 that the UN had discussed alternatives to Chinese representation. However, a few US allies (e.g., Canada and France) were no longer prepared to go along with any change in Chinese representation requiring a two-thirds majority. If the United States did not come up with new tactics, the next General Assembly would likely expel the ROC and invite the PRC to occupy the Chinese seat in all UN organizations.[34]

On November 5, Johnson asked Rusk to persuade Canada to alter its "One China, One Taiwan" proposal to a more acceptable one for the United States. This would involve a General Assembly Study Committee. The study committee would explore possibilities of a solution based on a seat for both the ROC and the PRC in the Assembly, with the Security Council seat going to Beijing.[35]

The United States attempted to convince the ROC that the shift in tactics might assure its continued representation in the UN. Johnson requested US ambassador to the ROC Walter McConaughy to persuade Taipei to change tactics.[36] ROC officials were indignant when McConaughy told them the United States found it necessary to support a study committee resolution. Foreign Minister Wei Tao-ming told McConaughy that a study committee resolution would be worse than a Two Chinas resolution. If such a resolution were adopted, his government would consider withdrawing from the UN. On November 26, Johnson sent a letter to Chiang Kai-shek declaring that the withdrawal from the UN by the ROC would be a tragedy.[37] The votes on November 29 moved in favor of the United States. The issue of PRC recognition remained an important question with a vote of 66 for, 48 against, and 7 abstaining. The General Assembly then voted to declare the study commission an "important question" (51 for, 37 against, 30 abstaining).[38] The representation issue was not altered.

Johnson and the PRC's Nuclear Development

One of the critical concerns of Johnson's presidency was the PRC nuclear test. Before the PRC's nuclear test, the JCS had studied options for military action, including the use of US nuclear weapons, and the CIA had plotted covert action against China's test facilities at Lop Nor.[39] Johnson had taken a backseat in the policy deliberations over a preemptive strike on PRC nuclear facilities. The option of attacking China, and the possibility of precipitating a US-PRC war, was a nightmare to him because he recalled the PRC intervention in Korea as well as the US involvement in the Vietnam War. Johnson told his advisors that the US position should not be provocative, but that the United States should not give the impression of being unconcerned either.[40] After the PRC's first test of a nuclear weapon, Johnson stated that this explosion came as no surprise to his government. The United States reaffirmed its defense commitments to its allies in Asia.[41]

Taiwan was very concerned about the PRC's nuclear capability. President Chiang Kai-shek believed that the primary PRC goal was to destroy the ROC.[42] On December 21, 1964, Johnson wrote a letter to Chiang Kai-shek stating that the United States was fully aware of the PRC's aggressiveness against Taiwan. Johnson believed that the continuing strength of the US alliance would deter the PRC from any thought of a nuclear attack on Taiwan,[43] and he would deploy additional fighter aircraft to Taiwan to enhance the strength of the US defense posture.[44] In September 1965, Madame Chiang Soong Mei-ling visited Washington and met with Rusk and McNamara. She pointed out that in the situation of increasing PRC nuclear power, the only US course of action was for the United States to take out the PRC nuclear installations before they reached dangerous proportions. McNamara responded that if the United States attacked the PRC nuclear weapons facilities, the PRC reaction would be violent, and that the United States would be condemned for starting a potential nuclear war.[45]

Johnson's China Policy During the Vietnam War

Johnson is remembered as the Vietnam War president who shifted a limited partnership with Saigon into a security commitment to preserving South Vietnam.[46] One of the reasons for the US involvement in Vietnam was that the Vietnamese Communists were the proxies of the PRC. Johnson believed that the North Vietnamese would not be able to attack South Vietnam without the PRC's deep involvement. He stated that the United States faced an aggressive PRC, but that the United States had the strength and determination to help US allies resist the PRC's ambition.[47]

Johnson believed that North Vietnam's attack against South Vietnam was part of the PRC's ambitious strategy, and Rusk agreed. He told Johnson that the US strategy in Vietnam was designed to contain the PRC and to keep it out of the conflict.[48] However, Johnson believed that the PRC was in a bellicose mood. The People's Liberation Army (PLA) trained militaries and rebels in the Southeast Asian countries. For example, the PLA was

92 Hedging the China Threat

training Thai guerillas. In Indonesia, Sukarno requested the PRC for support. Cambodia had become a principal supply point for PRC military equipment going to the North Vietnamese. Johnson's perception of the Chinese threat to Vietnam, and his determination to protect US global credibility, persisted during his administration.[49]

At first, the domestic atmosphere after Kennedy's assassination deterred the Johnson administration from escalating US involvement in Vietnam. However, US intelligence confirmed increased PRC intervention and, together with evidence of intensified Viet Cong activities in South Vietnam, the instability of Vietnam eroded Johnson's confidence in maintaining the status quo. In March 1964, Johnson sent McNamara and General Maxwell Taylor, the JCS chairman, to Saigon on a fact-finding mission. Their report affirmed that the close relationship between Hanoi and Beijing was creating trouble for the United States.[50] Johnson's military strategy in Vietnam would be shaped by one dominant consideration: nothing should be done that might provoke the PLA into engaging US forces.[51] US participation in the Vietnam War aimed to contain the PRC.

Johnson said privately in 1964 that the United States could not avoid recognizing the PRC forever. However, Beijing's lack of reciprocity was the main reason for the limited progress in bilateral relations. By 1966, US politics toward China had evolved away from unwavering opposition toward the possibility of détente with the PRC. However, Johnson had little hope for progress in the absence of a significant change of attitude on the part of the PRC and its presence in the Vietnam War, but he shared a desire to prevent the war in Vietnam from expanding.[52]

The State Level:
The US Military Confronts the PRC's Rising Threat

In 1964, the PRC continued to support Communists in Vietnam against the United States. The PLA deployed warplanes and conducted military exercises near the China-Vietnam border. In February 1965, the United States launched an air raid in North Vietnam to respond to its guerrilla attacks on US installations in South Vietnam. The US bombing gradually moved toward Hanoi in March, testing PRC responses.[53] In July, Premier Zhou instructed the PLA to enter North Vietnam. The PLA's assistance to North Vietnam aimed to break the US encirclement and defend the PRC.[54]

From 1965 to 1968, over 300,000 PLA troops were in Vietnam until Johnson announced that the bombing operation would halt on November 1, 1968, in anticipation of peace talks in Paris between South and North Vietnam.[55] After Johnson's announcement, "the tension began to deescalate, and China began to gradually withdraw parts of its troops." Throughout its intervention, the PRC restricted escalation. Beijing never publicized its presence in the North and controlled air combat over its own territory.[56]

Once the PRC acquired nuclear weapons, the US containment strategy against the Beijing regime became challenging. The US military explored different counteractive measures and the ROC government also increased its military buildup by acquiring advanced weapons from the United States.

During this period, Johnson convened the NSC meetings mainly to discuss Vietnam issues and the threat of China's involvement. Several participants charged that Johnson used the NSC as a "rubber stamp" to justify his military actions.[57] This section explores the US military's stance on the PRC's military actions in Vietnam, their response to the PRC's nuclear weapons, and disputes within the US military on an ROC defense buildup.

The US Stance on the PRC's Action in Vietnam

As the South Vietnam situation worsened, most of Johnson's advisors were worried about the PRC's intervention and suggested Johnson take strong counteractions. The stances of Johnson's key security advisors on the rising crisis in Vietnam deserve attention.

On October 2, 1963, Secretary McNamara and chairman of the JCS, General Maxwell Taylor, sent a memorandum to Johnson about their September mission to South Vietnam, concluding that the security of South Vietnam remained vital to the United States and that the Johnson government should reject communism in Vietnam and suppress the Viet Cong insurgency.[58] In December, Senate majority leader Mike Mansfield suggested a political settlement in Vietnam through negotiation, but Johnson's key security advisors believed this should not be considered until Hanoi and Beijing were defeated in South Vietnam. NSA Bundy argued that diplomacy would happen after the North Vietnamese believed that they could not conquer South Vietnam. McNamara stated that if the US withdrew from Vietnam, all the Southeast Asian countries would bow to Beijing. When more congressional members expressed their concern about getting bogged down in Vietnam, Johnson became reluctant to make any significant moves.[59]

When the Vietnam crisis intensified, McNamara revisited Saigon in March 1964. He suggested to Johnson that the US government might consider furnishing assistance to South Vietnam to bring the insurgency under control, which might require increasing the US forces by at least 50,000 troops.[60] He felt that unless the United States further supported South Vietnam, Southeast Asian countries would probably fall under communist dominance. On March 17, McNamara requested Johnson to authorize South Vietnamese ground operations into Laos for border control purposes, and to direct the preparation of Laotian border control actions and military actions to stabilize the situation in South Vietnam. Johnson agreed.[61]

On December 9, 1964, Senator Mansfield sent a memorandum to Johnson stating that the United States was "overcommitted" in its involvement in Vietnam. The president asked Bundy to comment on it. Bundy responded that he agreed with the senator that US interests were best served by the frugal use of US resources to forestall PRC domination of the area. The United States, however, did not see how its representatives could have helpful talks with the PRC in light of the bitter hostility of their comments about the United States.[62]

On March 2, 1965, North Vietnam started shelling South Vietnam. Six days later, the chairman of the JCS, General Wheeler, stated that if South Vietnam were lost, Southeast Asian countries would give way and look to the PRC. Secretary of State Rusk, Secretary of Defense McNamara, CIA director McCone, and US ambassador to South Vietnam, General Taylor, agreed.[63] In congressional testimony on March 11, McNamara emphasized the need to contain China through limited war and that there were two reasons why the United States must help Vietnam resist the aggression. First, a Communist victory in South Vietnam would open the way for further ventures by Hanoi and Beijing. Second, the United States needed to prove to the world that the form of aggression being tested in South Vietnam was not the wave of the future.[64]

During meetings on the Vietnam situation in mid-1965, McNamara reported to the president that if the United States did not strike China, Mao probably would not send ground forces or aircraft into the war. If the United States struck China, Mao would respond with conventional forces. Johnson asked whether the United States could cope with a "Korea-like" Chinese intervention. Army chief of staff, General Harold Johnson, did not think this was comparable to the Korean War. Secretary Rusk was asked how he thought the PRC would respond to a US preventative strike. Rusk responded that the PRC reaction would be violent. It would employ its principal weapons and enormous manpower in offensive retaliatory operations beyond its borders.[65]

In February 1966, chief of staff of the Army, General Harold Johnson, told McNamara that there appeared to be no clear position of the government on dealing with aggression along the Chinese southern border. McNamara requested JCS recommendations. In June, the JCS Study Group wrote a "long-range" report on the PRC's involvement in Vietnam. The report concluded that the PRC's objectives were to become a regional hegemony. It would launch a world revolution that would clash with US interests. The JCS supported a close-in containment involving a US military presence in Asia.[66]

Most of Johnson's advisors believed Vietnam had a significant geostrategic value in Southeast Asia. If Vietnam turned into a communist state, other countries in the region would be under the control of the Chinese Communists. Most military leaders embraced a close-in containment by sending US military forces to the region. They also watched the Chinese responses closely because of the Korean War experience.

The US Military's Response to the PRC's Nuclear Weapons

As the PRC prepared to test its atomic bomb in 1964, the State Department, the military, and the CIA prepared possible actions against this threat. The Policy Planning Council of the State Department led an interdepartmental study on PRC nuclear capability, which concluded that the PRC hoped its nuclear capability would put pressure on the US military presence in Asia. As counteractions, the council proposed the following approaches: a declaration of willingness to provide nuclear defense, assurances to allies under existing security commitments, bilateral planning for nuclear defense, and exploration of joint declarations with the Soviets.[67]

On April 14, 1964, the State Department examined possible actions against the PRC nuclear facilities. It concluded that US military action against the PRC nuclear facilities would put them out of operation for a few years. The Soviet Union, however, would be unlikely to agree to such US military action.[68] On September 15, Johnson, Rusk, McNamara, and McCone discussed the PRC nuclear weapons. They were not in favor of unilateral US military action against the PRC nuclear installations.[69]

After the PRC tested its nuclear bomb, the State Department and the JCS grew more concerned about its nuclear weapons development and delivery capability. The US military and intelligence community conducted several analyses of the PRC's nuclear development. On January 16, 1965, the JCS wrote a memorandum to McNamara regarding possible responses to the PRC nuclear threat, concluding that the present PRC nuclear capability had not affected the existing balance of military power between the United States and the PRC. The expansion of this capability, nonetheless, would pose challenging problems in the future.[70]

On February 10, a National Intelligence Estimate (NIE) on China's advanced weapons assessed that the PRC was developing a medium-range ballistic missile.[71] On March 10, another NIE on China's military establishment assessed that the PRC had given top priority to its nuclear weapons and missile programs.[72] Following the development of delivery vehicles for PRC nuclear weapons, the US Navy proposed in May 1965 that a PLA ballistic missile submarine be sunk on its maiden voyage. Early in 1966, US nuclear forces in the Pacific were increased by twenty additional B-52 bombers, to be based at Guam, and ten bombers that would fly the route loaded with nuclear weapons to provide improved coverage of PRC targets.[73] On November 3, 1966, a special NIE on China's advanced weapons program stated that the PRC had launched a guided missile, which could carry a nuclear warhead.[74]

96 Hedging the China Threat

In June 1966, the deputy secretary of defense and the deputy under secretary of state for political affairs produced the Special State-Defense Study report on the PRC's threat. The report showed that the most advanced weapons of the PRC over the next decade would be nuclear weapons. By the mid-1970s, the PRC may have deployed around sixty MRBMs and several intercontinental ballistic missiles (ICBMs). At that time, the PRC would possess a counterdeterrent force targeted against the United States. Three containment postures were available to the United States: (1) close-in containment and forward defense, including maintaining a significant military presence in Asia; (2) containment and defense from the offshore islands chain; (3) remote containment and mid-Pacific defense behind buffer zones.[75] The US planners argued that close-in containment was the most effective instrument.[76]

Disputes Within the US Military on the ROC Defense Buildup

After the PRC acquired its nuclear weapons, the ROC government increased its military buildup by acquiring advanced US weapons. From 1965 through 1968, the increased ROC military modernization prompted additional attention from the JCS.

In January 1965, the ROC requested that the United States approve the sale of eleven high-speed transports (destroyers) from the US reserve fleet, but the Johnson administration approved the sale of only six vessels.[77] In September, Minister Chiang Ching-kuo gave McNamara a list of weapons that Taipei wanted to purchase. It included F-5 fighters, submarines, PT boats, and a Mace missile squadron. In November, congressional budget cutting led McNamara to reduce FY 1966 grant aid for the ROC from $104 million to $94 million. Air Force chief of staff John McConnell requested to restore those funds. McNamara refused, reminding McConnell that there had been "many extraordinary demands" for Military Assistance Program appropriations.[78]

On December 29, 1965, General Wheeler called on President Chiang Kai-shek. At the meeting, they discussed the situation in Vietnam, deficiencies in ROC forces, and military assistance such as radar, submarines, and an accelerated F-5 program.[79] In 1966, fearing that the PRC could attack Taiwan, Chiang Kai-shek again stressed a need for radar and F-5s. In mid-April, he wrote to Johnson about an immediate PRC threat of an air attack against Taiwan. The United States found no supporting evidence, but temporarily deployed F-100s and F-4s to Taiwan. The ROC also asked permission to purchase five more transports. Assistant Secretary of Defense for International Security Affairs John McNaughton agreed, but only a two-ship sale was allowed.[80]

The ROC's large number of armed forces concerned the United States. The 1967 and 1968 Military Assistance Manuals advocated reducing the

ROC's army and marine corps from 452,000 to 307,000. In February 1968, the Office of the Secretary of Defense Systems Analysis suggested that army and air force personnel could be cut. For FY 1973, Systems Analysis proposed cutting army divisions from 22 to 13 and F-86s from 125 to 25, while increasing the F-5s from 54 to 72. The JCS concluded that this report contained many flaws. Systems Analysis had overstated the ROC's and underrated the PRC's capabilities.[81]

In August 1968, Minister Chiang Ching-kuo indicated that army cutbacks might be desirable if modernization could keep the ROC's combat capability. The ROC was interested in coproducing UH–1H utility helicopters. The Pentagon asked about the views of the JCS, triggering a debate within the JCS organization. The JCS endorsed a requirement for 236 helicopters. General Wheeler disagreed and argued that the success or failure of a PRC invasion would depend on aerial supremacy. ROC's reliance on helicopters for troop reinforcement could be disastrous. The Army chief of staff, General William Westmoreland, considered coproduction "most desirable." On November 7, the JCS advised Secretary of Defense Clark Clifford, McNamara's successor, that "a valid military requirement" for helicopters did exist since ROC troops depended on ground lines of communication. Eventually, the Pentagon did authorize coproduction, but President Chiang Kai-shek made no force reductions.[82]

During the Johnson administration, the US military assessed that the PRC would continue to be the strongest power in Asia. It would make continued efforts to achieve recognition as a major world power, and as the dominant power in Asia. Unless the United States stood firm before the PRC, the US allies in Asia would become more reluctant to assume a strong stand in opposition to China, in the absence of credible guarantees of US assertiveness against China's aggressive nature.[83]

The International Level: The Moscow and Beijing Split

After the end of the Chinese Civil War in 1949, Moscow and Beijing maintained a good relationship. In early 1950, both countries signed the Treaty of Friendship, Alliance, and Mutual Assistance, in which each state committed to providing military assistance. Thousands of Soviet military personnel went to China to train Chinese scientists and technicians, and 1,500 PLA went to the Soviet Union for training. The Soviet Union also transferred military and industrial technologies to the PRC.[84]

Tensions between Beijing and Moscow rose in 1956 after Nikita Khrushchev denounced Joseph Stalin. Mao defended Stalin against Khrushchev's charges because they threatened Mao's legitimacy in China. The Soviets proposed jointly building a long-wave radio transmission

98 Hedging the China Threat

center and a submarine fleet in China in 1958. Mao saw the Soviet requests as a threat to Chinese sovereignty and rejected them. In 1959, Moscow broke its promise to assist the PRC in developing an atomic bomb, informing Beijing that continued assistance in nuclear technology would jeopardize US-USSR efforts to limit nuclear weapons. In July 1960, Moscow informed Beijing that it would withdraw all of its technicians and scientists from China.[85] The following examines the USSR-PRC split and the US views on the split.

The USSR-PRC Divide

When Khrushchev attacked Mao as an adventurist in June 1960, their dispute became public. Their rift deteriorated after the Cuban Missile Crisis and the PRC-India border conflict in 1962. During the Cuban Missile Crisis, Beijing ridiculed Khrushchev for backing down before the US nuclear threat.[86] During the China-India War, the USSR stood behind India, which created a further Moscow-Beijing confrontation. In response to the Soviet charge of Mao's dividing the communist movement, the PRC accused Khrushchev of being the great divider. The United States concluded that the reconciliation of the two Communist leaders would unlikely happen quickly.[87]

The rift between Khrushchev and Mao was too wide to be fixed, but Khrushchev's fall in 1964 created an opportunity to bring a halt to the dispute. During the beginning of Leonid Brezhnev's leadership, the PRC expected a change in Soviet foreign policy, and Soviet leaders also wanted to improve their relations with Mao's regime.[88] Brezhnev was also more willing to support North Vietnam and less accommodating toward the United States. The State Department reported that the United States would not expect to see any early resumption of Soviet initiatives in disarmament negotiations with the United States. Nevertheless, Moscow had hinted at its willingness to be more conciliatory toward the PRC.[89]

US Views on the USSR-PRC Split

Johnson believed that the USSR-PRC split would impact US policy on Vietnam. Most officials in the Johnson administration felt that the aggressive nature of the PRC could destroy the trend toward Washington-Moscow détente and push the Soviet Union back to a militant hard-line. After Moscow announced Khrushchev's removal in October 1964, the Johnson administration became concerned about the new government's policy. The NSC staff and the US embassy in Moscow discerned that the new Brezhnev administration was reassuring Western governments of its intentions to continue Khrushchev's peaceful coexistence policy. The CIA concluded that the new leaders would continue the broad policy lines of Khrushchev.[90]

At an NSC meeting in September 1964, Johnson asked whether it was worth defending South Vietnam. General Wheeler remarked that if South Vietnam were lost, other countries in Southeast Asia would look toward the PRC. Director of policy planning at the State Department, Walt Rostow, argued in early 1965 that the United States could deepen the Soviet-PRC split to discourage the PRC from adopting a reckless course toward the United States. It was important that South Vietnam maintain its independence and that the North Vietnam offensive be frustrated. Other officials expressed similar ideas. Bundy argued that a noncommunist South Vietnam would defeat the PRC army and strengthen the emerging détente with the Soviet Union. Rusk argued that the United States should fight in Vietnam to convince the PRC that its subversion would not succeed. Otherwise, it would force Moscow to move toward Beijing.[91]

Faced with Beijing's challenge to Moscow's global leadership of the Communists, Soviet leaders would show their support for Hanoi. During a meeting with Soviet premier Alexei Kosygin in July 1965, US ambassador-at-large Averell Harriman stated that the United States would not stand by and see country after country fall under Beijing's control. Throughout 1964 and 1965, the perceived PRC expansionism in the developing countries, and the USSR-PRC conflict, led the Johnson administration to conclude that if the United States hoped to keep its credibility, it must dissuade the Soviet Union from moving toward the PRC hard-line approach. In the administration's view, the only way to do this was by meeting the threat from Hanoi and Beijing head-on in Vietnam. The China factor was a critical factor that determined US war efforts in Vietnam.[92]

Conclusion

The Johnson administration's cross-strait policy was similar to that of the Kennedy and Eisenhower administrations. Although President Johnson privately stated that the United States could not continue to avoid recognizing the PRC indefinitely, Beijing's lack of reciprocity regarding travel exchanges hampered bilateral relations. The US military believed that China would remain aggressive in Southeast Asia during the Johnson administration. As a result, the United States had to stand firm in the face of China's regional expansion. Tensions between Khrushchev and Mao began to surface after Khrushchev denounced Stalin in 1956.

The Johnson administration had two major cross-strait policies: (1) the main policy was a refusal to recognize the PRC in its bid to take over China's seat in the UN, and to support the ROC and use its influence to make certain the ROC retained the Chinese seat in the UN; and (2) in

100   Hedging the China Threat

response to the PRC's nuclear test, the United States dispatched additional fighter planes to Taiwan to strengthen the US defense posture.

In examining US policies and relationships during the Johnson administration at the individual level, I found that President Johnson demonstrated less success in improving the US-PRC relationship than he did with the Soviets. Johnson saw little chance of progress unless the PRC's attitude toward the United States changed. Both Johnson and Chinese leaders, on the other hand, shared a desire to keep the Vietnam War from escalating.

At the state level, the Johnson administration proposed travel exchanges with China, but China flatly rejected the US proposals. As a result, bilateral relations remained tense throughout the Johnson presidency. Military leaders in the United States believed that if Vietnam became a communist state, the Chinese Communists would gain control of the rest of the region. To prevent the domino effect of the communist expansion in Southeast Asia, most military leaders backed the deployment of US forces to the region. Military strategists believed that in the absence of credible guarantees of Western protection, Asian countries would be more hesitant to take a strong stance against China unless the United States stood firm in the face of the PRC.

At the international level, in 1960 when Khrushchev attacked Mao as an adventurist on the international stage, their disagreement and split became public. Following the Cuban Missile Crisis and the PRC-India border conflict in 1962, their schism widened. Beijing mocked Khrushchev during the Cuban Missile Crisis for capitulating in the face of a nuclear threat from the United States. During the China-India War, the USSR backed India, resulting in another clash between Moscow and Beijing. By 1964, the two Communist leaders had fallen out. The PRC accused Khrushchev of being the great divider in response to the Soviet charge that Mao was dividing the communist movement. The United States concluded that a quick reconciliation between the two Communist leaders was unlikely. The Johnson administration thought that it could use the schism to strengthen its political position.

Johnson had little hope for progress in the absence of the PRC's change of attitude toward the United States; nevertheless, Washington and Beijing shared a desire to prevent the war in Vietnam from escalating. Beijing's lack of travel reciprocity limited progress in US-PRC relations. USSR-PRC border clashes in 1969 furthered their split. This conflict pushed Beijing to seek ties with the United States, eventually ushering in Richard Nixon's historic visit to China in 1972.[93]

Notes

1. US Department of State, "Foreword," *FRUS, 1964–1968*, vol. 30, *China*, https://history.state.gov.

2. Ibid.

3. US Department of State, "60. Memorandum for the Record," October 19, 1964, *FRUS, 1964–1968,* vol. 30, https://history.state.gov.

4. US Department of State, "62. Report of Meetings," October 23–24, 1964, *FRUS, 1964–1968,* vol. 33, *China,* https://history.state.gov.

5. US Department of State, "76. Memorandum from the Joint Chiefs of Staff to Secretary of Defense McNamara," January 16, 1965, *FRUS, JCSM-41, 1964–1968,* vol. 30, *China,* https://history.state.gov.

6. US Department of State, "77. National Intelligence Estimate," February 10, 1965, *FRUS,* NIE 13-2-65, 1964–1968, vol. 30, *China,* https://history.state.gov; US Department of State, "80. National Intelligence Estimate," March 10, 1965, *FRUS, NIE 13-3-65, 1964–1968,* vol. 30, *China,* https://history.state.gov.

7. US Department of State, "198. Special National Intelligence Estimate," November 3, 1966, *FRUS, SNIE 13-8-66, 1964–1968,* vol. 30, *China,* https://history .state.gov.

8. Ibid.

9. US Department of State, "10. Telegram from the Embassy in Poland to the Department of State," January 29, 1964, 1964–1968, vol. 30, *China, FRUS,* https:// history.state.gov.

10. US Department of State, "22. Telegram from the Department of State to the Embassy in Poland," April 2, 1964, *FRUS, 1964–1968,* vol. 30, *China,* https://history .state.gov.

11. US Department of State, "Foreword."

12. US Department of State, "89. Action Memorandum from the Assistant Secretary of State for Far Eastern Affairs (Bundy) to Secretary of State Rusk," June 16, 1965, *FRUS, 1964–1968,* vol. 30, *China,* https://history.state.gov.

13. US Department of State, "Foreword."

14. US Department of State, "107. Memorandum of Conversation," September 26, 1965, *FRUS, 1964–1968,* vol. 30, *China,* https://history.state.gov.

15. US Department of State, "81. Telegram from the Embassy in the Republic of China to the Department of State," March 23, 1965, *FRUS, 1964–1968,* vol. 30, *China,* https://history.state.gov.

16. US Department of State, "82. Airgram from the Embassy in the Republic of China to the Department of State," April 14, 1965, *FRUS, A–801, 1964–1968,* vol. 30, *China,* https://history.state.gov.

17. US Department of State, "159. Letter from Secretary of Defense McNamara to Defense Minister of the Republic of China Chiang Ching-kuo," June 16, 1966, *FRUS, 1964–1968,* vol. 30, *China,* https://history.state.gov.

18. US Department of State, "Foreword."

19. US Department of State, "95. Memorandum from James C. Thomson, Jr., of the National Security Council Staff and the President's Special Assistant for National Security Affairs (Bundy) to President Johnson," August 5, 1965, *FRUS, 1964–1968,* vol. 30, *China,* https://history.state.gov.

20. US Department of State, "104. Memorandum of Conversation," September 22, 1965, *FRUS, I-26204/65, 1964–1968,* vol. 30, *China,* https://history.state .gov.

21. US Department of State, "115. Memorandum of Conversation," December 29, 1965, *FRUS, 1964–1968,* vol. 30, *China,* https://history.state.gov.

22. US Department of State, "126, Telegram from the Embassy in the Republic of China to the Department of State," February 22, 1966, *FRUS, 1964–1968,* vol. 30, *China,* https://history.state.gov.

102   *Hedging the China Threat*

23. US Department of State, "142. Memorandum for the Files," April 25, 1966, *FRUS, 1964–1968,* vol. 30, *China,* https://history.state.gov.

24. US Department of State, "Foreword."

25. William W. Newmann, "Kennedy, Johnson, and Policy Toward China: Testing the Importance of the President in Foreign Policy Decision Making," *Presidential Studies Quarterly* 44, no. 4 (December 2014): 649.

26. Ibid., p. 668.

27. Jonathan Colman, *The Foreign Policy of Lyndon B. Johnson: The United States and the World, 1963–1969* (Edinburgh: Edinburgh University Press: 2010), p. 128.

28. Mao Lin, "China and the Escalation of the Vietnam War: The First Years of the Johnson Administration," *Journal of Cold War Studies* 11, no. 2 (Spring 2009): 45.

29. US Department of State, "Foreword."

30. Newmann, "Kennedy, Johnson, and Policy," p. 657.

31. US Department of State, "Foreword."

32. Ibid.

33. US Department of State, "145. Memorandum from the President's Special Assistant (Rostow) to President Johnson," April 30, 1966, *FRUS, 1964–1968,* vol. 30, *China,* https://history.state.gov.

34. US Department of State, "149. Memorandum from Secretary of State Rusk to President Johnson," May 14, 1966, *FRUS, 1964–1968,* vol. 30, *China,* https://history.state.gov.

35. US Department of State, "200. Memorandum from Secretary of State Rusk to President Johnson," November 5, 1966, *FRUS, 1964–1968,* vol. 30, *China,* https://history.state.gov.

36. Ibid.

37. US Department of State, "Foreword."

38. Newmann, "Kennedy, Johnson, and Policy," p. 664.

39. Jim Mann, "U.S. Considered 64 Bombing to Keep China Nuclear-Free," *Los Angeles Times,* September 27, 1998.

40. Colman, *Foreign Policy,* p. 125.

41. Lyndon B. Johnson, "Statement by the President on the First Chinese Nuclear Device," October 16, 1964, *The American Presidency Project,* https://www.presidency.ucsb.edu/documents/statement-the-president-the-first-chinese-nuclear-device.

42. Colman, *Foreign Policy,* p. 125.

43. US Department of State, "74. Telegram from the Department of State to the Embassy in the Republic of China," December 21, 1964, *FRUS, 1964–1968,* vol. 30, *China,* https://history.state.gov.

44. Ibid.

45. US Department of State, "103, Memorandum of Conversation," September 20, 1965, *FRUS, 1964–1968,* vol. 30, *China,* https://history.state.gov.

46. Lin, "China and the Escalation," p. 43.

47. Robert Garson, "Lyndon B. Johnson and the China Enigma," *Journal of Contemporary History* 32, no. 1 (January 1997): 63.

48. Ibid., p. 77.

49. Lin, "China and the Escalation," pp. 47–48.

50. Ibid., p. 51.

51. Garson, "Lyndon B. Johnson," p. 64.

52. Colman, *Foreign Policy,* p. 132.

53. Allen S. Whiting, "China's Use of Force, 1950–96, and Taiwan," *International Security* 26, no. 2 (Fall 2001): 114.

54. Ibid.

55. "President Johnson Halts Bombing in Vietnam," NYPR Archive, October 31, 1968, https://www.wnyc.org.

56. Whiting, "China's Use of Force, 1950–96, and Taiwan," p. 115.

57. White House, "History of the National Security Council, 1947–1997," White House Archives, https://georgewbush-whitehouse.archives.gov.

58. US Department of State, "167. Memorandum from the Chairman of the Joint Chiefs of Staff (Taylor) and the Secretary of Defense (McNamara) to the President," October 2, 1963, *FRUS, 1961–1963*, vol. 4, *Vietnam*, https://history.state.gov.

59. Lin, "China and the Escalation," pp. 49–50.

60. US Department of State, "84. Memorandum from the Secretary of Defense (McNamara) to the President," March 16, 1964, *FRUS, 1964–1968*, vol. 1, *Vietnam*, 1964, https://history.state.gov.

61. US Department of State, "224. Memorandum from the Secretary of Defense (McNamara) to the President," June 25, 1964, *FRUS, 1964–1968*, vol. 1, *Vietnam*, 1964, https://history.state.gov.

62. US Department of State, "449. Letter from the President to Senator Mike Mansfield," December 17, 1964, *FRUS, 1964–1968*, vol. 1, *Vietnam*, 1964, https://history.state.gov.

63. Lin, "China and the Escalation," p. 62.

64. Ibid., p. 100.

65. Lyle J. Goldstein, "When China Was a 'Rogue State': The Impact of China's Nuclear Weapons Program on US–China Relations During the 1960s." *Journal of Contemporary China* 12, no. 37 (November 2003), p. 756.

66. Walter S. Poole, *The Joint Chiefs of Staff and National Policy: 1961–1964*. Washington, DC: Office of the Chairman of the Joint Chiefs of Staff, 2011, p. 255.

67. US Department of State, "30. Paper Prepared in the Policy Planning Council," undated, *FRUS, 1964–1968*, vol. 30, *China*, https://history.state.gov.

68. US Department of State, "25. Paper Prepared in the Policy Planning Council," April 14, 1964. *FRUS*, vol. 30, *China*, https://history.state.gov.

69. US Department of State, "49. Memorandum for the Record," September 15, 1964, *FRUS*, vol. 30, *China*, https://history.state.gov.

70. US Department of State, "76. Memorandum from the Joint Chiefs of Staff to Secretary of Defense McNamara," January 16, 1965, *FRUS*, JCSM-41-65, vol. 30, *China*, https://history.state.gov.

71. US Department of State, "77. National Intelligence Estimate," February 10, 1965, *FRUS*, NIE 13-2-65, vol. 30, *China*, https://history.state.gov.

72. US Department of State, "80. National Intelligence Estimate," March 10, 1965, *FRUS*, NIE 13-3-65, vol. 30, *China*, https://history.state.gov.

73. Goldstein, "When China," p. 750.

74. US Department of State, "198. Special National Intelligence Estimate," November 3, 1966, *FRUS, SNIE 13-8-66*, vol. 30, *China*, https://history.state.gov.

75. US Department of State, "161. Study Prepared by the Special State-Defense Study Group," June 1966, *FRUS*, vol. 30, *China*, https://history.state.gov.

76. Garson, "Lyndon B. Johnson," p. 75.

77. Poole, *Joint Chiefs of Staff*, p. 228.

78. Ibid.

79. US Department of State, "115. Memorandum of Conversation," December 29, 1965, *FRUS*, vol. 30, *China*, https://history.state.gov.

104 Hedging the China Threat

80. Poole, *Joint Chiefs of Staff*, p. 229.

81. Ibid., p. 229.

82. Ibid., p. 230.

83. Lin, "China and the Escalation," p. 47.

84. Michael S. Gerson, *The Sino-Soviet Border Conflict: Deterrence, Escalation, and the Threat of Nuclear War in 1969* (Alexandria, VA: Center for Naval Analyses, November 2010), p. 6.

85. Ibid., pp. 7–9.

86. Charles Dobbs, *Triangles, Symbols, and Constraints: The United States, the Soviet Union, and the People's Republic of China, 1963–1969* (Lanham: University Press of America, 2010), pp. 87–88.

87. Ibid., pp. 89–90.

88. Ibid., pp. 92–93.

89. Ibid., p. 101.

90. Lin, "China and the Escalation," pp. 55–60.

91. Ibid., pp. 62–68.

92. Ibid., pp. 61–69.

93. Colman, *Foreign Policy*, p. 132.

6

The Opening of China:
The Nixon Administration

DURING THE VIETNAM WAR, TAIWAN BECAME A VALUABLE STRATEGIC PARTNER TO the United States because it was an important logistics base and a listening post for intelligence gathering from China for US military operations in Indochina.[1] The US-Taiwan bonds, nonetheless, did not prevent Richard Nixon from taking a fresh approach in seeking US relations with China. In the past, Nixon had been among the harshest critics of the People's Republic of China (PRC) and a staunch supporter of the Republic of China (ROC). It was therefore ironic that it should fall to him, as president, to undertake a sweeping reassessment of China policy.[2]

Historical Events: The Process of Opening to China

In the 1960s, Beijing's foreign policy was hostile to both Washington and Moscow. Although the United States participated in negotiations with the PRC in Warsaw, their bilateral relations remained unchanged. During the Vietnam War, the PRC sent soldiers to North Vietnam, devastating US efforts to improve relations with Beijing. After the outbreak of the Cultural Revolution in 1966, the PRC's anti-imperialist and antirevisionist stance resulted in its isolation in the international arena. The triangular relations between Taipei, Washington, and Beijing began to change at the end of the 1960s.

Kissinger's Secret Trip to China

During his opening to China, President Nixon relied on more confidential channels to communicate with the PRC leaders.[3] Pakistan and Romania served as indispensable mediators for the US-PRC rapprochement. Nixon

106   *Hedging the China Threat*

and Henry Kissinger requested President Yahya Khan of Pakistan and President Nicolae Ceauşescu of Romania to act as the US-PRC intermediaries.[4] On October 26, 1969, President Nixon met with Romanian president Ceauşescu in Washington and expressed his interest in moving the US-PRC talks out of Warsaw. Nixon sought independent relations with Moscow and Beijing, and hoped Romania could serve as a "peacemaker" by talking to both parties.[5] Even more promising was making contact through Pakistan. After a two-year exchange of messages through Pakistani president Yahya Khan, the PRC welcomed Kissinger to China as the US representative.[6]

On April 21, 1971, PRC premier Zhou Enlai sent a message to President Nixon via Yahya Khan and reaffirmed his willingness to receive a special envoy of Nixon (including Kissinger) for direct discussions.[7] After receiving Nixon's confirmation that he would send Kissinger, Zhou wrote another letter to Nixon on May 29, welcoming Kissinger to China for a preliminary meeting to prepare arrangements for Nixon's visit to China. Beijing would guarantee secrecy. When the talks yielded results, the two sides agreed to a public announcement.[8] On June 4, Washington informed Beijing that Kissinger would visit China from July 9 to 11. Kissinger would be authorized to discuss all issues of concern to both countries prior to Nixon's visit to China.[9]

To secretly "smuggle" Kissinger into China, Nixon and Kissinger chose Pakistan, a country friendly with both China and the United States. To figure out his path to China via Pakistan, Kissinger called up Joseph Farland, a former Federal Bureau of Investigation (FBI) agent serving as US ambassador to Pakistan. Farland was instructed not to tell anyone about the trip, not even his boss, Secretary William Rogers.[10] Kissinger was simply "heading to Pakistan on a routine tour." When he was at the state dinner hosted by the Pakistani president with the media covering the event, Kissinger pretended to have an upset stomach and claimed he needed a few days to recuperate, buying time for visiting China.[11]

During his top secret trip to China in early July, Kissinger and Zhou held intensive dialogues, covering the issues of Taiwan, the USSR, Japan, and the establishment of communications. Taiwan issues were at the core of their discussions. Zhou claimed that Taiwan was an inalienable part of Chinese territory, and that the United States must recognize the PRC as the sole legitimate government and withdraw all its armed forces.[12] Kissinger responded that the United States had ended the Taiwan Strait patrol, removed a squadron of air tankers from Taiwan, and reduced the size of the US military advisory group by 20 percent. The United States was prepared to reduce forces in Taiwan as US-PRC relations improved. As for the political future of Taiwan, the United States was not advocating a Two Chinas solution or a "One China, One Taiwan" solution.[13]

The Opening of China   107

On July 14, Kissinger sent a memorandum to Nixon to report the critical points of his talks with Zhou. Kissinger said his team laid the groundwork for Nixon's summit with Mao Tse-tung to turn a page in history, but profound differences between the two countries persisted. Kissinger's assessment of Chinese leaders was "deeply ideological."[14] Nixon responded to Kissinger's efforts to facilitate the US-PRC talks by commenting that "history will record your visit as the most significant foreign policy achievement of this century."[15]

In his memoir, *Henry Kissinger: The White House Years,* Kissinger wrote that Taiwan was mentioned only briefly during the first session. In fact, nearly 20 percent of the first Zhou-Kissinger meeting mainly consisted of discussing Taiwan issues. Kissinger disagreed with Taiwan's independence and committed to withdrawing two-thirds of US forces from Taiwan once the Vietnam War ended. When Kissinger published his memoir in 1979, he did not want to provoke the US conservatives and ROC officials by disclosing what he had said to Zhou about Taiwan.[16]

After Kissinger's trip to China was revealed, the ROC ambassador to the United States, James Shen, lodged a strong protest to Assistant Secretary of State for East Asian and Pacific Affairs Marshall Green. Shen expressed regret for Kissinger's clandestine act that could hardly be described as friendly. Green responded by using Nixon's statement that Kissinger's visit would not be at the expense of the ROC. Shen said Taipei was upset at this development because the United States had chosen an unusual way to show its friendship with the ROC by accepting an invitation from the leader of a rebel regime.[17] On October 15, Ambassador Shen called on Kissinger to discuss his upcoming second visit to Beijing from October 20 to 27. Shen asked if Kissinger could say anything about the trip that had not been mentioned in the press. Kissinger assured him that there was no change in the US position.[18]

Kissinger's second trip to China in October 1971 was more rigid than the first one. Kissinger and Zhou had difficulties agreeing on the content of the draft communiqué for Nixon's visit. The United States provided the draft, but Zhou thought its content concealed the divergences, especially on the Taiwan issue. Zhou was dissatisfied with the US draft and decided to create a new one, but Kissinger felt that the Chinese version was aggressive. They were also unable to reach an agreement on Taiwan issues because the United States insisted on not breaking off diplomatic relations with Taiwan and withdrawing all troops. They did not obtain a consensus concerning the Taiwan issues and had to wait until Nixon's visit.[19]

After Kissinger's second visit to China, the ROC was worried that Kissinger and Zhou may have reached secretive deals that might damage Taiwan's interests. The ROC foreign minister, Chow Shu-kai, visited

108   *Hedging the China Threat*

Kissinger on October 29, and remarked that Nixon could reaffirm the Mutual Defense Treaty at a press conference, which Kissinger promised that he would do.[20]

The PRC's Admission to the United Nations

The PRC replaced the seat of the ROC in the UN General Assembly and Security Council on October 25, 1971. The decision on PRC's admission to the UN involved the "important question" and Albanian resolutions. In December 1961, the General Assembly approved the issue of Chinese representation as an important question resolution that required a two-thirds majority to pass. The Albanian resolution called for expelling the ROC and seating the PRC in the General Assembly and Security Council.[21] On September 17, 1969, the General Assembly agreed to consider the Albanian resolution. On October 17, the United States reintroduced China's representation as an important question. The resolution was passed on November 11 by 71 to 48, with 4 abstentions. The Albanian resolution also garnered a slim majority. On November 20, 1970, the important question resolution passed 66 to 52, with 7 abstentions. The Albanian resolution also passed 51 to 49, with 25 abstentions.[22]

The State Department struggled in mid-1971 to obtain ROC acceptance of a plan to allow the PRC to enter the UN while the ROC would continue to remain in the UN. Secretary Rogers told ROC officials that the only way of preserving the ROC's membership in the UN was for the United States to support a resolution that would provide representation for both Taipei and Beijing. Nixon asked Rogers to take the lead in handling the UN issue because he was engaging with China. He also asked the ambassador to the UN, George H. W. Bush, to fight hard to keep the ROC in the UN. The timing of the UN vote on Chinese representation and Kissinger's October trip to China worried the Nixon administration because the trip would reduce the chances for the ROC to remain in the UN. Kissinger believed that the votes had already been set. On October 12, the National Security Council (NSC) requested that the State Department inform all diplomatic posts that Kissinger's second trip was to arrange for Nixon's visit and that the United States supported the continued membership of the ROC in the UN.[23] Kissinger returned to China on October 20 for Nixon's visit, five days before the UN General Assembly met to vote on admitting the PRC. Although Bush tried to rally votes to keep the ROC's seat, Kissinger's visit to Beijing signaled US intentions. On October 25, Albania's motion to recognize the PRC as the sole legal China was passed as General Assembly Resolution 2758. The PRC replaced the ROC in the General Assembly and Security Council. The PRC was voted in, and the ROC was expelled from the UN.[24]

The Opening of China   109

Nixon's Historical Trip to China

From February 21 to 28, 1972, Nixon traveled to China. His visit not only was symbolic, but also substantive. Although Nixon met with Mao only once during the visit, the two had a dialogue on "philosophic problems" in the US-PRC relationship. Zhou Enlai chaperoned Nixon for most of the trip. The two sat down several times to exchange views from the Vietnam War to the USSR to the status of Taiwan. Nixon's trip ended with the Shanghai Communique.[25]

When meeting with Mao, Nixon said that most nations would approve of this historic meeting, but the Soviets and Indians would disapprove, and the Japanese would have doubts. He explained that both countries must examine why, and determine how their policies should develop to deal with the problems such as Korea, Vietnam, and Taiwan.[26] During the Nixon-Zhou talks, Nixon said that there were many differences between them. We could "lay the problems on the table, talk about them frankly . . . where we can agree, and where we cannot agree." Zhou responded that "we will invariably find common ground to promote the normalization of relations between us."[27]

Unlike the dialogues between Nixon and Mao and Nixon and Zhou, meetings between PRC Foreign Minister Chi Peng-fei and US Secretary of State Rogers were heated. Chi claimed that to normalize relations, the United States must recognize the PRC as the sole legal government of China and withdraw its forces from Taiwan. Rogers responded that if a statement of intention to solve the problem peacefully were made, the United States would reduce its troop levels. The United States had no predatory interest in Taiwan, and the United States had already reduced troop levels.[28]

Nixon's visit was a dramatic development in realpolitik and had been viewed as a "week that changed the world." His visit helped to break several decades of US-PRC hostility. The rapprochement altered the international balance of power, symbolized by Nixon's visit.[29]

The 1972 Shanghai Communiqué

As stated previously, drafting the 1972 Communiqué mainly took place on Kissinger's second visit to China. The result of Kissinger and Zhou's efforts was an unusual communiqué that stated differences and common ground. The key points of the tentative draft of the communiqué were related to Taiwan issues. The Chinese side reaffirmed its position that the PRC was the sole legal government of China and that US troops must withdraw from Taiwan. The US position was to settle the Taiwan question peacefully.[30]

On February 27, the US-PRC joint statement was released. The PRC side reaffirmed the following key positions: first, the PRC was the sole legal government of China. Second, the liberation of Taiwan was China's

110   *Hedging the China Threat*

internal affair, in which no other country had the right to interfere. Third, all US forces and military installations must be withdrawn from Taiwan. Fourth, the PRC opposed any activities aimed at creating One China, and One Taiwan; One China, and two governments; Two Chinas, and an independent Taiwan. The US key positions included: first, the United States reaffirmed its interest in a peaceful settlement of the Taiwan question by the Chinese themselves. Second, the two sides agreed that it was desirable to broaden the understanding between the two peoples. Third, the normalization of relations was not only in the interest of the Chinese and American peoples, but also contributed to the relaxation of US-China tension.[31]

The statement in the Shanghai Communiqué startled Taipei. The ROC was stunned by Nixon's intention to reduce US forces from Taiwan. It was a shocking blow to Taiwan since the ROC regarded the United States as its most important ally. The Ministry of Foreign Affairs condemned the communiqué in a statement: concerning the so-called Joint Communiqué issued by Nixon and Zhou, the ROC would consider this agreement null and void. The ROC was angered by this change in US interest. However, recognizing the continuing importance of the United States to the ROC, Taipei took no further action that would strain its relations with Washington.

Nixon drew criticism from his conservative Republican flank and several prominent Democrats, who expressed their concern that the communiqué was being interpreted as signaling the abandonment of the ROC.[32] To reverse congressional criticism, Nixon gave a briefing to leaders of both parties in Congress on February 29, assuring that he was not abandoning the ROC. To alleviate the fear of Asian allies, Nixon dispatched Marshall Green, assistant secretary of state for East Asian and Pacific affairs, and John Holdridge, a senior staff member of the NSC, to visit eleven Asian countries, including Taiwan. Green reassured Taipei that the United States would not give up the security commitments to the ROC and would honor all commitments, including US defense and other ties with the ROC.[33]

The Shanghai Communiqué was a document of both clarity and ambiguity: clarity in that the United States and the PRC agreed that all US forces would be withdrawn from Taiwan; and ambiguity in that the two sides did not agree on how the Taiwan issue should be settled. Since Nixon's trip to China, normalization of relations with the PRC had become a US foreign policy goal. Unfortunately, the PRC's preconditions for normalization with the United States were derecognition of the ROC, withdrawal of US troops from Taiwan, and abrogation of the US-ROC Mutual Defense Treaty.[34]

After Nixon's visit to China, the United States and the PRC had contact mainly through two channels of communication. Most of the daily business went through the Paris channel, with the United States and PRC ambassadors to France in charge of communication. Sensitive messages were passed through the back channel, through the PRC mission to the UN in New York. In February 1973, Kissinger went to Beijing to propose the establishment of liaison offices in Beijing and Washington. Both sides agreed.[35] In late 1973, bilateral relations began to deteriorate because of domestic problems on each side. A power struggle between moderate forces and the radicals occurred in the PRC. Mao's wife, Jiang Qing, attempted to weaken Zhou's political position. And Nixon's Watergate scandal prevented him from establishing full diplomatic relations.[36]

The Individual Level: The Nixon-Kissinger China Game

In 1946, Nixon had made his anticommunist sentiments publicly known from his first congressional campaign. He attacked his opponent, five-term incumbent Democrat, Jerry Voorhis, for being soft on Mao's regime. During his term as Dwight Eisenhower's vice president, Nixon remained firmly anticommunist. Despite such rhetoric, Nixon understood that with the PRC being a growing power, the United States should not try to keep it isolated from the international community.[37] During the 1950s and 1960s, Nixon had met with many prominent political leaders globally and visited most Asian countries. Before entering office, he developed a strong liking to the idea of garnering credit for a historic trip to China and expressed a need for a change in China's policy. In 1967, he wrote in *Foreign Affairs,* "We simply cannot afford to leave China forever outside the family of nations." [38] After accepting the Republican nomination for president, he reiterated that "we must always seek opportunities to talk with China."[39] Since he had a personal interest in seeking an opening toward China, Nixon asked his top security assistant, Henry Kissinger, to make it happen.

Behind Major Shifts in China's Policy

Nixon's views shifted as he approached the 1968 presidential campaign and later became president. The PRC's atomic test and the Vietnam War added fuel to interest in normalization of relations with the PRC. During the meeting with Kissinger on November 25, 1968, Nixon expressed the need to reevaluate US policy toward China. His reasons were as follows: first, Nixon acknowledged that a multipolar world was gradually replacing the US-USSR bipolar world.[40] He also recognized the urgent need for balance of power strategies, rather than unilateral action, in dealing with international affairs and crises.[41] Second, Nixon paid close attention to trends in public opinion and sensed a change in attitude toward the PRC. After he lost the presidential election to John F. Kennedy, Nixon traveled extensively from 1964 to 1968 and was influenced by the opinions of other leaders concerning the PRC. In

112   *Hedging the China Threat*

his talks with leaders in Asia and Europe, Nixon discovered that the Soviet Union was more militant and more of a threat to the United States than the PRC.[42] Third, Nixon's changing China policy reflected US domestic pressures from the Vietnam War. The war was unpopular among the young and liberal segments of the population in the United States. By mending relations with the PRC, Nixon hoped to convince the PRC's leaders to reduce their support for North Vietnam and assist the United States in pressing North Vietnam to agree on a settlement of the war.[43] Fourth, throughout the 1960s, Moscow's forces grew significantly. The 1969 USSR-PRC border conflict caused grave threats in China. Looking at that circumstance, Nixon played the "China card" to offset a Soviet military threat.[44] Nixon judged that a rapprochement with the PRC would give the United States strategic leverage for diplomatic maneuvers.[45] The PRC came to be viewed as a desirable counterweight to the USSR's threat.

The Nixon Doctrine

The PRC, the USSR, and Vietnam were three significant priorities in Nixon's foreign policy. On July 25, 1969, during his tour to Asia, Nixon met with reporters in Guam and outlined what was first called the "Guam Doctrine" and later the "Nixon Doctrine." He promoted the idea that the United States should continue to play a significant role in Asia. The United States should assist, but not dictate to the US allies. He would keep treaty commitments with the US allies, but the United States would prevent other countries, so dependent on the United States, from eventually being dragged into conflicts.[46] The doctrine had three key points: (1) the United States would not become involved in more wars like Vietnam; (2) it would reduce its military commitments throughout Asia; and (3) it would keep its treaty commitments and watch Asian developments.[47] The Nixon Doctrine provided a guide for action in Asia and paved the way for rapprochement with the PRC. The United States gradually lifted its economic sanctions on the PRC. Nixon initiated the idea of "negotiations instead of confrontation" as his China policy. In his February 1970 Foreign Policy Report to Congress, Nixon announced that "it is certainly in our interest, . . . that we take what steps we can toward improved practical relations with Beijing."[48] This policy developed because of the anti−Vietnam War movement in the United States. Recognizing that public backing for the war was crumbling, Nixon sought to disengage US forces from fighting with minimal damage to US prestige. An easing of the US-PRC hostility would achieve these objectives. Americans' views of Beijing had changed enough that an opening to Beijing would be generally applauded rather than condemned. However, this action would strain US relations with the ROC.

The Opening of China   113

Nixon's Calculation on the Opening of China

Since his presidency began in 1969, Nixon had been interested in changing relations with the PRC to take advantage of the adversarial USSR-PRC relationship. In September 1970, Nixon directed Kissinger to engage with the PRC. As noted earlier, the Pakistani channel produced a critical means for US-PRC engagement. In April 1971, both sides were sending goodwill gestures to each other, the Chinese with "Ping Pong diplomacy" by inviting US athletes to China, and Nixon with public statements of interest in visiting China. When the Pakistani ambassador delivered Zhou's reply, the Mao regime's interest in receiving Nixon's visit paved the way for Kissinger's secret dialogues with Mao and Zhou.[49]

After Kissinger's first trip to Beijing, on July 19 Nixon instructed Kissinger to talk with the press about Nixon's characteristics in crafting China's strategy. He wanted to be described as having "strong convictions, at his best in a crisis, a tough, bold, strong leader, a man who takes the long view, and a man who knows Asia."[50] In a private conversation on July 22, Nixon and Kissinger discussed views on relations with the PRC. Nixon declared, "We are doing the China thing to screw the Russians, help the United States in Vietnam, keep the Japanese in line, and get another ball in play. Furthermore, maybe way down the road, to have some relations with China."[51]

The potential US-PRC rapprochement was a threatening development for the USSR. Gambling that the PRC was more fearful of the USSR than of the United States, Nixon altered anti-Beijing rhetoric, reduced the US military presence in the Taiwan Strait, and made confidential overtures through third parties. Nixon, however, did not get what he most wanted from the PRC: a promise to stop sending military supplies to North Vietnam and to pressure Hanoi into negotiating a peace settlement for the Vietnam War.[52]

The Nixon-Kissinger Role

Henry Kissinger was one of the Cold War's most influential US foreign policymakers. After working closely with Kissinger during his first term, Nixon appointed Kissinger as his new secretary of state while also keeping him in the role of national security advisor (NSA), making Kissinger the first person ever to hold these two jobs concurrently.[53] Kissinger believed that the United States could utilize the USSR-PRC conflict split for its national interests, and assessed the future role of China within the triangular diplomacy. The United States needed to work with the Chinese against the Russians. The United States used the weaker China as a counterweight against the stronger Soviet Union. Kissinger claimed that he and Nixon realized that the

114 *Hedging the China Threat*

development of triangular relations between the United States, the USSR, and the PRC would provide a strategic opportunity for peace.[54]

One of the reasons why the United States secretly engaged with China was because Nixon and Kissinger were afraid that if it became public, domestic politics would terminate the initiative before it began. Once Nixon set a policy direction, he left it to Kissinger to implement it. Kissinger played the role of an advisor and executor, but not as a generator of ideas. Nixon was a strategic thinker, and Kissinger was a tactician carrying Nixon's ideas forward. Nixon provided fundamental guidance, and Kissinger was the shrewd negotiator.[55]

The State Level: US-PRC Relations and Conflicts within the Administration

During the administration's transition period, Nixon pursued reviving the efficiency of the NSC because he was upset with resistance to changes in the State Department. Thus, Nixon authorized Kissinger to reform the NSC to plan, analyze, and review policy options.[56] However, the increasing NSC influence over the China policy caused friction between the State Department and the Department of Defense (DoD).

Conflicts Between the State Department, the DoD, and the NSC

Kissinger presented a proposal to Nixon to reform the NSC. The new NSC became the leading organization for reviewing policy issues requiring presidential approval. On December 28, 1968, Nixon met with secretary of state-designate, William Rogers, and secretary of defense-designate, Melvin Laird, to discuss the Kissinger plan. Nixon agreed to increase the NSC's role. In his memorandum to the State Department, the DoD, and the Central Intelligence Agency (CIA) on January 16, 1969, Kissinger explained that the flow of policy papers was under the control of the NSC. All communication directed to the president should be delivered to the NSC office.[57] The State Department and the DoD disagreed with Kissinger's new role.

Secretary of Defense Laird objected to all intelligence being channeled through the NSC. Laird argued that the NSC approach would isolate not only the president from direct access to intelligence community outputs, but also the heads of the security apparatus.[58]

The announcement of Kissinger's trip and the invitation for a presidential visit to China generally garnered a positive response in the United States. Writing to Kissinger on August 13, Laird offered his department's support in normalizing relations with the PRC. He stressed the importance of keeping the DoD informed.[59] The Joint Chiefs of Staff (JCS) also emphasized the need for military participation in formulating plans and policies to normalize relations with China. They cautioned against a growing attitude that US military activities in Asia should be reduced to avoid provoking China.[60] Laird requested more information on China's policy and an opportunity to participate in deliberations, but Kissinger refused Laird's requests.[61]

State Department officials insisted that it should be their responsibility to formulate the foreign policy issues and bring them to the president's attention. Kissinger criticized the State Department for being unable to take the lead in managing interagency affairs because it was inadequate in long-term planning. Ultimately, Nixon's decision resolved the conflict. He urged that anyone who opposed his decision for the NSC reform should submit their resignation.[62]

During the process of building a relationship with China, the State Department was excluded because of Nixon's distrust of its leaks. The Warsaw meeting, scheduled for May 20, 1970, was canceled by the PRC because of the US invasion of Cambodia. It also marked the end of the State Department's operational involvement in the China initiative. Nixon relied on more confidential channels to communicate with Beijing.[63] The State Department did not know about Kissinger's trip to Beijing. Nixon told Rogers that the trip was a last-minute decision.[64]

Some State Department officials did participate in the drafting of the 1972 Communiqué for Nixon's visit to China. Kissinger realized that the Asian experts on his NSC staff would be unable to produce all the documents needed. Kissinger turned to Alfred Jenkins of the State Department. The State Department had also been involved with the implementation of easing trade and travel restrictions against the PRC. The Defense, Commerce, and Treasury Departments had all participated in implementing the relaxation of trade and economic relations with the PRC. The CIA also set up a back channel for Kissinger's secret China policy.[65]

Rogers did not fight hard in the rivalry with Kissinger over the control of foreign policy. Assistant Secretary Marshall Green did not get along with Kissinger. He was upset about Kissinger's undermining of the role of the State Department. Green criticized Kissinger's failure to learn from the experts, who had devoted their lives to working in East Asia, as a mistake. Green was angry about the secrecy of Kissinger's China initiative, without informing the State Department.[66] Kissinger was being criticized over the UN vote on the expulsion of the ROC and seating of the PRC, which occurred during his China visit. However, Kissinger blamed the State Department for mishandling the vote.[67] Even the NSC staff rarely saw Nixon because Kissinger gathered the information from his staff and delivered the briefing to the president himself, getting all the credit.[68]

116   *Hedging the China Threat*

Examining US-PRC Relations

The Nixon administration instituted the National Security Study Memoranda (NSSM), which were formal directives issued by Nixon or Kissinger, relating to US security and foreign policy. The memoranda mainly instructed departments or agencies to address or answer specific questions. The administration would then discuss these studies. The resulting policy decisions were often announced in the National Security Decision Memoranda (NSDM).[69]

Seeking rapprochement with the PRC. After Nixon came into office, he instructed the administration to seek rapprochement with the PRC. Nixon issued NSSM 14 on February 5, 1969, to focus on how the United States could reduce tension with China. While the State Department and the NSC advocated removing forces as the Vietnam War ended, the DoD voiced its concerns over withdrawing forces from Southeast Asia and Taiwan.[70] On February 16, 1971, the NSC's study showed that a growing number of foreign governments supported the PRC at the expense of the ROC. The increasing support for the PRC in the UN would lead to the seating of the PRC and the expulsion of the ROC.[71] On April 19, Nixon directed a study of diplomatic initiatives regarding improving US-PRC relations. The study came up with three suggestions: developing US–PRC relations to offset Soviet pressures, avoiding US-PRC armed conflict, and no change in the US policy of recognition for the ROC. Changes in the US military presence in Taiwan, however, had already taken place. For example, the Taiwan Strait naval patrol was stopped, and the Military Assistance Advisory Group was reduced. This constituted a major shift in US military policy in Taiwan.[72]

Rising irritants between the United States and Taiwan. As the United States improved its relations with the PRC, strained relations began to develop between the United States and the ROC. In early 1969, the United States limited aerial reconnaissance of the mainland. Following a raid by ROC forces on China, the State Department requested assurances from Taipei that prior notice would be given for any future military action on the mainland. In 1969, President Chiang Kai-shek complained to Secretary Rogers that his request for F-4s remained unfilled. Writing to Nixon on November 19, Chiang Kai-shek complained about Taiwan's inferiority to China's air and naval strength.[73] He also wanted submarines. The State Department and Pentagon had advised against this transfer because possessing them might encourage risky adventures in the Taiwan Strait. In April 1970, the State Department requested discussions with the Pentagon about terminating an annual exercise, Former Pioneer, due to changes in the political climate. The US Pacific Command (USPACOM) wanted it to continue, but the JCS disapproved of the exercises.[74]

Congressional support for normalization. In the early 1970s, congressional support for US security commitment to the ROC was firm. Nonetheless, Congress had a growing urge to revise the US containment policy toward the PRC. Congress welcomed Nixon's visit to China. As US congressional support for normalization began to rise, its support for Taiwan started to wane.[75] On October 11, 1974, Congress canceled the 1955 Formosa Resolution, which had given the president the power to intervene in the Taiwan Strait to defend Taiwan. The Nixon administration wanted Congress to repeal this resolution to normalize relations with the PRC. In addition, Congress had been supportive of the administration's policies of a gradual withdrawal of US troops from Taiwan.[76]

US Military Responses to the Changing Policy

The Joint Chiefs of Staff showed no interest in the changes in China policy that Nixon was about to impose. The JCS opposed the State Department's suggestion that the ROC abandon Quemoy and Matsu. Not only were these islands important intelligence-gathering posts, but abandoning them might cause the PRC to become more aggressive.[77] In February 1969, Nixon commissioned a review of the China policy. The interdepartmental study identified Taiwan as the obstacle to improving relations with China. Options were presented on Taiwan's future: develop US bases, reduce US military presence, carry out a withdrawal, and increase the use of Taiwan bases under an existing arrangement. The military supported the last option.[78]

State and Defense Department guidance to US political and military leaders in Taiwan emphasized pressing President Chiang Kai-shek to set the goal of the ROC defense budget that would not exceed 50 percent of the government's total budget to prevent any confrontation across the Taiwan Strait and to pave the way for US-PRC rapprochement.[79]

Nixon wanted to end the US combat role in Vietnam and restructure US policy in Asia. Close-in containment of China advocated by the JCS was unfavorable to Nixon.[80] In May, Kissinger mentioned three choices in dealing with China: continue the current course, intensify containment, and reduce tension. The JCS recommended staying with the current policy, but the NSC and State Department preferred reducing tension. On August 8, the interdepartmental group suggested that the United States end aerial surveillance over China and reduce US naval and air activity close to Chinese territory. The military found insufficient evidence to permit such a fundamental change. Military officials preferred close-in containment.[81]

In February 1972, with the president's trip to China only days away, the chief of naval operations, Admiral Elmo Zumwalt, urged his colleagues to send Nixon a memorandum that would clarify the importance of the Western Pacific to US security interests and a rationale for continuing a forward US

118   *Hedging the China Threat*

military presence.[82] The US military played a small part in designing the initial relationship with China. As US forces withdrew from Vietnam, China became less overtly hostile.[83]

On March 12, 1971, Kissinger led the Senior Review Group in discussing how to lessen military conflicts across the Taiwan Strait. The Army chief of staff, General William Westmoreland, noted that Taiwan remained a crucial link in the defense perimeter running along the Pacific Western Rim. The State Department's representative replied that removing or reducing US forces was the only effective means to reduce tension. Deputy Secretary David Packard asked the JCS about the implications of reducing the US military presence in Taiwan. The JCS responded that withdrawal could increase the difficulties of executing contingency and war plans. It might even drive Taiwan to seek rapprochement with the Soviets.[84]

The International level: Playing the China Card

During the Cold War, the United States deployed forces in East Asia against the military threat of the USSR, the PRC, North Korea, and North Vietnam. The US military presence projected a threatening image of the United States in the eyes of the PRC. Under the Nixon Doctrine, the United States decided to reduce its military presence in Asia.[85] In 1970, Nixon said it was in the United States' best interest to improve relations with China. His long-term (four- to eight-year) objectives were that the United States should avoid direct US–PRC armed conflicts, deter PRC aggression, and encourage a peaceful resolution of the Taiwan issue. For short-term (one- to three-year) objectives, he felt the United States should discourage the use of force by either the PRC or the ROC, achieve a relaxation of US-PRC tension, and initiate economic relations. As for the US policy toward Taiwan, the long-term goal was to encourage a peaceful resolution of the Taiwan issue. The short-term goal was to discourage China's use of force.[86] Chinese concern over the Soviet threat had motivated China to improve relations with the United States, and the war in Southeast Asia was a factor in the United States reassessing US-PRC relations.[87]

Exploiting the USSR-PRC Split

A worsening of USSR-PRC relations provided an incentive for a US-PRC thaw. Early in March 1969, a severe clash occurred over the border between Chinese and Soviet troops. On July 3, through NSSM 63, Nixon requested a study of the US choices related to this intensifying conflict.[88] Nixon perceived the conflict as both a risk and an opportunity for the United States. The NSC's Washington Special Actions Group (WSAG) and the Senior

Review Group (SRG) met in 1969 to discuss NSSM 63. Their study showed that the United States would emphasize its noninvolvement, urge both sides not to use nuclear weapons, call for negotiations, and take steps to avoid any provocative actions or accidental contact by US forces.[89]

The United States emphasized the Soviet threat to the PRC to encourage it to side with the United States. Even prior to Kissinger's July 1971 trip, the United States began to inform the PRC secretly of US-USSR relations. Throughout 1971 and 1972, Kissinger relayed messages through Paris and New York to the PRC, detailing US-Soviet discussions. For example, in July 1972 Kissinger discussed with the PRC ambassador to the UN, Huang Hua, a Soviet proposal for a nuclear nonaggression pact, stating: "You are the only government with which we have discussed it, and in our government, only the president and I, and my close associates, know about it."[90] Within the USSR-PRC divide, this provided the opening of relations between the United States and the PRC. Kissinger's Soviet card emphasized the Soviet threat to convince Beijing that it shared common security interests with Washington. It could also develop closer bilateral relations.[91]

Playing the China Card to End the War in Southeast Asia

Nixon hoped that he could reach an end to the Vietnam War. If the United States lost the war in Vietnam, it would deepen the division in the United States and place the United States in a position of weakness in dealing with the Soviets. Nixon turned to a dual strategy: pursuing a negotiated settlement while building up South Vietnamese forces and withdrawing US troops. This process was known as the "Vietnamization" of the war.[92] Nixon and Kissinger made ending the war in Southeast Asia a key goal of US-PRC rapprochement. In early 1972, the US defense attaché to France, Vernon Walters, was the channel to obtain PRC assistance with negotiations, including a request that the PRC arrange a meeting between Kissinger and an advisor to the North Vietnam leader.[93]

Kissinger sought to obtain PRC support for his proposals to the North Vietnamese for a cease-fire. For example, on May 8 Nixon wrote a letter to Zhou, explaining that the decision to mine North Vietnam's harbors was designed to end the conflict. Kissinger reported that Huang Hua's reaction was restrained. Under the noninterference stance, the PRC was careful to avoid any commitment to assist the United States in communicating with the North Vietnamese. Kissinger's visit to China in June 1972 was made to request PRC support in the hope of ending the war in Southeast Asia. However, Zhou stated that there had not been many constructive exchanges in the June talks. Through the latter half of 1972, Kissinger provided the PRC with US proposals for the Paris talks with the North Vietnamese. In a meeting with Huang Hua on October 24, Kissinger asked that the PRC convince

120   *Hedging the China Threat*

Hanoi that the US cease-fire proposal was not a trick. The United States requested that the PRC use its influence to help bring peace, but Kissinger's effort had little effect.[94]

Nixon and Kissinger were the two leading players at the beginning of normalizing relations with China. Nixon assured the PRC that he would establish diplomatic relations if elected for a second term. From 1973 to 1974, there were signs that the momentum had begun to slow. Kissinger's trips to Beijing in 1973, 1974, and 1975 were not as successful as his earlier ones. US defeats in Southeast Asia increased Chinese doubts about the United States' capability to confront Moscow. Beijing was annoyed when the United States appointed Leonard Unger as ambassador to Taiwan in 1974 instead of allowing the post to go unfilled. The United States also agreed with the ROC government to open three new consulates in the United States. Thus, the US-PRC relationship entered a stagnant period.[95] Nixon saw two benefits from US-China normalization. First, the improvement of US-PRC relations would help increase US leverage against the Soviet Union. Second, normalization with China might reduce the chances of Sino-Soviet rapprochement.[96]

Conclusion

Nixon's unprecedented trip to China in 1972 was a profound shift from his anti-China stance during the 1960s. Normalization of relations with the PRC became a US foreign policy goal, as Nixon feared the growing power of the USSR and saw US normalization with the PRC as a buffer against that power. In addition, international support for recognizing the PRC as the official Chinese representative to the UN had been growing. Nixon gave Henry Kissinger the authority to initiate a reform of the National Security Council. He also authorized Kissinger to plan, analyze, and review policy options regarding China issues. The NSC's growing influence over China's policy, however, changed the balance of power between the NSC, the State Department, and the Pentagon, which strained their working relationships. On the international stage, a deterioration in Moscow-Beijing relations provided the impetus for a US-PRC thaw. A major clash between Chinese and Soviet troops occurred near the border in early March 1969. The United States took advantage of that border crisis to provide further enhancements to US-China relations.

Nixon's primary policy achievements were: first, he made the decision to normalize relations with China, and his 1972 trip to China was historic. Second, in dealing with the challenging relationships with the PRC, USSR, and Vietnam, Nixon pioneered the concept of "negotiations rather than confrontation." This concept became the prototype for future US administrations.

The Nixon administration's China policy can be analyzed at three levels. At the individual level, Nixon had been interested in changing relations with China since the beginning of his presidency to capitalize on the adversarial USSR-PRC relationship. Nixon directed Kissinger to make personal efforts to engage the PRC in normalizing relations with China. At the state level, during his administration's early transition period, Nixon was frustrated with resistance to change and security leaks within the State Department. He became distrustful of the State Department, subsequently barring it from establishing relations with China. The Joint Chiefs of Staff were not on board with intended changes in the China policy. The Joint Chiefs also disagreed with the State Department's recommendation that the ROC abandon Quemoy and Matsu. Thus, there was much internal discord among the various departments. At the international level, the United States played the China card against North Vietnam and the Soviet Union. A deterioration in USSR-PRC relations provided an impetus for a US-PRC thaw. Kissinger's Soviet card emphasized the Soviet threat to persuade Beijing that it shared Washington's security interests and the need for stronger bilateral ties.

Notes

1. Ching-Peng Peng and Chien-Pin Li, "Myth or Reality: The Mutual Interest in Sino-American Relationship," in *R.O.C.-U.S.A. Relations, 1979–1989,* edited by Jaw-Ling Chang (Taipei: Institute of American Culture Studies, Academia Sinica, 1991), p. 112.

2. Ralph N. Clough, *Island China* (Cambridge: Harvard University Press, 1978), p. 24.

3. US Department of State, "Summary, 1969–1972," *FRUS, 1969–1976,* vol. E-13, *Documents on China,* https://history.state.gov.

4. Victoria Marine Kraft, *The US Constitution and Foreign Policy: Terminating the Taiwan Treaty* (New York: Green Press, 1991), pp. 32–33.

5. US Department of State, "94. Editorial Note," *FRUS, 1969–1976,* vol. 17, *China,* https://history.state.gov.

6. Jaw-ling Joanne Chang, *United States–China Normalization: An Evaluation of Foreign Policy Decision Making* (Baltimore: University of Maryland, 1986), p. 32.

7. US Department of State, "118. Message from the Premier of the People's Republic of China Chou En-lai to President Nixon," April 21, 1971, *FRUS, 1969–1976,* vol. 17, *China,* https://history.state.gov.

8. US Department of State, "130. Message From the Premier of the People's Republic of China Chou En-lai to President Nixon," May 29, 1971, *FRUS,* https://history.state.gov.

9. US Department of State, "132. Message from the Government of the United States to the Government of the People's Republic of China," June 4, 1971, *FRUS, 1969–1976,* vol. 17, *China,* https://history.state.gov.

10. Jane Perlez and Grace Tatter, "Plots and Private Planes: How Henry Kissinger Pulled Off a Secret Trip to China," WBUR, February 18, 2022.

11. Ibid.

12. US Department of State, "139. Memorandum of Conversation," July 9, 1971, *FRUS,* 1969–1976, vol. 17, *China,* https://history.state.gov.

13. Ibid.

14. US Department of State, "144. Memorandum from the President's Assistant for National Security Affairs (Kissinger) to President Nixon," July 14, 1971, *FRUS,* 1969–1976, vol. 17, *China,* https://history.state.gov.

15. Ibid.

16. William Burr, "The Beijing-Washington Back-Channel and Henry Kissinger's Secret Trip to China: September 1970–July 1971," *National Security Archive Electronic Briefing Book,* no. 66 (February 27, 2002), https://nsarchive2.gwu.edu.

17. US Department of State, "145. Telegram from the Department of State to the Embassy in the Republic of China," July 16, 1971, *FRUS,* 1969–1976, vol. 17, *China,* https://history.state.gov.

18. US Department of State, "159. Memorandum of Conversation," October 15, 1971, *FRUS,* 1969–1976, vol. 17, *China,* https://history.state.gov.

19. "Kissinger's Second Visit to China in October 1971," translated by Gao Bei, in *Xin Zhongguo waijiao feng yun* [Winds and Clouds in New China's Diplomacy], vol. 3, edited by Pei Jianzhang (Beijing: Shijie zhishi, 1994), pp. 59–70.

20. US Department of State, "169. Memorandum of Conversation," October 29, 1971, *FRUS,* 1969–1976, vol. 17, *China,* https://history.state.gov.

21. US Department of State, "167. Editorial Note," *FRUS,* 1969–1976, vol. 17, *China,* https://history.state.gov.

22. Ibid.

23. Ibid.

24. Chang, *United States–China Normalization,* p. 33.

25. Charles Kraus, "Nixon's 1972 Visit to China at 50," Wilson Center, February 21, 2022, https://www.wilsoncenter.org.

26. US Department of State, "194. Memorandum of Conversation," February 21, 1972, *FRUS,* 1969–1976, vol. 17, *China,* https://history.state.gov.

27. US Department of State, "195. Memorandum of Conversation," February 21, 1972, *FRUS,* 1969–1976, vol. 17, *China,* https://history.state.gov.

28. US Department of State, "198. Memorandum of Conversation," February 23, 1972, *FRUS,* 1969–1976, vol. 17, *China,* https://history.state.gov.

29. Kraus, "Nixon's 1972 Visit to China at 50."

30. US Department of State, "165. Memorandum from the President's Assistant for National Security Affairs (Kissinger) to President Nixon," *FRUS,* 1969–1976, vol. 17, *China,* https://history.state.gov.

31. US Department of State, "203. Joint Statement Following Discussions with Leaders of the People's Republic of China," February 27, 1972, *FRUS,* 1969–1976, vol. 17, *China,* https://history.state.gov.

32. Ibid.

33. "John H. Holdridge," *New York Times,* February 29, 1972.

34. Chang, *United States–China Normalization,* p. 4.

35. Ibid., pp. 104–106.

36. Ibid., pp. 36–37.

37. John Cooper, *A Quiet Revolution: Political Development in the Republic of China* (Lanham, MD: University Press of America, 1988), p. 33.

38. Iwan Morgan, "Richard Nixon's Opening to China and Closing the Gold Window," *History Today,* June 15, 2018.

39. Henry Kissinger, *The White House Years* (Boston: Little, Brown, 1979), p. 164.

The Opening of China   123

40. Richard M. Nixon, *RN: The Memoirs of Richard Nixon* (New York: Warner Books, 1978), p. 191.

41. Jen-ken Fu, *Taiwan and the Geopolitics of the Asian-American Dilemma* (New York: Praeger, 1992), pp. 50–51.

42. Nixon, *RN,* p. 281.

43. John Cooper, *Quiet Revolution,* p. 31.

44. Dennis Van Vranken Hickey, *United States–Taiwan Security Ties: From Cold War to Beyond Containment* (Westport, CT: Praeger, 1994), p. 23.

45. Nixon, *RN,* pp. 461–462.

46. US Department of State, "29. Editorial Note," *FRUS, 1969–1972,* vol. 1, https://history.state.gov.

47. Richard Nixon, *Public Papers of the Presidents of the United States: Richard Nixon,* vol.: 1 *1969* (Washington, DC: Government Printing Office, 1971), pp. 544–566.

48. Ibid., p. 546.

49. Burr, "The Beijing-Washington Back-Channel and Henry Kissinger's Secret Trip to China."

50. US Department of State, "147. Memorandum from President Nixon to His Assistant for National Security Affairs (Kissinger)," July 19, 1971, *FRUS, 1969– 1976,* vol. 17, *China,* https://history.state.gov.

51. Ibid.

52. Morgan, "Richard Nixon's Opening to China and Closing the Gold Window."

53. Ibid.

54. Yukinori Komine, *Secrecy in US Foreign Policy: Nixon, Kissinger and the Rapprochement with China* (Taylor and Francis Group, 2008).

55. Ibid.

56. Ibid.

57. Ibid.

58. Ibid.

59. Walter S. Poole, *The Joint Chiefs of Staff and National Policy 1973–1976* (Washington, DC: Office of the Chairman of the Joint Chiefs of Staff, 2015), p. 215.

60. Ibid., p. 216.

61. US Department of State, "Summary, Documents on China, 1969–1972."

62. Komine, *Secrecy in US Foreign Policy.*

63. US Department of State, "Summary, Documents on China, 1969–1972."

64. Chang, *United States–China Normalization,* p. 99.

65. Ibid., pp. 102–103.

66. Komine, *Secrecy in US Foreign Policy.*

67. US Department of State, "Summary, Documents on China, 1969–1972."

68. Komine, *Secrecy in US Foreign Policy.*

69. "National Security Study Memoranda (NSSM)," National Archives, https://www.nixonlibrary.gov.

70. US Department of State, "Summary, Documents on China, 1969–1972."

71. US Department of State, "105. Draft Response to National Security Study Memorandum 1061," February 16, 1971, *FRUS, 1969–1976,* vol. 17, *China,* https://history.state.gov.

72. US Department of State, "129. Response to National Security Study Memorandum 1241," May 27, 1971, *FRUS, 1969–1976,* vol. 17, *China,* https://history.state.gov.

73. Poole, *Joint Chiefs of Staff,* p. 218.

74. Ibid., p. 219.

124   Hedging the China Threat

75. Chang, *United States–China Normalization,* p. 132.

76. Ibid., p. 132.

77. Ibid., p. 217.

78. Ibid., p. 218.

79. Ibid., p. 211.

80. Ibid., p. 211.

81. Ibid., p. 212.

82. Ibid., p. 216.

83. Ibid., p. 217.

84. Ibid., p. 221.

85. US Department of State, "105. Draft Response to National Security Study Memorandum 1061."

86. Ibid.

87. Chang, *United States–China Normalization,* p. 67.

88. Poole, *Joint Chiefs of Staff,* p. 212.

89. US Department of State, "Summary, Documents on China, 1969–1972."

90. Ibid.

91. Evelyn Goh, "Nixon, Kissinger, and the 'Soviet Card' in the U.S. Opening to China, 1971–1974," *Diplomatic History* 29, no. 3 (June 2005): 475–501.

92. US Department of State, "1969–1976: The Presidencies of Richard M. Nixon and Gerald R. Ford," *Milestones in the History of U.S. Foreign Relations: 1969–1976,* https://history.state.gov.

93. US Department of State, "Summary, Documents on China, 1969–1972."

94. Ibid.

95. Chang, *United States–China Normalization,* pp. 36–38.

96. Ibid., p. 52.

7

Moving Slowly
Toward Normalization:
The Ford Administration

VICE PRESIDENT GERALD FORD ASSUMED THE PRESIDENCY IN AUGUST 1974, following Richard Nixon's resignation over the Watergate scandal. Ford inherited Nixon's foreign policy team, relying on National Security Advisor (NSA) and Secretary of State Henry Kissinger's foreign policy advice. In 1975, the US public and Congress both disapproved of concentrating foreign policy in the hands of Kissinger. President Ford named Lieutenant General Brent Scowcroft, Kissinger's deputy at the National Security Council (NSC), as NSA. Scowcroft did not seek to advocate policies in competition with Kissinger, and the two men continued to have a cordial working relationship assisting Ford.[1] During the Ford administration, the Beijing leaders believed that the resignation of Nixon in 1974 and the Communist victories in Indochina in 1975 had put the US domestic political situation in turmoil. Beijing thought that the United States seemed incapable of playing a superpower role in world affairs.[2]

Historical Events: Three Phases of the US-PRC Relations

During the Ford administration, there were three phases in dealing with relations between the United States and the People's Republic of China (PRC): the move toward normalization of relations (October 1974–July 1975), the summit in Beijing (August–December 1975), and Chinese domestic power struggles (January 1976–January 1977).

A Move Toward Normalization of Relations, October 1974-July 1975

During the 1960s, the PRC faced several security challenges with its neighboring countries. In 1962 China had a border war with India, and in 1969

126 *Hedging the China Threat*

it had an armed conflict with the Soviet Union over border disputes. In countering China, the Soviets established a close relationship with India. Considering the strategic calculation, the Chinese leaders decided to engage with the United States for their national interests.[3]

Early advances. After Nixon's summit with Chinese top leaders, the PRC increased its contact with the United States. The growth of trade and the expansion of exchanges gave public visibility to this growing relationship. Both countries opened liaison offices in their respective capitals. Since 1973, the PRC pressed the United States to deal with normalization on China's terms: break diplomatic relations with the Republic of China (ROC), withdraw all US troops from Taiwan, and abrogate the US-ROC defense treaty. Chairman Mao Tse-tung, Vice Premier Deng Xiaoping, and Minister of Foreign Affairs Qiao Guanhua asserted that China was patient with the timing of normalization and resolution of the Taiwan question. During Kissinger's visit to China, Mao told him, with irony, that "at this moment, it is better for the U.S. to maintain control over Taiwan." Deng and Qiao told Kissinger that the United States owed China a "debt" for their patience on this issue.[4]

The slowdown of the process. The opening of two ROC consulates in the United States in late 1973, and the appointment in early 1974 of a new US ambassador to Taiwan, Leonard Unger, raised objections in Beijing about US policy. In mid-1973, the ideological radicals in China attacked Premier Zhou Enlai's position and the Chinese government slowed down its exchange programs with the United States. Chinese elites, who had visited the United States were subject to criticism for being too close to the United States. Since Zhou's health was failing in late 1973, Vice Premier Deng Xiaoping assumed most of Zhou's responsibilities in foreign affairs. As a returned-to-power leader from the Cultural Revolution purges, Deng adopted a hard stance in his engagement with US officials. This was designed to lessen his vulnerability to criticism from his political rivals and to gain Mao's confidence.[5]

Senior Leaders' Dialogues Between the United States and the PRC, August-December 1975

In late 1975, there were numerous dialogues between the senior leaders of the United States and the PRC. The critical dialogues occurred when Ford and his delegation visited China from December 1 to 5. The bilateral relations, nonetheless, did not make any significant progress because of the domestic power struggles in China, which included the demise of Mao. Another concern was the upcoming 1976 presidential election in the United States.

The Mao-Kissinger conversation. On October 21, 1975, Kissinger visited Beijing, in preparation for Ford's trip to China. During a meeting with Deng, Kissinger was informed that Mao wanted to see him. Mao and Kissinger had an interesting conversation. Mao started his talk by stating, "I've already received an invitation from God." Kissinger smartly replied, "I hope you won't accept it for a long while."[6] Regarding the Taiwan issues, Mao grumbled, "What you are doing is leaping to Moscow by way of our shoulders." Kissinger answered, "We have nothing to gain in Moscow." Mao responded, "You can gain Taiwan." Kissinger replied, "We will settle that between us." Mao responded, "In a hundred years . . . it's better for it to be in your hands. And, if you were to send it back to me now, I would not want it. . . . There are a huge bunch of counterrevolutionaries there. In a hundred years, we will want it, and we are going to fight for it."[7]

The Kissinger-Deng dialogue. Kissinger and Deng discussed the withdrawal of US troops in Taiwan on November 26, 1975. Kissinger stated that after the United States and the PRC established diplomatic relations, the United States had no interest in keeping military bases in Taiwan. If the PRC could assure peaceful reintegration with Taiwan, the Ford administration would accept Beijing as the legal government of China and end diplomatic relations with Taiwan. Deng emphasized that the US-ROC defense treaty would need to be abolished. Kissinger argued that the defense treaty with Taiwan would not have its international status after normalization with China. Deng answered that it still had a "substantial meaning." Kissinger countered, "No, we do not need Taiwan."[8] Kissinger reminded Deng of Mao's statements that Beijing could wait for "one hundred years" to resolve the Taiwan issues. Deng explained that Mao meant "the solving of the Taiwan problem is an internal affair of China." Deng continued to illustrate that there were three principles on which they would not compromise: (1) Beijing refused Two Chinas or One China, One Taiwan; (2) the solution to the Taiwan question was an internal issue of the Chinese people; and (3) the PRC did not agree with any countries involved in solving the Taiwan question. Kissinger reacted to these three principles by stating that "in our judgment, there is no problem."[9]

The Ford-Mao talk. On December 2, 1975, Ford met with Mao during his trip to Beijing. During the summit, both leaders exchanged views mainly on the rising Soviet Union threat. Ford advocated that the countries could work together to keep pressure on the Soviet Union, the PRC from the East, and the United States from the West. The United States would maintain military capability and be prepared to use it. Mao replied, "Yes, a gentlemen's agreement." Regarding Japan, Mao said, "Japan also is threatened by the Soviet Union." Ford stated, "It is important that China and Japan have better relations." Mao agreed with Ford's view.[10]

128 *Hedging the China Threat*

The Ford-Deng dialogue. On December 4, 1975, the highlight of Ford's dialogues with the Chinese leaders was discussing Taiwan issues with Deng. At that time, Premier Zhou was on his deathbed. After a brief greeting, Ford directly spelled out five points regarding US policy toward Taiwan: support the unity of China, disagree with any independence effort by Taiwan, discourage any force from taking expansionist activities concerning Taiwan, reduce US military personnel on Taiwan, and move toward the normalization of relations along with the model of the Japanese arrangement.[11] Deng had taken note of Ford's solution to the Taiwan issue based on the Japanese formula. Deng emphasized that the Japanese formula included only the remaining people-to-people and trade relations with Taiwan. Ford said that the United States would anticipate that any solution would be by peaceful means. Deng responded, "The question of what method we will take to solve our internal problem is something that we believe belongs to the internal affairs of China, to be decided by China herself."[12]

During the top leaders' dialogues, Chinese leaders were firm concerning Taiwan. They perceived that the Ford administration wanted to speed up the process of normalizing relations. Consequently, the senior Beijing leaders skillfully and firmly pushed the US government to accept China's terms of normalization regarding Taiwan.

The Continuing Deterioration of US-ROC Relations

In January 1975, the interdepartmental group from the Pentagon, the State Department, and the Central Intelligence Agency (CIA), discussed the US military security assistance to the ROC under the changed context of US-China policy. Their study showed that Taiwan's survival was dependent on a continued US commitment to Taiwan's security. Losing confidence in the United States could lead the ROC government to increase its efforts to acquire a nuclear weapon.[13]

On October 9, 1974, the ROC ambassador to the United States, James Shen, delivered Premier Chiang Ching-kuo's letter about the importance of the Mutual Defense Treaty to Ford. The NSC staff agreed with the State Department that a response to the premier should be delayed until after Kissinger's trip to Beijing.[14] On January 6, 1975, Kissinger sent Ford a draft of a letter to Premier Chiang Ching-kuo. Kissinger suggested that a specific reaffirmation of the Mutual Defense Treaty would not be wise. The United States would want to move away from it as normalizing relations with the PRC progressed. On January 8, Ford wrote a letter to the premier, which stated that the United States reaffirmed its worldwide commitments, including the US commitment to the security of the ROC, a typical political cliché.[15]

During the Ford administration, it had become difficult for Ambassador Shen to meet with senior leaders in the Ford administration. On January 15,

1975, Richard Solomon and Richard Smyser of the NSC sent a memorandum to Kissinger. In this context, the NSC needed to decide about Shen's desire to pay calls on Vice President Nelson Rockefeller and NSA Brent Scowcroft. Shen believed Ford's trip to Beijing would result in developments unfavorable to ROC interests. This memorandum suggested the vice president refuse Shen's request because such a meeting would create unnecessary problems with the PRC. Ambassador Shen instead met with Assistant Secretary of State Philip Habib and the Deputy Secretary of State Robert Ingersoll.[16] Because the Ford administration sought to normalize relations with the Chinese government, relations between the United States and Taiwan continued to decline.

The Individual Level: Preparing Ford's Visit to China

Gerald Ford assumed the presidency during one of the gravest constitutional crises in the US history. The new president faced public discontent with the Watergate scandal and the defeat of the Vietnam War. Ford vowed to restore trust and confidence in the presidency.[17] In foreign policy, Ford continued Nixon's détente policy with the Soviet Union and reached an agreement on the Strategic Arms Limitation Talks (SALT).[18]

Ford reshaped his national security team at the end of 1975. Chief of the US Liaison Office to the PRC, George H. W. Bush, replaced CIA director William Colby. White House chief of staff Donald Rumsfeld replaced James Schlesinger as secretary of defense. Ford promoted Brent Scowcroft as NSA, with Kissinger continuing in his position as secretary of state.[19] Kissinger helped Ford adapt to the international scene. Kissinger was able to turn abstract wishes into concrete policies and praised Ford's analytic ability.[20] A good listener and an excellent judge of people, Ford treated his cabinet members in a trusting manner. However, if someone lost Ford's confidence, "you were in trouble."[21]

While Ford was in office, the key player forming US policy toward China was Kissinger. With the suggestion of Kissinger, Ford continued to improve US relations with the PRC by visiting Beijing in December 1975. However, before Ford's trip to China, Kissinger and senior Chinese leaders vastly disagreed on the content of the communiqué that was supposed to be released at the end of Ford's visit.

The Ford-Kissinger Relations

In mid-October 1975, Ford and Kissinger discussed Ford's December trip to China. Since the United States and the PRC had significant differences on Taiwan issues, the State Department suggested two options: the first was to let the PRC state its position, and the United States express its desire for normalization. Kissinger said his staff liked this idea, but he did not. The second option was to restate the Shanghai Communiqué, but instead of saying, "The U.S. does not challenge this position," the United States would affirm the One China idea. The president asked, "Which formulation is better here politically?" Kissinger replied, "I think mine is."[22] Kissinger successfully persuaded Ford to approve his option.

On October 24, after his talks with the Chinese leaders in Beijing, Kissinger reported to Ford that the relationship between the United States and the PRC had chilled. Since the two countries did not reach a consensus, the PRC foreign minister suggested a joint press statement rather than a communiqué after Ford's upcoming visit. Kissinger recommended the following procedure for Ford: reduce China's trip to three-plus working days in Beijing only. Work for a joint press statement that would eliminate contentious language. Proceed to the Philippines and Indonesia for a day each. Kissinger believed that reducing the China trip and adding the Philippines and Indonesia would be an appropriate reply. The US trip would strengthen relations with these two key countries in Southeast Asia.[23]

The next day, Kissinger reported details of his Beijing visit to Ford. Kissinger grumbled, "When I saw the Chinese drafted Communiqué, my first reaction was to cancel your trip. Bush's reaction was the same. However, when we thought about it, we changed our minds." Kissinger continued, "We would lose all our leverage with the Soviet Union. . . . It would give the Democrats a chance to say that you screwed up the Chinese policy." Ford asked, "How about adding India?" Kissinger reacted, "No. That's too big a shock."[24]

On October 31, Kissinger informed Ford about Beijing accepting the shortened version of the president's trip. Kissinger suggested two options, "Cancel, or else go, but get the word out that we don't expect anything of substance."[25] The president answered, "I think we should do the latter." Kissinger said, "I would tell the Chinese we find their communiqué unacceptable." George H. W. Bush thought that it was best not to have a communiqué. Ford said if the United States canceled the trip to China, it would be "a disaster both internationally, with the left, and with the right."[26]

Kissinger indicated that Ford might cancel his China trip. As a result, Beijing authorities became more conciliatory. On November 21, Kissinger told Ford, "What they respect is firmness. . . . I think we should tell the Chinese that I am going to Moscow. The Soviet angle keeps the Chinese under control." Ford responded, "When we hung tough on the Peking visit, it obviously worked." A week later, they met again, and Ford said, "I think the trip to China will be a good visit." Kissinger replied, "It is an important visit. Why have they insisted on your coming? These are unemotional people. Our kicking them around in October really paid off."[27]

Moving Slowly Toward Normalization   131

The loss of the Vietnam War sent shock waves throughout Asia Pacific. Ford and Kissinger faced criticism from a neoconservative movement. They had to balance these competing pressures into a competent foreign policy.[28] Ford valued Kissinger's judgment and the making of foreign policy. Ford stood by Kissinger's analysis as best he could. Kissinger also showed his respect for the president's analytic ability. They had a close working relationship.

Since engaging with China in the early 1970s, Kissinger had developed a good connection with the Chinese leaders. He was the only US leader who had in-depth conversations with Chairman Mao, Premier Zhou, and Vice Premier Deng. They thought that Kissinger was intelligent and persuasive. Kissinger represented the foreign policy of Nixon and Ford. While preparing for Ford's trip to China, Kissinger met extensively with Chinese leaders. They had a heated debate on the content of the communiqué. On October 23, Kissinger talked with Foreign Minister Qiao about the draft communiqué. Kissinger grumbled that the United States received the PRC draft near midnight. After reading the draft, Kissinger found it was difficult to find a reason for the president's visit. The American people would ask why the president visited China to sign a document that said, "The people of the third world countries have won a series of significant victories in their struggle against colonialism, imperialism, and hegemonism." He told them the document was unacceptable. Foreign Minister Qiao responded that the US document was also unacceptable to the PRC. Regarding the Taiwan issue, the US draft showed no substantial progress from the Shanghai Communiqué. The only change was in the wording of "does not challenge" to "agree."[29]

After Kissinger's communication with the Chinese leaders, the PRC began to tone down its stance. Both sides finally decided to have a joint statement instead of a communiqué. Ford did visit China in early October despite their differences. On December 4, Ford talked with Deng about Taiwan and bilateral relations. Ford said that the United States would anticipate that any solution to solve the Taiwan issues would be by peaceful means. The United States "can't just cast aside old friends."[30] Ford hoped that through joint efforts, both countries would overcome these differences and advance the cause of normalizing US-China relations.[31]

The State Level: The State Department's Influence

After Kissinger became secretary of state in September 1973, both the State Department and the NSC played an essential role in formulating US policy toward China and Taiwan. The Ford administration concluded that the United States and China rapprochement, together with the fall of South

132   *Hedging the China Threat*

Vietnam, had reduced the potential military conflict with China. The focus of US strategists was shifting away from Asia. In August 1974, Secretary of Defense James Schlesinger projected cutting the number of carriers in the Western Pacific from three to two, which took effect at the end of 1976.[32]

Military Support of Arms Sales to Taiwan

In October 1974, Ford directed a study of US policy on the transfer of US military equipment to Taiwan in the next three to five years. The study defined US interests and objectives and was based on the following assumptions: (1) the normalization process in US-PRC relations would continue; (2) there would be no radical change in the USSR-PRC relations; and (3) the United States would continue its defense commitment to Taiwan.[33]

On November 12, 1974, a study was prepared by the Interdepartmental Regional Group, chaired by Assistant Secretary of State for East Asian and Pacific Affairs Philip Habib. The study showed that the US objectives of supplying arms to Taiwan were to avoid actions that the PRC would interpret as inconsistent with normalization and mislead the PRC that the United States no longer had an interest in Taiwan's security.[34] The group suggested several options for their arms policy: first, impose a complete cutoff. Second, confine access to the replacement of current types of arms. Third, allow limited access to new weapons. A "lower range" policy would permit either replacement of or modest increases in existing stocks, or the acquisition of noncontroversial new equipment. An "upper range" policy would release some controversial items like Harpoons and C-130 transports. Fourth, authorize access to new weapons. The chairman of the Joint Chiefs of Staff (JCS), George Brown, and Deputy Secretary of Defense William Clement recommended the third option's upper range" as the best way to maintain Taiwan's stability while not impeding normalization with China. But Ford chose the third option's lower range, allowing the ROC to slightly improve its arsenal.[35]

The ROC's access to US arms was crucial to its national survival. Reduced access to US equipment would lead to a deterioration of Taiwan's military capabilities. Loss of confidence in the United States could lead Taipei to acquire a military nuclear capability. At the time, Taipei had not abandoned its covert military nuclear energy research program. It possessed most of the technological know-how for the development of a nuclear device.[36]

The study concluded that under international circumstances, there was little prospect of the ROC finding reliable third-country sources of primary weapons because such countries would risk endangering their (France, the Netherlands, and Israel) relationship with the PRC.[37] Thus, US military leaders suggested meeting Taiwan's defense basic needs without infuriating Beijing.

The US Military's Incremental Withdrawals from Taiwan

The White House pressed for further US military withdrawals from Taiwan. The NSC staff asked for plans to reduce the 4,000 nonintelligence personnel to either 2,550, or 100 percent by the end of 1976. In November 1974, the JCS endorsed a 25 percent reduction, which would require hiring civilians on contract, reducing a US Air Force communications group, and eliminating the 327th Air Division.[38] In February 1976, the NSC Senior Review Group discussed whether to cut the military presence from 2,200 to 1,100 by the end of 1976. The chairman of the JCS, General George Brown, asked, "What does the U.S. want to do in Taiwan?" Brent Scowcroft answered bluntly, "Getting all our troops out."[39]

In mid-May 1976, the JCS asked Secretary of Defense Donald Rumsfeld if the aim was to reduce US personnel in Taiwan, what defense commitments would remain? The DoD responded that the JCS would just remain as the smallest US military presence in Taiwan. On September 20, Ford decided that military and civilian strength in Taiwan would be reduced to 1,400 by the end of 1976. The JCS protested that Asian allies would see this decision as a mass exodus of the US security commitment to Asia. Rapid departures would also cause US personnel hardships in Taiwan. It suggested delaying it until March 31, 1977, when a new US communications facility would become operational in Taiwan. Deputy Secretary of Defense Robert Ellsworth supported the idea, and the White House agreed to an extension.[40]

The CIA's Warning

From 1974 to 1976, several CIA research papers cited the deterioration of US-PRC relations. The CIA estimates also recommended taking cautious approaches to implement the normalization process with the PRC because of the uncertainties of Chinese domestic power struggles during Mao's final years.

On October 26, 1974, Director of the CIA William Colby presented a paper to Kissinger titled "The Shift to Harness in Beijing's Policy toward the U.S." This paper noted that since mid-1973, progress in normalizing US-PRC relations had slowed markedly. The Chinese leaders had expressed dissatisfaction with the United States. The impetus for Beijing's shift mainly came from Mao himself. Other apparent reasons for the change included decreased fear of military attacks by the Soviet Union, and Mao's wish to synchronize foreign policy with the sharp leftward movement in Chinese domestic policies.[41]

In June 1976, Lewis Lapham, director of political research at the CIA, wrote a research paper titled "Foreign Policies of China's Successor Leadership." This paper suggested that Mao's successors would confront the

134 *Hedging the China Threat*

same foreign policy problem that Mao had faced. The research showed there was a desire to project China's influence globally, but that China had a limited capability to compete with the superpowers. If the post-Mao Politburo was dominated by an alliance of ideologues and opportunistic military leaders, the result might be a revolutionary attitude toward the United States. There might be more intense opposition to a broader range of US policies. They probably would prefer an equal balance of anti-US and anti-USSR policies. [42] On November 11, the CIA issued National Intelligence Estimate (NIE) 13-76 entitled "PRC Defense Policy and Armed Forces." This estimate concluded that the PRC perceived the United States as weakened and as less of a direct military threat than the Soviet Union. It also noted the PRC's fear of a compromise between the United States and the Soviet Union that would leave the PRC to confront the Soviets alone. [43]

The State Department's Increasing Impact

After Kissinger became secretary of state in September 1973, the State Department increased its influence in formulating China policy. With the resources, experience, staffing, and backing of Kissinger, the office of the assistant secretary of state for East Asian and Pacific affairs of the State Department began to play a vital part in planning and implementing the cross-strait policy.

On May 8, 1975, Assistant Secretary of State for East Asian and Pacific Affairs Philip Habib, Deputy Assistant Secretary of State for East Asian and Pacific Affairs William Gleysteen, Director of the Policy Planning Staff Winston Lord, and NSC staff member Richard Solomon completed a memorandum for Kissinger. They argued that the Chinese leaders were disturbed by contradictory statements on China policy made by President Ford, Secretary of State Kissinger, and Secretary of Defense Schlesinger—particularly the president's message in his press conference on May 10 that he intended to reaffirm US commitments to Taiwan. They suggested Kissinger state that the United States would continue adhering to the normalization process.[44] On July 3, the same group wrote another memorandum to Kissinger regarding US-China relations and the president's Beijing trip. They were convinced that there were solid reasons for attempting to negotiate a normalization agreement that would help to stabilize a nonconfrontational relationship with the PRC.[45]

On November 6, Chief of the Liaison Office in the PRC George H. W. Bush wrote a back-channel message to Kissinger. Bush articulated that the mood in his recent brief meetings with the PRC foreign minister, Qiao Guanhua, had been "noticeably chilly." The Chinese side rejected the US draft of the communiqué. They argued that they would not care if there was no communiqué and emphasized that "you owe us a debt."[46] Bush recommended that, in his statements, the president should strive to leave the Chinese leaders and the world audience with the unmistakable impression that "Gerald Ford is a straight-talking man, contemptuous of overblown rhetoric, and a man who sets policy based on our own view of what is right and of our interests . . . the president is a good decent man, but one who can be tough as nails with the Soviets, the Chinese, or others when necessary."[47]

The NSC's Insistence on Improving Relations with the PRC

During the Ford administration, the NSC's influence on China policy began to wane compared to the Nixon administration, but the NSC and State Department did develop friendly working relations between Scowcroft and Kissinger (Scowcroft had been Kissinger's deputy at the NSC).

The NSC started to see an enormous change in dealing with the ROC and the PRC. The NSC policy recommendations favored their new strategic partner, the PRC, over their old ally, the ROC. For example, on April 11, 1975, Richard Smyser and Richard Solomon of the NSC staff wrote a memorandum to Kissinger on the Chiang Kai-shek funeral delegation. They suggested that the vice president remain the best choice to head up the delegation to Taiwan. Habib later met with PRC ambassador Han Xu to inform him in advance of the public announcement about Nelson Rockefeller's attendance at Chiang Kai-shek's funeral. Habib explained that Rockefeller's visit had no political meaning. He emphasized that US policy continued to be governed by the Shanghai Communiqué, and Beijing could be confident the vice president would make no political comments in Taipei."[48]

On January 15, 1976, Scowcroft received a report titled "U.S. Policy Interests in the Asian-Pacific Area" written by William Kintner, former ambassador to Thailand. Ambassador Kintner warned, "The Chinese strategy for achieving global ascendancy is based on mobilizing the Third World against both the capitalist-imperialist power, the U.S., and the social-revisionist power, the USSR. . . . The PRC is continuing to foster the hardest revolutionary activity in many parts of the world." Kintner suggested "continuing liaison with the PRC and case-by-case cooperation."[49] On the issue of Taiwan, he wrote, "Do not recognize the PRC and concurrently derecognize the ROC in a manner or time frame that could lead both our adversaries and our friends to further doubt our interest in and commitment to retaining active and cooperative security, political and economic relations with other Asian states." Thomas Barnes of the NSC staff, who analyzed Kintner's study before passing the summary on to Scowcroft, wrote that it was the "first comprehensive review of our Asian posture."[50]

Despite some senior diplomats' and military leaders' warnings about normalizing relations with the PRC, the normalization had become a consensus between the White House and the State Department. Even though senior leaders had taken precautions, their overall policy of détente and engagement with China remained unchanged.

136   *Hedging the China Threat*

The International Level:
The United States Embraces the Détente Policy

Ford continued Nixon's foreign policy of détente with the Soviet Union. On September 18, 1974, while addressing the UN, Ford announced that the United States would strive to heal old wounds reopened in recent conflicts in Cyprus, the Middle East, and Indochina. On September 23, Kissinger outlined US efforts at the UN to broker peace in the Middle East and Cyprus and combat nuclear proliferation.[51] President Ford and Soviet leader Leonid Brezhnev reached an agreement on the Strategic Arms Limitation Talks. Both leaders set new limitations on nuclear weapons. The first months of Ford's presidency witnessed the final conquest of South Vietnam by North Vietnam in March–April 1975.[52] After Cambodia and South Vietnam ended in the hands of the Communists, Ford attempted to respond strongly to keep US influence in Asia. Preventing a new war in the Middle East was his other objective. By providing aid to both Israel and Egypt, the United States persuaded the two countries to accept an interim truce agreement.[53]

The Ford administration continued to develop US relations with the PRC; however, there were several reasons for the rising tension in their relationship. The leading cause was China's suspicion that the United States could provide an effective counterweight to Moscow's efforts to encircle China. The Chinese developed doubts about the ability of the United States to pursue its interests abroad.[54]

Détente with the Soviet Union

Ford and Kissinger made it clear to the Soviet leaders that despite Nixon's resignation, the Ford administration still hoped to pursue détente with Moscow. The détente strategy was an effort to lessen conflicts between the Soviet Union and the United States. The two nations explored feasible approaches to work together for national security and economic goals.[55]

In August 1975, Ford furthered détente when he joined with Brezhnev, and the heads of other European nations, to sign the Helsinki Accords in Finland. The participants reached a consensus and recognized the existing boundaries of European countries established at the end of World War II. The accords aimed to reduce tension between the Soviet and Western blocs. In the later years of the Ford administration, discussions between negotiators from Washington and Moscow regarding the details of SALT failed because of differences over limits on Soviet bombers and US cruise missiles.[56]

The criticism of détente in the United States, which had begun during the Nixon administration, grew louder during the Ford years. Conservatives in both political parties, and even members of the Ford cabinet such as Secretary Schlesinger, attacked détente. California's governor, Ronald Reagan, believed that Ford had underestimated the threat of the Soviet Union and had proven too willing to deal with the Soviets rather than confront them from a position of strength.[57] The Chinese leaders were also concerned about US-Soviet Union détente. Privately, the PRC feared that these developments would isolate them and strengthen the Soviet Union. Publicly, China was characterizing détente as appeasement of a growing Soviet threat. The senior Chinese leaders urged the Ford administration to move toward a more aggressive posture with Moscow. Such a policy would serve the Chinese interests because it would strengthen Western counterpressures against the Russians.[58]

The Fall of Vietnam

The Paris Peace Agreement of January 1973 established a cease-fire between North Vietnam and South Vietnam, but the war between the two sides resumed in 1973. By 1974, South Vietnam was on the brink of collapse.[59] Ford confronted this difficult situation when he succeeded Nixon. In late 1974, he reiterated Nixon's request for additional aid. Congress responded by granting South Vietnam $700 million in military and humanitarian assistance.[60] In Vietnam, an assault by Communist forces in North Vietnam in early 1975 brought South Vietnam to the brink of defeat. The end of the Vietnam War came in late April as North Vietnamese and North Vietnamese–controlled Viet Cong forces took over Saigon, the capital of South Vietnam. US allies in neighboring Cambodia and Laos were also falling from power. Ford ordered the evacuation of all US personnel.[61] For China, the Communist victories in Vietnam created significant momentum that would allow the PRC to play a more active role in Southeast Asia. Hanoi also showed delicate skill in playing a "two-handed" strategy of gaining interest from both Beijing and Moscow. Beijing was more concerned than ever about the Russians penetrating its backyard.[62]

The Worldviews of US and Chinese Leaders

Ford and Kissinger had several conversations with top Chinese leaders Mao Tse-tung and Deng Xiaoping. Their dialogues reflected the foreign policy and worldviews of the United States and the PRC, particularly their concern about the threat of the Soviet Union.

On October 21, 1975, Mao met with Kissinger and expressed his worldview. He identified only two superpowers in the world, the United States and the Soviet Union. Mao ranked the priority of world powers as the United States, the Soviet Union, Europe, Japan, and China.[63] Mao believed France was afraid of the reunification of West Germany and East Germany. He favored Germany's reunification, but he felt it would be prevented militarily

138 *Hedging the China Threat*

by the Soviet Union. Kissinger responded that the United States was not afraid of a unified Germany, but Soviet power in Europe should be weakened. Mao reacted, "Without a fight, the Soviet Union cannot be weakened." [64] Mao asked, "Do you think that the 300,000 troops the U.S. has in Europe at the present time are able to resist a Soviet attack?" Kissinger answered, "The weakness in Europe is not our troops, but European troops. I think with nuclear weapons we can resist the attack." Mao sarcastically reacted, "A considerable portion of Americans do not believe you'll use them. They do not believe Americans would be willing to die for Europe." [65]

On October 22, Kissinger and Deng discussed the South Asia situation. Kissinger stated that the United States would begin selling some equipment to Pakistan. [66] Deng asked, "How is your work going on with India?" Kissinger replied that India was eager to improve its relations with the United States. Kissinger stated that in the next five years, India might bring pressure on both Bangladesh and Pakistan and attack them. Kissinger leaked the information to Deng that "they are seriously considering engineering a coup in Bangladesh." [67]

During the Ford-Mao summit on December 2, Ford indicated if the PRC and the United States worked to meet the challenge from Moscow, it would develop more support in the United States toward continued progress for the US-PRC normalization. Both countries would have to convince the Soviet Union, not by words, but by actions. [68] Mao illustrated, "I went to Moscow twice, and Khrushchev came three times to Peking. On none of these occasions did the talks go really well." Ford responded, "I think it is in the best interests of your country and ours, if we are firm, which we intend to be." Mao asked about US-Japan relations. Ford replied that their relations were "the best they have been at any time since World War II. . . . I think it is important that China and Japan have better and better relations. . . . Are your relations with Japan very good?" Mao answered, "They are not bad, but they are not good." [69] Ford stated that in South Asia, "We continue to improve our relations with Pakistan. We have lifted our arms ban so that they can help themselves and develop sufficient military capability to convince India that it would not be a successful venture if the Indians should attempt any military operation." Mao responded, "If India took such action, the PRC would oppose it." These leaders also agreed that both countries should be more active in preventing the Soviet Union's expansion and driving out its influence. [70]

In the post-Mao era, Chinese foreign policy would continue to revolve around China's concerns regarding Moscow. The Russians would still be China's primary enemy. Even if Mao's successors chose to moderate their line toward Moscow, fear of the Soviet Union would continue to be the principal factor in their foreign relations. The successors would continue to view the US-PRC rapprochement in strategic terms. They would consider the United States as the only effective counterweight to the USSR. They would also view

Taiwan as a secondary issue in the US-PRC relationship, subordinated to the strategic US-Soviet-China triangle and China's security. Chinese successors would have to be patient with further US disengagement from Taiwan.[71]

Conclusion

Gerald Ford's administration gradually moved toward normalization with the PRC. Ford inherited Nixon's foreign policy team and relied on Kissinger's foreign policy advice. Ford stated that the United States expected any solution regarding Taiwan issues to be peaceful. After Kissinger was reappointed secretary of state, the State Department continued its increasing influence in shaping China's policy. At the international level, Ford continued Nixon's détente policy with the Soviet Union. Beijing was concerned about the détente between the United States and the Soviet Union, but the Communist victories in Vietnam and Cambodia provided momentum for China to play a more active role in Southeast Asia.

The primary policy outcomes were, first, Ford outlined five points of US policy toward Taiwan: support Chinese unity, oppose Taiwanese independence, discourage any force from engaging in expansionist activities concerning Taiwan, reduce US military personnel in Taiwan, and move toward normalization of relations with the PRC. Second, the US military decided that it would withdraw from Taiwan in stages.

At the individual level, Ford continued to improve US-China relations based on Kissinger's advice. Ford admired Kissinger's judgment in shaping US foreign policy. Kissinger also expressed admiration for President Ford's decisions. The United States anticipated that any solution to the Taiwan issues would be peaceful. At the state level, in comparison to the Nixon administration, the National Security Council's influence on US policy regarding relations with China began to wane during the Ford administration; however, National Security Advisor Brent Scowcroft and Secretary Kissinger developed friendly working relationships. Despite some senior diplomats' and military leaders' reservations about normalizing relations with the PRC, the White House and State Department reached an agreement to improve relations with China. Senior leaders' overall policy of détente and engagement with China remained unchanged. At the international level, Ford continued Nixon's détente policy with the Soviet Union. The Chinese leaders were concerned about the détente between the United States and the Soviet Union, as China feared that these developments would isolate it and strengthen the Soviet Union's influence in Southeast Asia.

In the 1976 presidential election, President Ford lost to his Democratic challenger, former Georgia governor Jimmy Carter. On December 21, Kissinger met with the chief of the PRC liaison office in Washington, Huang Zhen, who asked Kissinger for information about Cyrus Vance who Carter had

140 *Hedging the China Threat*

designated to be secretary of state in his upcoming administration. On January 8, 1977, Kissinger hosted a meeting between Huang and Vance. Huang declared that the PRC continued to insist on three actions that the United States must take before there could be an improvement in relations with the PRC: "sever the diplomatic relationship with Taiwan, withdraw US troops from Taiwan, and abrogate the Treaty." Vance responded that President Carter would stand firmly behind the implementation of the Shanghai Communiqué as the guiding principle from which they would govern bilateral relations.[72]

Notes

1. "History of the National Security Council, 1947–1997," White House, https://georgewbush-whitehouse.archives.gov.

2. US Department of State, "132. Memorandum from Secretary of State Kissinger to President Ford," November 20, 1975, *FRUS, 1969–1976*, vol. 18, *China,* https://history.state.gov.

3. Ibid.

4. Ibid.

5. Ibid.

6. US Department of State, "124. Memorandum of Conversation, Beijing," October 21, 1975, *FRUS, 1969–1976*, vol. 18, *China,* https://history.state.gov.

7. Ibid.

8. US Department of State, "94. Memorandum of Conversation," November 26, 1974, *FRUS, 1969–1976*, vol. 18, *China,* https://history.state.gov.

9. Ibid.

10. US Department of State, "134. Memorandum of Conversation," December 2, 1975, *FRUS, 1969–1976*, vol. 18, *China,* https://history.state.gov.

11. US Department of State, "137. Memorandum of Conversation," December 4, 1975, *FRUS, 1969–1976*, vol. 18, *China,* https://history.state.gov.

12. Ibid.

13. US Department of State, "90. Study Prepared by the Ad Hoc Interdepartmental Regional Group for East Asia and the Pacific," November 12, 1974, *FRUS, 1969–1976*, vol. 18, *China,* https://history.state.gov.

14. US Department of State, "100. Letter from President Ford to Republic of China Premier Jiang Jingguo," January 8, 1975, *FRUS, 1969–1976*, vol. 18, *China,* https://history.state.gov.

15. Ibid.

16. US Department of State, "101. Memorandum from Richard H. Solomon and W. Richard Smyser of the National Security Council Staff to Secretary of State Kissinger," January 15, 1975, *FRUS, 1969–1976*, vol. 18, *China,* https://history.state.gov.

17. "Gerald R. Ford Biography," Gerald Ford Foundation, https://geraldrford foundation.org.

18. US Department of State, "1969–1976: The Presidencies of Richard M. Nixon and Gerald R. Ford," *Milestones in the History of U.S. Foreign Relations: 1969–1976,* https://history.state.gov.

19. US Department of State, "Biographies of the Secretaries of State: Henry A. (Heinz Alfred) Kissinger (1923–)," Office of Historian of the State Department, https://history.state.gov.

Moving Slowly Toward Normalization   141

20. Philip Zelikow, "The Statesman in Winter Kissinger on the Ford Years," *Foreign Affairs* 78, no. 3 (May–June 1999): 123–128.

21. "Henry Kissinger," Gerald R. Ford Foundation.

22. US Department of State, "120. Memorandum of Conversation," October 17, 1975, *FRUS, 1969–1976,* vol. 18, *China,* https://history.state.gov.

23. US Department of State, "127. Memorandum from Secretary of State Kissinger to President Ford," October 24, 1975, *FRUS, 1969–1976,* vol. 18, *China,* https://history.state.gov.

24. US Department of State, "129. Memorandum of Conversation," October 25, 1975, *FRUS, 1969–1976,* vol. 18, *China,* https://history.state.gov.

25. US Department of State, "130. Memorandum of Conversation," October 31, 1975, *FRUS, 1969–1976,* vol. 18, *China,* https://history.state.gov.

26. Ibid.

27. US Department of State, "133. Editorial Note," *FRUS, 1969–1976,* vol. 18, *China,* https://history.state.gov.

28. Andrew Gawthorpe, "Ford, Kissinger and US Asia-Pacific Policy," *The Diplomat,* August 15, 2014.

29. US Department of State, "126. Memorandum of Conversation," October 23, 1975, *FRUS, 1969–1976,* vol. 18, *China,* https://history.state.gov.

30. US Department of State, "137. Memorandum of Conversation."

31. US Department of State, "102. Letter from President Ford to People's Republic of China Premier Zhou Enlai," January 23, 1975, *FRUS, 1969–1976,* vol. 18, *China,* https://history.state.gov.

32. Walter S. Poole, *The Joint Chiefs of Staff and National Policy 1973–1976* (Washington, DC: Office of Joint History, Office of the Chairman of the Joint Chiefs of Staff, 2015), p. 215.

33. US Department of State, "88. National Security Study Memorandum 2121," October 8, 1974, *FRUS, 1969–1976,* vol. 18, *China,* https://history.state.gov.

34. US Department of State, "90. Study Prepared by the Ad Hoc Interdepartmental Regional Group for East Asia and the Pacific."

35. Poole, *Joint Chiefs of Staff,* p. 219.

36. US Department of State, "90. Study Prepared by the Ad Hoc Interdepartmental Regional Group for East Asia and the Pacific."

37. Ibid.

38. Poole, *Joint Chiefs of Staff,* p. 217.

39. Ibid., p. 218.

40. Ibid.

41. US Department of State, "89. Paper Prepared in the Central Intelligence Agency," October 1974, *FRUS, 1969–1976,* vol. 18, *China,* https://history.state.gov.

42. US Department of State, "148. Paper Prepared in the Central Intelligence Agency," June 1976, *FRUS, 1969–1976,* vol. 18, *China,* https://history.state.gov.

43. US Department of State, "159. Editorial Note," *FRUS, 1969–1976,* vol. 18, *China,* https://history.state.gov.

44. US Department of State, "108. Memorandum from the Assistant Secretary of State for East Asian and Pacific Affairs (Habib), the Deputy Assistant Secretary of State for East Asian and Pacific Affairs (Gleysteen), the Director of the Policy Planning Staff (Lord), and Richard H. Solomon of the National Security Council Staff to Secretary of State Kissinger," May 8, 1975, *FRUS, 1969–1976,* vol. 18, *China,* https://history.state.gov.

45. US Department of State, "112. Memorandum from the Assistant Secretary of State for East Asian and Pacific Affairs (Habib), the Deputy Assistant Secretary of

142   *Hedging the China Threat*

State for East Asian and Pacific Affairs (Gleysteen), the Director of the Policy Planning Staff (Lord), and Richard H. Solomon of the National Security Council Staff to Secretary of State Kissinger," July 3, 1975, *FRUS, 1969–1976*, vol. 18, *China,* https://history.state.gov.

46. US Department of State, "131. Backchannel Message from the Chief of the Liaison Office in China (Bush) to Secretary of State Kissinger," November 6, 1975, *FRUS, 1969–1976*, vol. 18, *China,* https://history.state.gov.

47. Ibid.

48. US Department of State, "106. Memorandum from W. Richard Smyser and Richard H. Solomon of the National Security Council Staff to Secretary of State Kissinger," April 11, 1975, *FRUS, 1969–1976*, vol. 18, *China,* https://history.state.gov.

49. US Department of State, "138. Editorial Note," *FRUS, 1969–1976*, vol. 18, *China,* https://history.state.gov.

50. Ibid.

51. US Department of State, "44. Address by President Ford," September 18, 1974, *FRUS, 1969–1976*, vol. 38, Part 1, *Foundation of Foreign Policy,* https://history.state.gov.

52. US Department of State, "1969–1976: The Presidencies of Richard M. Nixon and Gerald R. Ford," *Milestones in the History of U.S. Foreign Relations: 1969–1976,* https://history.state.gov.

53. "Gerald R. Ford: The 38th President of the United States," White House, https://www.whitehouse.gov.

54. US Department of State, "132. Memorandum from Secretary of State Kissinger to President Ford."

55. John Robert Greene, "Gerald Ford: Foreign Affairs," Miller Center, September 30, 2023, https://millercenter.org.

56. Ibid.

57. Ibid.

58. US Department of State, "132. Memorandum from Secretary of State Kissinger to President Ford."

59. Greene, "Gerald Ford."

60. Ibid.

61. Ibid.

62. US Department of State, "108. Memorandum From the Assistant Secretary of State for East Asian and Pacific Affairs (Habib), the Deputy Assistant Secretary of State for East Asian and Pacific Affairs (Gleysteen), the Director of the Policy Planning Staff (Lord), and Richard H. Solomon of the National Security Council Staff to Secretary of State Kissinger."

63. US Department of State, "124. Memorandum of Conversation, Beijing."

64. US Department of State, "125. Memorandum of Conversation," October 22, 1975, *FRUS, 1973–1976*, vol. 18, *China,* https://history.state.gov.

65. US Department of State, "124. Memorandum of Conversation, Beijing."

66. US Department of State, "125. Memorandum of Conversation."

67. Ibid.

68. US Department of State, "134. Memorandum of Conversation."

69. Ibid.

70. Ibid.

71. US Department of State, "148. Paper Prepared in the Central Intelligence Agency," June 1976, *FRUS, 1969–1976, vol.* 18, *China,* https://history.state.gov.

72. US Department of State, "159. Editorial Note."

8

Establishing Diplomatic Relations with China: The Carter Administration

DURING GERALD FORD'S PRESIDENCY, THE DOWNFALL OF SOUTH VIETNAM CREated a difficult atmosphere for pursuing normalization with China because the United States might look weak. Nevertheless, when Jimmy Carter became president in January 1977, normalization seemed feasible because bilateral relations had improved. Carter believed that this window of opportunity might be brief. In early 1978, President Carter and National Security Advisor (NSA) Zbigniew Brzezinski determined to move toward normalization and therefore accepted China's three preconditions: the One China principle, the abrogation of the US-ROC Defense Treaty, and the withdrawal of US forces.[1]

On December 15, 1978, the United States and the People's Republic of China (PRC) announced that they would establish diplomatic relations on January 1, 1979. The United States recognized the PRC as the only legal government of China and maintained unofficial ties with Taiwan. After the United States shifted diplomatic recognition from Taiwan to China, Congress enacted the Taiwan Relations Act (TRA), which became US domestic law on April 10. The TRA stated that it was US policy to provide Taiwan with arms of a defensive character and to maintain the capacity of the United States to resist any use of force or coercion that would jeopardize the security of the people of Taiwan. Despite disagreement over the TRA, US-China relations improved as the two countries made progress on economic and security issues.[2]

This chapter explores the different phases of the United States establishing diplomatic relations with China, examines Carter's and Brzezinski's strong backing of normalization, analyzes the Carter administration's efforts to make it happen, and describes the changing US-Soviet-China triangular relations in the international environment.[3]

144 *Hedging the China Threat*

Historical Events: Phases of Normalization

The various stages of normalizing relations with China during the Carter administration were the discovery period, the drive period, and the framework period.

Discovery (January 1977–March 1978)

This period involved exploration by the National Security Council (NSC) of Richard Nixon and Henry Kissinger's memoranda of conversations regarding Chinese issues. From April to June 1977, the NSC decided to study normalization and engage in symbolic actions with China. The Presidential Review Memoranda (PRM), PRM 24 on China, was commissioned in April. On June 14, Brzezinski submitted a memorandum on initiatives for improving relations with China to President Carter. The memo outlined measures to restore ties with China in diplomacy, strategy, commerce, technology, and culture.[4]

PRM 24. On June 27, 1977, the State Department, Treasury Department, Defense Department, Central Intelligence Agency (CIA), and NSC held a Policy Review Committee Meeting regarding PRM 24. During the Carter administration, the NSC created the PRM and the Presidential Directives (PD) as part of the foreign policy development process. PRMs identified topics to be researched and defined the problems to be analyzed. The study's conclusions went to the president in a memorandum, which formed the basis for a Presidential Directive.[5]

PRM 24, Part I, presented four basic options from a diplomatic and political point of view: (1) make a significant effort to establish diplomatic relations by recognizing China and sustaining the US relationship with Taiwan; (2) seek to achieve qualitative movement toward full normalization by recognizing China while retaining official representation and keeping military forces in Taiwan; (3) advance the relationship, not through normalization, but through unilateral steps in Taiwan; and (4) maintain official relations at current levels. Secretary of Defense Harold Brown opened the discussion by encouraging participants to aim for the first option.[6]

Secretary of State Cyrus Vance asked Brown how the United States would benefit from normalization. Brown suggested two benefits: the United States would be better positioned in the triangle between the United States, the Soviet Union, and China; and the security of Taiwan would be enhanced if China would acknowledge a peaceful resolution of the issue.[7]

PRM 24, Part II, concerned the reduction of Taiwanese troops and offered several options. Secretary Brown thought that the first option (a complete reduction by December 1977) was impossible. He favored a tar-

Establishing Diplomatic Relations with China   145

get between the second (50 percent by December 31, 1977) and third option (50 percent by December 31, 1978). The chairman of the Joint Chiefs of Staff (JCS), General Brown, agreed. Brzezinski recommended some of the collateral steps in the fourth option (to accept an invitation for Secretary Brown to visit China, to keep the Chinese informed of US initiatives, to facilitate advanced technology sales by allies to the PRC, and to discuss deepening bilateral economic relations). Vance proposed that the United States had four options: demand from China a public renunciation of the use of force, assert US interest in the peaceful resolution of the issue, privately secure a pledge from China to the United States that it would not use force, and assert the interests of the United States.[8]

Vance's visit to China. Secretary Vance's visit to China from August 22 to 25, 1977, did not stimulate Beijing's interest in advancing its relations with the United States. On August 23, in a conversation on the normalization with the PRC foreign minister Huang Hua, Vance stated that Carter was prepared to normalize relations with the PRC. Following the 1972 Shanghai Communiqué and the peaceful resolution of the Taiwan issues, the United States was ready to establish diplomatic relations with the PRC.[9] Huang replied that the United States owed a debt to China and declared that to realize normalization, the United States must end diplomatic relations with Taiwan, withdraw all US troops from Taiwan, and abrogate the US-Taiwan defense treaty.[10] During the August 24 meeting between Vance and Deng Xiaoping, Deng emphasized, "Vance's formula is not a step forward from the original process of normalization. . . . It is, on the contrary, a retreat from it."[11]

US technology transfer to China. With the Chinese reaction to the Vance presentation and the bureaucratic divisions within the US government over Chinese policy, normalization entered a deadlock period. During this phase, Brzezinski was invited to China and attempted to make a breakthrough. The NSC also pushed a US technology transfer to China as an incentive to improve bilateral relations. On January 23, 1978, the president's special advisor for science and technology, Frank Press, proposed to Carter an approach to China through science and technology. Press stated that it was time to start the process for the following reasons: Chinese leaders emphasized building a strong science and technology foundation, and also acquiring foreign technology. A new wave of Chinese purchases of foreign technology could reach the billion-dollar mark in the first year. It would be beneficial to increase the US share of the China market and establish long-term economic relations. Carter agreed to Press's proposal.[12]

Brzezinski's trip to China. In mid-March 1978, Carter approved Brzezinski's trip to China from May 20 to 23. The four objectives of Brzezinski's

146 Hedging the China Threat

visit were: to deepen bilateral consultations on strategic matters, to expand cultural and economic ties, to set the stage for Ambassador Woodcock's meeting with Chinese leaders, and to acquire a personal feel for the Chinese leaders.[13] Brzezinski summarized the key talking points with Chinese leaders. The leaders demonstrated an eagerness to move forward with normalization. They linked normalization to their willingness to cooperate with the United States in matters of common strategic concern. Deng hinted at his understanding of the United States' need for a statement regarding the peaceful reunification of Taiwan. Hua Guofeng and Deng understood that the United States would retain commercial relations, including arms sales to Taiwan. The PRC appeared to offer the United States a choice—either continue arms sales to Taiwan without receiving China's statement indicating a desire to resolve the Taiwan issue peacefully, or to end arms sales coupled with a Chinese declaration of peaceful intent.[14]

The Drive Toward Normalization (April–December 1978)

The aftermath of Brzezinski's trip culminated in negotiations between Ambassador Leonard Woodcock and Chinese leaders in Beijing. Woodcock's efforts facilitated the final process of normalization.

Negotiations in Beijing. Woodcock and Chinese leaders held six sessions in Beijing from July 5 to December 4, 1978. Throughout the negotiations, Vance and Brzezinski instructed Woodcock. Chinese negotiators objected to US arms sales with Taiwan after normalization.[15] With Woodcock's sixth presentation on December 4, the United States extended an invitation to Deng to visit the United States. On December 13, the Woodcock-Deng meeting launched a new phase of the normalization process. Deng signaled that he would not let arms sales to Taiwan hinder normalization.[16] Deng agreed that the communiqué should be issued on January 1, 1979. He also accepted Carter's invitation to the United States.[17]

US-China scientific and technological relations. On November 3, 1978, a Presidential Directive created the first of the United States' and China's scientific and technological relationship. The following programs were approved: first, the United States would offer assistance and training for the PRC's development of energy resources, electric power, and cooperation in the high-energy physics areas. Second, the United States would receive up to 700 Chinese students, researchers, and visiting scholars by the fall of 1979. The United States would send 100 or more students and scholars to China to study and research in all fields. Third, the United States would offer to assist in the PRC purchase of, and provide launch services for, a telecommunications satellite. The technology transfer would be minimized by offering a low-capacity satellite. Fourth, the United States would seek a broadly cooperative relationship in agriculture. Fifth, programs would be developed in the fields of research in cancer, infectious diseases, and medical information.[18]

Establishing the Framework for Cooperation (January-August 1979)

During Deng's visit to the United States from January 29 to February 5, 1979, the US and Chinese representatives set the agenda for science and technology agreements, trade agreements, and cultural exchanges. The Carter administration reached science and technology agreements with China under the direction of the Office of Science and Technology Policy, the development of an economic relationship under the Treasury Department's encouragement, and the fostering of cultural ties under the Institute of Cultural Affairs.[19] Both the State Department and the NSC pushed for Most-Favored Nation (MFN) status for China. On March 22, Secretary of the Treasury Michael Blumenthal suggested to President Carter that the United States' emerging economic relationship with China should develop in a logical, orderly manner. Carter agreed.[20]

The Taiwan Relations Act

Carter announced that the United States would establish diplomatic relations with the PRC. The United States would also break diplomatic ties and terminate its defense treaty with Taiwan. After the announcement, Taipei and the US Congress were concerned about the future of Taiwan. As a result, Congress enacted the Taiwan Relations Act. No other country had ever severed relations with another country and then, by making a domestic law, maintain an unofficial relationship. However, in reality, it ensured security to Taiwan.[21]

Enactment of the TRA. On January 26, 1979, the Carter administration submitted to Congress the Taiwan Omnibus Bill to provide the framework for maintaining cultural, commercial, and other unofficial relations with Taiwan. Most members of Congress believed that the bill was inadequate for ensuring the security of Taiwan. Congress, also angered by Carter's failure to consult it, then decided to revise the bill.[22] In the months following normalization, the Senate put forth more than a dozen resolutions pledging varying levels of protection for Taiwan. Most Republicans on the Senate Foreign Relations Committee advocated for the protection of Taiwan and increased military assistance to Taiwan in the event of a PRC attack.[23]

Carter hastily signed a US-PRC Joint Communiqué that was deficient in several areas. The TRA attempted to remedy deficiencies in the following

148 *Hedging the China Threat*

ways: the first, the communiqué did not preserve the US right to continue selling defensive arms to Taiwan. To fix this deficiency, Congress stipulated Section 2(b)(5) of the TRA to provide that it is the policy of the United States to provide Taiwan with arms of a defensive character. Second, the communiqué failed to propose a response if the PRC attacked Taiwan. Congress amended Section 2(b)(4) to provide that it was the policy of the United States to consider any effort to determine the future of Taiwan by other than peaceful means, "a threat to the peace and security of the Western Pacific area and of grave concern to the United States." Third, the communiqué undermined the credibility of US security guarantees in Asia. Section 2(b)(2) was amended to read that it is the policy of the United States to declare that peace and stability in the area are in the political, security, and economic interests of the United States. Fourth, the communiqué did not contain a credible guarantee that Taiwan's future would be peacefully determined. As a result, Congress amended Section 2(b)(3) that the US decision to establish diplomatic relations with the PRC rests on the expectation that the future of Taiwan will be determined by peaceful means.[24]

The White House allowed Congress to include the security clause in its bill, but it objected to any language that might commit the United States to provide the same aid as it did in the 1954 Mutual Defense Treaty. Nevertheless, Senator Jacob Javits (R-NY) drafted an amendment to commit the United States to protect Taiwan in the event of the Chinese government using military force. Senator Charles Percy (R-IL) also submitted an amendment stating that the United States would consider any effort to resolve the Taiwan issue by other than peaceful means as a threat to the peace and security of the Western Pacific and to the security of the United States.[25]

On March 16, 1979, PRC foreign minister Huang Hua complained to Woodcock about the TRA. Woodcock commented to President Carter, "If the president decides to sign the bill, it is incumbent on us to reaffirm strongly to the Chinese prior to a signature that the bill is fully consistent with the spirit and letter of the normalization arrangement." Carter agreed and added, "Hold down public PRC complaints as much as possible." A House-Senate conference committee wrote the final version of the Taiwan omnibus legislation. The House adopted it on March 28 by a vote of 339 to 50, and the Senate did so on March 29 by an 85 to 4 vote.[26] Carter signed the TRA into law on April 10. His signing statement read in part: "upon the expectation that the future of Taiwan will be determined by peaceful means." The implementation section affirmed that the United States would make such defense articles and services available to Taiwan in such quantity as necessary to enable Taiwan to maintain a sufficient self-defense capability.[27]

In the absence of diplomatic relations and the Mutual Defense Treaty, the TRA became the legal framework for US-Taiwan relations. It illustrated a six-point statement that was US policy: (1) to preserve and promote commercial, cultural, and other relations between the United States and Taiwan; (2) to regard peace and stability in the area as essential to US political, security, and economic interests; (3) to establish diplomatic relations with Beijing based on the expectation that the future of the ROC would be determined solely by peaceful means; (4) to emphasize that attempt to determine that future by other than peaceful means would be of grave concern to the United States; (5) to continue to provide defensive arms to the ROC, but without consultation with the PRC; and (6) to resist any form of coercion exerted against the security, social, or economic systems of Taiwan.[28]

The TRA in operation. The political heart of the TRA was found in the statements of policy in Section 2 and the security guarantees contained in Section 3. The implementation of the TRA from 1979 to 1980, under the Carter administration, was difficult for Taiwan. The United States was oversensitive to any possible adverse reaction from the PRC government.[29] The security section, especially the part relating to arms transfer, was important to Taiwan's self-defense. Before normalization, the United States made it clear to the PRC that it would sell arms to the ROC. According to Carter, Deng told him to be prudent in selling weapons to Taiwan after 1979. During 1979, the United States delivered $598 million worth of military equipment already contracted for by the ROC. Then, Carter announced in early 1980 that the United States would sell $280 million worth of defensive weapons to Taiwan.[30] In June, Carter authorized Northrop and General Dynamics to conduct an FX aircraft sale to the ROC, but up to the end of his term, no decision was made on that sale.[31]

Carter ended all training within the United States of the ROC's military officers above the rank of major. Furthermore, the Taiwanese would receive instruction only on operating and maintaining defense equipment already purchased from the United States and would be excluded from training in military tactics or command.[32] Despite the difficulties in bilateral military relations, the TRA stood out in US-ROC relations as a rare example of bipartisan achievement on Capitol Hill. For the ROC, the TRA was the best that could be salvaged from the unilateral actions of the United States.[33]

The Individual Level: Carter's Push for Normalization

During the 1976 presidential campaign, Carter vowed to restore morality to domestic and foreign policy following Watergate and the Vietnam War.[34] Carter saw Asia in terms of the recent war in Vietnam, a disaster he pledged not to happen again. His three-fold policy was to avoid being drawn into a future Asian war, to shift military assets out of Asia to Europe

150 *Hedging the China Threat*

and the Middle East, and to encourage more local self-reliance.[35] During Carter's presidency, the most dramatic moment in US-China relations occurred on December 15, 1978, when the United States recognized the PRC as the sole legal government of China and declared it would withdraw diplomatic recognition from Taiwan.[36] Carter came into office intent on completing the process of shifting US diplomatic recognition from Taiwan to China. It was one of his top priorities. As the NSA, Brzezinski recalled that normalization was a critical strategic goal of Carter.[37]

Carter: Pressing Ahead for Normalization

On February 8, 1977, Carter met with the chief of the Liaison Office of the PRC, Huang Chen, regarding US-China relations. Carter stated, "We have made progress in recent years in strengthening the relations between our two peoples, and I want to see it continue to be strengthened."[38] Huang responded that since the United States still had diplomatic relations with Taiwan, Chinese leaders would not come to the United States under those circumstances. China opposed any activity to create Two Chinas or One China and One Taiwan. Carter stated, "We believe the Taiwan question rests in the hands of the PRC and in the people of Taiwan. Nothing would please us more than to see a peaceful resolution of this question. . . . We understand that this is an internal matter. . . . I hope we can see a strong movement toward normalization." Huang replied bluntly, "How to liberate Taiwan—whether by force or other means—is our internal affair. No outside power has the right to interfere just as we do not interfere in the internal affairs of others."[39] On June 14, Brzezinski wrote a memorandum to Carter on initiatives for improving relations with China. The message proposed measures to restore ties with China in five areas: diplomatic, strategic, commercial, technological, and cultural. On his visit to China, Vance could indicate to Chinese leaders that the United States intended to move in the direction of normalization over the coming 18–24 months. Carter agreed.[40]

Proceeding with normalization. Carter decided in late July 1977 to proceed with normalization. In August, he dispatched Vance to Beijing intending to conclude a deal.[41] Carter requested that Vance mention guidelines that he thought should govern US policy. First, the United States must not act unilaterally to improve relations with China. The process must be a reciprocal one. Second, the United States must behave with dignity. The United States could afford to be patient. And third, the US actions would not jeopardize the confidence of Taiwan.[42] Beijing, however, declined any compromise, making Vance's visit an unproductive experience. Carter decided to "put this project on the back burner."[43]

Establishing Diplomatic Relations with China   151

On July 30, Carter held a meeting on China policy with his national security team. Carter stated that the purpose of the meeting was to outline strategic considerations in dealings with China. His first question was: "What would the worldwide reaction be to normalization?" Vance answered that it would be positive. The Japanese would accept it. The Southeast Asians would welcome it. The Soviets would not be surprised. Carter asked, "Would Taiwan go independent?" Michael Oksenberg, a member of the NSC staff, responded: "They are unlikely to declare their independence . . . , what we do about normalization will be absolutely crucial. . . . We keep Taiwan from going nuclear, from developing relations with the Soviet Union, or from going independent." Carter asked, "What do you mean by that?" Oksenberg answered, "We act as a restraint on Taipei."[44] Carter stated, "If we are sure that our position is correct, I am prepared to move ahead as soon as possible. . . . I will talk to the congressional leadership; I will ask for their agreement. . . . We asked the Chinese . . . to pursue a peaceful settlement of the Taiwan issue. But I doubt they'll give it to us."[45]

The rise of Deng Xiaoping cleared the way by the beginning of 1978 for renewed rapprochement with the United States. Therefore. Carter began to take a new interest in Chinese matters and encouraged Brzezinski to hold regular conversations with Han Xu, chief of China's Liaison Office in Washington. In May 1978, a visit by Brzezinski to Beijing paved the way for an agreement on normalization.[46] On December 15, Carter stated that both countries agreed to recognize each other as of January 1, 1979. He also pressed ahead with a rapid expansion of commercial, academic, cultural, and other civilian contacts with the PRC.[47]

The Carter-Deng summit. On January 30, 1979, during Deng's visit to the United States, Carter talked with him about economic relations, technology transfer, nuclear testing, and Taiwan. Regarding economic ties, Carter stated that both countries would establish trade relations. Deng replied, "We could sign a long-term trade agreement, such as the long-term trade agreement we reached with Japan, at least equal in magnitude, in the trade volume." Carter agreed to have maximum trade with China. He emphasized that the trade opportunities would be affected by congressional decisions. Carter reminded Deng that his meetings with the leaders of Congress would be essential in determining the flexibility the United States had in trade with China.[48] Regarding technology transfer, Carter stated that the United States had restrictions on exporting high-technology items, but the United States would make these restrictions as flexible as possible. Concerning nuclear testing, Carter asked: "Is it possible for you to conduct such tests underground, as we ourselves do?" Deng responded, "For the time being, that is still difficult; but our atmospheric tests are very limited." To which Carter replied, "Dr. Press is an expert on this subject and . . . he would be

152   *Hedging the China Threat*

glad to consult with you on how the change to underground tests might be made more easily."[49]

Deng stated that the US and Japanese governments could contribute to a peaceful resolution of the Taiwan issues. That was to urge the Taiwanese authorities to negotiate with Beijing. Deng continued to say there were two conditions under which the PRC would be forced not to use peaceful means. One would be if the Taiwanese authorities refused to talk with China, and the other would be if the Soviet Union would go into Taiwan. As for Vietnam, Deng sent a verbal message to Carter. The armed provocations of Vietnamese troops inside Chinese territory had been escalating and China was forced to make the decision to undertake necessary self-defense operations against Vietnam, which would be restricted and limited in scope.[50]

Zbigniew Brzezinski: Faithful Implementation of Carter's Will

In August 1977, NSA Brzezinski held frequent talks with the deputy chief and chief of the PRC Liaison Office to the United States, Han Xu and Chai Zemin, to place the normalization in a strategic context. Brzezinski ensured that normalization would take place in a stable environment and helped keep Carter fully on board. After a bad meeting between Secretary Vance and Minister Huang on October 3, Brzezinski arranged for Carter to meet with only Ambassador Woodcock and himself on October 11, during which final details were nailed down. Brzezinski was the enforcer of secrecy on the president's behalf.[51]

The six Woodcock negotiating rounds produced cooperation among the State Department, NSC, and Defense Department. The Carter-Woodcock meeting on October 11, 1978, finalized the tactic. Brzezinski favored putting a January 15, 1979, date on the communiqué to show the seriousness of US intent. Vance preferred no date. Carter moved up Brzezinski's January 15 suggestion to January 1. Brzezinski then extended an invitation to Deng to visit the United States in January, and suggested Blumenthal would like to visit China early in the year. Carter agreed. The Deng-Woodcock meeting turned out to be successful. Brzezinski informed Carter that Deng agreed on normalization. Brzezinski then instructed the NSC staff to prepare to negotiate with China. Brzezinski's session with the chief of the PRC Liaison Office, Chai Zemin, finalized the Joint Communiqué. During Deng's visit to the United States, Brzezinski invited Deng to have dinner at his house. Brzezinski planned the three Deng-Carter meetings' talking points for Carter[52] and also kept the Chinese and Vietnam conflicts under control. Vance wanted the Blumenthal trip postponed, but Brzezinski recommended the visit go forward to respond to the Chinese invasion of Vietnam calmly. President Carter supported Brzezinski's position.[53]

The State Level: Different Voices for Normalization

During the normalization process, the NSC was firmly for normalization, but the State Department took a neutral approach. The military was more cautious in approaching China. Since NSA Brzezinski perceived Carter's determination to complete normalization, the NSC sought any opportunities possible to cater to China's demand for normalization.[54]

National Security Council: The Rising Influence of Decisionmaking

On January 25, 1977, Michel Oksenberg of the NSC staff wrote a memorandum to Brzezinski on US-China relations, commenting that US-Soviet relations moved forward while US-China relations languished. Oksenberg proposed a Carter-Huang meeting. Carter would indicate that the China issue of normalization concerned him. He would also write a letter to Premier Hua Guofeng, expressing his commitment to the principles of the Shanghai Communiqué. For the long term, the NSC would establish a working group to detail a strategy for dealing with China.[55]

The study of normalization relations. On March 8, 1977, Brzezinski reported to Carter on Nixon and Kissinger's memoranda of conversations with Mao Ise-tung and Zhou Enlai. All messages between Nixon-Kissinger and Mao-Zhou were being digested by the NSC staff. The Chinese had made no promises. Nixon-Kissinger repeated five points on normalization: (1) there is One China, and Taiwan is part of it; (2) the United States would not support any Taiwan independence movement; (3) the United States would use its influence to discourage Japan from moving into Taiwan; (4) the United States would support any peaceful resolution of the Taiwan issue; and (5) the normalization process would be completed by 1976.[56]

Brzezinski's trip to China. While he visited Beijing between May 20 and 23, 1978, Brzezinski had several conversations with senior Chinese leaders on normalization issues. On May 21, Brzezinski met with Deng. Brzezinski stated that the United States accepted the Chinese conditions and reaffirmed the five points made to Deng by the Ford administration. The United States believed it was important to solve the Taiwan issue by peaceful means. Deng replied, "We refused because the liberation of Taiwan is an internal affair of China." Brzezinski responded, "Although my visit here is not to negotiate normalization. I would like to think of it as contributing to a step forward and not a step backward."[57]

When Brzezinski met with Chairman Hua on May 22, he read a brief note from Carter, "a piece of the moon for you and the people of China,

154 *Hedging the China Threat*

symbolic of our joint quest for a better future." Hua replied that both countries shared common ground to cope with Soviet imperialism. Regarding Taiwan, he stated that "we think if Chiang Ching-kuo of Taiwan did not get U.S. equipment and weapons, there might have been a quicker and better settlement of this issue."[58] He further explained, "The normalization of relations between China and the U.S. is most beneficial to our efforts to deal with the Polar Bear . . . the U.S. should not use China as a pawn to improve its relations with the Soviet Union." Brzezinski responded, "I agree with that. . . . Exchange of trade and military delegations, visits by Cabinet members from the U.S. to China, at this stage are all things which I have mentioned to your Foreign Minister and which Ambassador Woodcock is prepared to pursue."[59]

Brzezinski wrote a report on his China visit for Carter. He observed that the Chinese appeared ready to offer the United States a choice if the United States wished for normalization—either to continue arms sales to Taiwan after normalization without receiving a Chinese statement indicating their intent to resolve the Taiwan issue peacefully, or no further US arms sales coupled with a Chinese declaration of peaceful pursuit.[60] During the normalization process with China, the NSC garnered a strong backing from Carter. Under Brzezinski's leadership, the NSC understood that Carter wished to complete the process during his first term.

The State Department: Implementation of Normalization

Before President-elect Carter took office, Secretary of State-designate Vance spoke with the chief of PRC Liaison Office, Huang Chen, on January 8, 1977. Huang asked Vance how he saw the Carter administration's approach to normalizing relations with China. Vance replied that Carter would follow the Chinese policy of the previous administration.[61] Huang stated that the Shanghai Communiqué constituted the foundation of bilateral relations. Their relations could be improved if both sides strictly observed all the principles. Vance replied, "I fully accept the principle of one China."[62] As a result, US-Taiwan relations were chilled during the Carter administration.

The Decline of US-Taiwan Relations

On February 9, 1977, the ROC ambassador to the United States, James Shen, called on Under Secretary Philip Habib, complaining about the US statements on the China issue. He was disappointed over the absence of any reference by the Carter administration about the US–ROC diplomatic and security ties. He grumbled about the lack of response to his request for a meeting with Vance.[63] On February 14, Habib met with Shen to provide a reply to the ROC requests. Shen reiterated his request for a summary of Carter's talk with Huang Chen, noting that the United States used to brief ROC on details of the Warsaw and Geneva meetings. Habib rejected it.[64] On August 18, Vance wrote a telegram to the US ambassador to Taiwan Leonard Unger on briefing Premier Chiang Ching-kuo on Vance's trip to China. The purpose was to notify Taiwan that the United States began a process that may result in the US-PRC normalization. Talking points included the following: (1) the United States hoped normalization issues would deal with trade and cultural exchanges; (2) the United States did not expect to conclude a normalization agreement during the secretary's visit; and (3) the normalization did not have a timetable; and (4) the US approach to normalization would not undercut Taiwan's security.[65]

The Taiwan Nuclear Program

In February 1977, the US nuclear team found that Taiwan would have the capacity to detonate a nuclear device in the next two to four years. The team suggested that the United States should terminate all ROC nuclear research programs.[66] On March 26, the State Department sent a telegram to Ambassador Unger stating that the US team found out about nuclear activities at the Institute of Nuclear Energy Research (INER) in Taiwan. Unless the ROC's nuclear program was to eliminate all proliferation risks, the US government would not be able to continue cooperation on peaceful nuclear energy matters. Other important relationships would also suffer.[67] With the instruction from the State Department, Unger called on Chiang Ching-kuo. Premier Chiang reiterated his support for Carter's nonproliferation policy. The US embassy in Taiwan later reported that the ROC accepted the demands of the Carter administration regarding the suspension of the operation of the Taiwan research reactor.[68]

Vance's Visit to China

On his August 23–24, 1977 visit, Vance had a heated argument with Minister Hua. Vance stated that after normalization, the United States would want to ensure that the United States could continue to engage in trade, investment, travel, and private contacts with Taiwan. The United States would also make a statement on the US interest in a peaceful settlement of the Taiwan question by the Chinese.[69] Huang responded that the Taiwan issue was an obstacle to normalization between the two countries because of US aggression against China. He felt the views the United States put forward concerning the normalization could only give China the impression that the United States wanted to interfere with Chinese internal affairs. Huang continued, "The Chinese people will liberate Taiwan sooner or later."[70] On

156 *Hedging the China Threat*

August 24, Deng received Vance, and both had an unpleasant conversation about normalization. Vance stated, "What I said to Minister Huang on normalization is a very serious proposal which the president and I have talked about many times. That proposal is worth serious study." Deng responded, "We are prepared to seek peaceful means of settling this issue without the participation of the U.S. . . . But we do not exclude the forceful liberation of Taiwan under military means."[71] On August 25, Vance telegrammed Carter, reporting critical points of his meetings with Chinese leaders. First, Huang was responsive to the suggestion that the United States look for ways to increase bilateral trade. Huang and Vance agreed that a formal communiqué was not necessary. Second, during the meeting with Hua Guofeng, Hua commented favorably on Carter's statement on acceptance of the principles of the Shanghai Communiqué as the basis of the bilateral relationship and enhancing understanding.[72] Indeed, during the trip to China, Vance recognized a big difference between the United States' and China's views on Taiwan issues, but his report to Carter diluted the differences.

Woodcock's Negotiations

On June 13, 1978, Vance wrote a memorandum to Carter on the next moves regarding China. Ambassador Woodcock would undertake negotiations with Chinese leaders on normalization. Vance thought both sides needed to determine the target date for the public announcement of establishing diplomatic relations. Then, they would address the remaining issues: relations with Taiwan after normalization, statements on peaceful settlement, and arms sales to Taiwan. The State Department and the NSC would instruct Woodcock to inform Beijing.[73]

After meeting several times with the acting foreign minister, Han Nianlong, Woodcock noted that despite disagreements, Han avoided any explicit reference to arms sales and observed that the Chinese did not seem to slam the normalization door.[74] On December 4, 1978, Woodcock informed Vance and Brzezinski of his meeting with Han who presented the following Chinese views: (1) Carter must agree to meet the three Chinese conditions, which should be included in the Joint Communiqué; (2) China will agree to issue a communiqué on January 1, 1979; (3) nongovernmental agencies can be maintained in Taiwan, but all official and semiofficial links must be severed; (4) there should not be arms sales to Taiwan after normalization; (5) the United States should not let Taiwan acquire atomic weapons; and (6) a Chinese commitment to peaceful liberation is not only impossible, but would not serve the United States' interests in a peaceful solution.[75]

Brzezinski informed Carter of the Woodcock-Han talks, emphasizing the crucial importance of following Han's conditions. He felt this was an opportunity not to be lost. Brzezinski recommended several talking points for Carter's approval, which included altering the US agreements with Taiwan; the date on which embassies would be established; what the text of the communiqué would be; and whether Woodcock should raise the possibility of Deng visiting the United States. Carter agreed to all the proposals.[76]

On December 13, Woodcock sent a message to Vance about his meeting with Deng. Deng accepted the US draft of the Joint Communiqué, but proposed including an antihegemony clause. He also agreed that the communiqué should be issued on January 1, 1979, and accepted Carter's invitation to the United States. Deng asked that the United States make no sales of defensive weapons to Taiwan during this period.[77] Woodcock commented that his meeting with Deng launched a decisive normalization phase. Deng was determined to pin down a normalization agreement at an early date, and signaled that he would not let the arms sales to Taiwan block normalization.[78]

On December 15, Woodcock met with Deng to discuss the arms sales issue. When Woodcock confirmed the US intention to continue selling arms to Taiwan after 1979, Deng would not agree. Continued arms sales would amount to retaining the essence of the Mutual Defense Treaty and such sales would block efforts to find a rational means of settling the Taiwan issue peacefully. He urged the United States to act in ways compatible with peaceful reunification.[79] Brzezinski informed Woodcock that the United States would be restrained on arms sales but that, within the US political process, it would be impossible for the United States not to reaffirm its position on this subject.[80]

The End of Formal US-Taiwan Relations

Vance and Brzezinski wrote to Ambassador Unger on December 15, 1978, informing him to request an immediate meeting with President Chiang Ching-kuo in the strictest confidence. Carter asked Unger to notify Chiang Ching-kuo that the United States and the PRC agreed to establish diplomatic relations effective January 1, 1979. Carter wished to assure Taiwan that there needed to be no interruption in practical ties between people in Taiwan and the United States. These relationships could be facilitated through nongovernmental agencies.[81] Also, on December 15, Unger met with President Chiang Ching-kuo and read the message about the US unilateral statement and the Joint Communiqué. The Taiwanese president said that the US solution would lead to the internal instability of Taiwan. The US government's decision was dishonest. It made a critical decision and gave the ROC government only seven hours' notice and no opportunity for discussion.[82]

In late December 1978, Carter requested that Deputy Secretary of State Warren Christopher go on a mission to Taiwan. Christopher and Chiang Ching-kuo would discuss the arrangements for the US-Taiwan unofficial

158   *Hedging the China Threat*

relations.[83] On January 1, 1979, a massive demonstration in Taiwan was held one block from the US embassy. The commander in chief, Pacific (CINCPAC), Admiral Maurice Weisner, who accompanied Christopher, described the disturbances when they arrived on December 28, 1978: "Upon arrival in Taipei, our motorcade, en route from the Taipei airport, passed through crowds of several thousand young people who were not adequately controlled."[84]

The US Military

The normalization process caused concern from the Joint Chiefs of Staff because it would damage their long-standing military-to-military relationship with Taiwan. The JCS position was that the United States should treat China and the Soviet Union the same, using military contacts to improve relations with both countries. The chairman of the JCS, General George Brown, in a memorandum to Secretary of Defense Harold Brown, provided initiatives for developing future contacts with the PRC. The JCS chairman wanted to establish an exchange program between the National Defense University/National War College and its PLA equivalent and offer to host PLA personnel to be observers during US military exercises in the Pacific.[85]

Toward the end of 1977, the new Director of the Joint Staff, Vice Admiral Patrick Hannifin, asked the Defense Intelligence Agency (DIA) to estimate the global reactions should the United States recognize the PRC. The DIA concluded that most countries would view US efforts to normalize relations with the PRC "favorably or with relative indifference." At the same time, the Soviet Union would express "some concern," and Taiwan would "vigorously oppose it." By late September 1978, with negotiations on recognition entering their final stage, Secretary Brown asked the JCS for their views on the impact of terminating the treaty with Taiwan. The chiefs' position remained in favor of normalizing relations, providing it could be done without jeopardizing the security of the people of Taiwan.[86]

Arms sales to Taiwan. As a result of normalizing relations with the PRC, the US military realized Taiwan would be on its own. During the Nixon-Ford years, the United States found low-profile approaches to selling weapons to Taiwan. However, it became difficult for Taiwan to buy weapons from the Carter administration. In March 1977, Carter placed a "hold" on an $8 million sale of improved Hawk missiles to the ROC forces. The arms sale to Taiwan concerned the CINCPAC, Admiral Maurice Weisner, who exercised responsibility through a Military Assistance Advisory Group (MAAG) in Taiwan. According to the MAAG's estimate, Taiwan's capacity to maintain deterrence was based on acquiring new weapons systems. Following the submission of MAAG's report, CINCPAC, in late Sep-

Establishing Diplomatic Relations with China **159**

tember 1977, urged the JCS to approach the secretaries of state and defense to provide more military assistance to Taiwan.[87]

The chief of the ROC General Staff, Admiral Soong Chang-Chih, sent JCS chairman Brown a letter requesting US approval to sell F-16 aircraft, Harpoon antiship missiles, and Chaparral missiles. General Brown realized it was impossible to provide the weapons requested by Admiral Soong. In March 1978, the joint State-Defense paper established criteria for providing arms aid to Taiwan. The premise was that the US arms sale to Taiwan was only defensive, so it did not pose a threat to normalizing relations with China.[88]

Though interested in acquiring the F-16, in December 1977 Taiwan submitted a request, following advice from the CINCPAC, to purchase sixty-eight F-4s. The CINCPAC felt this older type might not be as controversial as the F-16. Despite the JCS's endorsement of the F-4, the State Department and the White House delayed the decision because of normalization talks with China. In late August 1978, while visiting the CINCPAC, Admiral Soong stated that while his government preferred the F-16, F-18, or F-4, it was willing to entertain the possibility of other planes so long as they were high-performance models. Consequently, Secretaries Vance and Brown and NSA Brzezinski tentatively settled on offering Taiwan a yet unbuilt aircraft, designated the F-5G. Although inferior to the F-4 in speed and altitude capabilities, the F-5G promised advantages in range and maneuverability. In October, Carter held up the sale of the F-5Gs and offered additional F-5Es instead. In November, the president added that the United States would agree to coproduce up to forty-eight F-5Es and sell Taiwan 500 Maverick missiles and 400 laser-guided bombs.[89]

In August 1979, Taipei submitted a new request for weapons, including the all-weather fighter and air and sea defense weapons, as its urgent requirements. In November, Taiwan sent a high-level delegation to Washington to plead its case. The State Department viewed even the most minor issue involving arms sales to Taiwan as having repercussions for US-China relations.[90]

The Withdrawal from Taiwan. For the JCS, ending the US recognition of Taiwan posed problems. The immediate one involved overseeing the withdrawal of the US military presence—the closing of facilities, the termination of the MAAG, and the relocation of war reserve materiel stockpiled in Taiwan. Under the terms agreed on in 1978 for recognition of the PRC, a speedy withdrawal of all US personnel became unavoidable.[91]

On November 20, 1978, the JCS wrote a memorandum on normalization to Secretary Brown. The JCS believed that if the PRC could give adequate assurances of security for the people of Taiwan, the United States could accept the three PRC preconditions for normalization.[92] On

December 23, Brown wrote a memorandum to Brzezinski. Regarding the withdrawal of the US military presence, the military saw no problems managing the withdrawal of all US forces from Taiwan, although the four-month schedule would be tight.[93]

On December 28 and 29, Admiral Weisner met with President Chiang Ching-kuo to discuss the arrangements the United States was prepared to make for maintaining unofficial relations with Taiwan. First, the Mutual Defense Treaty would end or lose effect. Second, the United States would submit appropriate legislation confirming the continuing eligibility of the people of Taiwan to maintain unofficial relations. Third, the United States would like to discuss the continued leasing of the US Military Assistance Advisory Group compound as the site of the new offices to be maintained by the United States.[94]

During committee hearings in February and March 1979 over the TRA, the chairman of the JCS, General Jones, explained that Taiwan's security posture could deter any attack from China for a considerable future. Congress was skeptical. The TRA incorporated provisions more explicit than the administration had proposed, assuring Taiwan that it could count on the United States to make available defense weapons and services to maintain a sufficient self-defense capability.[95] The US military enjoyed a more positive relationship with Taiwan than the State Department or the White House during the Carter years. The JCS supported Taiwan's arms requests, wanting to preserve Taiwan's self-defense to help offset the PRC's growing military power.[96]

Conflicts between the State Department and DoD. On September 18, 1979, Vance wrote Carter a memorandum on the China policy. Vance was concerned that US strategic policies leaned toward China's favor rather than maintaining the balance. The United States also had a significant interest in seeing the Soviet Union contained in its efforts to gain a strategic advantage in troubled areas of the world. The triangular policy of balance that best served US interests should be based on certain principles: US relations with Moscow and Beijing must remain better than the relationship between the two adversaries, and it would not be to the US advantage for the Soviet-China rivalry to end. A trip to China by Secretary Brown would need to be carefully considered. In Vance's view, it should come the next year, after Premier Hua's trip to the United States, and after preparatory groundwork regarding public perceptions, allied consultations, and foreshadowing with the Soviets.[97]

On the same day, Brzezinski wrote a memorandum to Carter about conflicting memos from Vance and Brown. He enclosed two memoranda, one from Brown outlining his planned visit to China and one from Vance recommending postponing the visit until next year. Brzezinski did not believe that the United States should have the same relations with the Soviet Union, a country that threatened the United States, as with China. The Brown visit was proposed to the Chinese leaders by the vice president with Carter's approval. The United States did invite Soviet defense minister Dmitriy F. Ustinov to visit the United States, but he declined. The United States also hinted to the Soviets that they could invite Secretary Brown to visit the Soviet Union, but they did not respond. Brzezinski recommended that Carter approve the visit.[98] Carter saw no reason to reverse this agreement and suggested that Vance remind the Soviets of the US long-standing offer of an exchange of defense minister visits with the Soviet Union and informed them that Secretary of Defense Harold Brown would accept such an invitation from China.[99]

The Military's objection to US technology transfer. On December 13, 1979, Secretary Brown wrote a memorandum to Carter on US policy toward China. Brown suggested that the development of security cooperation with Beijing must be managed carefully, considering allied and Soviet reactions. Concerning export controls and technology transfers, the Pentagon would forgo arms sales to China at this time, and the same condition applied to military end-use technology. As for dual-use equipment and technology, the Pentagon agreed that the United States should preserve a case-by-case approach. Regarding assistance for China's nuclear test program, the United States should proceed cautiously in this area because China's motives were unlikely to be limited to learning how to avoid the environmental costs of atmospheric testing. [100]

The CIA Assessment

After Carter took office, the CIA conducted several assessments on China's economy, security, and Taiwan issues. In February 1977, the CIA prepared a report on the post-Mao economic situation, which showed that China's new leadership had begun its reign with economic issues high on the agenda.[101] In March, a report on security issues indicated that the US connection was essential to China as a deterrent to a major Soviet attack. Mao's successors did not expect that US military forces would be used on China's behalf in the event of a major Soviet attack on China.[102] Then, on July 26, the CIA prepared another memorandum on the prospects of Taiwan after normalization: (1) Taiwan should be able to control the shock that would accompany the normalization; (2) So long as US postnormalization trade and financial arrangements with Taiwan were close, Taiwan's foreign trade opportunities should remain good; (3) China could be expected to continue tactics designed to erode Taiwan's stability in the postnormalization period; (4) the PRC was unlikely to attempt a direct military attack on

162   *Hedging the China Threat*

Taiwan during the next five years; (5) Taiwan would be able to sustain a limited military deterrent against China if the United States continued to supply military hardware; and (6) Taiwan believed that retaining a close relationship with the United States would be the key to its survival.[103]

The International Level:
The China-Vietnam Border Dispute

During the Carter administration, there was a growing technological gap between Washington and Moscow as the United States enjoyed technological advantages. In the military field, the goals of the US strategy were to preclude the Soviets from using force, to develop NATO's conventional strength, and to maintain a balance of power in East Asia. In May 1978, Carter asked Brzezinski to undertake an assessment of the global balance of power to provide the basis for the US global strategy. The conclusions included: first, US-Soviet relations involved elements of both competition and cooperation. Second, the United States remained the strongest nation in the world; the Soviet Union was second. Of the following five most important countries in the world, four (France, the United Kingdom, West Germany, and Japan) were allies of the United States. Third, the PRC was an antagonist of the Soviet Union.[104]

Soviet-Chinese Competition

On November 14, 1978, US intelligence produced a memorandum on Soviet-Chinese competition in Indochina. This region was divided into two camps, with the Soviets backing Vietnam and Laos and China supporting Kampuchea (Cambodia). The cause of the China-Vietnamese confrontation was the Vietnam-Kampuchea border war. China considered Kampuchea allied with China as a buffer against the expansion of Vietnam and, by extension, Soviet influence. The Soviets took advantage of the opportunity to make Vietnam dependent on Moscow, thereby establishing a sphere of influence on China's southern boundary. Vietnam had moved closer to Moscow by signing a friendship and cooperation treaty.[105]

The China-Vietnam Border Disputes

On January 29, 1979, Carter and Deng discussed the China-Vietnam crisis. Deng said, "We find that Vietnam has become Soviet-controlled, and the fact of its flagrant invasion of Cambodia, its plot to establish an Indochinese Federation under Vietnamese control, is graver than you think. . . . Two-thirds of the Vietnamese forces are in the South; one-third are in the

North. Some punishment over a short period will put a restraint on Vietnamese ambitions. . . . We need your moral support in the international field." Carter responded, "It could result in an escalation of violence and a change in the world posture from being against Vietnam to partial support for Vietnam. It would be difficult for us to encourage violence." Deng pointed out, "What we plan to do is a limited short time action, to teach them a lesson. If done properly, it might even give rise to some changes within Laos and Vietnam. . . . There is not too much difficulty in teaching them a lesson along the border."[106]

On January 30, Carter responded to Deng about China's possible punitive strike against Vietnam. Carter thought it would be a mistake for the following reasons: success would be unlikely; the Chinese peaceful image would be changed; a serious incident may escalate into a regional conflict; if China were given an ultimatum to withdraw, it would be tough to withdraw; and armed conflict initiated by China would cause serious issues in the United States concerning the future peaceful settlement of Taiwan.[107] Deng said, "China must teach Vietnam a lesson. . . . The action will be very limited. The action will be quick, lasting 10–20 days, followed by withdrawal."[108]

On February 19, 1979, the NSC held a Special Coordination Committee (SCC) meeting on the China-Vietnam conflict. At the time, the Chinese military had penetrated 10 kilometers on two different fronts of the Vietnam border. To avoid any US involvement, most of the participants suggested that the United States should: minimize the adverse effect of the conflict on US relations, either with Beijing or Moscow; deter a Soviet escalation of the conflict; secure the withdrawal of both Vietnam from Kampuchea and China from Vietnam; and seek the emergence of a neutral Kampuchea. Carter approved the US objectives, which the SCC had recommended.[109] In March 1979, the CIA prepared a research paper on the China-Vietnam border disputes. The paper indicated that Beijing escalated the confrontation by instructing its border guards in late December 1978 to begin forward patrolling and to open fire on Vietnamese border posts and personnel. Although confronted with military attacks by regular Chinese troops at the border, the Vietnamese military held its positions and fought back.[110]

US-Soviet-China Relations

On March 23, 1979, Secretary Brown wrote a memorandum on US-China relations to Brzezinski. After the United States had normalized relations with China, the United States faced issues regarding future military defense contacts with China. As relations with China deepened, it would affect US relations with the Soviets. The United States could broaden security ties

164   *Hedging the China Threat*

with the PRC in limited ways without triggering a strong Soviet reaction. The United States had similar contacts with the Soviets. However, to go beyond this level of US–PRC security interaction could risk a reaction from Moscow that would not serve US interests.[111]

The Chinese viewed the United States as a source of help in their modernization, as a facilitator in their increasing relations with Japan and Western Europe, and as a deterrent to Soviet military threats.[112] China also regarded US- PRC security relations within a superior-subordinate framework, in which the stronger partner was expected to protect the weaker partner. The weaker partner sought to manipulate its protector and felt betrayed when the patron failed to provide support. Chinese leaders saw the United States as a strategic counterweight to the Soviet Union. This was Deng's intent during China's invasion of Vietnam. The Chinese used their strengthened ties with the United States not only to enhance China's modernization programs, but also to provoke tension in Moscow's relations with the United States and thereby divert Soviet pressure away from the PRC.[113]

Conclusion

During the Carter administration, Jimmy Carter wanted to establish diplomatic relations with China as soon as possible. Under Zbigniew Brzezinski's leadership, the National Security Council supported Carter's plan to accept China's demands. The State Department remained neutral. The Pentagon, concerned that supporting normalization would endanger Taiwan's security, proposed that the United States sell more advanced arms to Taiwan; however, that plan was denied. Many members of Congress were enraged by Carter's decision.

The Carter administration's main policy outcomes included the normalization of relations with China and the passage of the Taiwan Relations Act in 1979 by the US Congress.

On an individual level of analysis, in his desire to normalize relations with China, Carter felt that it would be necessary to comply with all of China's demands regarding Taiwan, including the abolishment of the Mutual Defense Treaty, the withdrawal of all troops, and the acceptance of the One China principle. At the state level, Carter's decisions gave rise to conflicts between different branches of the US government. At the international level, Deng consolidated his power and emerged as the leading player in the Chinese Communist Party. Deng attempted to convince the United States not to sell arms to Taiwan, but he was unsuccessful.

Carter appeared to have unilaterally proceeded with the normalization concessions in defiance of the US Congress, prompting Congress to respond with the Taiwan Relations Act. China under Deng agreed to normalization if

Establishing Diplomatic Relations with China **165**

the United States met China's previously stated conditions. Individual decisionmakers implemented the policy modifications. Prior to Carter's taking office, there were no significant domestic or international crises that pressured him to initiate the fundamental policy changes he strongly supported. It appears that Carter needlessly caved in to China's demands. There is no evidence that US-China relations would not have progressed essentially in the same manner without Carter's concessions to China. Given the domestic and international changes Deng desired to implement, he required closer ties with the United States than his predecessors.

Notes

1. US Department of State, "1977–1980: China Policy," *Milestones in the History of U.S. Foreign Relations: 1977–1980*, https://history.state.gov.
2. Ibid.
3. Steven L. Rearden and Kenneth R. Foulks Jr., *The Joint Chiefs of Staff and National Policy 1977–1980* (Washington, DC: Office of Joint History, Office of the Chairman of the Joint Chiefs of Staff, 2015), p. 141.
4. US Department of State, "31. Memorandum from the President's Assistant for National Security Affairs (Brzezinski) to President Carter," June 14, 1977, *FRUS, 1977–1980*, vol. 13, *China*, https://history.state.gov.
5. "Presidential Review Memoranda (PRM)," Jimmy Carter Library, https://www.jimmycarterlibrary.gov.
6. US Department of State, "34. Summary of Conclusions of a Policy Review Committee Meeting," June 27, 1977, *FRUS, 1977–1980*, vol. 13, *China*, https://history.state.gov.
7. Ibid.
8. Ibid.
9. US Department of State, "48. Memorandum of Conversation," August 23, 1977, *FRUS, 1977–1980*, vol. 13, *China*, https://history.state.gov.
10. US Department of State, "49. Memorandum of Conversation," August 24, 1977, *FRUS, 1977–1980*, vol. 13, *China*, https://history.state.gov.
11. US Department of State, "50. Memorandum of Conversation," August 24, 1977, *FRUS, 1977–1980*, vol. 13, *China*, https://history.state.gov.
12. US Department of State, "75. Memorandum from the President's Special Adviser for Science and Technology (Press) to President Carter," January 23, 1978, *FRUS, 1977–1980*, vol. 13, *China*, https://history.state.gov/historicaldocuments/frus1977-80v13/d75.
13. US Department of State, "113. Memorandum from the President's Assistant for National Security Affairs (Brzezinski) to President Carter," May 25, 1978, *FRUS, 1977–1980*, vol. 13, https://history.state.gov.
14. Ibid.
15. US Department of State, "159. Backchannel Message from the Chief of the Liaison Office in China (Woodcock) to Secretary of State Vance and the President's Assistant for National Security Affairs (Brzezinski)," December 4, 1978, *FRUS, 1977–1980*, vol. 13, *China*, https://history.state.gov.
16. US Department of State, "167. Backchannel Message from the Chief of the Liaison Office in China (Woodcock) to Secretary of State Vance and the President's

166   *Hedging the China Threat*

Assistant for National Security Affairs (Brzezinski)," December 13, 1978, *FRUS, 1977–1980,* vol. 13, *China,* https://history.state.gov.

17. US Department of State, "166. Backchannel Message from the Chief of the Liaison Office in China (Woodcock) to Secretary of State Vance and the President's Assistant for National Security Affairs (Brzezinski)," December 13, 1978, *FRUS, 1977–1980,* vol. 13, *China,* 1028Z, https://history.state.gov.

18. US Department of State, "150. Presidential Directive/NSC 431," November 3, 1978, *FRUS, 1977–1980,* vol. 13, *China,* https://history.state.gov.

19. US Department of State, "327. Memorandum from Michel Oksenberg to the President's Assistant for National Security Affairs (Brzezinski)," December 19, 1980, *FRUS, 1977–1980,* vol. 13, *China,* https://history.state.gov.

20. US Department of State, "232. Memorandum From Secretary of the Treasury Blumenthal to President Carter," March 22, 1979, *FRUS, 1977–1980,* vol. 13, *China,* https://history.state.gov.

21. Robert G. Sutter, "The TRA and the United States's China Policy." In *A Unique Relationship: The United States and the Republic of China Under the Taiwan Relations Act,* edited by Ramon H. Myers (Stanford: Hoover Institution Press, 1989), p. 54.

22. James Shen, "The Taiwan Relations Act," *Tamkang Journal of American Studies*1, no. 4 (Summer1985): 37–38.

23. Jen-ken Fu, *Taiwan and the Geopolitics of the Asian-American Dilemma* (New York: Praeger, 1992), p. 71.

24. Victoria Marine Kraft, *The U.S. Constitution and Foreign Policy: Terminating the Taiwan Treaty* (New York: Green Press, 1991), pp. 124–126.

25. Martin Lasater, *U.S. Interests in the New Taiwan* (Boulder: Westview, 1993), p. 15.

26. US Department of State, "235. Editorial Note," *FRUS, 1977–1980,* vol. 13, *China,* https://history.state.gov.

27. Ibid.

28. Harvey Feldman, "A New Kind of Relationship," in *A Unique Relationship: The United States and the Republic of China* under *the Taiwan Relations Act,* edited by Ramon H. Myers (Stanford: Hoover Institution Press, 1989), p. 28.

29. Ibid., p. 33.

30. Shen, "The Taiwan Relations Act," p. 42.

31. Robert L. Dowen, *The Taiwan Pawn in the China Game* (Washington, DC: Georgetown University Press, 1979), pp. 75–76.

32. Ibid., p. 78.

33. Rearden and Foulks, *Joint Chiefs of Staff,* p. 147.

34. US Department of State, "1977–1981: The Presidency of Jimmy Carter," *Milestones in the History of U.S. Foreign Relations: 1977–1980,* https://history.state.gov.

35. Rearden and Foulks, *Joint Chiefs of Staff,* p. 141.

36. US Department of State, "1977–1980: China Policy," *FRUS,* https://history.state.gov.

37. Rearden and Foulks, *Joint Chiefs of Staff,* p. 142.

38. US Department of State, "5. Memorandum of Conversation," February 8, 1977, *FRUS, 1977–1980,* vol. 13, *China,* https://history.state.gov.

39. Ibid.

40. US Department of State, "31. Memorandum from the President's Assistant for National Security Affairs (Brzezinski) to President Carter," June 14, 1977, *FRUS, 1977–1980,* vol. 13, *China,* https://history.state.gov.

41. Rearden and Foulks, *Joint Chiefs of Staff,* p. 144.

42. US Department of State, "43. Letter from President Carter to Secretary of State Vance," August 18, 1977, *FRUS, 1977–1980,* vol. 13, *China,* https://history .state.gov.

43. Rearden and Foulks, *Joint Chiefs of Staff,* p. 145.

44. US Department of State, "41. Memorandum of Conversation," July 30, 1977, *FRUS, 1977–1980,* vol. 13, *China,* https://history.state.gov.

45. Ibid.

46. Rearden and Foulks, *Joint Chiefs of Staff,* p. 145.

47. US Department of State, "104. Address by President Carter to the Nation," December 15, 1978, *FRUS, 1977–1980,* vol. 1, *Foundations of Foreign Policy,* https://history.state.gov.

48. US Department of State, "208. Memorandum of Conversation," January 30, 1979, *FRUS, 1977–1980,* vol. 13, *China,* https://history.state.gov.

49. Ibid.

50. US Department of State, "212. Oral Message from Chinese Vice Premier Deng Xiaoping to President Carter," *FRUS, 1977–1980* vol. 13, *China,* https:// history.state.gov.

51. US Department of State, "327. Memorandum from Michel Oksenberg to the President's Assistant for National Security Affairs (Brzezinski)."

52. Ibid.

53. Ibid.

54. US Department of State, "1977–1981: The Presidency of Jimmy Carter."

55. US Department of State, "3. Memorandum from Michel Oksenberg of the National Security Council Staff to the President's Assistant for National Security Affairs (Brzezinski)," January 25, 1977, *FRUS, 1977–1980,* vol. 13, *China,* https:// history.state.gov.

56. US Department of State, "16. Memorandum from the President's Assistant for National Security Affairs (Brzezinski) to President Carter," March 8, 1977, *FRUS, 1977–1980,* vol. 13, *China,* https://history.state.gov.

57. US Department of State, "110. Memorandum of Conversation," May 21, 1978, *FRUS, 1977–1980,* vol. 13, *China,* https://history.state.gov.

58. US Department of State, "111. Memorandum of Conversation," May 22, 1978, *FRUS, 1977–1980,* vol. 13, *China,* https://history.state.gov.

59. Ibid.

60. US Department of State, "113. Memorandum from the President's Assistant for National Security Affairs (Brzezinski) to President Carter," May 25, 1978, *FRUS, 1977–1980,* vol. 13, *China,* https://history.state.gov.

61. US Department of State, "2. Memorandum of Conversation," January 8, 1977, *FRUS, 1977–1980,* vol. 13, *China,* https://history.state.gov.

62. Ibid.

63. US Department of State, "7. Telegram from the Department of State to the Embassy in the Republic of China," February 10, 1977, *FRUS, 1977–1980,* vol. 13, *China,* https://history.state.gov.

64. US Department of State, "10. Telegram from the Department of State to the Embassy in the Republic of China," February 16, 1977, *FRUS, 1977–1980,* vol. 13, *China,* https://history.state.gov.

65. US Department of State, "44. Telegram From the Department of State to the Embassy in the ROC," August 18, 1977, *FRUS, 1977–1980,* vol. 13, *China,* https:// history.state.gov.

66. US Department of State, "12. Memorandum from Michel Oksenberg of the National Security Council Staff to the President's Assistant for National Security

168 *Hedging the China Threat*

Affairs (Brzezinski)," February 16, 1977, *FRUS, 1977–1980,* vol. 13, *China,* https://history.state.gov.

67. US Department of State, "22. Telegram from the Department of State to the Embassy in the Republic of China," March 26, 1977, *FRUS, 1977–1980,* vol. 13, *China,* https://history.state.gov.

68. US Department of State, "23. Editorial Note," *FRUS, 1977–1980,* vol. 13, *China,* https://history.state.gov.

69. US Department of State, "48. Memorandum of Conversation."

70. US Department of State, "49. Memorandum of Conversation."

71. US Department of State, "50. Memorandum of Conversation."

72. US Department of State, "52. Telegram From Secretary of State Vance to the Department of State and the White House," August 25, 1977, *FRUS, 1977–1980,* vol. 13, China. https://history.state.gov.

73. US Department of State, "119. Memorandum from Secretary of State Vance to President Carter," June 13, 1978, *FRUS, 1977–1980,* vol. 13, *China,* https://history.state.gov.

74. US Department of State, "141. Memorandum from the President's Assistant for National Security Affairs (Brzezinski) to President Carter," October 11, 1978, *FRUS, 1977–1980,* vol. 13, *China,* https://history.state.gov.

75. US Department of State, "159. Backchannel Message from the Chief of the Liaison Office in China (Woodcock) to Secretary of State Vance and the President's Assistant for National Security Affairs (Brzezinski)," December 4, 1978, *FRUS, 1977–1980,* vol. 13, *China,* https://history.state.gov.

76. US Department of State, "162. Memorandum from the President's Assistant for National Security Affairs (Brzezinski) to President Carter," December 5, 1978, *FRUS, 1977–1980,* vol. 13, *China,* https://history.state.gov.

77. US Department of State, "166. Backchannel Message from the Chief of the Liaison Office in China (Woodcock) to Secretary of State Vance and the President's Assistant for National Security Affairs (Brzezinski).'"

78. US Department of State, "167. Backchannel Message from the Chief of the Liaison Office in China (Woodcock) to Secretary of State Vance and the President's Assistant for National Security Affairs (Brzezinski)."

79. US Department of State, "170. Backchannel Message from the Chief of the Liaison Office in China (Woodcock) to Secretary of State Vance and the President's Assistant for National Security Affairs (Brzezinski)," December 15, 1978, *FRUS, 1977–1980,* vol. 13, *China,* https://history.state.gov.

80. US Department of State, "172. Backchannel Message from the President's Assistant for National Security Affairs (Brzezinski) to the Chief of the Liaison Office in China (Woodcock)," December 15, 1978, *FRUS, 1977–1980,* vol. 13, *China,* https://history.state.gov.

81. US Department of State, "171. Backchannel Message from Secretary of State Vance and the President's Assistant for National Security Affairs (Brzezinski) to the Ambassador to the Republic of China (Unger)," December 15, 1978, *FRUS, 1977–1980,* vol. 13, *China,* https://history.state.gov.

82. US Department of State, "173. Backchannel Message from the Ambassador to the Republic of China (Unger) to Secretary of State Vance and the President's Assistant for National Security Affairs (Brzezinski)," December 15, 1978, *FRUS, 1977–1980,* vol. 13, *China,* https://history.state.gov.

83. US Department of State, "181. Memorandum from the President's Assistant for National Security Affairs (Brzezinski) to the Deputy Secretary of State (Christopher)," December 26, 1978, *FRUS, 1977–1980,* vol. 13, *China,* https://history.state.gov.

84. US Department of State, "183. Telegram from the U.S. Pacific Command to the Department of State and the White House," December 30, 1978, *FRUS, 1977–1980,* vol. 13, *China,* https://history.state.gov.

85. Rearden and Foulks, *Joint Chiefs of Staff,* pp. 142–143.

86. Ibid., p. 145.

87. Ibid., p. 148.

88. Ibid., p. 149.

89. Ibid., pp. 150–151.

90. Ibid., p. 153.

91. Ibid., p. 151–152.

92. US Department of State, "154. Memorandum from the Joint Chiefs of Staff to Secretary of Defense Brown," November 20, 1978, *FRUS, 1977–1980,* vol. 13, *China,* JCSM-335-78, https://history.state.gov.

93. US Department of State, "179. Memorandum from Secretary of Defense Brown to the President's Assistant for National Security Affairs (Brzezinski)," December 23, 1978, *FRUS, 1977–1980,* vol. 13, *China,* https://history.state.gov.

94. US Department of State, "183. Telegram from the U.S. Pacific Command to the Department of State and the White House," December 30, 1978, *FRUS, 1977–1980,* vol. 13, *China,* https://history.state.gov.

95. Rearden and Foulks, *Joint Chiefs of Staff,* p. 152.

96. Ibid., p. 154.

97. US Department of State, "272. Memorandum from Secretary of State Vance to President Carter," September 18, 1979, *FRUS, 1977–1980,* vol. 13, *China,* https://history.state.gov.

98. US Department of State, "273. Memorandum from the President's Assistant for National Security Affairs (Brzezinski) to President Carter," September 18, 1979, *FRUS, 1977–1980,* vol. 13, *China,* https://history.state.gov.

99. US Department of State, "274. Letter from President Carter to Secretary of State Vance, Secretary of Defense Brown, and the President's Assistant for National Security Affairs (Brzezinski)," September 19, 1979, *FRUS, 1977–1980,* vol. 13, *China,* https://history.state.gov.

100. US Department of State, "283. Memorandum from Secretary of Defense Brown to President Carter," December 13, 1979, *FRUS, 1977–1980,* vol. 13, *China,* https://history.state.gov.

101. US Department of State, "4. Intelligence Report Prepared in the Office of Economic Research, Central Intelligence Agency," February 1977, *FRUS, 1977–1980,* vol. 13, *China,* ER 77-10049, https://history.state.gov.

102. US Department of State, "14. Intelligence Memorandum Prepared in the Central Intelligence Agency," March 1977, *FRUS, 1977–1980,* vol. 13, *China,* https://history.state.gov.

103. US Department of State, "38. National Intelligence Analytical Memorandum," July 26, 1977, *FRUS, 1977–1980,* vol. 13, *China,* https://history.state.gov.

104. US Department of State, "108. Memorandum of Conversation," May 20, 1978, *FRUS, 1977–1980,* vol. 13, *China,* https://history.state.gov.

105. US Department of State, "152. Interagency Intelligence Memorandum," November 14, 1978, *FRUS, 1977–1980,* vol. 13, *China,* NI IIM 78-10024, https://history.state.gov.

106. US Department of State, "205. Memorandum of Conversation," January 29, 1979, *FRUS, 1977–1980,* vol. 13, *China,* https://history.state.gov.

107. US Department of State, "206. Oral Presentation by President Carter to Chinese Vice Premier Deng Xiaoping," January 30, 1979, *FRUS, 1977–1980,* vol. 13, *China,* https://history.state.gov.

170   *Hedging the China Threat*

108. US Department of State, "207. Memorandum of Conversation," January 30, 1979, *FRUS, 1977–1980,* vol. 13, *China,* https://history.state.gov.

109. US Department of State, "219. Summary of Conclusions of a Special Coordination Committee Meeting," February 19, 1979, *FRUS, 1977–1980,* vol. 13, *China,* https://history.state.gov.

110. US Department of State, "226. Research Paper Prepared in the National Foreign Assessment Center, Central Intelligence Agency," March 1979, *FRUS, 1977–1980,* vol. 13, *China,* https://history.state.gov.

111. US Department of State, "233. Memorandum from Secretary of Defense Brown to the President's Assistant for National Security Affairs (Brzezinski)," March 23, 1979, *FRUS, 1977–1980,* vol. 13, *China,* https://history.state.gov.

112. US Department of State, "312. National Intelligence Estimate," June 5, 1980, *FRUS, 1977–1980,* vol. 13, *China,* NIE 11/13–80, https://history.state.gov.

113. US Department of State, "233. Memorandum from Secretary of Defense Brown to the President's Assistant for National Security Affairs (Brzezinski)."

9

Arms Sales Disputes and Reassurances: The Reagan Administration

AFTER ESTABLISHING DIPLOMATIC RELATIONS ON JANUARY 1, 1979, THE PEOple's Republic of China (PRC) desired to attain US technology for its modernization program. The United States wanted to access the enormous Chinese market. Both countries were also interested in confronting the rising Soviet military expansion in Asia.[1] In April 1979, Deng Xiaoping responded positively when a visiting US senator, Joe Biden, proposed establishing a joint intelligence-listening post in China to monitor Soviet military activities. After Secretary of Defense Harold Brown's visit to China in early January 1980, a post was established in Xinjiang with Chinese personnel and US equipment.[2]

During Jimmy Carter's presidency, several actions reflected his disinterest in the alliance system in East Asia, including planning to withdraw US troops from South Korea, ending diplomatic relations with Taiwan, neglecting consultations with allies, and decreasing the US naval presence in the Pacific.[3] Criticism rose over Carter's lack of foreign policy leadership. During the 1980 presidential campaign, candidate Ronald Reagan stated that the United States must remain a Pacific power. If he was elected, his administration would restore the United States' vital role in the region.[4] When Reagan took office in 1981, US strategic interests in Asia moved toward an anti-Soviet coalition. As part of its efforts, the Reagan administration implemented limited military cooperation and provided defensive arms assistance to China.

Historical Events: US-PRC Negotiations on US Arms Sales

During his first presidential campaign, Reagan repeated his call for restoring official relations with Taiwan. In response, China warned that if the United

172 *Hedging the China Threat*

States reestablished diplomatic relations with Taiwan, it would destroy the foundation of US-China relations. Reagan's chief foreign policy advisor, Richard Allen, was eager to defuse the issue before the fall campaign. Allen suggested that vice presidential candidate George H. W. Bush should visit Beijing in August 1980 to use his connection with Chinese leaders, as former head of the US Liaison Office in Beijing, to smooth bilateral ties.[5] Speaking to PRC foreign minister Huang Hua, Bush explained that Reagan did not want to reestablish diplomatic relations with Taiwan or recognize Two Chinas. On August 22, Bush met with Deng. During the meeting, an aide handed Deng a small sheet of paper with news from the United States: Reagan had just made another campaign statement, suggesting that he favored an official relationship with Taiwan. Deng angrily remarked, "If you do what Reagan suggests, you will set the clock back."[6] On August 25, Reagan made an important statement on US-China relations, pointing out the importance of bilateral relations. He stressed that US relations with Taiwan would develop under US domestic law, the Taiwan Relations Act (TRA). After taking office in January 1981, the Reagan administration sought to advance its relations with China and ensure Taiwan's security.

China Opposes US Arms Sales to Taiwan

During the negotiations for normalization with China, one of the US conditions was to continue to sell defensive weapons to Taiwan. National Security Advisor (NSA) Zbigniew Brzezinski instructed the US ambassador to China, Leonard Woodcock, to meet with Deng. When Woodcock informed Deng about the United States continuing arms sales to Taiwan, Deng furiously responded that China would never agree with the US intentions. Completing the normalization, however, was China's priority.[7] In mid-1980, the Carter administration authorized Northrop and General Dynamics aircraft manufacturers to discuss possible FX aircraft sales to foreign countries, including Taiwan. Beijing opposed the FX decision.

The US government insisted on continuing arms sales to Taiwan based on the following considerations: (1) arms sales would give Taiwan more confidence in its capability against China; (2) Taiwan would not seek radical solutions such as reconsidering its nuclear option that would be contrary to US interests;[8] (3) arms sales to Taiwan could also reduce suspicion from other US allies about its reliability in keeping its defense commitments; (4) if Taiwan remained strong militarily, China would be less likely to initiate an attack on Taiwan;[9] and (5) arms sales were a lucrative business for the US defense industry.

Reagan's first secretary of state, Alexander Haig, was convinced of the importance of the strategic relationship with China against the Soviet Union. By the summer of 1981, if the United States decided to sell the FX

Arms Sales Disputes and Reassurances   173

aircraft to Taiwan, China would downgrade its relations with the United States. By October, PRC foreign minister Huang Hua proposed not exceeding the level of sales during the Carter years. It reduced that level annually and set a date for the termination of transfers. Reagan rejected this proposal.[10] After taking the suggestions from the State Department and Pentagon, Reagan decided to veto the FX sale. The US conservative wing was outraged at what it considered harmful to the security of Taiwan.[11]

Arms Sales Negotiations

On August 17, 1982, the United States and China issued a Joint Communiqué in which the US government promised to reduce and eventually terminate arms sales to Taiwan. Beijing was delighted to get the Reagan administration to accept the principle of limiting arms sales, even if no specific date was set.[12] Even though Taipei opposed the US-PRC deal, this agreement was finalized after ten months of negotiations between the US and PRC governments. There were several stages of negotiations.

The first stage. From January to September 1981, China tested the intentions of US arms sales to Taiwan. The critical issue was the FX aircraft for export. White House counselor Edward Meese and NSA Richard Allen were among those who supported the sale to Taiwan. Secretary Haig proposed to permit China to purchase US defensive weapons as a "gift" during his China visit in June 1981. He considered selling arms to China for its consent to FX sales to Taiwan. Beijing opposed it. Deng warned Haig of a possible rupture in bilateral relations over the issue of arms sales to Taiwan. Deng also complained about the US slowness in its technology transfer and military purchases. In July 1981, the US ambassador to China, Arthur Hummel, was informed by China that if the United States continued to sell arms to Taiwan, this would force China into a strong reaction with grave consequences. In September, China canceled General Liu Huaqing's visit to the United States to discuss arms purchases.[13]

The second stage. To extend an olive branch to Taiwan leaders, on September 30, 1981, Ye Jianying, chairman of the Standing Committee of the National People's Congress, stated the policy concerning reunification with Taiwan. He announced a "Nine-Point Proposal": (1) talks would be held between China and Taiwan on a reciprocal basis to accomplish reunification; (2) the two sides would facilitate the exchange of mail, trade, air, shipping services, family reunions, and academic and cultural exchanges; (3) after the country was reunified, Taiwan could enjoy a high degree of autonomy as a special administrative region; (4) Taiwan's social and economic system would remain unchanged; (5) leaders in Taiwan could take

174   *Hedging the China Threat*

up posts of leadership in China; (6) when Taiwan encountered financial difficulties, the PRC might subsidize it; (7) arrangements would be made for people in Taiwan who wished to come and settle on the mainland; (8) businesspeople would be welcome to invest in China, and their rights would be guaranteed; and (9) China's reunification and prosperity would be in the interests of the Chinese people on the mainland and in Taiwan.[14] Taiwan turned down China's Nine-Point Proposal. President Chiang Ching-Kuo reiterated the Three No's policy of no contact, no compromise, and no negotiation with Beijing.[15]

In late October 1981, Reagan met with Chinese premier Zhao Ziyang in Mexico during a summit meeting of North-South leaders. A private meeting was arranged. Zhao stated that China wanted a long-term strategic relationship with the United States, but Taiwan was a problem. Reagan replied that the United States had been closely associated with the people of Taiwan and would not abandon old friends. Zhao then revealed that China offered Taiwan the Nine-Point Proposal for peaceful reunification. As Zhao recited it, pausing every few sentences while the interpreter translated, he watched Reagan's face closely.[16]

On October 29, Foreign Minister Huang added the requirement that the United States would give Beijing assurances of ceasing the arms sales by a specified date in the future. Haig protested Minister Huang's threat. However, Haig agreed with Huang's suggestion for high-level talks on the sale of arms dilemma. Negotiations began on December 4, when the US ambassador, Arthur Hummel, met PRC deputy foreign ministers Zhang Wenju and Han Xu. The United States agreed that arms sales would not exceed the level of the Carter years, but it was unwilling to specify a date to terminate arms sales. Sales would decline until there was a peaceful resolution of the Taiwan question.[17]

The third stage. In January 1982, Reagan decided to veto the FX aircraft sale. The State Department sent John Holdridge, assistant secretary of state for East Asian and Pacific affairs, to Beijing to inform Chinese leaders of the aircraft decision. During the early months of 1982, the United States and China exchanged many new drafts of the proposed Joint Communiqué, but no agreement was reached. Beijing insisted on a specified date for the cessation of arms sales. It also refused to accept any linkage between a peaceful resolution of the Taiwan issue and the reduction of US arms sales. During the spring of 1982, the negotiations were deadlocked.[18]

The fourth stage. Bargaining began in May 1982, when Vice President George H. W. Bush visited Beijing to discuss the issue of arms sales. The United States hoped that his visit would convince Chinese leaders that the United States was committed to reaching an agreement. Bush did not bring any new ideas. The White House also publicized letters from Reagan to three Chinese leaders, Deng Xiaoping, Zhao Ziyang, and Hu Yaobang. Reagan reinforced the US reduction of arms sales to Taiwan if China maintained its peaceful policy.[19] After the Bush-Deng meeting, the United States remained silent for six weeks because of strong domestic opposition and a change of leadership in the State Department. After the announcement of Haig's resignation in June, Beijing realized that there was no room left for further maneuvering and that Reagan would make no further concessions.[20] By the end of July, Chinese officials dropped their insistence that the United States agree to a date for the termination of arms sales.[21] The Chinese strategy was to threaten the United States by downgrading US-PRC relations if the United States failed to comply. During the negotiation process, the Beijing regime launched an extensive lobbying effort by inviting former US leaders to China, such as former presidents Gerald Ford and Jimmy Carter, former vice president Walter Mondale, and former NSA Brzezinski. Carter also urged Reagan not to sell Taiwan anything.[22]

The 1982 US-PRC Communiqué

Since January 1982, the United States and China had discussed arms sales to Taiwan. As the two countries exchanged drafts of a communiqué, disagreements were evident. The first was that China insisted that the United States finally end all arms sales to Taiwan. The second centered on US arms sales reductions depending on a China policy of maintaining peaceful relations with Taiwan, but Beijing refused to commit to the United States on its future policy toward Taiwan. On August 17, the United States and China issued a Joint Communiqué. The agreement on the communiqué did not signal consensus because both parties offered different interpretations. The United States focused on the correlation between the reduction of arms sales and China's peaceful policy. China focused on the US pledges to respect its sovereignty and gradually reduce arms sales.[23]

The communiqué included the following key points. First, the United States recognized the PRC as the sole legal government. Second, the Message to Compatriots in Taiwan, issued by China, promulgated a fundamental policy of striving for peaceful reunification. Third, the United States had no intention of infringing on Chinese territorial integrity. Fourth, the United States would not exceed the level of arms supplied since the establishment of diplomatic relations. It intended to gradually reduce its sale of arms. Finally, the two sides were determined to strengthen their ties in the economic, cultural, educational, scientific, and technological fields.[24]

After the signing of the communiqué, differences in interpretation of its provisions emerged. Assistant Secretary of State John Holdridge stated

176 *Hedging the China Threat*

that the US reduction of arms sales was predicated on a continued peaceful China approach toward Taiwan. Beijing denied its statement of seeking a peaceful solution to the Taiwan question. Taiwan also opposed the communiqué, arguing that it violated the spirit of the TRA. With reducing arms sales and China modernizing its military, the military balance would shift toward China's favor and place Taiwan's security at risk.

US-China Military Relations

The United States and China made progress in military relations during the Reagan administration due to the rise of the Soviet military threat. Secretary of Defense Caspar Weinberger visited China in September 1983. In his talks with Chinese leaders, Weinberger agreed to provide military hardware such as antitank, antiaircraft, and radar equipment to China. Both sides also agreed to exchange working-level military training.[25]

In June 1984, PRC defense minister Zhang Aiping visited the United States. Both sides agreed to improve military cooperation. US officials promised China avionics for its jet interceptors and training for its pilots at US bases. In response, China sold half a squadron of its copied version of the Soviet MiG-21 fighter to the United States. The Chinese also obtained approval to secure the technology to manufacture rocket-propelled shells and high-explosive, armor-piercing ammunition for their artillery. In October 1984, a high-level US military training delegation traveled across China, visiting military facilities in Beijing, Shanghai, and four other cities.[26]

Events in January 1985 further confirmed US-China military cooperation. In the wake of a six-week visit to various military sites in the United States by Chinese naval officers, the United States agreed to sell sonars, torpedoes, turbine engines, and antimissile technology. The chairman of the Joint Chiefs of Staff (JCS), General John Vessey, visited China. Vessey held three days of talks with military and civilian leaders in Beijing. He also traveled to Shenyang, Hangzhou, Shanghai, and Canton for a look at the Chinese army, navy, and air force units in the field.[27] He lectured at the military academy, inspected military equipment, observed a mock battle, and held meetings with Chinese officials. Vessey became the highest-ranking military officer to visit China since 1949.[28]

China relied on the United States for technology in carrying out modernization agendas. Another reason that encouraged China to maintain close ties with the United States was the threat of the Soviet military. So long as China needed science and technology from the United States, and so long as the problems in China-Soviet relations persisted, friendly US-China relations seemed reasonable.[29]

The Individual Level:
President Reagan's Support for Taiwan

In the 1970s, Reagan was ranked as one of the strongest supporters of Taiwan in US politics, opposing US-China normalization. He believed that Carter had gone too far in his concessions in Taiwan.[30] During the 1980 campaign, Reagan's speeches frequently ended with an emotional declaration: "There's one message I want to deliver more than anything in the world as president, no more Taiwan, no more Vietnam, no more betrayal of friends and allies by the U.S. government." Reagan claimed that he would support reestablishing official relations with Taiwan if elected. His advisors grew worried about his support for Taiwan because the Democrats warned that Reagan would cause a breakup in US-China relations.[31]

Reagan's View of Taiwan

In July 1971, Richard Nixon announced his normalization policy to China. Nixon asked then governor Reagan to travel to Taiwan as his envoy to lessen conservatives' anger in the United States. Reagan informed Chiang Kai-shek that the United States would never sell out Taiwan. After the United Nations expelled the Republic of China (ROC) in October 1971, Reagan insisted that Nixon cut US funding for the UN. In 1975, Reagan told President Ford of his opposition to abandon Taiwan while normalizing relations with China. In April 1978, Reagan visited Taiwan. He declared that it was hard to believe that any American would let his government abandon an ally whose only "sins" were being small and loving freedom. Reagan predicted that Carter would lose credibility if he improved relations with China at Taiwan's expense. When Carter established diplomatic relations with China, Reagan condemned Carter's act of betrayal.[32]

Reagan's advisors, Richard Allen and James Lilley, drafted a statement for the Republican candidate on the Taiwan issue that acknowledged that Reagan would not reverse the US formal recognition of China. When they showed it to Reagan, he replied, "Oh, no, I'm not making that statement."[33] George H. W. Bush and Richard Allen informed Reagan that they had to make the Taiwan controversy diminish during the presidential campaign. Reagan then began to draft his own statement on China. Lilley thought that if Reagan's words had ever been uttered, the United States and China might have come close to war.[34] After amending the draft, Reagan's campaign chief of staff, Ed Meese, urged Reagan to deliver his advisors' statement. Reagan asked, "You still think I ought to make this statement?" Everyone in the room agreed. He then read it to the press. Reagan emphasized that the US-China partnership should be global and strategic. The United States

178   *Hedging the China Threat*

would develop relations with Taiwan following "the law of our land, the Taiwan Relations Act." He emphasized, "I would not pretend, as Carter does, that the relationship we now have with Taiwan, enacted by our Congress, is not official." Reagan would not disturb Carter's recognition of China.[35]

Reagan's Six Assurances to Taiwan

Reagan won the presidency in November 1980, intensifying China's concerns that his China policy would damage bilateral relations. Pushed by Haig, Reagan notified Beijing of his desire to maintain close official ties with China and unofficial relations with Taiwan.[36] In a memorandum to Reagan on November 26, 1981, Haig recommended that the United States should not increase arms sales to Taiwan. According to a Pentagon study, which concluded that the FX aircraft was not crucial to the Taiwan defense, Reagan decided not to sell the FX to Taiwan. Instead, Reagan permitted Taiwan to continue coproducing the F-5E and to purchase military parts from the United States.[37]

In August 1982, Washington and Beijing signed a communiqué stating that the United States would reduce and finally end weapons sales to Taiwan. Though he agreed to sign the communiqué, Reagan was disturbed by its negative security consequences against Taiwan. Reagan placed a memorandum underscoring that the US reduction of its arms sales was conditioned on the commitment of China to the peaceful solution of Taiwan. Reagan reassured Taiwan that the United States would not abandon it.[38]

Before the release of the communiqué, James Lilley, newly assigned as the head of the American Institute in Taiwan (the de facto embassy of the United States in Taiwan), called on President Chiang Ching-kuo on July 14, 1982. His visit came as US negotiations with China were close to concluding. In Reagan's name, Lilley delivered "Six Assurances" regarding US policy toward Taiwan.[39] The Reagan administration had made the following points: the United States has not agreed to set a date for ending arms sales to Taiwan; has not agreed to hold prior consultations with China on arms sales to Taiwan; will not play any mediation role between Taipei and Beijing; has not decided to revise the TRA; has not altered its position regarding sovereignty over Taiwan; and will not exert pressure on Taiwan to enter into negotiations with China.[40]

On July 26, Lilley again called on Chiang Ching-kuo and delivered the following "nonpaper" instructed by Reagan. First, the United States would prepare to discuss military requirements with Taiwan's representatives. Second, before the end of August, the United States would inform Congress of the extension of joint manufacturing of the F5-E. Third, the United States had purchased sixty-six F-104G aircraft from West Germany, out of which twenty-three would be delivered to Taiwan. Lilley said that the

United States did not agree to Beijing's demand to have prior consultations with it on arms sales. He concluded that the United States would sell military items, as needed by Taiwan, following the TRA.[41]

On August 16, the day before the issuance of the communiqué, Lilley delivered another nonpaper to Chiang Ching-kuo, which stated the following: Reagan wanted Lilley to assure Taipei that he was committed to the moral and legal obligations in the TRA; the security of Taiwan would continue and providing Taiwan with sufficient arms to enable its self-defense capability was a solemn responsibility of the US legislative and executive branches;[42] and, finally, the United States would monitor Beijing's intentions toward Taiwan.[43]

After the communiqué with China was issued, Reagan moved secretly to his Taiwan policy. He dictated a one-page memorandum. The United States would restrict arms sales to Taiwan, so long as the balance of cross-strait military power was preserved. If China upgraded its military capabilities, the United States would help Taiwan to match improvements.[44] Reagan stated that the United States could increase arms sales if China threatened Taiwan. If relations improved, the United States could exercise restraint. Reagan believed he had kept faith with Taiwan. He emphasized, "We have done everything we have always done. The shipments are regularly going on. Our Taiwan friends will get everything they need for their self-defense."[45] The TRA would guide US policy toward Taiwan. If China launched attacks on Taiwan, the United States would increase arms sales to counter the threat. The Six Assurances, however, only gave cold comfort to Taiwan because the communique had greatly limited the US arms sales to Taiwan.

After Paul Wolfowitz replaced John Holdridge, and George Shultz replaced Alexander Haig, they implemented the communiqué differently from what Holdridge or Haig had conceived. The Six Assurances provided flexibility for the US security policy toward Taiwan.

Reagan's Visit to China

In early 1983, Reagan and his advisors began discussing a visit to China. They believed that such a trip not only would enhance bilateral cooperation, but also would bolster Reagan's foreign policy credentials for his 1984 reelection campaign.[46] At that time, Reagan repeatedly called Taiwan a US ally. Beijing considered it offensive. General Secretary Hu Yaobang stated that if Reagan wanted a successful trip to China to boost his reelection, it would be better for him to keep his mouth shut about Taiwan.[47]

In 1983, several US cabinet members visited China, but no senior Chinese leader agreed to come to Washington. US officials suggested that PRC premier Zhao Ziyang pay a visit to the United States, but China did not

180   *Hedging the China Threat*

agree. Paul Wolfowitz argued that if Reagan flew to Beijing to court its leaders after US cabinet members did, his trip would undermine the reciprocity. Reagan backed Wolfowitz and said he would go to China, but not until Zhao came here first. Later, Beijing announced that Premier Zhao would visit Washington in January 1984, opening the way for Reagan to go to China in April.[48] When Zhao visited the White House on January 10, Reagan described him as capable. Reagan was pleased that Chinese Communism had made room for some private enterprise and told Zhao that using force against Taiwan would change US-China relations beyond repair. Both "got along fine from then on."[49]

In April 1984, Reagan traveled to China. Senator Barry Goldwater, returning from a trip to Taiwan, met with Reagan in Guam. Goldwater feared the president would be selling out Taiwan. Reagan recalled in his memoirs, "Barry was upset about my visiting China and made little attempt to hide it. . . . He suspected I was getting ready to give up on Taiwan."[50] Reagan assured him that he would not forsake old friends to make new ones.[51]

Besides meeting with Deng and Zhao, Reagan met with General Secretary Hu Yaobang who informed him that Chinese politics was stable. The United States need not fear chaos after Deng's departure. In his public remarks in China, Reagan criticized the Soviet Union and praised democracy, but attempted to say less about Taiwan. In Shanghai, Reagan had denounced the Soviet Union as an expansionist power that had engaged in an invasion of Afghanistan. He had also praised the US values of faith in God and free markets.[52]

US relations with China continued to improve during Reagan's second term. Beijing sent thousands of graduate students to attend US universities. Chinese exports to US consumers grew from almost nothing in 1980 to $13 billion in 1988. The anticommunist rhetoric Reagan voiced in the late 1970s gave way to a closer relationship with China. During his presidency and especially in his second term, Reagan's China policy moved from the right toward the center.[53]

The State Level:
Negotiation of the US-PRC Arms Communiqué

The key players in the Reagan administration's foreign policy making included Secretary of State Alexander Haig, Secretary of Defense Caspar Weinberger, and NSA Richard Allen.[54] The secretary of state was instrumental in creating and implementing the US foreign policy. Haig first occupied the position, but his poor relations with his colleagues and Reagan caused him to resign earlier. George Shultz replaced Haig and was regarded as an effective bureaucratic leader. Weinberger served as secretary of defense for seven years. He played critical roles in the foreign policy arena. The position of the NSA was downgraded when Reagan was in office.[55]

The disputes regarding the China policy issue reemerged during the first Reagan term. The problem originated from differences among major players in the administration. Haig pushed for closer relations with Beijing against Moscow, but there were conflicts between Haig, Richard Allen (who resigned in December 1981), and William Clark. Allen and Weinberger voiced sympathy for improving relations with Taiwan. Both recognized the friendship Reagan felt for Taiwan.[56]

The State Department Under Haig: Pressing a Close Tie with China

Haig believed that China might be the most crucial country in the world regarding US strategic interests. At the time of Reagan's election, US-China relations were fragile, a result of what the Chinese called "the Three Disappointments." The first disappointment was the US passivity in confronting the Soviet Union in the post-Vietnam period. The second was unequal treatment. Instead of receiving credits and technical assistance from the United States, China received an influx of US businesspeople seeking profits. The third was that its relations with the United States had not solved Taiwan's issues.[57]

Haig's Visit to China

In June 1981, Deng invited Haig to visit China. Reagan instructed Haig to inform the Chinese leaders that the United States was following a policy to counter Soviet expansion and to emphasize the permanent nature of the US presence in Asia.[58] From June 14 to 17, 1981, Haig visited China. He received approval from Reagan to bring a gift to the Chinese leaders: the Reagan administration was ready to treat China as friendly, and eligible to receive more US technology.[59] The United States also explored the possibilities of continuing arms sales to Taiwan, but Deng confided to Haig that arms sales to Taiwan were a sensitive issue. Beijing had a limit to its tolerance.[60]

Before his China trip, Haig pressed the State Department to develop ideas. For example, the United States would be ready to consider selling weapons systems to China. The White House had cleared this idea, but without reviews within the bureaucracy. The National Security Decision Directive declared that the arms sales proposal was not to be revealed until after a follow-up trip by a Chinese defense official to the United States. Haig, however, announced that the United States would sell weapons to

182   *Hedging the China Threat*

China at a press conference in Beijing. Haig's decision upset James Lilley of the NSC staff and Richard Armitage of the Pentagon specialists on East Asia. Lilley secretly reported to NSA Richard Allen in Washington that Haig had gone too far. Armitage also sent a similar message back to Secretary of Defense Caspar Weinberger. Allen took the news of Haig's unapproved disclosure to Reagan.[61] A few hours before Haig was to depart from China, Reagan declared that the United States had a law called the TRA that provided for the sale of defense equipment to Taiwan. He intended to live up to the act. Beijing was shocked. Haig was furious that the White House had undercut him. He even tried to bar Lilley and Armitage from returning home on his Air Force plane.[62]

Friends of Taiwan in the United States conducted a publicity campaign in preparation for FX aircraft sales. The Northrop Corporation had expectations of the Reagan administration's sale of the FX because Northrop had a thousand employees in the Reagan state of California, and its president, Tom Jones, was Reagan's friend. Northrop and the Taiwanese authorities worked together to persuade the White House. NSA Richard Allen spoke with the Taiwanese through private channels. He said that Taiwan would get the FX fighters.[63] After Haig's unpleasant trip to China, he argued that by selling arms to China, the United States might be able to end China's objections to the United States selling the FX to Taiwan. When Assistant Secretary John Holdridge said he was having trouble gaining approval from the Pentagon to sell China the missiles and armored personnel carriers, Haig rebuked: "We're going to sell arms to China in September so that we can sell arms to Taiwan in January!" The Beijing leaders opposed both of Haig's ideas. Chinese foreign minister Huang Hua warned Haig that China would not accept US weapons as a bribe.[64]

In a meeting with Reagan, Huang said that the United States should stop selling all arms supplies to Taiwan until after it negotiated with Beijing. If not, China would downgrade its relations with the United States. Haig, who was present in the meeting, was also irritated with China's demands. Haig warned Hua that he was risking everything that had been built up between China and the United States over the previous decade.[65]

Beijing increased pressure on Taiwan not to receive weapons systems from the United States. In early July 1981, China protested to the US ambassador in Beijing, Arthur Hummel, regarding the US arms sales to Taiwan. China stated that if the United States continued to sell arms, it would force China into a very strong reaction.[66] On October 29, Minister Huang repeated similar demands and added another requirement that US sales to Taiwan cease by a specified date. Haig replied, "No American President, and especially not Ronald Reagan, would specify a day in the future on which the U.S. would stop helping a friend and former ally, especially not knowing what danger the friend might be in that day."[67]

Arms Sales Disputes

The Central Intelligence Agency (CIA) and Defense Intelligence Agency (DIA) warned of dire consequences should Taiwan get its arms. An intelligence report warned that the sale of the FX would be perceived in China as the US policy to hinder unification with Taiwan. China would probably downgrade US relations and become more bellicose with Taiwan.[68] Another CIA report assumed that the weapons sale could mean the fall of Deng, which might bring reconciliation with Moscow. Richard Allen disagreed with the CIA and called its reports disinformation. In mid-November 1981, the Pentagon report concluded that Taiwan did not need the FX aircraft to meet its defense needs. Its defense security could be met through continued coproduction of F-5E aircraft on a factory line that existed in Taiwan and by the provision of used F-104Gs in possession of a NATO ally.[69] Reagan then decided against the FX sale. Taipei was upset about Regan's decision and continued to lobby its friends in Congress and the military-industrial complex in the United States.

After offering China a major concession, Assistant Secretary John Holdridge was dispatched to Beijing to inform Chinese officials of the FX decision. He notified Chinese leaders that the United States would not export aircraft to Taiwan. The Chinese leaders, however, did not express appreciation for the Reagan administration. Instead, they criticized the decision to extend the joint production of F-5Es.[70]

By early 1982, China tested how much more the United States would compromise. Richard Allen resigned from the NSC in a scandal over his acceptance of Japanese gifts, strengthening Haig's influence. During this period, China pressed the United States to set a date to cut off all sales to Taiwan.[71] James Lilley, who served as the head of the American Institute in Taiwan since the beginning of 1982, was instructed to see if Taiwan might accept this idea. The State Department wanted Lilley to convince Taiwan that there could be a terminal date for arms sales. Instead, he cabled back that the idea would not work. His message annoyed Vice President George H. W. Bush. Bush said Taiwan did not count as much as China.[72]

Reagan believed that a frank statement of US good intentions would produce positive results. He wrote to Premier Zhao, suggesting that Vice President George H. W. Bush visit Beijing in May to discuss arms sales. The State Department drafted proposals. Reagan worked over the draft with the new NSA, William Clark, who toughened the US terms.[73] Bush urged Chinese leaders to recognize that the United States would not set a date for the termination of arms sales. Minister Huang told the US delegation that nothing had been accomplished since his trip to Washington last autumn. The State Department officials were stunned because they had made significant concessions.[74] During Bush's visit, the State Department emphasized the importance of US-China relations, which caused fierce opposition from those loyal to Taiwan.[75]

184   *Hedging the China Threat*

Paul Wolfowitz, head of policy planning at the State Department, sent a memo to Haig opposing the communiqué. Haig ignored it, but pro-Taiwan congressmen and officials in the White House were becoming worried that the negotiations would restrict arms sales to Taiwan.[76] In July, an article in the *Washington Times* claimed that the State Department was preparing secret drafts of joint agreements limiting weapon sales, one of which contained the US promise to reduce such sales and eventually terminate them. Senator Goldwater inquired whether the State Department had such documents and the reply was that it had never created this kind of draft. However, the State Department did prepare it, which infuriated the conservatives in Congress. They demanded that Reagan fulfill his campaign promise to execute the provisions on arms sales in the TRA.[77]

Haig resigned saying, "If the President faltered in his relations with China, the Democratic opposition would leap on this situation and turn it into a major issue in the 1984 election." After Haig's resignation, NSA William Clark stated that the president would not retreat regarding relations with Taiwan and would not put a time limit on weapons sales.[78] In the end, the issue was settled by Reagan. In July, aides brought the president the memo from former secretary Haig, arguing that the United States should agree to end arms sales to Taiwan. Reagan refused to sign it. He was willing to agree to limits on the sales, but not to a cutoff. Instead, he approved a written agreement that spoke vaguely of the US hopes for a final resolution of the dispute over arms sales, but set no date for the sales to end. The Chinese government agreed to the deal, which was enshrined in a communiqué on August 17, 1982.[79]

Shultz and Wolfowitz: The Dilution of China's Importance

Haig's replacement, George Shultz, forged better working relations with Reagan. Shultz played a crucial role in guiding US diplomacy during his six-year tenure in office. He was suspicious about the value of enhanced US-China military relations. Shultz believed that China could be a helpful ally in stabilizing Asia and leveraging US efforts to reduce Soviet power, but the United States did not need to make fundamental concessions to China. US priorities in Asia should remain centered on bolstering trade and military ties with its ally, Japan.[80]

As a former secretary of the treasury, Shultz focused more on economic strength than military power. As a former labor negotiator, Shultz understood the bargaining process. In early 1983, Shultz laid out his Asia policy: Japan, not China, should be the focus of US attention.[81] Before his first trip to China in February 1983, the State Department highlighted that Shultz was not carrying any policy changes. In Beijing, Shultz confronted a group of US executives eager to do more business with China. They asked Shultz why the US government was not doing more to help them win business contracts. One of them stated that Japan and West Germany issued export licenses for China much more quickly than did the United States. Shultz bluntly replied, "Why don't you move to Japan or Western Europe?"[82]

The Reagan administration's conflicts over arms sales to Taiwan were divided into two factions. The pro-China faction included men like former assistant to the secretary of state John Holdridge, Director for China William Rope, and the deputy chief of mission at the US embassy in Beijing, Charles Freeman. The pan-Asia faction included Reagan's aides, William Clark and Gaston Sigur at the NSC, Paul Wolfowitz and James Lilley at the State Department, and Richard Armitage at the Pentagon. The pan-Asia faction accused the pro-China faction of abandoning Taiwan. Conversely, pan-Asia was depicted by its adversaries as people who could not understand China. In the aftermath of the 1982 Communiqué, the pan-Asia cohort triumphed. Wolfowitz became assistant secretary of state and Armitage oversaw Asia policy at the Pentagon.[83]

Military Relations Between the Defense Department and the PLA

Secretary of Defense Caspar Weinberger shared Reagan's conviction that the Soviet Union posed a grave threat and that the defense establishment needed to be modernized. Improving relations with China was one of the principal international goals of Weinberger. During his visit to China in September 1983, Weinberger arranged for China's premier and defense minister to visit the United States and for Reagan to travel to China in June 1984. Weinberger and his PRC counterpart also signed a military-technical cooperation agreement.[84]

Weinberger's trip to China. In 1983, the Reagan administration loosened its controls on high-technology exports to China. US defense and high-technology industries swarmed into China for a lucrative market. In September 1983, Secretary Weinberger traveled to China to revive the US-China military relationship. He found that the Chinese military leaders were more interested in obtaining US technology than talking about an anti-Soviet alliance. They pressured the United States to approve the export of entire categories of defense technology so that China did not have to ask for each item. Weinberger was unwilling to go that far. He did announce that the administration approved export licenses for thirty-two military and dual-use technology items the Chinese had been trying to buy.[85]

China acquires US weapons systems. In June 1984, Reagan made China eligible for the US Foreign Military Sales program, enabling it to buy

186 *Hedging the China Threat*

weapons from the US government. In the following five years, the Chinese military acquired various US weapons systems so that it could modernize its factories to produce artillery ammunition and projectiles, buy torpedoes and artillery-locating radar, and modernize its jet fighters. China also received several commercial transactions such as buying hardware from US defense industries. The most notable of these was the purchase of twenty-four Sikorsky S-70C helicopters. These US arms sales helped the People's Liberation Army (PLA) to modernize its defense military capabilities. In fear of the rising close military tie between the United States and China, Taiwan actively lobbied against US arms sales to the PLA, even though the Pentagon insisted these sales would not undermine Taiwan's security.[86]

The State Department Against One Country, Two Systems for Taiwan

During the talks between China and the United Kingdom on the future of Hong Kong in 1982, Deng conveyed his proposal for a One Country, Two Systems formula in a meeting with former US NSA Zbigniew Brzezinski, who visited China. Deng tried to persuade Brzezinski that this formula was good for Taiwan and that the United States should agree with it.[87] US officials watched the talks between the PRC and the UK over Hong Kong issues. Charles Freeman, the PRC embassy's deputy chief of mission, was assigned this responsibility. When the talks launched in the summer of 1982, Freeman felt that the United States could not intervene. In 1983, as US-China relations improved, Freeman became more active in the future of Hong Kong.[88] UK prime minister Margaret Thatcher signed the Hong Kong agreement in December 1984, during a trip to Beijing. Deng gave her a message to deliver to Reagan, "Why don't we apply the same formula of one country, two systems to Taiwan?" Deng hoped that Thatcher would use her influence with Reagan to get him to think about Taiwan, but she did not deliver it.[89]

At the State Department, Paul Wolfowitz found that there was lobbying at high levels to persuade George Shultz to consider Deng's idea. Among those was Henry Kissinger, and the idea of a One Country, Two Systems settlement for Taiwan gathered momentum. Wolfowitz opposed any bargaining with China over Taiwan because future Chinese leaders would be less willing than Deng to carry out such an agreement. Wolfowitz noted that if the United States embraced this system for Taiwan, it would be violating promises of the Six Assurances. The Reagan government agreed that it would not pressure Taiwan to negotiate with China, or to serve as an intermediary between China and Taiwan. Deng's initiative finally failed.[90]

The International Level:
Demonstration of the Reagan Doctrine

The Reagan foreign policy insisted on the superiority of representative government, free-market capitalism, and freedom over communism. This approach was branded the Reagan Doctrine, which advocated opposition to communist-supported regimes. Reagan utilized his rhetorical skills to frame the Cold War contest as a war between good and evil.[91] While Reagan was in office, there were several crises. For example, on April 2, 1982, Argentine forces invaded the Falkland Islands. Thatcher ordered the deploying of a naval task force to the region. Haig went to the United Kingdom and Argentina for talks, but failed to broker a peaceful solution. The United States supported the British position and the suspension of aid to Argentina. A British victory ended the 1982 Falklands Crisis. Other major crises included the US-Soviet confrontation and the continuing Soviet invasion of Afghanistan, which enhanced US-China relations.

From Confrontation to Détente

The significant growth of Soviet military power in Asia Pacific occurred during the Carter administration. Fifty-one Soviet army divisions, one-fourth of its ground forces, were deployed in the Far East. Its bombers, with a range encompassing Japan, Korea, and China, augmented more than 2,000 Soviet aircraft based in Asia. The Soviet naval fleet in the Pacific comprised 319 warships and 50 nuclear submarines.[92] The expansion of the Soviet military posed a serious threat to China and the US allies.

The Soviets invaded Afghanistan, causing President Carter to withdraw a strategic arms limitation treaty, boycott the 1980 Olympic Games in Moscow, and ban US grain sales to the USSR. Committed to restoring US strength, President Reagan pursued a modernization of US nuclear and conventional forces. During Reagan's first term, he labeled the Soviet Union an "evil empire" and introduced the Strategic Defense Initiative (Star Wars), which Soviet leaders viewed as a threat. In the fall of 1983, the Soviets shot down a Korean Airlines flight over the Sea of Japan, and NATO deployed intermediate-range nuclear missiles in Western Europe.[93]

The Reagan administration advocated various initiatives that intensified confrontation with Moscow. Reagan increased defense spending to modernize US forces and achieve technological advances. For example, the US military built a larger navy with advanced weaponry and deployed intermediate-range nuclear missiles in Europe. The United States supported Afghan resistance organizations opposing the Soviet-backed regime, anticommunist forces in Angola, and the Contras in Nicaragua. The United States also increased spending on the US Information Agency,

188 *Hedging the China Threat*

especially Voice of America, countering communist ideology throughout the world.[94]

Rising US-Soviet tensions led the Reagan administration to attempt conciliatory measures to reduce the threat of confrontation, especially nuclear war. In 1982 Reagan proposed decreasing nuclear weapons stockpiles, which resulted in the Strategic Arms Reduction Treaty (START). The emergence of Mikhail Gorbachev also provided Reagan with a partner to engage in negotiations.[95] Secretary Shultz advocated that US-Soviet negotiations would enhance US security. Reagan shared Shultz's ideas for talks. In October 1986, Gorbachev and Reagan discussed abolishing all nuclear weapons. In December 1987, they signed the Intermediate-Range Nuclear Forces Treaty, which eliminated an entire class of missiles.[96]

The CIA and China

Between 1983 and 1988, the Reagan administration forged a more substantial working relationship with Beijing than the previous US governments. After the Soviet invasion of Afghanistan in 1979, the CIA armed and trained the Afghan resistance. China was a partner in these covert operations. After CIA director Stansfield Turner visited China in late 1980, both intelligence agencies formed a close relationship and wanted the Soviet Union to pay a heavy price for the invasion.[97]

The Afghan resistance discovered that there were not enough mules to support its military operations. The CIA studied the possibility of transporting mules from the United States to Afghanistan, but found that the idea would not work. The CIA then turned to its Chinese partners and agreed to buy mules from China. The mules, loaded with weapons, provided support for the Afghan resistance, contributing to the Soviets' failed operation in Afghanistan. Through the first half of the 1980s, US policy ensured that the weapons used by Afghan resistance came from communist countries so that Moscow could not accuse the United States of involvement in the war. A large share of the CIA's arms purchases for Afghanistan came from China. The Chinese government made $100 million yearly through its weapons sales to the CIA.[98]

Reagan advocated increasing the Pentagon budget by 35 percent during his two terms in office. The United States supported the Afghan resistance opposing the Soviet-backed regime in Kabul. The Reagan administration also increased spending on the US Information Agency, signaling the importance of challenging Soviet ideology. The accomplishments of this administration occurred after Reagan left office in 1989. Within a year, the Berlin Wall fell and, by the end of 1991, the Soviet Union had collapsed, signaling the end of the Cold War. Reagan and his foreign policy advisors played critical roles in this turn of events.[99]

Conclusion

During his presidency and especially in his second term, Ronald Reagan's China policy moved from the conservative right toward the politically moderate center. He emphasized that the US-China partnership should be global and strategic. Reagan's first secretary of state, Alexander Haig, supported close relations with China. Haig's replacement, George Shultz, was suspicious about the value of enhanced US-China military relations. He felt that the United States did not need to make further concessions to China. After the Soviet invasion of Afghanistan in 1979, the Reagan administration supported Afghan resistance organizations fighting against the Soviet troops. The CIA armed and trained the Afghan resistance. China was a partner in these covert operations. The Reagan administration forged a more substantial working relationship with the Chinese government than previous US administrations.

Policy outcomes included: first, the United States and China signed the 1982 US-PRC Joint Communiqué. China insisted that the United States reduce its arms sales to Taiwan. Second, the Reagan administration made Six Assurances to Taiwan.

At the individual level, in the 1970s Reagan was recognized as one of the strongest supporters of Taiwan in US politics, opposing US-China normalization. Despite Reagan's strong support of Taiwan, US relations with China continued to improve during Reagan's second term. The anticommunist rhetoric that Reagan voiced in the late 1970s gave way to a closer relationship with China because the rising Soviet threat led Reagan to improve his relations with Chinese leaders.

At the state level, Reagan's key policymakers included Secretary of State Alexander Haig, Secretary of Defense Caspar Weinberger, and NSA Richard Allen. The State Department under Haig pressed for close ties with China. Haig's replacement, George Shultz, forged better working relations with President Reagan regarding China policy. Secretary Shultz believed that China could be a helpful ally in stabilizing Asia and in leveraging US efforts to reduce Soviet power without making fundamental concessions to China.

At the international level, the Reagan administration advocated various initiatives that intensified confrontation with Moscow. Reagan increased defense spending to modernize US forces and achieve technological advances. The emergence of Gorbachev provided Reagan with a partner to engage in negotiations. In October 1986, Gorbachev and Reagan discussed abolishing all nuclear weapons. In December 1987, they signed the Intermediate-Range Nuclear Forces Treaty, which eliminated an entire class of missiles.

Notes

1. Hong N. Kim and Jack L. Hammersmith, "U.S.-China Relations in the Post-Normalization Era, 1979–1985," *Pacific Affairs* 59, no. 1 (Spring 1986): 70.

190   *Hedging the China Threat*

2. Ibid., p. 73.

3. Robert L. Downen, "Reagan Policy of Strategic Cooperation with China: Implication for Asian-Pacific Stability," *Journal of East Asian Affairs* 2, no. 1 (Spring–Summer 1982): 45.

4. Ibid., pp. 47–54.

5. James Mann, *About Face: A History of America's Curious Relationship with China from Nixon to Clinton* (New York: Knopf, 1999), p. 116.

6. Ibid., p. 117.

7. Jaw-ling Joanne Chang, "Negotiation of the 17 August 1982 U.S.-PRC Arms Communique: Beijing's Negotiating Tactics," *China Quarterly*, no. 125 (1991): 35–36.

8. Zbigniew Brzezinski, *Power and Principles: Memoirs of the National Security Adviser 1977–1981* (New York: Farrar, Straus, Giroux, 1985), p. 218.

9. Chang, "Negotiation," p. 66.

10. Alexander M. Haig Jr., *Caveat: Realism, Reagan, and Foreign Policy* (New York: Macmillan, 1984), p. 210.

11. Barnett Doak, *US Arms Sales: The China-Taiwan Tangle* (Washington, DC: Brookings Institution, 1982), p. 30

12. Michael Schaller, "Ronald Reagan and the Puzzles of 'So-Called Communist China' and Vietnam," in *Reagan and the World: Leadership and National Security, 1981–1989,* edited by Bradley Lynn Coleman and Kyle Longley (Lexington: University Press of Kentucky, 2017), p. 199.

13. Chang, "Negotiation," pp. 39–40.

14. "Ye Jianying on Taiwan's Return to Motherland and Peaceful Reunification," China.org.cn, September 30, 1981.

15. Dong Xing, "Taiwan-China Relations over 40 Years: Policies Which Changed the Landscape," January 6, 2019, Special Broadcasting Service, https://www.sbs.com.au.

16. Haig, *Caveat,* pp. 209–210.

17. Chang, "Negotiation of the 17 August 1982 U.S.-PRC Arms Communique: Beijing's Negotiating Tactics," *China Quarterly,* p. 41.

18. Ibid., p. 42.

19. US Department of State, "The August 17, 1982, US-China Communiqué on Arms Sales to Taiwan," *Milestones in the History of US Foreign Relations: 1981–1988,* https://history.state.gov.

20. Chang, "Negotiation," pp. 42–43.

21. US Department of State, "August 17, 1982."

22. Chang, "Negotiation," pp. 43–46.

23. US Department of State, "August 17, 1982."

24. Ibid.

25. Kim and Hammersmith, "U.S.-China Relations," p. 84.

26. Ibid., p. 87.

27. "The Chairman of the U.S. Joint Chiefs of Staff," UPI Archives, January 19, 1985, https://www.upi.com.

28. Kim and Hammersmith, "U.S.-China Relations," p. 88.

29. Ibid., p. 91.

30. Haig, *Caveat,* p.198.

31. Mann, *About Face,* p. 116.

32. Schaller, "Ronald Reagan," pp. 193–195.

33. Mann, *About Face,* p. 117.

34. Ibid., p. 118.

35. Ibid.

36. Kim and Hammersmith, "U.S.-China Relations," p. 75.

37. Ibid., pp. 78–80.

38. Harvey Feldman, "President Reagan's Six Assurances to Taiwan and Their Meaning Today," Heritage Foundation, October 2, 2007, https://www.heritage.org.

39. Ibid.

40. "President Reagan's Six Assurances to Taiwan," June 13, 2023, Congressional Research Service, https://sgp.fas.org.

41. Harvey Feldman, "Taiwan, Arms Sales, and the Reagan Assurances," *American Asian Review* 19, no. 3 (Fall 2001).

42. Ibid.

43. Feldman, "President Reagan's Six Assurances."

44. Mann, *About Face,* p. 127.

45. Schaller, "Ronald Reagan and the Puzzles," p. 200.

46. Mann, *About Face,* p. 143.

47. Schaller, "Ronald Reagan and the Puzzles," p. 202.

48. Mann, *About Face,* p. 144.

49. Schaller, "Ronald Reagan and the Puzzles," p. 201.

50. Mann, *About Face,* p. 145.

51. Schaller, "Ronald Reagan and the Puzzles," p. 202.

52. Mann, *About Face,* pp. 145–146.

53. Schaller, "Ronald Reagan and the Puzzles," pp. 203–206.

54. Qingminy Zhang, "The Bureaucratic Politics of US Arms Sales to Taiwan," *Chinese Journal of International Politics* 1, no. 2 (Winter 2006): 243.

55. US Department of State, "1981–1988: The Presidency of Ronald W. Reagan," *Milestones in the History of U.S. Foreign Relations: 1981–1988,* https://history.state.gov.

56. Schaller, "Ronald Reagan and the Puzzles," p. 198.

57. Haig, *Caveat,* pp. 194–196.

58. Ibid., pp. 205–206.

59. Mann, *About Face,* p. 120.

60. Haig, *Caveat,* p. 207.

61. Mann, *About Face,* p. 121.

62. Ibid., p. 122.

63. Zhang, "Bureaucratic Politics," p. 245.

64. Mann, *About Face,* p. 122.

65. Ibid., p. 124.

66. Haig, *Caveat,* p. 208.

67. Ibid., p. 210.

68. Chang, "Negotiation of the 17 August 1982 U.S.-PRC Arms Communique: Beijing's Negotiating Tactics," *China Quarterly,* pp. 47–48.

69. Haig, *Caveat,* p. 212.

70. Zhang, "Bureaucratic Politics," p. 248.

71. Mann, *About Face,* pp. 124–125.

72. Ibid., 126.

73. Haig, *Caveat,* p. 212.

74. Mann, *About Face,* p. 125.

75. Zhang, "Bureaucratic Politics," p. 248.

76. "Alexander Haig's Fall from Grace," Association for Diplomatic Studies and Training, June 13, 2016, https://adst.org.

77. Zhang, "Bureaucratic Politics," p. 249.

78. Ibid.
79. Mann, *About Face,* p. 127.
80. Schaller, "Ronald Reagan and the Puzzles," p. 200.
81. Mann, *About Face,* p.130.
82. Ibid., p. 131.
83. Ibid., p. 132.
84. "Caspar W. Weinberger," Office of the Secretary of Defense, https://history .defense.gov.
85. Mann, *About Face,* pp. 139–140.
86. Ibid., pp. 141–143.
87. Feldman, "President Reagan's Six Assurances."
88. Mann, *About Face,* p. 153.
89. Ibid., p. 153.
90. Ibid., p. 154.
91. US Department of State, "1981–1988: The Presidency of Ronald W. Reagan."
92. Downen, "Reagan Policy," p. 44.
93. US Department of State, "U.S.-Soviet Relations, 1981–1991," *Milestones in the History of U.S. Foreign Relations: 1981–1988,* https://history.state.gov.
94. US Department of State, "1981–1988: The Presidency of Ronald W. Reagan."
95. Ibid.
96. US Department of State, "1981–1991: U.S.-Soviet Relations."
97. Mann, *About Face,* pp. 134–136.
98. Ibid., pp. 136–137.
99. US Department of State, "1981–1988: The Presidency of Ronald W. Reagan."

10

Dealing with the
Tiananmen Square Crisis:
The George H. W. Bush Administration

ON NOVEMBER 8, 1988, GEORGE H. W. BUSH WON THE PRESIDENTIAL ELEC-
tion. Bush was committed to improving the relationship between the United
States and the People's Republic of China (PRC). When Jimmy Carter
established diplomatic relations with China in 1978, Bush had argued that
Carter had given away too much. In the 1980 election, when Ronald Reagan suggested his new administration might recognize Taiwan, Bush who
was Reagan's running mate, opposed the idea. Bush had ample experience
working with Chinese leaders. From 1974 to 1975, he was the chief of the
US Liaison Office to China, the de facto ambassador to China. As president-elect, Bush visited the PRC ambassador to the United States, Han Xu,
in Washington, which reflected his attitude toward a closer working relationship with China.[1]

Bush built up his team of foreign policy advisors, which included Secretary of State James Baker, Secretary of Defense Dick Cheney, and
National Security Advisor (NSA) Brent Scowcroft, who all usually worked
well together. Bush approached foreign affairs with pragmatism. He relied
on the frequent contacts of foreign leaders that he established as ambassador to the United Nations, director of the Central Intelligence Agency
(CIA), and vice president. In early June 1989, the People's Liberation
Army (PLA) cracked down on a pro-democracy student movement demonstrating in Tiananmen Square. Although Bush loathed Beijing's forceful
reaction, he did not want to ruin bilateral relations. The US Congress
called for a harsh response to the PLA's massacre of peaceful protestors.
Later, Bush sent Brent Scowcroft and Deputy Secretary of State Lawrence
Eagleburger to China to maintain the relationship. [23]

194 *Hedging the China Threat*

Historical Events: Turmoil Breaks Out in China

After Japan's emperor Hirohito died on January 7, 1989, his funeral on February 24 offered newly elected president Bush an opportunity to travel to China. Bush was looking forward to visiting Beijing, where he had lived and worked for two years.[4] His visit to China, soon after taking office, showed his efforts to nurture good relations with the Chinese leadership.

After the Tiananmen Square incident, the Bush administration imposed sanctions against China. Bilateral relations worsened. Bush knew that if he further exacerbated the relationship, it would be against US interests because China was an important player in international affairs. After the United States adopted sanctions, Bush sent Scowcroft and Eagleburger on secret missions to China in July and December 1989 to mend the deteriorated relationship.[5]

The Student Demonstration in Tiananmen Square

The students demonstrated in front of Zhongnanhai, the compound that houses most of the PRC's senior leaders and the offices of the important bureaucracies. When the newly chosen ambassador James R. Lilley arrived in Beijing, he conversed with protesting students. These students were determined to remove corrupt leaders in government. They wanted a better China, but not necessarily a noncommunist China.[6] On April 19, 1989, the confrontation between student protesters and the government escalated into violence. Protesters asked Premier Li Peng to discuss political reform in China. Some called for his resignation. In response, the chairman of the Central Military Commission (CMC), Deng Xiaoping, ordered 9,000 soldiers to reinforce the police in Beijing.[7]

Bush asked Lilley, "Is this a genuine movement?" Lilley responded that the demonstrations could threaten the Chinese Communist Party (CCP) regime.[8] On April 23, the Politburo Standing Committee members briefed Deng about student protests in major cities such as Beijing, Xi'an, and Changsha. Deng believed that these students had been influenced by the collapse of communist regimes in East Europe. The objective of the protesting students was to overthrow the CCP.[9]

General Secretary Zhao Ziyang sympathized with the students' demands for accelerating reform. Zhao insisted that the CCP had to change. At a Politburo Standing Committee meeting on May 1, 1989, Zhao stated that the student slogans upholding the constitution, promoting democracy, and opposing corruption echoed the party's principles. Opposing Zhao's ideas was hard-liner premier Li Peng. He feared that the CCP was losing control of the situation. Li asserted that the government should first maintain stability. Then, Beijing could discuss reforming the political system if social stability was achieved.[10]

From May 15 to 18, Soviet leader Mikhail Gorbachev visited China. The US embassy in Beijing closely monitored Gorbachev's meetings with Chinese leaders.[11] At the time, the US State Department was planning a visit to the United States by the PRC chairman of the National People's Congress (NPC), Wan Li. His official visit was to counter the impact of Gorbachev's trip. Pentagon officials also planned for US warships to make a port call in Shanghai to showcase US-China military cooperation. However, Gorbachev's trip, Wan Li's visit, and the US Navy's visit lost their spotlight during the student protests in Beijing.[12]

By the time Gorbachev arrived in Beijing on May 15, almost half a million people had swarmed into Tiananmen Square. That evening, members of the Standing Committee of the Politburo voted to impose martial law in Beijing. Deng cast the deciding vote for restoring order. He said that if 1 billion people held multiparty elections, China would have chaos like the Cultural Revolution.[13] On May 19, Zhao Ziyang showed up at Tiananmen Square and apologized to the hunger-striking students, "We have come too late." He urged the students to end their fast. As a result, Zhao was dismissed by the party elders on May 21.[14]

Bush thought that violence could be avoided since Deng was in charge of Chinese politics. Lilley viewed it differently because Chinese leaders were being humiliated by the demonstrators. He felt there would be bloodshed.[15] By purging Zhao Ziyang, Deng overcame an obstacle to using force against the demonstrators. He shored up the support of the military in the last days of May. On the evening of June 3, Deng, through President Yang Shangkun, ordered the military force to end the protest.[16] The PLA launched its assault by shooting civilians and students. The number of causalities was over a thousand, according to US sources.[17]

The Bush Administration's Responses

Bush announced a ban on new weapons sales and suspension of military personnel contacts with China on June 5, 1989.[18] He attempted to send messages to the Chinese leadership by urging them to act with restraint, but he could not access China's senior leadership. Lilley could only deliver presidential communications through the regular Chinese Foreign Ministry channels.[19]

Bush condemned China's use of force by halting the US-China military relationship. The State Department also informed US allies that the United States intended to cut off international loans to China. The Bush administration hoped other countries would do likewise. This effort was successful. But Congress was upset with Beijing's brutality, and wanted to impose severe sanctions.[20]

During the weeks following the massacre, thousands of dissidents were arrested. The US-China communication channels, cultivated over

196 Hedging the China Threat

the previous ten years, remained closed. Lilley's calls to the PRC Foreign Ministry, on behalf of President Bush, fell on deaf ears.[21] On June 20, Secretary Baker testified before the Senate Foreign Relations Committee and revealed sanctions against China. He stated that the United States would seek to freeze lending to China by the World Bank and other international financial institutions. He had recommended to Bush that the United States suspend high-level contacts. The White House later agreed with Baker.[22]

Secretary Baker's Visit to China

Despite the worsening US-China relationship, both governments sought to progress in their interactions. James Roy, the newly appointed US ambassador to China, and Asian affairs director of the National Secretary Council (NSC), Douglas Paal, worked to persuade Secretary of State James Baker, who was reluctant about traveling to China. Paal sought China's assistance in dealing with North Korea's nuclear issues. In September 1991, Baker told Foreign Minister Qian Qichen that he and Bush thought the time was ripe for him to make a trip to China.[23] When Baker arrived in Beijing on November 15, he encountered many obstacles.

In his first meeting with Foreign Minister Qian Qichen, Qian demanded that the United States end all sanctions against China and stop interfering in Chinese domestic affairs. In response, Baker presented what he wanted from China, including pressure on North Korea to allow international inspection of its nuclear facilities at Yongbyon and progress on human rights. Baker told Qian, "I need concrete results—not promises, not meetings, not delays. . . . If I am seen as having failed, Congress will take China policy away from the president." Qian did not yield or compromise.[24] On November 16, Baker met with Premier Li Peng. The two men argued about human rights in general. Baker referred to the Tiananmen crackdown as a tragedy. Li countered that the response in Tiananmen Square was a good thing for China's stability.[25] Douglas Paal described the tense conversation between Baker and Li as "the worst meeting I have ever been to in my life."[26]

Baker and Qian had a long meeting on the last day of Baker's visit. Both made the following concessions:[27] first, on missile sales, the Chinese agreed orally to disallow the sales of M-9s to Syria and M-11s to Pakistan. In return, Baker agreed that the United States would remove the sanctions that prohibited licensing high-speed computers and satellite technology for China. Second, the Chinese stated their earlier support for a "non-nuclear" Korean Peninsula. Third, China agreed to prevent goods made by prison labor from reaching the United States. And it would send a delegation to Washington to negotiate the US charges of massive piracy and intellectual property rights violations. Fourth, the Chinese agreed to continue human rights dialogue with Assistant Secretary of State Richard Schifter.[28] Baker hoped to meet with Deng, as he was carrying a letter from Bush to Deng. Baker asked that he be permitted to deliver letter in person, but that was rejected by China.[29] Baker was disappointed about his trip to China. He agreed with the press's characterizations of his trip as a failure, and gave apologetic briefings to Congress on his return. His distrust of the Chinese grew because of his trip.[30]

Democratic Reforms in Taiwan

Taiwan transformed its political rule from an authoritarian regime to a democratic government in the 1980s.[31] In 1985, President Chiang Ching-kuo implemented political reforms. In September 1986, the opposition Democratic Progressive Party (DPP) was established. Martial law was lifted in July 1987. Later, newspapers freely opened, and television and radio broadcasting ended the ruling party's monopoly. The DPP demanded that the legislative bodies be chosen in general elections. It also proposed revisions to the constitution to refocus the state's mission toward Taiwan rather than retaking China.[32]

The National Affairs Conference. During Chiang Ching-kuo's presidency, Taiwan experienced profound political, social, and economic changes. The leader of the ruling party Kuomintang (KMT), Lee Teng-hui, who had succeeded Chiang Ching-kuo when he died in January 1988, became president.[33] In March 1990, Lee completed his term as Chiang Ching-kuo's replacement and a new presidential election was held. Choosing the president was the National Assembly's responsibility and, given the KMT's enjoyment of a majority, the ruling party's nominee easily won.[34]

In 1990, Lee proposed a National Affairs Conference (NAC). Representatives of political parties, scholars, and business leaders discussed and sought a consensus on how Taiwan should proceed toward constitutional reform. Their goal was to create a blueprint for Taiwan's democratization that would be acceptable to all the major players. They discussed four topics: the local government system, the central government system, constitutional revision, and the policies of China. The DPP pushed the KMT to have a direct popular election of the president and began to promote the idea that Taiwan should rejoin the United Nations.[35]

The New China policy and pragmatic diplomacy. Challenges facing Taiwan in the 1990s were its international status and cross-strait relations. Beginning in October 1987, Taiwan residents were allowed to travel to China. At first, visits were restricted to visiting relatives in China. The door then

198   Hedging the China Threat

opened to scholars, cultural groups, and tourists. Taiwanese doing business in China followed. The increase in cross-strait interactions led to an urgent demand for institutions to handle China's affairs. In September 1990, Taiwan established a presidential advisory council on mainland affairs. The Executive Yuan also approved the council's National Unification Guidelines, which laid out a three-stage process for unification, including private exchanges; direct postal, transport, and commercial links; and a consultation period to work out an agreeable framework for unification.[36]

In 1991, Taipei announced the end of hostility toward Beijing. In January, Taiwan established the Mainland Affairs Council (MAC), responsible for planning, evaluating, and implementing China policy. In May, Lee canceled the Period of Mobilization for the Suppression of Communist Rebellion, ending China's Civil War. No longer would Taiwan claim to be China's rightful government. Instead, Taiwan took the position that China and Taiwan were divided into two areas under the jurisdiction of two states.[37]

Organizations were set up to formulate cross-strait policy and to conduct semiofficial contacts. Taiwan created the Straits Exchange Foundation (SEF); China established the Association for Relations Across the Taiwan Strait (ARATS). Progress was paused by disagreements over the definition of the One China principle. The two sides, however, addressed that in 1992 by agreeing that there was One China, but each could have its own interpretation.[38]

An approach to improve international relations was gaining strength in Taiwan. Known as "pragmatic diplomacy," this strategy aimed to increase Taiwan's international visibility. It encompassed two approaches: forging relationships with other countries and joining international organizations. It undertook public diplomacy in the United States and other countries, promoting Taiwan as a democratic nation deserving of support and a voice in the international community. Under the new "divided China" formula, Taipei no longer insisted that only One China could be represented in international organizations. Instead, Taiwan referred to the examples of East and West Germany to argue that the dual recognition of divided states was acceptable to Taiwan. Beijing, nevertheless, rejected dual recognition and the One Country, Two Entities formula.[39]

Cross-strait relations improved in the early 1990s. After 1987, millions of Taiwanese visited China. Both governments established procedures for managing bilateral relations. In March 1992, they set up document verification procedures. A year later, the leaders of the agencies met in Singapore, SEF's Koo Chen-fu and Wang Daohan of ARATS. Despite these improvements, the two sides were far apart on fundamental issues. Beijing insisted on the following points: "One China" means the PRC, and Taiwan is a province of the PRC. Taipei rejected that, arguing that Taiwan and China represented two equal parts of a divided nation.[40]

The Individual Level:
President George H. W. Bush and China

Bush had an exceptional resume when he took office: director of the CIA, congressman, US ambassador to the UN, and vice president. His experience in various governmental positions made him familiar with policy formulation.[41] Bush believed that friendships could smooth over diplomatic difficulties. In times of crisis, leaders who knew each other would resolve problems more easily. He enjoyed meeting with foreign dignitaries and diplomats to develop personal relations. He was also good at telephone diplomacy to get things done.[42] Regarding relations with China, Bush had rich experiences dealing with leaders in Beijing. His experience as head of the US Liaison Office in China gave him a deeper understanding of Chinese politics and ideology. He believed in the strategic importance of China in the Cold War between the United States and the Soviet Union. Bush expressed concern about a thaw in Moscow-Beijing relations and sought opportunities to enhance the Washington-Beijing strategic relationship.[43]

Bush's Dialogues with Chinese Leaders

After attending the Japanese emperor Akihito's funeral, Bush arrived in Beijing on February 25, 1989. Bush met with President Yang Shangkun, who assured him that future Chinese relations with the Soviet Union would not be like they were in the 1950s. Beijing and Moscow would not establish a military alliance.[44] On February 26, Bush had a meeting with Premier Li Peng. Li emphasized that the upcoming Gorbachev visit was part of China's effort to normalize relations with the Soviet Union, but both countries would not seek an alliance. As for relations with the United States, Li hoped to accomplish more economically, increasing US investments. However, he warned against Americans trying to influence China's domestic policies by stating that it "smacks of interference in China's internal affairs, and we are not happy about it."[45]

The highlight of Bush's visit was his meeting with Deng Xiaoping. Both leaders spent much time talking about the Soviet-China relationship. Deng assured Bush that the upcoming Gorbachev trip was not meant to signal the renewal of an old alliance against the United States. Deng said the United States and China might not see eye to eye on everything, but that he hoped for a new pattern in bilateral relations. Both countries could build mutual trust to minimize the problems.[46] The Chinese leaders wanted to develop a pragmatic working relationship with the United States. Bush hoped both countries could build trust and encourage positive action. Bush left Beijing optimistic that his delegation had laid important groundwork

200 *Hedging the China Threat*

for better bilateral relations. However, a few months later, the Tiananmen Square events would badly damage US-China relations.[47]

Bush's Reactions to the Tiananmen Massacre

On June 4, 1989, the PLA entered Tiananmen Square, dispersing demonstrators. Bush was frustrated that he could not get a message to Chinese leaders during the crisis. This led Bush to send a secret mission to Beijing.[48] Bush met with Secretary Baker and NSA Scowcroft to discuss how to respond to the crisis. He wanted a rational response from those who had implemented the use of force, the hard-liners and the military. Bush decided to suspend military sales and contacts, but did not want to disrupt US-China relations.[49] On June 5, former president Richard Nixon and Bush discussed the US responses to the Tiananmen massacre over the phone. Nixon suggested that the United States should not disrupt the relationship and should look at the long haul. Bush told Nixon he did not think the United States should stop trade with China.[50]

A difficult situation was made worse when Chinese activist, Fang Lizhi, appeared at the US embassy in Beijing asking for refuge. The Chinese government criticized the Bush administration's intervention in its domestic affairs and then deployed security forces near the embassy. Bush believed that good US-China relations were in the fundamental interests of both countries. On June 10, Bush sent a letter to Deng, requesting an emissary to get their relationship back on track.[51] In the letter, Bush expressed that he did not want to get involved in China's internal affairs and to burden the Chinese people through economic sanctions. When Bush heard Fang Lizhi was in the US embassy, he knew a huge wedge would be driven between the United States and China. Bush asked Deng if he could send a special emissary on his behalf, who could speak with candor to Deng. This mission was kept top secret. Bush hoped his personal relations with Deng would make a difference in their communications.[52]

Under pressure from Congress and the media, on June 20 Bush extended the ban between military officials to include all high-level official contacts with Beijing and suspended US support for all loans to China through the World Bank and the Asian Development Bank. However, as he was criticizing China publicly, Bush maintained engagements with Chinese leaders in private. Deng agreed through diplomatic channels to receive Bush's emissary.[53]

Bush's First Emissary to China

The idea for Scowcroft's secret trip to China had come from Bush. Secretary Baker had not told Bush that he planned to announce a ban on high-

Dealing with the Tiananmen Square Crisis   201

level officials' exchanges, until minutes before testifying in Congress. When Scowcroft heard about the prohibition on contacts of high-level officials, he was very surprised.[54]

Bush sent NSA Scowcroft and Deputy Secretary of State Eagleburger as his special emissaries. They landed in Beijing on July 1. The next day, they had several long conversations with Chinese leaders, including Chairman of the Central Military Commission Deng Xiaoping, Premier Li Peng, Vice Premier Wu Xueqian, and Foreign Minister Qian Qichen.[55] Deng began the meeting with a long speech. He said, "The reason I have chosen President Bush as my friend is because since the inception of my contact with him, I found that his words are rather trustworthy." He continued that after Bush took office, turmoil broke out in China. It was unfortunate that the United States was deeply involved. Deng complained that the US Congress had acted against China. US-China relations were in a dangerous situation. He added that Beijing still needed to put down the counterrevolutionary leaders. China would persist in punishing those instigators of the rebellion and its behind-the-scenes boss under Chinese laws. China would never allow outsiders to interfere in its internal affairs.[56]

Scowcroft delivered Bush's messages. First, Bush asked Deng to ease up on the crackdown. Further arrests of Chinese students would lead to a strong US response. Second, he hoped Deng would reopen a direct channel between leaders of both governments. During the crisis, Bush could not send direct messages to Chinese leaders. Scowcroft's mission was designed "to keep channels open." Third, the sanctions the United States imposed on China would be restrained or temporary.[57] Bush wanted to preserve the steady relationship, but the United States had to sanction China because of public pressure. Fourth, he wanted Deng to know that the president was not the only factor in the US democratic system. Congress was a coequal branch of government. Finally, the Bush administration wanted to continue its security cooperation with China against the Soviet Union, and to continue the operation of the intelligence facilities in China that monitored Soviet military activities.[58]

Regarding the events of Tiananmen Square, Scowcroft continued, "What the American people perceived in the demonstrations they saw, rightly or wrongly, was an expression of values which represent their most cherished beliefs, stemming from the American Revolution."[59]

The US Congress and press attacked Bush for not acting strongly enough. Three days before, the House of Representatives had voted to impose stiffer sanctions on China by 418 to 0. Bush vetoed this legislation, and his veto was only narrowly sustained in the Senate.[60] Deng argued that the United States must understand that China is an independent country, which rejects interference by foreigners. China must see what actions the Bush administration would take. With those words, Deng left

202 Hedging the China Threat

the discussion to Premier Li Peng to decide how to handle future discussions between both governments.[61]

Premier Li Peng said that he recognized the differences between the two cultures and traditional values. Li was convinced that the United States did not have a clear picture of what had been happening, or accurate information about the Tiananmen event. He insisted that the death toll in the crackdown given in the West was wrong; it was not tens of thousands, but 310, and the number included members of the PLA as well.[62]

For Bush, the main purpose of sending his emissary was not for negotiations, but to keep the lines of top leaders' communication open. Both sides were determined not to let the Tiananmen events disrupt their relationship. Bush was pleased with the visit[63] and, after it, power over China policy shifted from the State Department to the White House. Baker later focused on issues of the Soviet Union and the Middle East, leaving the White House to deal with China issues. It became a joke with the government's desk officer for China that Bush handled the details of relations between the United States and China.[64]

Bush Sends Scowcroft to China Again

Frustrated that both countries had made little progress since Scowcroft's trip to Beijing in July 1989, Bush wrote another letter to Deng emphasizing that he respected China's nonintervention position in its internal affairs. Nonetheless, the US-China relationship demanded the candor with which only a friend could speak. Despite the US Congress trying to compel Bush to cut off economic ties with China, he "kept the boat from rocking."[65] On August 11, 1989, Deng replied with a letter stressing that China acted under its laws to abolish the "rebellion." He continued that US sanctions against China were still in place, which was interfering in China's domestic affairs and damaging US-China relations.[66]

At the end of 1989, Bush sent Scowcroft and Eagleburger to China for the second time to restore bilateral relations. Bush's envoy arrived in Beijing on December 11. The Scowcroft delegation held many conversations with Chinese leaders. Scowcroft emphasized that both sides should not focus on placing blame for problems; instead, they must take bold measures to break their stagnant relations.[67] Eagleburger and Scowcroft encouraged the Chinese leadership to explore a road map toward better relations. Scowcroft met twice with Qian Qichen. Their first meeting was frustrating, with each side complaining about the other. The second meeting finalized the terms of a road map of reciprocal moves toward normalization.[68]

During Scowcroft's meeting with Premier Li Peng, Li argued that if the Chinese government had not adopted resolute measures on the Tiananmen event, the present situation in China would be even more turbulent.

Li told Scowcroft that China was ready to improve bilateral relations. He explained that they understood the Bush administration's repeated explanation of the difficulties faced by Bush, but they were also under restraint.[69] When Scowcroft's delegation met with General Secretary Jiang Zemin, he understood that Bush was trying to improve the current situation. Jiang told Scowcroft that both governments should find common ground while resolving differences. They should not let ideology hinder their efforts to restore relations.[70]

After dialogues with Jiang, Scowcroft engaged in a dialogue with Deng Xiaoping. Deng understood that both sides had to justify their actions to their people. He said the United States should not antagonize China because it did not consider the United States a rival. Deng reminded him that since 1972, China had done nothing to hurt the interests of the United States. Deng suggested that if a solution could be found, Jiang should come to the United States to end the dispute. Deng added that he was retired and did not intend to interfere in the work of the new leadership.[71]

Bush hinted that his second emissary mission had achieved an understanding with the Chinese to improve bilateral relations. On January 10, 1990, China announced it would lift martial law in Beijing. On January 11, State Department spokesperson Margaret Tutwiler announced that the United States would support World Bank lending to China on a case-by-case basis for "humanitarian, basic human needs-type loans."[72] The Bush emissary mission paved the way toward getting assurances on China's stopping missile sales, lifting martial law, and releasing people detained after Tiananmen.[73] However, the mission was greeted with criticism. Congress criticized Bush for not consulting with its members before sending his emissary. The visit was contrary to the ban on high-level contact with China. Senator George Mitchell denounced the mission as an embarrassing kowtowing to a repressive Communist government.[74]

Bush's Decision on the F-16 Sale

The Bush administration's sanctions against arms sales to China after Tiananmen pushed China's decision to buy Su-27 aircraft from Russia.[75] The Soviet Union's disintegration and urgent need for financial support offered a shopping opportunity for China. In March 1992, Russia agreed to sell China twenty-four Su-27 fighters, which caused grave concern in Taiwan. The sale led to increased lobbying by Taiwan and its friends in the United States for a change in US policy on selling the F-16. For a decade, Taipei had asked for F-16s, emphasizing that its aging fighters crashed regularly. However, the US government rejected the request because it would violate the 1982 Communiqué with China.[76]

204   Hedging the China Threat

While Bush was in office, Taiwan's image in the United States improved. For decades, US opinion was critical of Taiwan's authoritarian rule. With Taiwan's democratization beginning to take shape in the late 1980s, in contrast to China's poor human rights record, US political and security support for Taiwan improved.[77] Taiwan pressured the Bush administration to sell it F-16s by purchasing French Mirage fighters. In 1991, France also agreed to sell Taiwan sixteen naval frigates in a deal worth more than $4 billion. Taiwan officials visited Washington for the annual review of their needs for military equipment. F-16s were at the top of the list. The State Department informed Taiwan officials that the F-16s were off-limits.[78]

In May 1991, Lilley stepped down as US ambassador to China. In November, Bush appointed Lilley as the assistant secretary of defense for international security affairs, responsible for military relations between the United States and Asian countries. By 1992, there was a rising voice in the Bush administration that Taiwan should buy new planes. For example, NSC Asian director Douglas Paal said, "Taiwan has lost 150 aircraft over the past ten years. It has gone from about 500 planes to 350, and then China goes out and buys Su-27s."[79]

Lilley argued that Taiwan needed F-16s. He told Under Secretary of Defense for Policy Paul Wolfowitz and Douglas Paal to consider arms sales to Taiwan. In May 1992, Lilley also raised the issue with Secretary of Defense Dick Cheney. Lilley told Cheney that the State Department had turned down Taiwan's request for F-16s, but that the PRC was purchasing Su-27s from the Soviets, France was marketing the Mirage-2000, and Taiwan's Indigenous Defense Fighter (IDF) was not developing well. Cheney agreed. The Pentagon began pushing hard for the F-16 sale to Taiwan.[80] US foreign defense contractors also began to press Bush for the opportunity to market systems to Taiwan that had long been off-limits.[81]

Bush's reelection consideration. During the 1992 presidential campaign, Democratic candidate Bill Clinton's campaign theme was Bush's poor performance in the US economy. Senator Lloyd Bentsen and Governor Ann Richards also blamed Bush's China policy for preventing the F-16 sale to Taiwan. Polls showed Bush running 20 percentage points behind Clinton. As the reelection campaign looked unfavorable for Bush, he started to pay more attention to domestic matters.[82] Clinton criticized Bush for not standing up for democracy, but instead sending his aides to toast China's leaders.[83]

At the end of July 1992, Bush accepted the invitation of Senator Joe Barton (R-TX) to campaign at the Texas F-16 manufacturing plant. Before Bush arrived, General Electric announced on July 29 that it would lay off 5,800 employees by 1994 because of a reduction in F-16 orders. The next day, Bush told reporters that he would consider whether the United States could export F-16s to Taiwan.[84] The day after Bush said he was "taking a new look" at the F-16 issue, Douglas Paal, at the president's behest, invited Ambassador Zhu Qizhen and visiting MFA North American and Oceanian Affairs Department director general, Yang Jiechi, to the White House residence for a drink with the president. Zhu complained about Bush's remarks on the F-16 issue, to which the president replied, "This is going ahead. It's political. Tell Deng Xiaoping that this is something I have to do."[85]

On September 2, Bush appeared at the General Dynamics plant in Fort Worth, Texas, under a banner saying "Jobs for America. Thanks, Mr. President," to announce that he had decided to sell 150 aircraft to Taiwan for an estimated $6 billion. "This F-16 is an example of what only America and Americans can do," Bush told the cheering crowds, several thousand of whose jobs he had just saved.[86] The F-16 episode came from a determined Bush. He later indicated that he hoped to be able to "make it up" to Beijing after the election.[87]

Beijing's responses. Beijing's reaction to the F-16 sales to Taiwan was strong. On September 4, 1992, the vice minister of foreign affairs, Liu Huaqiu, called Ambassador Roy to protest the F-16 decision. Beijing stopped bilateral discussions of nonproliferation issues. It also dropped out of a US-sponsored forum to discuss how to restrict arms sales to the Middle East.[88] The assistant secretary of state for East Asian and Pacific affairs, William Clark, suggested that the White House send a presidential envoy to explain to Chinese leaders about the F-16 sales to Taiwan. The NSC approved Clark's idea of sending a presidential envoy and chose him for the job.[89]

When Clark arrived in China on September 7, he offered four initiatives for Chinese leaders to consider: a return of equipment stored in the United States from the aborted Peace Pearl program, an agreement to reopen military-to-military talks, an agreement to resume Joint Committee on Commerce and Trade talks, and an agreement to resume Joint Committee on Science and Technology talks. Nevertheless, China failed to appreciate the initiatives. China broke its agreement with Baker about shipping missiles to Pakistan. China also signed an agreement to provide Iran with a nuclear power reactor.[90]

In 1992, Bush was facing an arduous reelection campaign. He needed Texas, where General Dynamics produced the F-16 that Taiwan had been seeking to purchase for over a decade.[91] Taiwan's defense minister hailed the sale as a breakthrough. Beijing did not downgrade relations because it hoped Bush would win reelection and would not create problems for the renewal of MFN tariff status, which was coming up for a congressional vote.[92] Any harsh Chinese protest might have hurt Bush's reelection. China did not want Clinton, who had been more critical of China's human rights practices, to get elected.[93]

206 *Hedging the China Threat*

The F-16 sale increased the seniority of Taiwanese government visitors to the United States and US visitors to Taiwan. Beijing began to put pressure on Washington, and stated that no US arms sale to Taiwan would go uncontested, and no US officials' visit to Taiwan unprotested.[94]

The State Level:
The Tension Between the
Bush Administration and Congress

Bush's key national security team was comprised of James Baker, Richard Cheney, and Brent Scowcroft. A collegial approach to foreign policy making was the norm, especially in the "breakfast group" of Baker, Cheney, and Scowcroft, which met weekly to resolve problems.[95] They all had rich experience working in governmental agencies. Baker had been under secretary of commerce under Richard Nixon and Gerald Ford, and Reagan's chief of staff. He was Bush's right-hand man. Scowcroft was deputy NSA for the NSC when Henry Kissinger was NSA, and when Kissinger became secretary of state, Scowcroft took on the role of NSA. Bush said Scowcroft handled that job with total dedication and skill. This group emphasized loyalty and teamwork.[96]

Bush favored strengthening presidential powers in the conduct of US foreign policy. His administration endeavored to ease the tension with the Democratic-controlled Congress. Scowcroft established a Congressional Liaison Office within the NSC as a conciliatory gesture toward Congress. After Tiananmen, Scowcroft realized that Congress would become a major problem because it was upset with Beijing's brutality.[97] Congress wanted to impose severe sanctions against China.

Nancy Pelosi's Bill

Although troubled by the Tiananmen crackdown, the Bush administration wanted to restore US-China relations because of China's strategic importance. As Congress was considering more punitive sanctions than the Bush administration had imposed, the administration emphasized that good relations with China were in the best interest of the United States.[98] On June 20, 1989, Secretary Baker testified and revealed sanctions against China before the Senate Foreign Relations Committee. He stated that the United States would seek to freeze lending to China by the World Bank and other international financial institutions.[99] On June 21, Nancy Pelosi introduced the Emergency Chinese Adjustment of Status Facilitation Act of 1989. The bill set a major showdown between Congress and the Bush administration over control of China's policy.[100]

By July 1989, the Chinese student movement began shifting its focus from Tiananmen Square to the US Congress. Zhao Haiqing, working on his Harvard doctorate, became a lobbyist for Chinese students. He worked closely with congressional members and introduced bills on behalf of the Chinese students. Senator Slade Gorton suggested giving these students permanent resident status in the United States, but Zhao supported a moderate bill that suspended the requirement that Chinese students return home. Pelosi sponsored this bill. On July 20, at a congressional hearing, Zhao argued that students who supported the demonstrations would be threatened if they returned to China.[101] By the fall of 1989, Bush had paid little attention to the Pelosi bill. Jeffrey Bader, deputy director of the China Desk at the State Department, informed the White House that this bill should be called to the president's attention. Bader warned that Pelosi's student legislation might soon be approved. Administration officials feared that the legislation, if enacted, might endanger future US-China educational exchanges.[102]

As the administration reviewed the situation following the veto on November 30, there was no chance of sustaining the veto in the House. The only hope was in the Senate. In his final efforts, Bush invited Republican senators to breakfast at the White House. The House voted 390 to 25 on January 24, 1990, to override. On January 25, Bush's efforts in the Senate prevailed, 62 to 37, 3 more votes than the minimum required to sustain the veto.[103]

The MFN Disputes

At the beginning of 1990, Bush tried to restore relations with China, but these efforts caused problems. On February 7, Deputy Secretary of State Lawrence Eagleburger testified before the Senate Foreign Relations Committee on US policy toward China. Eagleburger asserted China's importance in dealing with global issues such as the proliferation of missiles, nuclear and chemical weapons, and environmental pollution.[104] In March, Pelosi circulated a letter inviting colleagues to join a congressional working group to oppose Bush's policies toward China. The Chinese students, backed by Pelosi, pressed for overturning China's Most-Favored Nation (MFN) status. A compromise emerged. Congress would renew China's MFN for a year, but impose a series of human rights conditions that China would have to meet for renewals.[105]

On May 2, 1990, Pelosi submitted a bill establishing strict conditions for China to be accorded MFN treatment. The act prohibited Bush from recommending a continuation of the MFN unless he reported to Congress that China had made significant progress in human rights, trade, and nonproliferation policies.[106] On May 11, Beijing released 211 Tiananmen prisoners. Bush took preemptive action, telling Republican legislators and reporters on May 15 that he intended to renew MFN for China. Bush left little room for doubt

208 *Hedging the China Threat*

in his remarks to reporters. "I want to see MFN for China, . . . We do not want to isolate China."[107] After Bush's announcement on June 3 that he would renew MFN, Beijing released another ninety-seven prisoners. On October 18, the Pease bill, which passed the House by a vote of 384 to 30, proposed that MFN not be extended unless the president submitted a report to Congress stating that China had released all of the Tiananmen prisoners. The formal resolution of disapproval of the president's decision to extend the MFN passed the House in October 1990, but only by a vote of 247 to 174, short of the two-thirds majority needed to override a promised Bush veto.[108]

On November 16, the Senate passed a bill to impose sanctions, including bans on arms sales, satellite exports, police equipment, and nuclear cooperation. The Bush administration was certain that such legislation would result in China terminating the student exchange program. On November 19, the Pelosi bill passed the House by a vote of 403 to 0. The next day in the Senate, it passed by a unanimous voice vote. Bush vetoed the bill. His veto set the executive and legislative branches on a collision course.[109] In November 1992, Bush lost his reelection to Bill Clinton. The veto represented not Bush's strength, but his vulnerability.[110]

The International Level: The Demise of Communist Regimes

With the end of the Cold War, the Bush foreign policy team faced radical global shifts. The collapse of communism in Eastern Europe and the Soviet Union, the reunification of Germany, and the Gulf War stretched the ability of the US foreign policy establishment. Despite Gorbachev's perestroika and glasnost (reconstruction and openness), the Soviet Union still disintegrated. The Chinese Communist Party was afraid that its regime might be next. The United States struggled to follow the rapid changes in international politics.[111]

The Fall of Communist Regimes

Gorbachev said at the Warsaw Pact meeting on July 16, 1988, that each nation should pursue its solution to national problems. Russian troops would begin to be withdrawn. Eastern Europeans freed themselves of one-party dictatorships, without the fear of Soviet intervention in their domestic affairs. Hungary's legislature changed its constitution to allow opposition parties. In November 1989, the Czech government resigned after antigovernment demonstrations. Czechoslovakia had a new government under Vaclav Havel. During the same period, Bulgaria's Communist Party government resigned, and the party surrendered its dominant role. Chinese

Dealing with the Tiananmen Square Crisis   209

leaders viewed these events with alarm. China's media stopped reporting on what was happening in Berlin, Prague, and Warsaw. Chinese party elders were worried about the Western-style economic reforms that Deng and his followers proposed, such as free markets and private enterprise. Chinese conservatives believed that the capitalist West was hostile to China and the United States would take every opportunity to undermine it.[112]

The Gulf War

On August 2, 1990, the Iraqi forces invaded Kuwait. After Iraq's invasion, the Bush administration assembled a coalition to oppose Iraq. Bush articulated the principles that guided Operation Desert Shield: the immediate withdrawal of Iraq from Kuwait, the restoration of the Kuwaiti government, the stability of the Middle East, and the protection of Americans abroad. In November, the UN Security Council passed Resolution 678, which authorized member states to make Iraq withdraw from Kuwait if it had not done so by January 15, 1991. On January 12, the US Congress voted to authorize a coalition of military forces against the Iraq invasion. Operation Desert Storm began on January 17, when US-led coalition forces conducted air strikes against Iraq. On February 24, they launched the ground war and overwhelmed the Iraqi forces. On February 27, coalition troops reached Kuwait City. The next day, a cease-fire was declared. On March 3, General Norman Schwarzkopf, commander in chief of the US forces, met with the Iraqi leadership to dictate the terms of the cease-fire. Operation Desert Storm ended in less than two months. The Iraqi forces were defeated.[113]

Saddam Hussein's invasion of Kuwait allowed the United States and China to cooperate on this crisis. Assistant Secretary of State Richard Solomon flew to Beijing for consultations. Both countries agreed that Iraq's action violated international norms and joined in passing a UN Security Council resolution calling on Baghdad to withdraw. On August 5, Beijing imposed an arms embargo on Iraq, but hesitated when Bush ordered US warships to the Gulf to enforce the embargo. Although it voted in favor of a Security Council resolution in late August to authorize a blockade, China would not support US military activities, nor would it support a joint UN force. China hoped its contribution toward a peaceful resolution would put it in a position to press the European Union and the United States for the reduction of post-Tiananmen sanctions.[114]

By November 1990, the UN resolution set a deadline for Iraqi troops to be withdrawn from Kuwait and authorized the use of force if they were not. On November 7, Baker met Qian in Cairo. Qian indicated that China would not block the passage of a resolution authorizing the use of force. On November 29, with Baker in the chair at the UN Security Council meeting, Qian abstained on the vote, saying China had difficulty voting in favor of

210   *Hedging the China Threat*

using force. The final tally was 12 votes in favor, 2 opposed, and 1 abstention. Baker was furious about China's abstention. Baker told Qian on November 30 that he could not get him on the president's schedule. Qian was outraged and asked Ambassador Zhu Qizhen to call China Desk chief Kent Wiedemann after midnight to find out before 7 A.M. whether Bush would see him. If not, he would not come to Washington. Zhu called Douglas Paal at 1 A.M., demanding to speak with Scowcroft. Scowcroft answered the phone at about 3 A.M. and agreed that Qian could see Bush.[115] Qian became the first senior PRC official to meet Bush since June 1989. Bush told reporters with Qian that both countries had differences in human rights, but they had many things in common.[116]

As the military preparation of US forces in the Gulf region continued, China's sense of alarm grew. Its cooperation with the US-led alliance decreased. After the air attacks on Baghdad began in mid-January 1991, China increased its support for Soviet efforts to resolve the conflict. In early February, Deng described the Gulf War as "big hegemonists beating up small hegemonists."[117] The US military victory in the Gulf War was an enormous shock for the PLA. US technological superiority over Iraq's Chinese-made weapons was overwhelming. It led to great concern among China's leaders about the inferiority of their military technology. In the wake of the Gulf War, the PLA high command overhauled China's concept of warfare, adopting the concept of preparing to fight "modern local wars under high-tech conditions."[118]

Conclusion

While President George H. W. Bush despised Beijing's brutal reaction to the protesting students during the 1989 Tiananmen Square protests, he did not want to worsen the fragile US-China relations. The US Congress demanded harsh retaliation for the PLA's massacre of protestors. The National Security Council and State Department attempted to defuse tensions within the Democratic-controlled Congress. With the end of the Cold War, the Bush administration's foreign policy team faced radical global shifts. They struggled to keep up with the rapid changes in international politics.

There were two particularly significant policy decisions during the Bush administration: first, after the Tiananmen Square crackdown, NSA Brent Scowcroft went to China to keep leaders' lines of communication open; and, second, President Bush decided to sell F-16 fighter jets to Taiwan, which outraged Beijing.

At the individual level, President Bush recognized that China was of strategic importance to both the United States and the Soviet Union. He looked for opportunities to strengthen strategic ties between the United

Dealing with the Tiananmen Square Crisis **211**

States and China. After the PLA raided Tiananmen Square on June 4, 1989, Bush dispatched a covert mission to Beijing to mend relations following US sanctions and the extremely negative US media coverage of the massacre. Concerning Taiwan's issues, Bush decided to sell 150 fighter jets to Taiwan, which would revitalize the US military industry and boost his popularity prior to his reelection campaign.

At the state level, due to the increased tension between the Bush cabinet and Congress, the Bush administration advocated for greater presidential authority in the conduct of US foreign policy. NSA Scowcroft established a Congressional Liaison Office within the NSC to improve relations with Congress. After the Tiananmen Square event, the Pentagon suspended military relations with China. The State Department planned to stop making international loans to China. Congress also imposed harsher economic and technological sanctions on China.

At the international level, there were radical global shifts at the end of the Cold War. The fall of communism in Eastern Europe and the Soviet Union, Germany's reunification, and the war in Iraq tested the US foreign policy establishment. The Chinese Communist Party feared that its regime would follow suit. The United States had overwhelming technological superiority over Iraq's Chinese-made weapons, which raised concerns among China's senior military leaders.

The Chinese had made little secret of their preference for Bush over Bill Clinton, even though they may have felt betrayed by Bush over the F-16 deal. Bush lost the November 1992 presidential election to Clinton.[119] In December 1992, Barbara Franklin, Bush's commerce secretary, traveled to China in hopes of restarting a bilateral trade commission and to facilitate Chinese access to US products. Because Bush was a lame duck president with one month left in office, this trip was criticized back home. The Franklin visit was overshadowed by the November unofficial visit to Taiwan of the US trade representative, Carla Hills, the first US cabinet-level official to travel to Taiwan since 1979. At the close of the Bush administration, both China and the United States desired to improve their relationship, but neither could get the job done.[120]

Notes

1. James Mann, *About Face: A History of America's Curious Relationship with China from Nixon to Clinton* (New York: Knopf, 1999), pp. 175–176.

2. Stephen Knott, "George H. W. Bush: Foreign Affairs," University of Virginia Miller Center, September 30, 2023, https://millercenter.org.

3. Ibid.

4. Mann, *About Face,* p. 177.

5. Qingmin Zhang, "The Bureaucratic Politics of US Arms Sales to Taiwan," *Chinese Journal of International Politics* 1, no. 2 (Winter 2006): 254.

212   Hedging the China Threat

6. James R. Lilley and Jeffrey Lilley, *China Hands Nine Decades of Adventure, Espionage, and Diplomacy in Asia* (New York: Public Affairs, 2005), p. 298.

7. Robert L. Suettinger, *Beyond Tiananmen: The Politics of U.S.-China Relations 1989–2000* (Washington, DC: Brookings Institution Press, 2003), pp. 29–31.

8. Mann, *About Face,* p. 186.

9. Suettinger, *Beyond Tiananmen,* pp. 33–34.

10. Lilley and Lilley, *China Hands Nine Decades,* p. 300.

11. Mann, *About Face,* p. 184.

12. Ibid., p. 187.

13. Lilley and Lilley, *China Hands Nine Decades,* pp. 301–302.

14. Ibid., p. 305.

15. Ibid., pp. 190, 310.

16. Ibid., pp. 315–316.

17. Mann, *About Face,* p. 191.

18. Lilley and Lilley, *China Hands Nine Decades,* p. 324.

19. Mann, *About Face,* p. 191.

20. Ibid., pp. 193–197.

21. Lilley and Lilley, *China Hands Nine Decades,* p. 336.

22. Mann, *About Face,* p. 205.

23. Suettinger, *Beyond Tiananmen,* p. 129.

24. Ibid., p. 130.

25. Mann, *About Face,* p. 251.

26. Suettinger, *Beyond Tiananmen,* p. 130.

27. Ibid., p. 130.

28. Ibid., p. 131.

29. Mann, *About Face,* p. 251.

30. Suettinger, *Beyond Tiananmen,* p. 131

31. Shirley A. Kan, *Democratic Reforms in Taiwan: Issues for Congress* (Washington, DC: Congressional Research Service, May 26, 2010), p. 1.

32. Shelley Rigger, *Politics in Taiwan: Voting for Democracy* (London: Routledge, 2002), p. 131.

33. Kan, *Democratic Reforms in Taiwan,* p. 6.

34. Rigger, *Politics in Taiwan,* pp. 150–151.

35. Ibid., pp. 151–153.

36. Ibid., pp. 153–154.

37. Ibid., pp. 152–154.

38. Richard Bush, *At Cross Purposes: U.S.-Taiwan Relations Since 1942* (London: Taylor and Francis Group, 2004), p. 224.

39. Rigger, *Politics in Taiwan,* pp. 154–155.

40. Ibid., p. 168.

41. Zhang, "Bureaucratic Politics," p. 254.

42. George H. W. Bush and Jeffrey A. Engel, *The China Diary of George H. W. Bush: The Making of a Global President* (Princeton: Princeton University Press, 2008), p. 417.

43. Suettinger, *Beyond Tiananmen,* p. 24.

44. George H. W. Bush and Brent Scowcroft, *A World Transformed* (New York: Vintage Books, 1998), p. 91.

45. Ibid., p. 92.

46. Ibid., p. 94.

47. Ibid., p. 97.

48. Lilley and Lilley, *China Hands Nine Decades,* p. 336.

Dealing with the Tiananmen Square Crisis   213

49. Bush and Scowcroft, *World Transformed,* p. 89.
50. Ibid., p. 98.
51. Ibid., pp. 99–100.
52. Ibid., pp. 101–102.
53. Lilley and Lilley, *China Hands Nine Decades,* p. 338.
54. Mann, *About Face,* pp. 205–206.
55. Bush and Scowcroft, *World Transformed,* pp. 104–105.
56. Ibid., pp. 106–107.
57. Mann, *About Face,* p. 207.
58. Ibid., p. 208.
59. Bush and Scowcroft, *World Transformed,* p. 107.
60. Ibid., p. 108.
61. Ibid., p. 109.
62. Ibid., p. 109.
63. Ibid., pp. 110–111.
64. Mann, *About Face,* p.209.
65. Bush and Scowcroft, *World Transformed,* p. 156.
66. Ibid., p. 157.
67. Mann, *About Face,* pp. 221–216.
68. Bush and Scowcroft, *World Transformed,* pp. 174–175.
69. Ibid., p. 175.
70. Ibid., p. 176.
71. Ibid., p. 176
72. Suettinger, *Beyond Tiananmen,* pp. 100–101.
73. Bush and Scowcroft, *World Transformed,* p. 178.
74. Mann, *About Face,* pp. 222–223.
75. Ibid., p. 257.
76. Suettinger, *Beyond Tiananmen,* p. 140.
77. Bush, *At Cross Purposes,* pp. 222–224.
78. Mann, *About Face,* p. 265.
79. Ibid., pp. 264–265.
80. Zhang, "The Bureaucratic Politics of US Arms Sales to Taiwan," pp. 255–256.
81. Bush, *At Cross Purposes,* p. 224.
82. Mann, *About Face,* p. 266.
83. Suettinger, *Beyond Tiananmen,* p. 39.
84. Zhang, "Bureaucratic Politics," p. 256.
85. Suettinger, *Beyond Tiananmen,* p. 141.
86. Ibid., p. 139.
87. Alan D. Romberg, *Rein In at the Brink of the Precipice: American Policy Toward Taiwan and U.S.-PRC Relations* (Washington, DC: Henry L. Stimson Center, 2003), p. 153.
88. Suettinger, *Beyond Tiananmen,* p. 142.
89. Ibid., p. 141.
90. Ibid., pp. 142–143.
91. Romberg, *Rein In,* p. 50.
92. Ibid., p. 152.
93. Mann, *About Face,* p. 271.
94. Suettinger, *Beyond Tiananmen,* p. 143.
95. "President Bush and Secretary Baker," in *A Short History of the Department of State,* US Department of State, https://history.state.gov.

214   *Hedging the China Threat*

96. Zhang, "Bureaucratic Politics," pp. 252–253.
97. Mann, *About Face,* pp. 193–197.
98. Suettinger, *Beyond Tiananmen,* pp. 93–94.
99. Mann, *About Face,* p. 205.
100. Suettinger, *Beyond Tiananmen,* p. 95.
101. Mann, *About Face,* pp. 210–212.
102. Ibid., p. 214.
103. Bush and Scowcroft, *World Transformed,* p. 178.
104. Mann, *About Face,* pp. 227–228.
105. Ibid., pp. 231–232.
106. Suettinger, *Beyond Tiananmen,* p. 119.
107. Ibid., p. 120.
108. Ibid., pp. 109–110.
109. Bush and Scowcroft, *World Transformed,* pp. 158–159.
110. Suettinger, *Beyond Tiananmen,* p. 133.
111. US Department of State, "Bush's Foreign Policy," Office of Historian of the State Department, https://history.state.gov.
112. Ibid., p. 106.
113. Knott, "George H. W. Bush."
114. Suettinger, *Beyond Tiananmen,* pp. 111–123.
115. Ibid., pp. 113–114.
116. Mann, *About Face,* pp. 249–250.
117. Suettinger, *Beyond Tiananmen,* p. 115.
118. Ibid., p. 117.
119. Ibid., p. 143.
120. Mann, *About Face,* p. 272.

11

The 1995–1996 Taiwan Straight Crisis: The Clinton Administration

FROM 1995 TO 1996, THE WORLD WITNESSED CHINESE MILITARY COERCION against Taiwan. The conflict began with Taiwan president Lee Teng-hui's visit to the United States to attend his college reunion at Cornell University.[1] Following his visit, the People's Liberation Army (PLA) conducted military exercises and missile tests that reached a climax during Taiwan's presidential election in March 1996.[2] Taiwan's initial responses to the 1995 crisis focused on downplaying the threat and increasing readiness, but in 1996 the Taiwanese military strengthened offshore garrisons and established a high-level crisis management mechanism.[3]

China's military intimidation resulted in President Bill Clinton's approval of ordering two aircraft carrier battle groups to the coastal waters of Taiwan to deter the PLA aggression. This crisis reflected the interaction of the Chinese military threat and the US deterrent policy. The Chinese leaders used military exercises to pressure the United States and Taiwan to change their policies. In response, the Clinton administration used deterrence and diplomacy to maintain the security and stability of Taiwan.[4] This chapter explores the major events of the 1995–1996 Taiwan Strait Crisis, Clinton's interest in diminishing the crisis, his administration's crisis management, and the international responses to the crisis.

Historical Events: The Prelude to the Taiwan Strait Crisis

On June 1, 1995, the US State Department granted Lee Teng-hui an entry visa to visit his alma mater from June 7 to 12. In his keynote speech at Cornell, "Always in My Heart," Lee talked about Taiwan's successful democratic

216   *Hedging the China Threat*

reforms and the sovereignty that belonged to the people of Taiwan. His speech resulted in a harsh verbal attack against him by Beijing, accusing him of promoting Taiwan's independence.[5]

Before the Crisis: The Culmination of Discontent

Early in his administration, Lee extended an olive branch to China. He promised to reduce the ROC military's size and to recognize the PRC's jurisdiction over China. In late October 1992, the unofficial Taiwanese Straits Exchange Foundation (SEF) conducted a dialogue with the Chinese Association for Relations Across the Taiwan Strait (ARATS) in Hong Kong. Both organizations aimed to deal with matters created by the cross-strait exchanges, but China pressed Taiwan to engage in political dialogues on One China.[6] The cross-strait conflict was ready to erupt with different beliefs of One China and the US grant of Lee's visa.

Disputes over One China. Although the governments of Taiwan and China adhered to the principle of One China, each government had its own interpretation. Beijing viewed it to be "the People's Republic of China." After unification, Taiwan would become a Special Administrative Region, following the Hong Kong and Macau model, under PRC jurisdiction. Taipei rejected this model, arguing that One China referred to "the Republic of China" from 1912 to the present. Under the ROC constitution, its sovereignty covered the whole of China, but at present its governing geography only extends to Taiwan and some offshore islands. Taipei contended that both the ROC and the PRC were parts of One China. During the SEF-ARATS negotiations, the resulting agreement to disagree was dubbed "the 1992 Consensus." Both sides stated that there was One China, even though they disagreed about what One China meant. Lee insisted that there were two separate sovereign states: the ROC on Taiwan and the PRC on the mainland.[7] His policy on China upset the Chinese leaders.

Taiwan policy review. In 1993, the Clinton administration reviewed the US policy toward Taiwan. Since 1979, the United States had maintained "unofficial" relations with Taiwan. Discontent surfaced, however, over how officials could meet and manage ties with a government that had a strong economy and democracy, but no official status. Some US officials complained that they could not meet with their Taiwanese counterparts in their offices and had to meet them in restaurants to do business. Taiwan's top leaders, such as the president and premier, could not travel to the United States. The policy review was intended to be revised based on the changing circumstances and Taiwan's growing economic importance to the United States.[8]

The 1995–1996 Taiwan Straight Crisis   217

In May 1994, the National Security Council (NSC) and the State Department examined the Taiwan Policy Review. Although aware of growing congressional support in bolstering US ties with Taiwan, they had been proposing changes because of growing concerns about China's reaction and Taiwan's expectations. In early September, Clinton approved changes that included: changing the name of Taiwan's unofficial mission to the Taipei Economic and Cultural Representative Office (TECRO); Taiwan's officials could call on their US counterparts in their offices, except for the State Department and the White House; US representatives could call on the Taiwanese president, premier, and foreign minister in their offices; and Taiwan's top leadership would be permitted to make transit stops in the United States under approved conditions. Beijing's reaction was very negative. The People's Republic of China (PRC) vice foreign minister, Liu Huaqiu, called on the US ambassador to China, J. Stapleton Roy, on September 11, 1994, to protest the changes in the US Taiwan policy.[9]

Taiwan's pragmatic diplomacy. President Lee believed Taiwan should increase its international recognition. His "pragmatic diplomacy" involved seeking to expand contacts with other countries. In 1993, he called for Taiwan to be readmitted to the United Nations and to have access to international organizations. In early 1994, President Lee and Vice President Lien Chan engaged in "vacation diplomacy." They traveled to Southeast Asian countries to meet with senior officials. They also visited Central America, Africa, and Europe, asking for permission to make a transit stop in the United States.[10]

China warned the Clinton administration against allowing Lee to visit the United States. When Lee planned to visit Costa Rica and South Africa, his government asked permission to spend a night in Hawaii for transit. In response, the State Department informed the American Institute in Taiwan (the unofficial US embassy) to inform the Republic of China (ROC) foreign minister, Chien Fu, that Lee's itinerary should not include a stop in the United States. When American Institute in Taiwan (AIT) director Lynn Pascoe informed Chien Fu, Chien angrily responded and called US officials "a bunch of spineless jellyfish" for giving in to Beijing's intimidation.[11]

The Lee administration began lobbying Republican Party leaders that a better balance was needed in US relations with China and Taiwan. Later, the State Department agreed that Lee's aircraft could make a refueling stop in Honolulu on the way to Central America. Fearing that Taiwan supporters would attract media attention at the Honolulu International Airport, it arranged for Lee's plane to be refueled at nearby Hickham Air Force Base. Lee remained on his plane because of the lack of courtesy when it landed to refuel on May 4. The chairman of AIT, Natale Bellocchi, went aboard and found an angry Lee. The story spread to the news media like wildfire. Some

218   *Hedging the China Threat*

members of Congress began to intervene. Senator Paul Simon wrote to Clinton, criticizing his administration for not treating Lee properly. Simon called for cabinet-level exchanges with Taiwan and support for its UN membership. Senators Frank Murkowski and Hank Brown invited Lee to visit the United States. Senator Brown inserted amendments in bills to require the United States to approve a visa for Taiwan's president and other high-level officials.[12]

Lee's visit to his alma mater. The US constraints on the travel of Taiwan's leaders banned Lee from visiting the United States. However, TECRO officials in the United States had established close ties with members of Congress. US lobbying firms were also used to promote Taiwan's interests. The contrast between a democratic Taiwan and an authoritarian China caused Americans to support Taiwan. Congress pressured Clinton on Taiwan issues. On January 12, 1995, the chair of the House International Relations Committee, Benjamin Gilman, held hearings. He and former secretary of state James Baker expressed support for Lee to visit the United States. On March 6, thirty-six members of Congress introduced a resolution in the Senate and House, recommending that Clinton welcome a private visit by Lee to his alma mater.[13] In May, the Senate voted 97 to 1 and the House 360 to 0 in support of a visa. Clinton agreed.[14]

After China was informed of the United States' approval of Lee's visit, the PRC Foreign Ministry called on the US ambassador and demanded that Washington revoke the decision. The United States refused to reverse it. Beijing postponed Defense Minister Chi Haotian's trip to Washington in June 1995. Lee's visit also created US-Taiwan tension. Washington identified Lee's trip as unofficial, but Taiwan wanted it to be official. On June 8, Lee arrived in Los Angeles. Three US senators joined the local officials and crowds in welcoming Lee. In discussions with TECRO, the State Department wanted Lee's speech to be a memory of Lee's years at Cornell and a brief introduction to Taiwan's economic reform. A draft was to be made available for review by US officials, but it arrived the day before the speech was to be delivered. Lee advocated the Taiwan experience and emphasized that communism was dying. He concluded with a request for more contact from international organizations.[15] Benjamin Lu, Taiwan's representative in the United States, assured Winston Lord that Lee's visit would be low key, but Lee made a political speech emphasizing Taiwan's sovereignty. Lord felt betrayed and never agreed to see Lu again.[16]

Beijing reacted furiously by blaming Lee for splitting up the country and mobilizing its propaganda apparatus to demonize him. Within the Politburo Standing Committee, voices calling for retaliation grew stronger. To lessen the tension, Clinton invited the PRC's ambassador to the United States, Li Daoyu, to the White House for a meeting on June 8, even though

Clinton seldom met privately with foreign ambassadors. He emphasized that the Cornell visit did not mark a change in US policy. Li reacted angrily, clenching his fists and pumping his legs. Li was summoned back to Beijing because he was under attack in China for not warning the leadership about Lee's visit. [17]

Three Phases of Military Intimidation

The crises occurred in the Taiwan Strait between July 1995 and March 1996. The PLA conducted three phases of missile tests and military exercises to intimidate Taiwan and influence US policy toward Taiwan.[18]

The first stage (July–August 1995): Military exercises and verbal attacks. Chinese leaders considered the United States granting of the Lee visa as challenging China's opposition to Taiwan's independence. They wanted to push the United States to commit to the One China policy. Foreign Minister Qian stated that the United States must eliminate the effects of Lee's visit. Premier Li Peng demanded that the United States take measures to correct its wrong decision.[19] Lee's visit also worsened China-Taiwan relations. Tang Shubei, vice chairman of ARATS, was in Taipei at the end of May 1995 to plan for the second round of bilateral talks, scheduled to be held on July 20 in Beijing. However, Beijing canceled the talks to protest Lee's visit to the United States In the first stage, China's military objectives were to ensure that the US "One China policy" remained unchanged.[20]

The PLA reportedly presented the military options to President Jiang Zemin, Premier Li Peng, and Central Military Commission (CMC) vice-chairmen Liu Huaqing and Zhang Zhen. This group then presented the options to the Politburo Standing Committee, which decided on the missile-firing exercises.[21] The first military exercise, called East Sea No. 5, was conducted by the navy and air force on Dongshan Island on June 30, 1995. On July 18, China announced that the PLA would conduct missile tests in a target area, eighty-five miles north of Taiwan, from July 21 to 28. China informed foreign aircraft and vessels to stay away from the exercise areas. On July 21 and 22, China launched four short-range M-9 ballistic missiles. On July 24, two medium-range DF-21 ballistic missiles were launched.[22] In late July, in response to China's military actions, Taiwan conducted its own missile launches and naval exercises. In August, the PLA launched the second round of missile tests. Vessels and aircraft conducted live-fire exercises off the coast of Fujian. The Shensheng-95 exercises, which ran from August 15 to 25, included maritime maneuvers of at least 59 naval ships and 192 air sorties. [23] The exercises coincided with Taiwan's Party Congress of the Kuomintang (KMT), during which it nominated its presidential candidate. After Lee received the party endorsement,

220   *Hedging the China Threat*

Beijing leaked news that the PLA was preparing exercises to force Taiwan to cancel the presidential election.[24]

While the PLA engaged in military exercises, Beijing delivered a barrage of verbal attacks against Lee. Beijing accused Lee of harboring a political agenda. His push for democratization, constitutional reform, and pragmatic diplomacy were all designed to lead Taiwan toward independence. Beijing asserted that the Taiwan issue was a domestic affair and warned that the United States should not interfere. In response to Beijing's mounting threat, Taipei mobilized its military for a red alert contingency. The military responded in late July with a naval exercise north of Taiwan. Lee called for building an effective deterrent and rapid-reaction defense force. He announced that the Taiwan military would conduct an exercise in September and October. Beijing responded to Lee's speech with more militant rhetoric at the August 1 celebration of the PLA's founding, with the announcement of a missile exercise on August 11.[25]

The second stage (September–November 1995): Military threat against Taiwan's legislative elections. From September 5 to October 20, the PLA conducted amphibious landing maneuvers in the Yellow Sea. Beijing declared that these exercises were designed to resist separatist activities of pro-independence forces in Taiwan. The PLA conducted additional military exercises from October 31 to November 23. The exercises were conducted south of the Taiwan Strait and included an amphibious landing on Dongshan Island with two air force divisions, 300 navy vessels, and 17,000 troops participating.[26] The exercises simulated an amphibious landing on a Taiwan-held offshore island and attacks on a mock-up of Taiwan's airport. Beijing was satisfied with the outcome of its military threat against Taiwan.[27]

The US media were sympathetic and gave Taiwan positive press. They emphasized that the United States must reject military bullying from Beijing against Taiwan. They suggested that the US strategy needed clarity rather than ambiguity. After months of congressional hearings and editorial discourses, Clinton decided to take military action to warn China not to miscalculate the situation. As early as December 1995, the US aircraft carrier *Nimitz* battle group passed through the Taiwan Strait. Pentagon officials claimed that the *Nimitz* had been scheduled to sail along Taiwan's east coast but changed its route to the Taiwan Strait because of bad weather. However, there was no record of a tropical storm off Taiwan at that time.[28]

The third stage (January-March 1996): Increased military coercion to affect the election. Beijing closely observed Taiwan's presidential election in March 1996. Beijing was concerned that the election would legitimize Lee using the independence issue to secure his presidency. Premier Li Peng stated that China's commitment to using force was directed against foreign forces to bring about Taiwan's independence. President Jiang said that if Taiwan did not abandon its independence activities, the China-Taiwan struggle would not stop. From late January through February 1996, the PLA amassed more than 100,000 troops in Fujian Province. Their size raised alarm in the United States. The US military did not believe the exercises were a prelude to a military attack against Taiwan, but they warned China not to take military action. On March 4, China announced that the PLA would conduct missile tests from March 8 to 18.[29]

The exercises simulated an invasion of Taiwan that occurred in three waves. The first wave took place on March 8. The PLA fired three DF-15 missiles into two target areas less than fifty miles from the northern port of Keelung and the southern port of Kaohsiung.[30] The Clinton administration believed that if it did not respond strongly, Beijing would doubt the US commitment to Taiwan's security. On March 10, Clinton agreed to deploy two aircraft carrier battle groups toward Taiwan.[31] The second wave occurred on March 12 when the PLA conducted live-fire exercises at the southern end of the Taiwan Strait. The third wave, from March 18 to 25, centered on a joint amphibious assault exercise near the Haitan Islands, at the northern end of the Taiwan Strait. The PLA assembled 150,000 troops and 300 aircraft and navy vessels. The PLA finished its exercises after Taiwan's election on March 23.[32]

US Reactions to China's Military Coercion

In 1995, the Clinton administration responded during the first stage with the purpose of restoring its relations with China. US officials interpreted China's July missile tests and subsequent military exercises as an effort by the Beijing authority to send a warning to Lee. US responses were restrained and sought to avoid escalation. They consisted of statements and reassurances to Beijing that the US policy toward China had not changed. US officials reacted to the missile tests by stating that "they do not contribute to peace and stability" in the region.[33]

In January 1996, Chas Freeman, former assistant secretary of defense, heard of an indirect PLA nuclear threat against the United States over Taiwan. Lieutenant General Xiong Guangkai, deputy chief of the PLA General Staff, stated that in the 1950s, the United States threatened nuclear attacks on China. The United States could do that because China was unable to retaliate. He continued, "Now we can. So, you will not threaten us again because you care more about Los Angeles than Taipei."[34]

In early February, the US Office of Naval Intelligence reported that the PLA began to mobilize missiles, heavy equipment, and several brigades to Fujian Province. Undersecretary of State Peter Tarnoff warned his Chinese

222   *Hedging the China Threat*

counterpart, Deputy Foreign Minister Li Zhaoxing against military aggression. Tarnoff read from the Taiwan Relations Act, which directed the White House to resist any military threat against Taiwan.[35] The Clinton administration believed that if the United States did not respond with strength, Beijing would doubt the US commitment to Taiwan's security. On March 10, Clinton ordered two aircraft carrier battle groups to the Taiwan Strait to deter the PRC from escalating the crisis.[36]

Taiwan's Reactions to China's Military Exercises

After the PLA's July 1995 missile launches, Taiwan established a high-level crisis management team consisting of officials from the President's Office, the NSC, and the Executive Yuan. Under guidance from the President's Office, the NSC set up a staff-level team focused on the crisis, the military established an intelligence support team, and the National Security Bureau (NSB) set up a team to collect intelligence. The NSC believed China had three objectives for the 1996 exercises: to push Lee to step down, to force Taiwan to postpone the presidential election, and to minimize votes for Lee. The National Security Bureau (NSB) saw three levels of intensity. The lowest level action was propaganda. Medium-intensity actions would include limited military actions such as missile launches, disrupting resupply to offshore islands, and aircraft flights over the middle line in the Taiwan Strait. High-intensity actions would include a blockade of Taiwan or the offshore islands. The military was prepared, but avoiding actions that might escalate tensions.[37]

US-Taiwan Communications

The United States and Taiwan had three main communication channels during the crisis. The most important was between the State Department and the Ministry of Foreign Affairs (MOFA), working through the AIT and TECRO. The second channel was between Pentagon officials and the Taiwan military mission in Washington. A third channel was established between the United States and Taiwan's NSCs in New York.[38]

The State Department-Ministry of Foreign Affairs channel. The first channel was MOFA (represented in the United States by TECRO) and the State Department (represented in Taiwan by the AIT). AIT director Lynn Pascoe regularly interacted with President Lee, Foreign Minister Fred Chien, and NSC secretary general Ding Mou-shih. The AIT Liaison Affairs Section, whose representatives were de facto defense attachés, had good access to the Taiwan military. The Central Intelligence Agency (CIA) station chief in Taipei had a good relationship with Taiwan's National Security Bureau.

The other side of this channel was in Washington between TECRO and the State Department.[39]

The Pentagon-TECRO military mission channel. The second communication channel was between the two militaries. This channel involved the TECRO military mission meeting with Deputy Assistant Secretary of Defense Kurt Campbell and the director for China in the Office of the Secretary of Defense, Karl Eikenberry, to discuss arms sales and security cooperation. The Taiwan military mission received briefings about US assessments of the PLA force activities through this channel during the crisis. The military mission kept TECRO representative Benjamin Lu informed about its conversations with the Pentagon.[40]

The National Security Council channel. The third channel, the US-Taiwan NSCs, was established in March 1996, with secret meetings between Deputy NSA Sandy Berger, Undersecretary of State Tarnoff, and Taiwan NSC secretary general Ding Mou-shih in New York. Berger sought to ensure that Taiwan's leadership understood the rationale for the US carrier deployments, to reiterate US support for Taiwan, and to persuade Taiwan's leaders to cancel military exercises planned for March. Ding agreed that Taiwan would delay the exercises, diminishing US concern about escalating actions after the PLA's March exercises concluded.[41] Neither TECRO nor the AIT had been informed of the meeting. Ding delivered Washington's messages to President Lee. After an intelligence briefing on the PLA exercises, Berger and Tarnoff went straight to the main points. The United States was deploying two aircraft carrier battle groups (CBGs) to the region as a demonstration of the US commitment to the security of Asia Pacific. Ding assured them that Taiwan did not want to provoke Beijing and would cooperate with the United States to ease tensions.[42]

During the 1996 Taiwan Strait Crisis, Taipei exchanged a wide range of intelligence with Washington. Observers have speculated that the US reaction to China's coercion of Taiwan encouraged the Clinton administration to shift from strategic ambiguity to strategic clarity.

The Post-1996 Taiwan Strait Crisis

To avoid escalating the crisis, the United States requested that Taipei and Beijing exercise restraint and resume dialogue that would lead to a peaceful resolution. On March 25, 1996, Beijing declared the completion of its military exercises. The US battle groups also departed the Taiwan Strait as the tension subsided.[43]

Strengthening Taiwan's security. A series of PLA missile tests and exercises in 1996 raised concerns over Taiwan's security. US security experts stated

224   *Hedging the China Threat*

the need to strengthen Taiwan's missile defense and antisubmarine capability. During their visit in April 1998, former CIA director James Woolsey and a specialist on China, Michael Pillsbury, offered their advice to enhance Taiwan's security. Woolsey urged Taiwan to enhance its intelligence and surveillance, to work on its air defense in the short term, and to improve its missile defense system in the long term. Pillsbury said that his meetings with the PLA generals gave him the impression that Taiwan was preparing for the wrong war. He said Taiwan's military focused on air, coastal, and antisubmarine defense. The PRC strategy, however, was to destroy Taiwan's radar warning sites and electrical power grids.[44]

The United States pushes for the resumption of cross-strait dialogues. In early 1998, some former US officials suggested that China and Taiwan should resume their dialogue and improve relations. For example, while visiting Taiwan in January, former assistant secretary of defense for international security affairs Joseph Nye, advocated that Taiwan not seek independence, Beijing renounce the use of force, and the United States not recognize Taiwan's independence. On the heels of Nye's visit, a delegation led by former secretary of defense William Perry arrived in Taipei. The delegation brought a message from China that Beijing would resume negotiations with Taipei. From 1998, the United States pushed Taiwan and China to resume dialogue. Anthony Lake, a former national security advisor (NSA), stated that it was in the interests of China and Taiwan to resume their dialogue. Taipei and Beijing did resume their suspended dialogue in April 1998, when a deputy negotiator from the Taiwan semiofficial Straits Exchange Foundation met with his China counterpart on the first fence-mending trip in nearly three years.[45]

The Individual Level: Clinton's Consent to Lee's Visit and Clinton-Jiang Summits

During the 1992 presidential campaign, Clinton approved of George H. W. Bush's decision to sell F-16 aircraft to Taiwan. Clinton also voiced his support for the US commitment to help Taiwan defend itself under the TRA.[46] On November 3, Clinton was elected president. His campaign theme had emphasized that economic issues counted most for US voters, and he had criticized Bush for not paying enough attention to US values such as human rights.[47] Clinton had a good impression of Taiwan when he was governor of Arkansas. Before taking the presidency, he visited Taiwan four times, where he witnessed Taiwan's economic and political progress. He was treated as an honorable political celebrity in Taiwan. Clinton's interactions with China's top leaders, however, had been tense. During his first meet-

The 1995–1996 Taiwan Straight Crisis   225

ing with President Jiang in Seattle in 1993, Jiang lectured Clinton on the hegemonic nature of US interference in China's domestic affairs.[48]

Clinton's Consent to Lee's Visit

The United States' decision to issue Lee Teng-hui a visa reflected the president's sentiments toward Taiwan. Clinton defended his decision by suggesting that turning Lee down would have violated his fundamental rights. In the United States, people had the constitutional right to travel. Clinton argued, "It is very difficult in America to justify not allowing a citizen of the world . . . to come to his college reunion and to travel around our country."[49] In the spring of 1995, Clinton did not want to yield to China's pressure. He had enough lectures from Beijing. "Just as the Chinese demanded us to respect their own way, they have to respect our way," Clinton said at one of the discussions with national security teams about Lee's visit. He emphasized that the United States was supposed to be sensitive to China, and that they also "needed to be sensitive to us."[50]

Clinton decided to support an unprecedented visit by Lee. Clinton held a round of talks with congressional leaders and his foreign policy team. On May 8, Clinton discussed the US budget with several senators. Senator Charles Robb then raised the subject of the State Department's refusal to permit Lee to attend his reunion. Clinton assured the senators he was leaning toward granting Lee a visa. By the time the Clinton foreign policy team realized it, they had little choice but to approve Lee's trip. Anthony Lake also said, "We just can't be absolutely steamrolled by Beijing or let Beijing's sensitivities totally dominate us as we make these decisions."[51]

On May 22, 1995, a White House spokesman announced that Lee would be given a visa to visit the United States as a private individual. By saying no to Beijing, Clinton could improve his domestic position. That was important after the Democratic Party's setback in the mid-term elections of 1994. For the first time since 1948, Republicans seized control of both Houses of Congress. The Republican Congress attacked Clinton on China policy. Both parties were sympathetic to Taiwan. Clinton had to deal carefully with Congress.[52] Risking Beijing's anger, Clinton allowed Taiwan's president to visit the United States. In Beijing, the Foreign Ministry condemned the decision as "an extremely serious act of brazenly creating two Chinas," and called on Washington to rescind its action.[53]

The Clinton-Jiang Summit

The China policy under Clinton was grounded on engagement and enlargement. He believed US-China relations were important because China was too strong to ignore. Since Clinton took office in 1992, he and Jiang held

226 *Hedging the China Threat*

eleven meetings between 1993 and 2001. Their main topics of discussion covered US-China relations, Taiwan issues, and international issues of common concern. Regarding the Taiwan issues, several summits stood out.[54]

Unofficial summit meetings from 1993 to 1995. During his 1992 presidential campaign, Clinton accused Bush of "coddling dictators" in its policy toward Beijing. On November 19 and 20, 1993, Clinton met with Jiang during the informal Asia-Pacific Economic Cooperation (APEC) summit in Seattle.[55] Clinton was preoccupied with US complaints about human rights violations in China. He showed no emotion as photographers shot the beginning of the meeting with Jiang.[56] Their talks focused on North Korea's nuclear developments, human rights, arms proliferation, and the US trade deficit with China. On Taiwan's issues, Clinton promised to pursue the One China policy and observe the principles enshrined in the three US-China communiqués.[57] Both sides declared the meeting a successful beginning, but they admitted that there was a long way to go.[58]

On November 14, 1994, Clinton met with Jiang at a summit meeting at the APEC forum in Jakarta. Jiang complained to Clinton about US policy toward Taiwan because the Clinton administration announced an upgrading of the US policy on contacts with Taiwan.[59] Jiang said that China would not "sit idly by" if Taiwan were to pursue "Taiwan independence" with the assistance of foreign intervention. Clinton responded with the mantra that the United States would abide by the three communiqués and maintain the One China policy.[60] On October 24, 1995, Jiang and Clinton had an unofficial summit in New York that focused on trade disputes, arms proliferation, and human rights issues. Regarding Lee's visit to the United States, Clinton stated that such visits would be "unofficial, private, and rare" and decided on a case-by-case basis. Clinton offered confidential assurances that Washington would not support Taiwan's independence and membership in the UN.[61]

The 1997 Jiang visit to the United States. On October 29, 1997, Jiang visited the White House and was hosted at a state dinner. During the summit, both leaders reached the following agreements: to have dialogues between cabinet officials on security issues, establish a presidential hotline, urge North Korea to join four-party talks, and strengthen bilateral military contacts.[62] Clinton assured Jiang that the United States did not support a Two China policy, Taiwan independence, or Taiwan membership in the UN or other international organizations requiring statehood. Although China could not get the United States to agree to include Clinton's assurances in an official statement, this was the first time the US government publicly stated that it did not support Taiwan's independence.[63] Clinton emphasized that a key to Asia's stability was a peaceful China-Taiwan relationship, hoping that Beijing and Taipei would resume a constructive dialogue. In response,

The 1995–1996 Taiwan Straight Crisis   227

Jiang stated that Deng Xiaoping proposed One Country, Two Systems to settle the Taiwan question. China would not commit to renouncing the use of force. The reasons for China's use of force were directed against the external forces that interfered in China's internal affairs and those who wanted to achieve the independence of Taiwan.[64]

In July 1999, President Lee described China and Taiwan's relationship as a "special state-to-state relationship." Outraged by Lee's actions, Beijing canceled the upcoming cross-strait meeting, conducted extensive military exercises in Fujian, and sent its aircraft over the midline of the Taiwan Strait. Concerned that Lee's statement could lead to renewed tension, the United States pressured him to modify his policy and to allow the dialogue to resume. Clinton had postponed arms sales to Taiwan to avoid worsening the situation. When Clinton met with Jiang in New Zealand in September 1999, he cautioned China not to use military force against Taiwan. He reasserted US support for its One China policy and complained about Lee's statement.[65]

The State Level:
The Clinton Administration Responds to the Crisis

The NSC and Pentagon, and particularly their leaders, played a significant role in dealing with the Taiwan Strait Crisis. NSA Anthony Lake maintained friendly relations with Secretary of State Warren Christopher. Lake initially kept a low profile, avoiding public appearances, but in response to criticism that Clinton had not adequately explained his foreign policy, Lake began to appear as a public speaker.[66] Secretary of Defense William Perry was well received in the Pentagon. After taking office, Perry endeavored to improve relations with China. However, when China threatened Taiwan during the Taiwan presidential election, he suggested Clinton send two aircraft carrier groups to counter China's military threat.[67]

The NSC's Decisionmaking During the Crisis

On March 6, 1995, thirty-six members of Congress introduced a concurrent resolution in the Senate and House, recommending that Clinton indicate that the United States would welcome a private visit by Lee. On May 2, the House passed the resolution calling on Clinton to allow Lee to come to the United States on a private visit by a vote of 396 to 0. A week later, the Senate passed the resolution by a margin of 97 to 1.[68] Christopher, Perry, and Lake realized that Clinton felt strongly that Lee should have the right to travel to Cornell. They feared that if they continued to deny his visa, Congress would enact binding legislation requiring it to permit Lee's trip.[69]

228   *Hedging the China Threat*

The NSC's recommendation for Lee's visa. The main concern of Anthony Lake was that the administration was driven by Congress on Lee's visit. At the meeting with Christopher and Perry on May 17, 1995, the three agreed to find a way for Lee to get his visa, yet minimize damage to US-PRC relations. The director for Asian affairs at the NSC, Robert Suettinger, had prepared a memorandum for Clinton. Suettinger's memo included two alternative recommendations: first, to hold out against allowing Lee's visit; and, second, to work quietly with Taipei and Beijing to structure a visit that would be manageable. However, Lake wanted Suettinger to reverse the order of the recommendations, giving preference to granting a visa. Suettinger asked to include an annotation on the likely PRC reaction to Lee's visit: another deep freeze for US-China relations, a decline in PRC-Taiwan relations, and the PRC conducting military exercises and missile tests. Lake agreed. The memorandum moved to the president's office. Clinton approved it.[70] Before the decision was made public, the administration attempted to minimize the damage. ROC officials were informed that Lee could travel to the United States, but that his visit was strictly private. On May 20, Lake and Tarnoff called in the PRC ambassador, Li Daoyu, to deliver the news.[71]

The NSC's Three No's policy. The NSC was taken aback by Beijing's strong reaction to Lee's visit and sought ways to restore US-China relations.[72] Henry Kissinger led a delegation of the America-China Society to China. He had meetings with President Jiang, Premier Li, and Foreign Minister Qian in early July 1995. Premier Li criticized the United States for shaking the foundation of bilateral relations. Kissinger later met with Clinton and advised him that the United States should engage with the Chinese in "strategic" terms based on US interests to improve bilateral relations. China specialists in the State Department and the NSC considered inviting Jiang to the United States.[73] The NSC prepared a draft letter for Clinton to Jiang. Christopher would deliver the letter to Qian at the APEC ministerial meeting. It included hope for improved bilateral relations and the US Three No's policy. The Three No's stated that the United States did not support: (1) efforts to create Two Chinas or One China, One Taiwan; (2) Taiwan's independence; or (3) Taiwan's admission to the United Nations. China interpreted the Three No's policy to mean "oppose" rather than "support" Taiwan's independence.[74]

The Pentagon Under Perry's Leadership: Countering China's Threat

William Perry had emerged as a strong proponent of developing strong relations with the Chinese leadership. During the Jimmy Carter administration, he was involved in US defense cooperation with China against the Soviet Union. During the 1980s, he visited China while working for a Stanford

The 1995–1996 Taiwan Straight Crisis   229

University center on arms control. Perry referred to Liu Huaqing, vice chairman of the Central Military Commission, as "my old friend." He also knew Jiang Zemin when he was the minister in charge of the electronics industry.[75]

Perry's visit to China. In October 1994, Perry visited China, erasing the restrictions on high-level military contacts that had been in place since 1989. Perry encouraged more transparency of the PLA budget to ease US concerns.[76] He argued that joint efforts on defense exchanges could be a positive step toward new cooperation between the two militaries. Perry's top priority in Beijing was obtaining China's assistance in dealing with North Korea. In June 1994, China told North Korea that it might go along with a UN resolution imposing sanctions. During Perry's visit to China, North Korea was hesitating to sign a written agreement to close its nuclear installations. Perry asked China to convey a US message to Pyongyang. The message was that the United States was prepared to take strong sanctions against North Korea, that it was prepared to send more troops to South Korea, and that it was prepared to risk a war. North Korea agreed, in writing, to dismantle its nuclear installations.[77] Perry's visit to China, however, did not prevent the confrontation between the two militaries. In October 1994, the US aircraft carrier *Kitty Hawk* had been cruising in international waters in the Yellow Sea when its antisubmarine aircraft detected a PLA submarine. US planes tracked the submarine. In response, the PLA sent jet fighters toward the US aircraft. A Chinese official informed the US defense attaché that the next time such an incident occurred, the PLA would give the order to shoot.[78]

The Pentagon sends carriers to Taiwan waters. After the November 1995 PLA exercises, the CIA set up a special task force to monitor Chinese military activities in the Taiwan Strait. The CIA assessment concluded that military action by the PLA could not be ruled out.[79] By early December 1995, US officials had gathered intelligence of PLA plans for a March 1996 exercise. The NSC, the State Department, and the military were proceeding with contingency planning. The process began with meetings between NSC Asian affairs director Robert Suettinger, State Department Office of Chinese Affairs director Jeff Bader, and Joint Chiefs of Staff (JCS) J5 deputy director for Asia Robert Foglesong. The Pentagon soon took over military planning. In late February 1996, Clinton was briefed by General John Shalikashvili on military options to respond to PLA military aggression, which included the possible use of nuclear weapons. Clinton observed the risks of escalation to the nuclear level and said, "We've got to do all we can to avoid this."[80]

In December 1995, the assistant secretary of defense for international security affairs, Joseph Nye, visited China. When a Chinese official asked how the United States would respond to China's attack on Taiwan, Nye replied that it would depend on the circumstances. He stated that in 1950 the United States had said it would not become involved in Korea, then reversed

230   *Hedging the China Threat*

itself.[81] By the end of 1995, the Pentagon was taking steps to counter the PLA intimidation. On December 19, the aircraft carrier *Nimitz* sailed through the Taiwan Strait. It was the first time the US carrier had appeared in the Taiwan Strait since 1979.[82] In February 1996, a Pentagon-established Taiwan-China situation task force determined that the PLA was not preparing to attack Taiwan, but was trying to influence Taiwan's presidential election.[83]

On March 7, a Chinese delegation headed by the director of the Office of the Central Foreign Affairs Working Committee, Liu Huaqiu, arrived in Washington. Perry and Lake warned that any military action against Taiwan would have "grave consequences."[84] On March 8, China began a new round of missile firings. The US reconnaissance aircraft had monitored three PLA ballistic missiles that were fired toward waters adjacent to Taiwan's two largest ports: Kaohsiung and Chilung.[85] US intelligence assessed it as a major escalation. Lake urged China to cease provocative missile testing and return to the cross-strait dialogue.[86] Perry told Liu that China was "bracketing" Taiwan. This technique could precede a direct attack. Perry notified Liu that China's military exercises were reckless and unacceptable.[87]

On March 9, Perry and Shalikashvili from the military, Christopher and Lord representing the State Department, and Lake and Berger from the NSC gathered at Perry's office to consider how the United States should respond to China's missile tests. Perry initially favored an aggressive reaction, sending one or more carrier battle groups through the Taiwan Strait to demonstrate that the United States would not be intimidated. Shalikashvili objected because it was provocative, and carrier assets were already fully deployed. But in the end, the participants agreed that two carrier battle groups would be deployed.[88] Perry later explained, "We considered sending one carrier, but decided that wasn't strong enough. We considered sending two carriers and docking them by Taipei. We decided that was provocative."[89] Later in the afternoon, the group briefed the president, who concurred with the decision.[90]

Secretary Christopher appeared on NBC on March 10 and confirmed that the *Independence* would be sent closer to Taiwan. He did not mention the redeployment of the *Nimitz*. That announcement was confirmed by the Pentagon on March 12. Since the *Nimitz* was stationed in the Gulf, it was expected to arrive in the waters bordering Taiwan on March 23, the date of Taiwan's presidential elections.[91] "It was very tense. . . . We were up all night for weeks. We prepared the war plans, the options," said a senior defense official. In Honolulu, Admiral Joseph Prueher ordered the Pacific Command to form a "crisis action team" to coordinate intelligence and air-and-sea operations around the clock.[92] "Beijing should know, and this US fleet will remind them, that while they are a great military power, the strongest military power in the Western Pacific is the U.S.," Perry said to Congress.[93] The deployment of the two carriers would signal to the Chinese that the United States had a national interest in regional stability.[94]

The 1995–1996 Taiwan Straight Crisis   231

Taiwan's presidential elections took place on March 23, and Lee garnered 54 percent of the popular vote among the four candidates.[95] No further exercises were scheduled. Taipei canceled its exercise at Washington's suggestion. The US carriers returned to regular duty stations shortly after the election, and the crisis quietly ended.[96] The Clinton administration believed that if the US military had not responded, Beijing would have doubted the US commitment to Taiwan's security. China would have been encouraged to escalate its military activities in a future confrontation. Perry believed that the United States had to demonstrate its military resolve. Christopher also stated that because Asia Pacific countries looked to the United States to preserve stability in the region, the United States had to take action to calm down the situation.[97]

The International Level:
Responses from the Regional Countries

The impact of the 1995–1996 Taiwan Strait Crisis went beyond the boundary of Taiwan. China's military coercion became the focus of worldwide attention because commercial flights and shipping in the Taiwan Strait had to be rerouted for safety considerations. Asian leaders began to speculate on the possible impact of a military conflict on the regional economy and security. After the crisis, Clinton visited Tokyo and signed an agreement with Japanese prime minister Ryutaro Hashimoto in April 1996. Clinton and Hashimoto extended the security treaty even though the Cold War rationale had disappeared. The PLA's military coercion against Taiwan helped solidify the US-Japan alliance. Clinton delivered a speech when he boarded the aircraft carrier *Independence* in Japan, emphasizing that the presence of the carrier near Taiwan had helped to "calm a rising storm." [98] The US military response had attracted the attention of leaders throughout Asia.

Japan's Responses

The Japanese government expressed its concern publicly and urged Beijing to exercise restraint concerning the cross-strait tension. Japan had made a bilateral defense pact with the United States, considering the enhanced prospect of military conflicts in its neighborhood.[99] The Japanese government summoned the PRC ambassador to Japan, Xu Dunxin, to voice its concern about the Chinese threat that caused the tension in the Taiwan Strait. On March 1, 1996, Prime Minister Ryutaro Hashimoto conveyed to Premier Li Peng that Japan hoped that China and Taiwan would resolve their conflicts peacefully. He asked China for self-restraint. Hashimoto later confided that he could not sleep well during the crisis because of the intense tension.[100] Foreign Minister

232 Hedging the China Threat

Yukihiko Ikeda told his Chinese counterpart, Qian Qichen, that he did not approve of China's war games and hoped the Taiwan issue could be settled through dialogue. Some Foreign Ministry officials admitted that if US forces decided to protect Taiwan and asked Japan to provide logistical support, Japan could not say no. Hideo Usui, director general of the Japan Defense Agency, said Japan would keep a close eye on China's missile tests. After the Taiwan Strait Crisis, the US-Japan security partnership was redefined. The US-Japan Alliance for the 21st Century was signed in Tokyo on April 17, 1996. The new alliance relations required Japan and the United States to promote a more robust policy coordination. It included studies on cooperation in dealing with situations that may emerge in the areas surrounding Japan. The scope of the treaty has later broadened beyond its previous focus on the defense of Japan to the East China Sea, including Taiwan.[101] Many in Japan believed that China's use of force against Taiwan would destabilize East Asian security.[102]

Australia's Responses

Australia's concerns were more direct. When the John Howard government took office on March 11, 1996, a crisis between China and Taiwan had escalated with the deployment of two US aircraft carrier groups to the region. On March 12, the PRC ambassador in Canberra was called in to hear expressions of concern from Foreign Minister Alexander Downer. In an unprecedented step, Downer declared clear support for the US forces deployed in the region, stating: "We have seen in the last few days a very clear demonstration by the U.S. that it is interested in maintaining its involvement in the security of the region and we obviously welcome that."[103] Defense Minister Ian McLachlan also endorsed the strong US naval response in support of Taiwan. The US-Australia Strategic Partnership for the 21st Century was declared at the US-Australia defense talks in Sydney on July 30. Australia was the only country in the region to publicly ally itself with the United States against China over the Taiwan issue.[104]

Responses from the Regional Countries

China's coercion came at a price. The region's countries were forced to intensify their focus on "the rise of China" and its implications for regional stability. As for Southeast Asian countries, they aired their concern about the increasing China threat. The image of a China threat had already emerged in the minds of Asian people before the missile crisis, especially those of China's neighboring countries. The missile intimidation, however, solidified that image and rendered it a reality.[105] Apart from Australia, countries in the Asia Pacific region did not openly criticize China's behavior. For example, South Korea was carefully neutral. The Philippines was worried by what it

The 1995–1996 Taiwan Straight Crisis   233

perceived to be the manifestation of China's assertiveness on territorial issues. Russia, Malaysia, Thailand, and Indonesia expressed the view that as the Taiwan issue was an internal Chinese matter, it should be resolved by China and Taiwan themselves, and outside powers should not interfere.[106]

Conclusion

During the Clinton administration, the president believed that US-China relations must be a major priority simply because China was too powerful to ignore. Nonetheless, Clinton reversed a policy that had denied the hosting of Taiwanese dignitaries in the United States when he agreed to allow the president of Taiwan, Lee Teng-hui, to visit his alma mater, Cornell University. In response, the PRC launched a military threat against Taiwan that ushered in the 1995–1996 Taiwan Strait Crisis. China's military coercion became the focus of worldwide attention when commercial flights and shipping in the Taiwan Strait had to be rerouted for safety considerations.

Primary policy outcomes during the Clinton years include: first, President Clinton's consent to Lee's visit to the United States; second, the United States sending two carriers to the Taiwan Strait during the 1995–1996 crisis; and third, the Clinton administration releasing the Three No's Policy (no US support for Taiwan independence, no support for a Two China or One China, One Taiwan policy, and no support for Taiwan's admittance into any international organization that requires statehood for membership).

At the individual level, Clinton had a good impression of Taiwan. As a governor of Arkansas, Clinton visited Taiwan four times and witnessed Taiwan's economic and democratic progress. Clinton's interactions with China's top leaders, however, had been tense. During his first meeting with President Jiang Zemin, Jiang criticized the hegemonic nature of US interference in China's domestic affairs.

At the state level, the CIA set up a special task force to monitor PLA activities during the Taiwan Strait Crisis. In late February 1996, Clinton was briefed by the chairman of the JCS, General Shalikashvili, on military options to respond to PLA military aggression. In March, the Pentagon, the State Department, and the NSC decided to send two carriers to the waters near Taiwan. Clinton supported the decision.

At the international level, after the Taiwan Strait Crisis, Clinton signed an agreement with Japanese prime minister Hashimoto in April 1996. The agreement extended the security treaty even though the original Cold War rationale had disappeared. In general, regional countries' reactions to the PRC military coercion against the Taiwan presidential election was negative, especially those of Japan and Australia. As a result, Japan and Australia tightened their ties with the United States against future Chinese aggression.

234   Hedging the China Threat

The 1995–1996 Taiwan Strait Crisis showed that China and Taiwan's confrontation could easily draw the United States and China into military conflict. After a series of US-China negotiations and the US show of force to deter China's military escalation, the crisis began to lessen. Following the crisis, the United States and China began to engage in economic cooperation and military engagement. Because 1996 was a US presidential election year, Republican hopeful, George W. Bush, began to criticize the Clinton administration for appeasing Beijing, sacrificing Taiwan's interests, and putting Taiwan in the hands of the Chinese Communist regime.

Notes

1. Shao-cheng Sun, "A Study on the United States Military Security Commitments to the Republic of China (1949–1998)" (Master's thesis, National Defense University, Taipei, 1998), p. 153.

2. Robert S. Ross, "The 1995–96 Taiwan Strait Confrontation: Coercion, Credibility, and the Use of Force," *International Security* 25, no. 2 (Fall 2000): 87.

3. Kristen Gunness and Phillip C. Saunders, *Averting Escalation and Avoiding War: Lessons from the 1995–1996 Taiwan Strait Crisis* (Washington, DC: National Defense University Press, December 2022), p. 2.

4. Ross, "1995–96 Taiwan Strait Confrontation," pp. 87–89.

5. David Chou, ed., "U.S. Roles in the 1995–1996 Taiwan Strait Crisis," in *Security Relationship Between the U.S. and Taiwan: After the 1996 Mini-Crisis,* edited by David Chou (Taipei: Mei-de, 1997), p. 23.

6. Ted Galen Carpenter, *America's Coming War with China: A Collision Course over Taiwan* (New York: Palgrave Macmillan, 2005), pp. 62–64.

7. Ibid., pp. 64–65.

8. Robert Suettinger, *Beyond Tiananmen: The Politics of U.S.-China Relations 1989–2000* (Washington, DC: Brookings Institution Press, 2003), pp. 205–206.

9. Ibid., pp. 206–207.

10. Ibid., pp. 202–203.

11. Ibid., p. 204.

12. Ibid., pp. 204–205.

13. Ibid., pp. 211–214.

14. Ross, "1995–96 Taiwan Strait Confrontation," p. 91.

15. Suettinger, *Beyond Tiananmen,* pp. 218–220.

16. Barton Gellman, "U.S. and China Nearly Came to Blows in 1996," *Washington Post,* June 21, 1998.

17. Suettinger, *Beyond Tiananmen,* pp. 220–221.

18. Gunness and Saunders, *Averting Escalation and Avoiding War,* pp. 8–14.

19. Ross, "1995–96 Taiwan Strait Confrontation," pp. 91, 94.

20. Gunness and Saunders, *Averting Escalation and Avoiding War,* p. 14.

21. Ibid., pp. 14–15.

22. Suettinger, *Beyond Tiananmen,* pp. 225–226.

23. Gunness and Saunders, *Averting Escalation and Avoiding War,* pp. 15–16.

24. Sun, "Study," p. 155.

25. Suettinger, *Beyond Tiananmen,* pp. 224–226.

26. Gunness and Saunders, *Averting Escalation and Avoiding War,* pp. 16–17.

The 1995–1996 Taiwan Straight Crisis   235

27. Ross, "1995–96 Taiwan Strait Confrontation," pp. 102–103.
28. Chou, "U.S. Roles," p. 26.
29. Ross, "1995–96 Taiwan Strait Confrontation," pp. 104–107.
30. Gunness and Saunders, *Averting Escalation and Avoiding War,* pp. 17–18.
31. Hidenori Ijiri, "The China-Taiwan Problem in Lieu of U.S.-Japan Leadership Sharing," *Issues and Studies* 33, no. 5 (May 1997): 68–69.
32. Gunness and Saunders, *Averting Escalation and Avoiding War,* p. 18.
33. Ibid., pp. 18–19.
34. Gellman, "U.S. and China."
35. Ibid.
36. Ijiri, "China-Taiwan Proble," pp. 68–69.
37. Gunness and Saunders, *Averting Escalation and Avoiding War,* pp. 24–26.
38. Ibid., p. 28.
39. Ibid., pp. 28–29.
40. Ibid., p. 31.
41. Ibid., pp. 30–31.
42. Ibid., pp. 257–258.
43. Michael Kau, "The Challenge of Cross-Strait Relations: The Strategic Implications of the Missile Crisis," in *The Security Environment in the Asia-Pacific, ed. Hung-mao Tien and Tun-jen* (Armonk, New York: M.E. Sharpe, 2000), pp. 245–246.
44. Sun, "Study," pp. 162–163.
45. Ibid., pp. 169–170.
46. Martin Lasater, *The Changing of the Guard: President Clinton and the Security of Taiwan* (Oxford: Westview, 1993), p. 128.
47. Suettinger, *Beyond Tiananmen,* p. 155.
48. John W. Garver, *Face Off: China, the United States, and Taiwan's Democratization* (Seattle, WA: University of Washington Press, 1997), p. 67.
49. James Mann, *About Face: A History of America's Curious Relationship with China from Nixon to Clinton* (New York: Knopf, 1999), p. 323.
50. Ibid., p. 323.
51. Ibid., p. 324.
52. Ibid., pp. 67–68.
53. Mark Matthews, "Clinton OKs Visit by Taiwan President," *Baltimore Sun,* May 23, 1995.
54. "Backgrounder: Chronology of Meetings Between Chinese President Jiang and US Presidents," China.org.cn, February 21, 2002.
55. "Chinese President Jiang Zemin Attends Seattle Summit," China.org.cn, July 12, 2011.
56. Jim Mann and Charles Wallace, "Clinton, Chinese President Meet Before Summit," *Los Angeles Times*, November 14, 1994.
57. "Backgrounder."
58. Nick Driver, "Clinton Holds Summit Meeting with Jiang," UPI Archives, November 20, 1993, https://www.upi.com.
59. Mann and Wallace, "Clinton."
60. Suettinger, *Beyond Tiananmen,* p. 210.
61. John F. Harris, "Clinton, Jiang Confer," *Washington Post,* October 25, 1995.
62. Xiaobo Hu, "A Milestone as Well as a Milestone: The Jiang-Clinton Summit," *Issues and Studies* 33, no. 12 (December 1997): 1.
63. Ross, "1995–96 Taiwan Strait Confrontation," p. 115.
64. "President Clinton and President Jiang Zemin Joint Press Conference, 1997," USC US-China Institute, October 29, 1997, https://china.usc.edu.

236   *Hedging the China Threat*

65. Ross, "1995–96 Taiwan Strait Confrontation," p. 116.
66. "History of the National Security Council, 1947–1997," White House, https://georgewbush-whitehouse.archives.gov.
67. Suettinger, *Beyond Tiananmen,* pp. 215.
68. Mann, *About Face,* p. 324.
69. Ibid.
70. Suettinger, *Beyond Tiananmen,* pp. 215–216.
71. Mann, *About Face,* p. 325.
72. Suettinger, *Beyond Tiananmen,* p. 227.
73. Ibid., p. 231.
74. Ibid., p. 232.
75. Mann, *About Face,* p. 331.
76. Suettinger, *Beyond Tiananmen,* p. 209.
77. Mann, *About Face,* pp. 331–332.
78. Ibid., p. 333.
79. Suettinger, *Beyond Tiananmen,* p. 249.
80. Gunness and Saunders, *Averting Escalation and Avoiding War,* pp. 19–20.
81. Ross, "1995–96 Taiwan Strait Confrontation," p. 103.
82. Mann, *About Face,* p. 335.
83. Ross, "1995–96 Taiwan Strait Confrontation," p. 108.
84. Mann, *About Face,* p. 336.
85. Gellman, "U.S. and China."
86. Suettinger, *Beyond Tiananmen,* p. 254.
87. Gellman, "U.S. and China."
88. Suettinger, *Beyond Tiananmen,* p. 255.
89. Ibid., pp. 336–337.
90. Suettinger, *Beyond Tiananmen,* p. 255.
91. Ibid., p. 256.
92. Gellman, "U.S. and China."
93. Mann, *About Face,* p. 337.
94. Ross, "1995–96 Taiwan Strait Confrontation," p. 110.
95. Virginia Sheng, "Lee Sweeps to Victory in Presidential Poll," *Free China Journal* 13, no. 12 (March 1996): 1.
96. Suettinger, *Beyond Tiananmen,* p. 260.
97. Ross, "1995–96 Taiwan Strait Confrontation," p. 109.
98. Mann, *About Face,* p. 338.
99. Taifa Yu, "Taiwan Democracy Under Threat: Implication and Limit of China's Military Coercion," *Pacific Affairs* 70, no. 1 (Spring 1997): 21.
100. Keiji Nakatsuji, "How Did or Did Not Japan Respond to 1995–1996 Taiwan Strait Crisis," (Kyoto: Ritsumeikan University, December 2018).
101. Gary Klintworth, "Crisis Management: China, Taiwan, and the United States—The 1995–96 Crisis and Its Aftermath," Parliament of Australia, https://www.aph.gov.au.
102. Qinfxin Ken Wang, "Japan's Balancing Act in the Taiwan Strait," *Security Dialogue* 31, no. 3 (September 2000): 338.
103. Roy Campbell McDowall, *Howard's Long March: The Strategic Depiction of China in Howard Government Policy 1996–2006* (Canberra: ANU Press, 2009), p. 9.
104. Klintworth, "Crisis Management."
105. Ross, "The 1995–96 Taiwan Strait Confrontation," pp. 116–117.
106. Klintworth, "Crisis Management."

12

From Strategic Competitor to Strategic Partner: The George W. Bush Administration

BEFORE GEORGE W. BUSH BECAME PRESIDENT IN 2001, REPUBLICANS WERE critical of President Bill Clinton's pro-China policy. They denounced the Clinton administration for pushing Taiwan to negotiate with Beijing.[1] After Bush took office, his administration prioritized its allies and partners in Asia, including Taiwan, and the Bush security team decided to strengthen its political and military ties with Taiwan.[2] The US-China relationship, however, began to change when, on April 1, 2001, a US EP-3 reconnaissance aircraft collided with a Chinese F-8 fighter jet in the South China Sea. The F-8 and its pilot were lost in the open sea. The EP-3 made an emergency landing on Chinese soil. Beijing demanded an apology for the accident. Bush requested the release of the crew and plane, while the Chinese demanded the United States cease its reconnaissance missions. Bush said his administration would not apologize for the accident because the Chinese pilot provoked the US aircraft.[3]

After the EP-3 incident, US-China relations began to deteriorate. However, after the September 11 attacks in the United States, the Bush administration became preoccupied not only with the global war on terror, but also with the US military involvement in Iraq and the nuclear crisis with North Korea.[4] The United States and China later improved their relations because the US government needed China's assistance with international security issues.

Historical Events:
The US Balancing Role in China-Taiwan Relations

In its first years, the Bush administration developed close ties with Taiwan, more than any other administration since 1979, because of Taiwan's vibrant democracy, containment of China, and the rising China threat against Taiwan.[5]

237

238   *Hedging the China Threat*

The Bush Administration's Policy Toward Taiwan

In February 2000, the Taiwan Affairs Office of the People's Republic of China (PRC) issued a white paper on Taiwan, which warned that should Taiwan indefinitely refuse to negotiate a peaceful settlement, the PRC would be compelled to use force to achieve unification. In his inaugural speech on May 20, President Chen Shui-bian stated that if China did not intend to use military force against Taiwan, he would not do the following: declare independence, change the national title, include a "state-to-state" description in the constitution, promote a referendum to change the status quo regarding independence or unification, and abolish the National Unification Council or the Guidelines for National Unification.[6]

Beijing realized that any use of force against Taiwan would be met with opposition from the United States and Taiwan. Chi Wang, a professor at Georgetown University, stated that he had many opportunities to talk with Chinese leaders, including Deng Xiaoping, and generals. During their talks, the Taiwan issue was the most important topic to the Chinese leaders. Since the 1990s, leaders in Beijing had become more flexible in their approach to reconciliation with Taiwan. Wang claimed that Beijing demanded only that Taipei accept the One China principle as a basis for negotiations. If Taiwan accepted it, the PRC would be open to political arrangements.[7]

In 1999, Republic of China (ROC) president Lee Teng-hui announced that cross-strait relations were a "special state-to-state relationship." China interpreted Lee's statement as a move toward independence and mounted strong opposition. Beijing considered Chen Shui-bian, who succeeded Lee in 2000, to be a longtime advocate of Taiwan independence, and a more serious challenge. Chen's Democratic Progressive Party (DPP) also aimed to seek Taiwan's independence.[8]

Distrustful of China's ambitions and refusal to adopt democratic values, Bush labeled China a "strategic competitor." Under his leadership, the US policy toward Taiwan gradually shifted from strategic ambiguity to strategic clarity. In April 2001, Bush stated the US security commitment to Taiwan as an obligation to do whatever it took to help Taiwan defend itself.[9]

The arms sales policy toward Taiwan. The Bush administration's arms sales policy toward Taiwan triggered US-China friction. The first major dispute occurred in April 2001 over the proposed sale of the Aegis system. Taiwan requested four Arleigh destroyers manned with the Aegis, a radar system that could track 100 targets simultaneously, forming the theater missile defense system to defend Taiwan. Beijing opposed this sale.[10] When he visited the United States in March 2001, People's Republic of China (PRC) deputy prime minister Qian Qichen said that selling the Aegis would violate the US-China communiqué on US arms sales to Taiwan. Bush later deferred a decision on the Aegis, but he approved an arms package totaling more than $4 billion. It was the largest since his father, George H. W. Bush, sold 150 F-16 fighter jets to Taiwan in 1992. George W. Bush also approved the sale of four Kidd class destroyers, twelve antisubmarine planes, eight submarines, and twelve minesweeping helicopters.[11]

Traveling controversy of Taiwan's president. In August 2000, the Clinton administration had granted newly elected president Chen Shui-bian a visa to stop in Los Angeles, on his way to South America and Africa. The Bush administration expanded the range of unofficial contacts with Taiwan leaders. In 2001, the administration granted Chen approval to land in New York from May 21 to 23, and in Houston from June 2 to 3 on the way to and from Latin America.[12] In 2003, the US government granted Chen's requests for a stopover to and from Panama through New York from October 31 to November 2, and Anchorage from November 4 to 5.[13] In New York, Chen received a human rights award on November 1. In his award address, Chen stated that the insufficiency of Taiwan's constitutional framework was the rationale for hastening the birth of a new constitution for Taiwan.[14] Chen used this New York trip to garner domestic support for his reelection in March 2004. This trip was covered by the media, which gave the impression of US support for Taiwan.[15] In China's view, US approval of stopovers was a violation of the One China principle.

Opposing Chen. The Bush administration not only provided better treatment for Chen to land on US soil, but also permitted high-ranking Taiwanese officials to visit the United States. For example, in March 2002 Taiwan's minister of defense, Tang Yiau-ming, made a business trip to Florida to attend a conference and talked to Deputy Secretary of Defense Paul Wolfowitz.[16] On September 11, 2002, the US flag was flown at the American Institute in Taiwan (AIT) for the first time since the Jimmy Carter administration broke diplomatic relations with Taiwan in 1979.[17]

The Bush administration embraced the following elements in its policy toward China and Taiwan: the One China policy in the context of the three US-China joint communiqués, the 1979 Taiwan Relations Act (TRA), and the 1982 Six Assurances to Taiwan. The United States expected China and Taiwan to act responsibly for regional stability by encouraging cross-strait dialogues on political and security issues. The United States assisted Taiwan in seeking opportunities for international participation such as with the World Health Organization (WHO).[18]

Beijing's basis for cross-strait relations had been the One China principle. In January 2002, Vice Premier Qian Qichen emphasized that "there is One China in the world; the Mainland and Taiwan both belong to one China; China's sovereignty and territorial integrity have no separation."[19]

240 Hedging the China Threat

However, on August 3, in a televised conference of the World Federation of Taiwanese Associations meeting in Tokyo, President Chen advocated "one country on each side" and called for a referendum on Taiwan's future. He argued that only its 23 million people should decide Taiwan's future.[20]

After Chen's remark, the Bush administration expressed concern because "one country on each side" conflicted with the US One China policy. To calm the situation, Chen sent the minister of the Mainland Affairs Council, Tsai Ing-wen, to Washington. Tsai assured the Bush administration that the Taiwan policy toward China would not be changed. In response, Bush told PRC president Jiang Zemin, while visiting the White House in October, that the United States "opposes" Taiwan's independence. Bush stated that the One China policy, based on the three communiqués and the TRA, remained unchanged.[21]

During the presidential campaign in Taiwan, Bush administration officials were dissatisfied with Chen taking advantage of Bush's pro-Taiwan policy. They believed Chen wanted to sabotage US-China relations and trigger cross-strait tension. They felt this would garner more votes from his supporters for his reelection by holding referendums concerning Taiwan's efforts to proclaim independence. The Bush administration was disturbed about the comments of the Taiwan leaders.[22] For example, Vice President Annette Lu remarked to the press in June 2003 that the United States had no right to oppose Taiwan's decision to hold referendums, and President Chen said: "Taiwan is not a province of any country."[23]

In September 2003, Chen proposed the creation of a new constitution, to be ratified by referendum. He encouraged a large turnout of DPP supporters to increase the chances of his reelection the following year.[24] Frustrated by Chen, the Bush administration opted to send a warning to him. James Moriarty, the Asian advisor of the National Security Council (NSC), went to Taiwan to persuade Chen to change his position on holding referendums simultaneously with the presidential election. Moriarty carried a letter from Bush expressing discontent with Chen's actions, but his trips to Taiwan were futile. In response, PRC premier Wen Jiabao visited the United States at the invitation of Bush. Wen requested Bush's cooperation in restricting Chen on the independence movement. On December 9, while meeting with Wen, Bush stated that the United States opposed any unilateral decision to change the status quo across the Taiwan Strait.[25]

After President Chen decided to conduct the referendum, the Bush administration sent a clear warning to the Chen administration. Deputy Assistant Secretary of Defense Richard Lawless told Taiwan's deputy defense minister Chen Chao-min, in February 2003, that Taiwan should not view the US commitment to Taiwan as a substitute for investing the necessary resources in its defense. In June 2003, Chen sent Foreign Minister Eugene Chien to the United States, where he met with Vice President Dick

Cheney. Cheney opposed the referendum, fearing that it could affect US-PRC relations.[26] In November, Deputy Secretary of State Richard Armitage said that the TRA was not a defense treaty. It guided policy in providing Taiwan "sufficient defense articles for her self-defense." He reaffirmed that the US commitment to assist Taiwan's self-defense "doesn't go beyond that in the TRA."[27]

After the US opposition to the referendum during the 2004 Taiwan presidential election, Chen changed the wording of the referendum. The Taiwanese voters would be asked whether Taiwan should buy more weapons if China did not remove its missiles aimed at Taiwan. The change of words attempted to lessen the anger of the Bush administration and gain support from the United States by suggesting more weapon purchases from the United States.[28] In April 2004, Assistant Secretary of State James Kelly warned Taiwan not to dismiss Beijing's statements as "empty threats." In September 2005, the Pentagon clarified the mutual obligations under the TRA and limited the United States' ability to assist Taiwan. Deputy Under Secretary of Defense Richard Lawless stressed the TRA's focus on Taiwan's self-defense. He declared that under the TRA, the United States was obligated to "enable" Taiwan to maintain sufficient self-defense.[29]

The controversial Taiwan election. The result of the Taiwan presidential election was a slim victory for the DPP over the Kuomintang (KMT). The legality of Chen's victory shadowed the election. Before the election, polls showed Chen's likely defeat. A day before the election, Chen and Vice President Lu were shot during their campaign rally. Following the announcement of Chen's victory, the KMT charged that he had stolen the election. The Bush administration congratulated Taiwan on its democratic election, but it did not congratulate Chen.[30] Chen requested the Bush administration to recognize his victory. Armitage said the election was a "great example of the democratic process," but he did not mention a winner. After the election results were certified, the State Department authorized Therese Shaheen, director of the AIT, to telephone Chen with a congratulatory message.[31]

The State Department was angry at Taiwan over the issue of Chen pushing ahead with a proposal to write a new constitution in 2006. In April 2004, Assistant Secretary of State James Kelly said, about the issue of Taiwan proclaiming independence, that it would "carry the potential for a military response by China." The State Department expressed grave concern about what Chen would say in his inauguration speech on May 20. Chen yielded to US pressure and changed his inaugural address to a conciliatory tone. He used the term *the ROC* more than Taiwan, mentioning "reengineering" the ROC constitution rather than writing a new one. Chen even spoke of Taiwan's future possibly being linked to China.[32]

242   *Hedging the China Threat*

The Taiwan Problem in the
Second George W. Bush Administration

Chen won reelection with a campaign emphasizing Taiwan's determination against perceived Chinese coercion. He committed to deepening the reforms that defined Taiwan as a country separate from China.[33] On May 17, 2004, the Taiwan Affairs Office of the PRC issued a statement that gave Taiwan leaders a choice between two roads. One was to reaffirm the One China principle and to end separatist activities. In return, dialogues and exchanges would resume, and economic cooperation would deepen. If not, none of that would happen.[34]

The Bush administration endeavored to deter China from using force against Taiwan and deter Taiwan from moving toward independence. The administration acknowledged the importance of supporting Taiwan in deterring China from using military power to threaten Taiwan, but criticized Chen's unilateral change in Taiwan's status, which risked US military conflict with China. The National Security Council (NSC) and State Department issued statements before Taiwan's legislative elections in December 2004, warning Taiwan voters that US support for Taiwan was not unconditional.[35]

The PRC National People's Congress enacted the Anti-Secession Law in March 2005. The law stipulated that if Taiwan independence forces act under any name to cause Taiwan's secession from China, China would employ nonpeaceful means to protect its sovereignty.[36] In response, the United States settled into a policy of dual deterrence. On the one hand, the Bush administration strengthened US military forces, enhanced US-Taiwan military cooperation, and improved Taiwan's military preparedness to deter China's military threat. On the other hand, the United States intervened in the Chen government's assertiveness toward Taiwan's nationalism because it seemed to endanger US interests.[37]

To diminish the rising cross-strait tension, in April 2005 Lien Chan visited Beijing, the first time a KMT chairman had been in China since the KMT's defeat in 1949. The leaders of the KMT and the Chinese Communist Party (CCP) agreed to uphold the 1992 Consensus, oppose Taiwan's independence, and promote the development of cross-strait relations. If the KMT became the ruling party at the next presidential election, the KMT and the CCP proposed to resume cross-strait negotiations, end the state of hostilities, and conclude a peace accord.[38] Taiwan's opposition leaders pursued engagement with China.

The Individual Level:
Bush's Policy Toward Beijing and Taipei

Before taking office, Bush aimed to counter China's rise. Considering that Clinton had jeopardized US interests by favoring engagement with China over

Japan, Bush pursued a balanced US policy in Asia. His administration bolstered relations with Japan and emphasized Taiwan's importance to US interests. However, following the 9/11 terrorist attacks, building a global coalition to combat terrorism fostered closer ties with China. As a result, Bush's policy evolved to benefit the US-China relationship over its ties to Taiwan.[39]

Presidential Campaigning

In US presidential campaign discourse, anti-PRC critiques of incumbents for not being "tougher" on China have become common. This enabled presidential candidates to align themselves with democratic values against the Chinese Communist regime. Identifying Chinese leaders as "the butchers of Beijing," Bush asserted that China was a competitor, not a strategic partner. He condemned the Clinton administration's handling of China relations as ineffective and soft. On November 19, 1999, Bush described China's policies as "alarming abroad and appalling at home." He rebuked Beijing as an enemy of religious freedom and a sponsor of forced abortions. Bush claimed that if he was elected president, "China will know that America's values are always part of America's agenda."[40]

Bush questioned the policy of strategic ambiguity and claimed that his administration would be clear about Taiwan. He criticized it as an espionage threat to the United States.[41] While he portrayed the PRC as a symbol of the repulsive nature of communism, Bush described Taiwan as representing a free country that the United States would defend from possible Chinese aggression.[42]

While Bush promised to treat the PRC as a "competitor" rather than a "partner" if elected, he was careful to clarify that the PRC was not an "enemy." He cautioned that if the United States made China an enemy, it would become one. Bush recognized that "competitors can find areas of agreement such as in trade." Throughout the campaign, Bush asserted that the United States' "greatest export is freedom" and that trade with China would increase its freedom. Connecting Taiwan's growing democracy to its booming economy allowed Bush to mention that Taiwan could be a role model for China's future.[43]

From "Strategic Ambiguity" to "Strategic Clarity"

On April 25, 2001, President Bush was interviewed by the ABC network on whether the United States was obliged to defend Taiwan if China attacked it. He replied, "Yes, we do, and the Chinese must understand that." When asked if this meant protecting Taiwan "with the full force of the American military," Bush replied, "whatever it took to help Taiwan defend itself."[44] By publicly committing the US military to Taiwan's defense, Bush left no

244   *Hedging the China Threat*

doubt that the United States would intervene in response to the PRC's use of force against Taiwan.[45] No US president had made such a commitment to Taiwan. Kenneth Lieberthal, Clinton's director of Asian affairs at the NSC, maintained, "This does go beyond what any previous administration has indicated either orally or in writing." Lieberthal said Bush had even gone beyond the abrogated 1954 US-ROC Mutual Defense Treaty.[46] Political opponents were critical of Bush's remarks. For example, Senator John Kerry (D-MA) accused Bush of abandoning the policy of strategic ambiguity with "absolutely no consultation with members of Congress or with our allies in the region."[47]

In a CNN interview, Bush supported the One China policy and opposed a Taiwanese declaration of independence. He said that his statements on ABC did not break new ground and that he only restated what other US presidents had said.[48] Phillip Reeder, a spokesman for the Department of State, said, "Our policy hasn't changed today, it didn't change yesterday, and it didn't change last year. It hasn't changed in terms of what we have followed since 1979 with the passage of the TRA."[49] US officials argued that Bush's statement did not represent a change in US policy concerning Taiwan. National Security Advisor (NSA) Condoleezza Rice explained, "The Taiwan Relations Act makes very clear that the U.S. has an obligation that Taiwan's peaceful way of life is not upset by force. What he said is how seriously and resolutely he takes this obligation."[50]

Bush altered the US policy of strategic ambiguity by proclaiming that the United States would aid Taiwan's defense. He stated that the United States' role in the China-Taiwan conflict was "to use our prestige in the world to make sure the One China policy remains intact." Bush supported the status quo in US relations with China and Taiwan.[51] He stated that his administration would drop strategic ambiguity, for outright support for Taiwan. Bush's defense policy had moved from "strategic ambiguity" to "strategic clarity."[52] The continuity is that US presidents continued to say or signal clearly that they would come to Taiwan's defense against an unprovoked attack. That is what Clinton did by sending the carriers in 1995–1996.

Bush's Defense Policy Toward Taiwan

On Taiwan's defense issues, Bush believed the United States was interested in the security of Taiwan's democracy. US arms sales to Taiwan had been significant. In April 2001, Bush announced that he had decided on an arms sales deal with Taiwan. Bush approved the sale of four Kidd-class destroyers and twelve P-3C Orion submarine-killer aircraft. He also agreed to help Taiwan secure eight diesel submarines.[53] In a February 2002 speech to the US-Taiwan Business Council meeting, Deputy Secretary of Defense Paul

Wolfowitz noted that, as Bush said, the United States was committed to helping Taiwan defend itself. At this conference, Wolfowitz and Assistant Secretary of State for East Asian and Pacific Affairs James Kelly met with the Taiwanese defense minister, Tang Yao-ming. This was the first visit of a Taiwanese defense minister to the United States since the breaking of official relations with Taiwan in 1979. This meeting established a new precedent in the defense relationship.[54]

After the 9/11 terror attacks, the Bush administration's 2002 National Security Strategy Report called for better relations with China, but warned against any power seeking to challenge US interests with military force. US military contacts remained restricted while other departments were resuming engagement. Observers speculated about differences among Bush administration officials concerning policy toward China. They viewed Secretary Colin Powell and the State Department as seeking to manage differences with China that would avoid disruption and allow for greater development. However, Defense Secretary Donald Rumsfeld was seen leading a hard-line approach in dealing with contingencies involving US forces in a Taiwan conflict.[55]

In 2002, Bush authorized the assignment of active duty military personnel to AIT in Taiwan. He also permitted Taiwanese security-related officers to attend classes at the Pentagon-funded Asia-Pacific Center for Security Studies. Bush relaxed restrictions on US military officers traveling to Taiwan. US military representatives were involved in dozens of programs in Taiwan, including classroom seminars and training in the field. US officers advised Taiwan's military at all levels in policy, implementation, and training. Pentagon officials were involved in helping Taiwan reform its military, including training and improving interservice operability. The two militaries established a hotline for communicating in case of an emergency.[56]

Bush signed legislation to enhance military ties between Taipei and Washington. In 2002, he signed the Foreign Relations Authorization Act of Fiscal Year 2003. Taiwan was designated a major non-NATO ally for the transfer of defense articles and services. Bush also signed an act calling on the administration to study the feasibility of expanding military ties, including combined operational training exercises and the exchange of senior officers. The United States sent its military specialists to Taiwan to assess the situation and to help Taiwan integrate weapons systems. In April 2003, Admiral Dennis Blair, former commander in chief of the US Pacific Command, accompanied a twenty-person US military delegation to Taiwan.[57] Bush's defense policy toward Taiwan embraced the concepts of supporting the TRA and the Six Assurances to Taiwan. Bush expected China and Taiwan to act responsibly to support regional stability, and the United States would encourage cross-strait dialogue on political and security issues.[58]

246 *Hedging the China Threat*

Bush on Taiwan's Independence

On April 25, 2001, when Bush stated the US commitment to defend Taiwan, he added that "a declaration of independence is not the One China policy, and we will work with Taiwan to make sure that doesn't happen." Visiting Beijing in February 2002, Bush emphasized the US commitment to the TRA and a peaceful resolution, along with opposition to provocations by either Beijing or Taipei after President Chen said on August 3 that there was "one country on each side" of the Taiwan Strait. Bush later stated during a summit with PRC president Jiang in Crawford, Texas, in October, that the United States did not support Taiwan's independence.[59]

During campaigns for Taiwan's 2004 presidential election, Chen advocated holding referendums and amending the constitution regarding Taiwan's sovereignty. The Bush administration called on Chen to adhere to his pledges of Five No's in his 2000 inaugural address, including not promoting a referendum. On October 14, 2003, Condoleezza Rice said that nobody should try unilaterally to change the status quo. On November 29, Chen announced that he would still hold a defensive referendum on election day because it would allow Taiwan's people to express their opposition to China's threat. However, he would not touch the issue of independence.[60] Bush criticized Chen for having contradicted his earlier commitment.

The Bush administration took a clearer stance on December 1, 2003, when the State Department opposed any referendum that would move toward independence. On December 9, Bush stood next to visiting PRC premier Wen and expressed opposition to Chen's proposal of the referendum. Chen responded that he would hold the referendums as planned and that he intended to keep Taiwan's status quo from being changed.[61] On January 16, 2004, Chen altered the wording of the referendums that would ask citizens the two questions: (1) whether the government should acquire more missile defense systems if China does not withdraw missiles and renounce the use of force against Taiwan; and (2) whether the government should negotiate with China on a framework for cross-strait peace and stability. On March 20, the two referendums were deemed invalid because only 45 percent of eligible voters cast ballots in favor of them. After the election, the White House sent the senior director for Asian affairs, Michael Green, to Taiwan to urge Chen to exclude sovereignty-related issues from constitutional changes. Chen responded to US concerns in his inaugural address on May 20. In Chen's second term, Bush did not support Taiwan's independence or membership in the United Nations and opposed changes to the status quo.[62]

Chen was reelected president by a narrow margin of votes. Soon after his victory, the DPP aimed to win the legislative elections in December and to proceed with the constitutional reform, even with US opposition.

Facing Chen's insistence on independence rhetoric, the White House emphasized that the United States did not support independence for Taiwan or unilateral moves that would change the current status. For both sides, it meant no statements or actions would unilaterally alter Taiwan's status. The United States urged Beijing and Taipei to pursue dialogue through any available channels.[63]

In April 2004, just before his inauguration, Chen sent Secretary General Chiou I-jen to Washington. He met with Deputy Secretary of State Richard Armitage to convince the Bush administration of constitutional reform. Taiwan would not change its official name, flag, or sovereignty. The proposal was rejected by the Bush administration. On October 25, as a sign of US irritation, Secretary Powell stated, "There is only one China. Taiwan is not independent. It does not enjoy sovereignty as a nation, which remains U.S. policy." Although Bush had reaffirmed the promise to defend Taiwan, he stated, "We're for a One China policy based upon what they call the Three Communiques, and we adhere to the Taiwan Relations Act, which means this: Neither side will unilaterally change the status quo. . . . If China were to invade unilaterally, we would rise up in the spirit of the Taiwan Relations Act. If Taiwan were to declare independence unilaterally, it would be a unilateral decision that would change the U.S. equation."[64]

In February 2006, the Bush administration was surprised when Chen declared his wish to abolish the National Unification Council and proposed the admission of the ROC to the UN under the name "Taiwan." The US government alerted Chen that he had to consult with Washington before making such an announcement, but Chen refused. Bush took retaliatory measures. In May 2006, when Chen applied for a transit visa to the United States during his visit to Latin America, Washington allowed him to transit only in Honolulu and Anchorage. Bush also obstructed the sale of the F-16 C/D to Taiwan. During a meeting with PRC president Hu Jintao in 2006, Bush assured Hu that he did not support Taiwan's independence.[65]

The second term of George W. Bush continued the shift in the administration's approach to dealing with China. When Condoleezza Rice became secretary of state, she garnered greater support for more engagement with Beijing. Strategic priorities in the war on terror, the war in Iraq, and the threat of nuclear proliferation in North Korea made for significant anchors in this shift. Undersecretary of State Robert Zoellick called for China to become a responsible stakeholder. Bush's trust in Secretary Rice was significant to this flexibility because her diplomacy prioritized dialogue with Beijing. Bush supported engagement, noting that the United States and China could coexist in a "cooperative and constructive, yet candid" manner.[66]

248   *Hedging the China Threat*

The State Level: The EP-3 Incident

The early months of the Bush administration comprised three themes in China policy: a reversal of Clinton's China coddling, increases in US military capabilities, and recognition of the China threat. The conservative hawks, Vice President Dick Cheney and Secretary of Defense Donald Rumsfeld, favored expansive military policies and assertive diplomacy against a rising China. Conservative pragmatists, NSA Condoleezza Rice, Secretary of State Colin Powell, and Deputy Secretary of State Richard Armitage were considered less hostile to China.[67] Powell, in his confirmation testimony in January 2001, affirmed that he would maintain the capacity to resist any form of coercion that jeopardized the security of Taiwan.[68] Even though differences between Rumsfeld and Powell over policy toward US-Taiwan and US-China military exchanges existed, they were not major. They viewed China as a rival, especially after the EP-3 accident.[69]

The Collision and Detention of US Crew

On April 1, 2001, US EP-3 reconnaissance aircraft took off from Kadena Air Base in Okinawa. The EP-3 and a People's Liberation Army (PLA) navy F-8 jet fighter collided in international airspace about seventy miles off China's Hainan Island. When the US crew made an emergency landing on the island at the PLA navy's Lingshui airfield, the security guards detained the twenty-four US crew members for eleven days. The F-8 fighter crashed into the sea, and the pilot Wang Wei was lost.[70] The Chinese government was humiliated by the US "hegemony."

According to the US military, the PLA pilots had flown aggressively against US aircraft. In particular, the pilot Wang Wei had constantly intercepted the US aircraft. The US Pacific Command had complained to the PLA, warning that its flights were dangerous. The PLA said the US aircraft encroached on its sovereign airspace. On April 1, Wang's fighter jet maneuvered too close to the EP-3. His aircraft got sucked in by one of the EP-3's propellers and plummeted into the South China Sea. After the accident, the PRC Ministry of Foreign Affairs reprimanded the US military because the EP-3 had turned toward the PLA fighter and caused the collision.[71] The US flight crew was interrogated daily by the PLA security guards. The Chinese told the crew that they would be thrown into prison in China indefinitely.[72] They also wanted the EP-3 crew to accept full responsibility for the collision.[73]

The Bush Administration's Response to the Crisis

The Bush administration faced a foreign policy crisis, while the president focused on the crew's return. Admiral Dennis Blair, commander in chief,

Pacific Command, reported that the EP-3 was on a routine operation in international airspace over the South China Sea when it was intercepted by PLA fighters. Admiral Blair declared that the plane had "sovereign immunity," and expressed frustration at the lack of Chinese cooperation.[74] On April 2, Bush appealed to PRC leaders, expressing that he was troubled by the lack of a timely Chinese response to the US request for this access. He also expressed concern about the PLA's pilot, offering to assist in search and rescue. On April 3, President Jiang demanded that the United States stop reconnaissance flights in the airspace along China's coast. On the same day, the US defense attaché in Beijing, Brigadier General Neal Sealock, gained access to the detained crew members. After hearing from Sealock, Bush stated, "Now is the time for our servicemen and women to return home. And it is time for the Chinese government to return our plane."[75] As spokesperson at a press briefing on April 4 at the Pentagon, Rear Admiral Craig Quigley pushed back against the argument that the United States should implement a security response. The military believed that there was a diplomatic solution to this incident and not a military one.[76]

During the crisis, the US military provided information and photographs showing that the PLA pilot who was lost had previously flown risky interceptions close to the US aircraft. General Sealock met with the crew and briefed Bush. After several rounds of negotiations, on April 11 Ambassador Joseph Prueher expressed "sincere regret" over the missing PLA pilot, and that the United States was "very sorry" for the pilot's loss. On April 12, the US crew was released. After the crew's return, the United States continued to fly in the South China Sea. Deputy Secretary of State Richard Armitage asserted to China the right to fly these routes.[77] After the EP-3 episode, the Bush administration began a poor relationship with China. The administration reacted to the crisis by seeing China as a threat.[78]

The Responses from the US Congress and the Public

The US Congress responded strongly to China's detention of US personnel. Representative Duncan Hunter (R-CA) suggested legislation canceling China's trading status. He stated that "while the U.S. traded with China, they prepared for war."[79] Representative Dana Rohrbacher (R-CA) stated that China attacked a US surveillance aircraft in international waters and held it hostage for two weeks. The US massive investment in China created not a more democratic China, but an aggressive "nuclear-armed bully." If the United States did not change fundamental policies, there would be conflict.[80]

In February 2001, before the collision, 48 percent of participants in a Gallup poll indicated they had an unfavorable view of China. During the incident, a poll from April 1 to 4 showed 68 percent of participants indicated

250   *Hedging the China Threat*

China as an "extreme/somewhat threat." It showed a spike in the unfavorable perception of China's government. An *ABC News/Washington Post* poll from April 5 showed another result, with 57 percent judging China as unfriendly and an enemy. An overwhelming majority (74 percent) agreed that trade should be restricted if China did not return the crew and plane.[81]

The International Level: US-China Relations After 9/11

After 9/11, the Bush administration launched an antiterrorism campaign. The antiterrorism campaign provided an opportunity to improve bilateral cooperation between the United States and China. Bush expressed bilateral relations in new terms. Both countries shared the burden of waging a war on terror.[82] Due to the 9/11 terrorist attacks and the North Korean nuclear crisis, the Bush administration sought cooperation with Beijing to deal with these issues. The United States also wanted more stable cross-strait relations.[83] Bush pursued "constructive, cooperative, and candid" relations with China. As relations improved, Bush welcomed the PRC's support in the antiterrorism campaign and anti-North Korean nuclear development.[84]

US-China Counterterrorism Cooperation

When 9/11 occurred, President Jiang offered condolences and helped track down the culprits. Beijing sought to improve its relationship with Washington by supporting the UN resolution to use force in Afghanistan and sending a counterterrorism team to the United States to share intelligence. Beijing also aided Washington in bringing Pakistan to the war effort by allowing the US military bases to be close to Afghanistan. By October 2002, Bush met with Chinese leaders twice in the United States, representing an unprecedented level of engagement.[85]

The State Department announced that US and Chinese leaders had fostered a robust partnership to confront global terrorism. Their initiatives included the establishment of an FBI liaison office in Beijing, the signing of the Container Security Initiative, and the announcement of reconstruction aid for Afghanistan. Along with China's aid in convincing Pakistan to accept US basing rights, US and China counterterrorism officials were working together. In return for agreeing to open an FBI liaison office in Beijing, Attorney General John Ashcroft declared the East Turkistan Islamic Movement (ETIM) in Xinjiang a terrorist movement, legitimizing China's fight against "splittists."[86] Beijing could then legitimately crack down on the ETIM, which had advocated for self-determination. ETIM, which desired the creation of East Turkestan, an independent nation-state, was labeled as a terrorist group by both Beijing and Washington.[87]

The 9/11 terrorist attacks impacted US foreign policy. The PRC supported the US-led antiterrorist campaign; ensured Pakistan's cooperation in the war on terror; shared intelligence with the United States on militant Islamic groups based in Asia; and froze its bank accounts in Hong Kong. As Li Zhaoxing, China's vice minister for foreign affairs, explained, "China is also a victim of terror." Beijing fought against Islamic separatist groups based in Xinjiang for over a decade. The PRC revealed that US troops had captured some Chinese Muslims during operations in Afghanistan. Secretary Powell pointed out that the 9/11 attacks helped improve US-China relations. Li contended that both countries should cooperate more on common regional interests, including the reconstruction of Afghanistan, and the reduction of India-Pakistan tensions.[88] As the host of the 2008 Summer Olympic Games, China committed to antiterror initiatives. This created a greater recognition of the need to challenge extremism.[89]

North Korea's Nuclear Program

Since the 1990s, North Korea's nuclear program has been a concern of East Asian countries. Bush named North Korea a member of the "axis of evil" in 2002. The East Asian countries feared that a US military attack on North Korea would lead to a massive migration of refugees into China. North Korea also serves as a buffer that provides some strategic depth for China. Beijing began to play an active role in negotiating a peaceful resolution. This motivated the Chinese to cooperate with the United States to find a solution to prevent the collapse of the Kim Jong Il regime.[90]

Pyongyang's decision to leave the Nuclear Non-Proliferation Treaty (NPT) and pursue nuclear weapons in January 2003 caused the Bush administration to deepen its engagement with China to prevent the rising threat of North Korea. China had influence over the regime, providing 80 percent of North Korea's economic needs. The Bush administration found that Beijing could pressure Pyongyang into dialogues. The US-China relationship, by the end of the second Bush administration, appeared to improve toward a stable partnership, particularly related to China's urging North Korea to turn toward denuclearization.[91]

The counterterrorism relationship was instrumental in improving US-China ties following 9/11. The war against terror and the North Korean crisis helped the United States and China work together. President Bush met with President Jiang three times within one year. These summits facilitated the resumption of military exchanges that had been suspended after the EP3 collision.[92]

The reason for Bush's departure from a pro-Taiwan stance was the US preoccupation with urgent problems of the antiterrorism campaign and the United States' desire to avoid potential conflicts in the Taiwan Strait.[93]

252 *Hedging the China Threat*

As the two countries moved closer, Chinese officials expressed hopes that the United States might make concessions on the Taiwan issue. General Liang Guanglie, the PLA chief of staff, explained that the Taiwan issue was the most important sensitive issue of bilateral relations. Beijing hoped Washington would properly handle the Taiwan issue and contribute to the reunification of China. Deputy Secretary of State Richard Armitage contended that "China is operating under the mistaken assumption that the war against terrorism and Iraq will get them something in return on Taiwan, that the U.S. will make concessions in Taiwan. This won't happen."[94]

Conclusion

During the George W. Bush administration, the US policy toward Taiwan gradually shifted from strategic ambiguity to strategic clarity. In April 2001, President Bush stated the US security commitment to Taiwan as a US obligation to "do whatever it takes" to help Taiwan defend itself. However, during the 2004 Taiwan presidential campaign, the Bush administration was unhappy when the Chen administration took advantage of Bush's pro-Taiwan policy by proposing an amendment to the constitution. Moreover, the US policy toward China before and after the 9/11 terrorist attacks was substantially different. The Bush antiterrorism campaign provided an opportunity to improve US-China security cooperation.

The Bush administration's cross-strait policy included: first, embracing the One China policy in the context of three significant US-China joint communiqués, the 1979 TRA, and the 1982 Six Assurances to Taiwan. Second, the Bush administration encouraged China and Taiwan to act responsibly for regional stability by facilitating cross-strait dialogues.

In considering the US-Taiwan relationship at the individual level during the George W. Bush years, it is apparent that even before taking office Bush was planning to counter China's goal of becoming the leading world power. After taking office, Bush suggested that his administration should drop its defense policy of strategic ambiguity to one of strategic clarity in support of Taiwan. During his administration, the United States continued the same overall defense policy as that of previous US presidents: the United States signaled that it would come to Taiwan's defense in the event of an unprovoked attack from China. Following the 9/11 terrorist attacks in the United States, the building of a global coalition to combat terrorism fostered closer ties with China. As Bush's policy evolved to meet the increased threats of terrorism, the US-China relationship improved regarding Taiwan.

At the state level, the early months of the Bush administration comprised three themes in China's policy: a reversal of Clinton's China coddling, an increase in military capabilities, and a recognition of the China threat. During the EP-3 event in 2001, the US Congress condemned China's detention of the US aircraft crew following a forced landing on Hainan Island. During the incident, a poll revealed that 68 percent of US participants saw China as a threat to US security.

At the international level, due not only to the 9/11 terrorist attacks but also to the North Korean nuclear crisis, the Bush administration sought closer cooperation with Beijing. As bilateral relations improved, the Bush administration welcomed Chinese support in carrying out the antiterrorism campaign and in dealing with North Korea's nuclear program. As the US government was committed to dealing with the antiterrorism campaign, it needed more stable cross-strait relations.

By the end of the Bush administration, *the China threat* had become a common term because of China's ever rising economic expansion and military buildup. As the 2008 US presidential election approached, Barack Obama's campaign team perceived that the United States needed to shift its focus from the Middle Eastern and European regions to East Asia. Their proposed policy would include bolstering security alliances, strengthening relationships with rising world powers, increasing trade and investments, and enhancing the US military presence in Asia. This redirection of focus to East Asia caused grave concern to the Chinese leaders, which continued into the Obama administration.

Notes

1. Shirley A. Kan et al., "China-U.S. Aircraft Collision Incident of April 2001: Assessments and Policy Implications," *Report for Congress* (Washington, DC: Congressional Research Service, October 10, 2001), p. 1.

2. John F. Cooper, "United States Taiwan Policy: How the 2004 (Taiwan) Presidential Election Put It to the Test," in *Sources of Conflict and Cooperation in the Taiwan Strait*, edited by Yongnian Zheng and Raymond Ray-Kuo Wu (World Scientific, 2006), p. 155.

3. Aiden Warren and Adam Bartley, *U.S. Foreign Policy and China: Security Challenges During the Bush, Obama, and Trump Administrations* (Edinburgh: Edinburgh University Press, 2021), pp. 36–37.

4. Robert G. Sutter, "The Taiwan Problem in the Second George W. Bush Administration—US Officials' Views and Their Implications for US Policy," *Journal of Contemporary China* 15, no. 48 (August 2006): 418.

5. Chi Wang, *George W. Bush and China: Policies, Problems, and Partnerships* (Lanham, MD: Lexington Books, 2009), p. 52.

6. Ibid.

7. Ibid., 59.

8. Richard Bush, *Uncharted Strait: The Future of China-Taiwan Relations* (Washington, DC: Brookings Institution Press, 2013), pp. 15–16.

9. Cooper, "United States Taiwan Policy," p. 155.

10. Wang, *George W. Bush and China,* pp. 52–53.

11. Ibid., pp. 53–54.

254 Hedging the China Threat

12. Dennis Van Vranken Hickey, "Continuity and Change: The Administration of George W. Bush and US Policy Toward Taiwan," *Journal of Contemporary China* 13, no. 40 (August 2004): 471–472.

13. Shirley A. Kan, *China/Taiwan: Evolution of the "One China" Policy—Key Statements from Washington, Beijing, and Taipei,* Report for Congress (Washington, DC: Congressional Research Service, June 1, 2004), p. 13.

14. "Mainland Policy and Work," Mainland Affairs Council, https://www.mac.gov.tw.

15. Frank Muyard, "Taiwan: The Birth of a Nation?" *Open Edition Journals* (May–June 2004), https://journals.openedition.org.

16. Cooper, "United States Taiwan Policy," p. 156.

17. Hickey, "Continuity and Change," p. 472.

18. Peter Brookes, *U.S.-Taiwan Defense Relations in the Bush Administration,* Heritage Foundation, November 14, 2003, https://www.heritage.org.

19. Bush, *Uncharted Strait,* p. 20.

20. "Taiwan Communique," International Committee for Human Rights in Taiwan, September 2002. https://www.taiwandc.org/twcom/tc102-int.pdf.

21. Kan, *China/Taiwan,* p. 23.

22. Cooper, "United States Taiwan Policy," p.157.

23. Ibid., p. 158.

24. Bush, *Uncharted Strait,* p. 17.

25. Cooper, "United States Taiwan Policy," pp. 158–159.

26. Ben Lian Deng, "US Taiwan Policy During the George W. Bush Administration (2001–2009)," *Cadernos Argentina Brasil* 7, no. 1 (2018): 7.

27. Kan, *China/Taiwan,* p. 23.

28. Cooper, "United States Taiwan Policy," p. 160.

29. Kan, *China/Taiwan,* p. 23.

30. Cooper, "United States Taiwan Policy," pp. 160–161.

31. Ibid., pp. 162–163.

32. Ibid., p. 164.

33. Robert G. Sutter, "The Taiwan Problem in the Second George W. Bush Administration-US Officials' Views and Their Implications for US policy," *Journal of Contemporary China* 15, no. 48 (August 2006): 421–422.

34. Bush, *Uncharted Strait,* p. 19.

35. Sutter, "Taiwan Problem," pp. 417–419.

36. Bush, *Uncharted Strait* pp. 19–20.

37. Sutter, "Taiwan Problem," p. 419.

38. Bush, *Uncharted Strait,* p. 20.

39. Michelle Murray Yang, "Tracing Rhetorical Shifts in US-Sino Relations: George W. Bush's Discourse Regarding Taiwan and the PRC," in *The George W. Bush Presidency,* edited by Meena Bose and Paul Fritz (Washington, DC: Nova Science, 2016), p. 147.

40. Ibid., pp. 147–150.

41. Hickey, "Continuity and Change," p. 464.

42. Yang, "Tracing Rhetorical Shifts," p. 150.

43. Ibid., p. 152.

44. Hickey, "Continuity and Change," p. 469.

45. Yang, "Tracing Rhetorical Shifts," p. 152.

46. Wang, *George W. Bush and China,* p. 55.

47. Yang, "Tracing Rhetorical Shifts," p. 153.

48. Wang, *George W. Bush and China,* p. 55.

From Strategic Competitor to Strategic Partner   255

49. Hickey, "Continuity and Change," p. 469.
50. Yang, "Tracing Rhetorical Shifts," p. 153.
51. Ibid., p. 150.
52. Warren and Bartley, *U.S. Foreign Policy and China,* pp. 26, 33.
53. Hickey, "Continuity and Change," p. 466.
54. Brookes, *U.S.-Taiwan Defense Relations.*
55. Robert G. Sutter, "Bush Administration Policy Toward Beijing and Taipei," *Journal of Contemporary China* 12, no. 36 (August 2003): 486–487.
56. Wang, *George W. Bush and China,* pp. 60–61.
57. Hickey, "Continuity and Change," p. 468.
58. Brookes, *U.S.-Taiwan Defense Relations.*
59. Kan, *China/Taiwan,* p. 12.
60. Ibid., p. 13.
61. Ibid., pp. 13–14.
62. Ibid., p. 15.
63. Deng, "US Taiwan Policy," pp. 7–8.
64. Ibid., p. 8.
65. Ibid.
66. Warren and Bartley, *U.S. Foreign Policy and China,* p. 78.
67. Ibid., pp. 19–24.
68. Brookes, *U.S.-Taiwan Defense Relations.*
69. Warren and Bartley, *U.S. Foreign Policy and China,* pp. 21–22.
70. Kan et al., "China-U.S. Aircraft Collision," p. 1.
71. Kim Zetter, "Burn After Reading," *The Intercept,* April 10, 2017.
72. Ibid.
73. Jim Turnbull, "Lt. Shane Osborn: Looking at a Miracle," *Naval Aviation News,* September 27, 2011.
74. Kan et al., "China-U.S. Aircraft Collision," p. 2.
75. Ibid., p. 3.
76. Jarrod Hayes, *Constructing National Security: U.S. Relations with India and China* (London: Cambridge University Press, 2013), p. 145.
77. Kan et al., "China-U.S. Aircraft Collision," pp. 4–7.
78. Sutter, "Bush Administration Policy Toward Beijing and Taipei," p. 480.
79. Hayes, *Constructing National Security,* pp. 147–149.
80. Ibid., pp. 150–154.
81. Ibid., pp. 154–155.
82. Warren and Bartley, *U.S. Foreign Policy and China,* p. 26.
83. Deng, "US Taiwan Policy," pp. 6–7.
84. Sutter, "Bush Administration Policy," pp. 486–487.
85. Warren and Bartley, *U.S. Foreign Policy and China,* p. 41.
86. Ibid., pp. 53–55.
87. Kurt M. Campbell, Nirav Patel, and Richard Weitz, *The Ripple Effect: China's Responses to the Iraq War* (Washington, DC: Center for a New American Security, October 2008), p. 9.
88. Hickey, "Continuity and Change," pp. 472–474.
89. Campbell, Patel, and Weitz, *Ripple Effect,* p. 38.
90. Ibid., p. 19.
91. Warren and Bartley, *U.S. Foreign Policy and China,* pp. 72–79.
92. Hickey, "Continuity and Change," p. 474.
93. Cooper, "United States Taiwan Policy," p. 156.
94. Hickey, "Continuity and Change," p. 474.

13

Seeking a Rebalanced Policy: The Obama Administration

THE BARACK OBAMA ADMINISTRATION ADVOCATED A "PIVOT," AND LATER A "rebalanced" policy to the Asia Pacific region. During her first visit to Beijing in February 2009, Secretary of State Hillary Clinton stated that it was crucial for the world that the United States and the People's Republic of China (PRC) work together on security and economic issues.[1] President Obama sought to establish a constructive engagement with the PRC. He met with PRC president Hu Jintao at the sidelines of the Group of 20 (G-20) summit in London in April 2009. They agreed on establishing "constructive and cooperative" relations for both countries.[2] Despite attempts at further cooperation, differences between the two countries persisted.

Historical Events: The Normalization of Cross-Strait Relations

Newly elected Republic of China (ROC) president Ma Ying-jeou shifted Taiwan's approach to China from confrontation to engagement. The normalization of relations became a priority for Ma. The ruling party (Kuomintang, or KMT) believed that improved cross-strait relations not only would reinforce Taiwan's security, but also would increase economic opportunities.

Cross-Strait Détente

In his inaugural address on May 20, 2008, President Ma asserted that there would be "no reunification, no independence, and no war" during his four-year term. He called for a return to cross-strait dialogues based on the 1992 Consensus.[3] As a result, Beijing expressed a willingness to resume dialogues with Taiwan.

257

258   *Hedging the China Threat*

The Economic Cooperation Framework Agreement (ECFA). The two sides resumed talks in June 2008 under the banners of Taiwan's Straits Exchange Foundation (SEF) and China's Association for Relations Across the Taiwan Straits (ARATS). These two semiofficial government organizations produced sixteen agreements on various functional and economic issues. Among them, ECFA, a preferential trade agreement that aimed to reduce tariffs and commercial barriers, stood out.[4] The pact, signed on June 29, 2010, in Chongqing, China, was considered the most important cross-strait agreement since 1949. Under the agreements, Taiwan and China would reach a zero-tariff goal on goods within two years after its implementation.[5] ECFA was important for cross-strait relations, both politically and economically. The opposition parties in Taiwan, the Democratic Progressive Party (DPP) and Taiwan Solidarity Union (TSU), however, criticized ECFA as being inadequately protective of Taiwan's sovereignty. In response, the KMT government released the results of a poll conducted shortly after the agreements were concluded, reporting 60–70 percent approval of the accords. The Obama administration welcomed the increased cross-strait interaction that the ECFA agreement represented.[6]

Confidence-building measures. After Obama assumed the presidency in 2009, his administration expressed support for cross-strait confidence-building measures (CBMs).[7] On July 14, the ROC's minister of the Mainland Affairs Council (MAC), Lai Shin-yuan, indicated that Taiwan public opinion polls in 2009 showed that more than 70 percent of the people supported the cross-strait negotiation mechanism; and 60–80 percent of the population was satisfied with the cross-strait agreements.[8]

On December 31, 2008, Hu Jintao's speech on the PRC's thirtieth anniversary of opening-up and economic reform included a six-point proposal calling for peace in the Taiwan Strait. The points included: abiding by the One China principle, strengthening commercial ties, promoting personnel exchanges, stressing cultural links, allowing Taiwan's reasonable participation in international organizations, and negotiating a peace agreement.[9] Hu stated that both sides could engage in exchanges on military matters and discuss establishing military security CBMs.[10] On September 16, 2010, Taiwan's coast guard conducted a joint maritime rescue drill with its Chinese counterpart.[11] The joint exercise at sea was an initial step for cross-strait CBMs.

The Sunflower Movement

In March 2014, protests broke out against the Taiwan ruling party's attempt to push a new Cross Strait Service Trade Agreement (CSSTA) through the legislature. Ma hoped for an approval process, but faced opposition. The protestors, who called the protests the "Sunflower Movement," were wary of the economic consequences of CSSTA. They criticized Ma's lack of efforts to oversee cross-strait relations.[12] During his first term, Ma worked toward a closer relationship with China. Shortly after winning the reelection, Ma wanted the trade deal to pass, but his decision came with a political price.[13] The ECFA went into effect in 2011, but in 2013 the government experienced growing opposition to this economic integration. On March 18, 2014, the protesters staged a rally outside the Legislative Yuan. They occupied the legislative chamber and succeeded in preventing attempts by police to expel them.[14]

Before students occupied the legislative building, they wanted the CSSTA bill to be sent back to the "article-by-article review and voting" stage. On March 20, they issued new demands: to withdraw the CSSTA and to legislate a supervisory law for cross-strait negotiations. On March 22, Premier Jiang Yi-huah met with student leader Lin Fei-fan, but Jiang refused the demand to withdraw the trade agreement. The next day, President Ma held a press conference and stressed the economic advantages of the free-trade agreement with China. After several futile negotiations, some protestors decided to occupy the Executive Yuan. On March 23, they broke into the government building, but the next day the police dispersed them. On March 29, Ma held another press conference and commented on the movement as youth demonstrating their social concern and democratic participation. Since the end of March, the movement experienced a drop in protestors, so the Sunflower leadership knew that the passion of protestors had faded. On April 10, protestors departed from the legislative chamber.[15] This social movement seriously damaged the ruling KMT party's image and boosted the opposition DPP's morale. Accordingly, the KMT lost the presidential election to the DPP in 2016.

Cross-Strait Relations During the Obama Administration

During the Obama administration, Beijing and Taipei expanded trade links and cultural ties as a means of reducing tension. In a 2011 poll conducted by Taiwan's Mainland Affairs Council, more than 60 percent of participants expressed a positive view of the pace of cross-strait exchanges. Despite improving relations, China continued its military buildup to prepare its future Taiwan contingency.[16] Obama was elected the same year that Ma assumed the ROC presidency. Ma came to the office pledging closer cross-strait ties that reduced bilateral tensions. The Obama administration expressed its support for reconciliation between Taiwan and China.[17] In 2015, China's strategy toward Taiwan was influenced by what it saw as positive cross-strait developments. For example, a summit between Xi Jinping and Ma Ying-jeou occurred in Singapore in November, the first meeting since 1946.[18]

China's security approach to Taiwan. The Chinese government deferred using force, as long as it believed unification over the long term remained possible. It argued that the threat of using force was important to prevent

260 Hedging the China Threat

Taiwan from moving toward independence.[19] Beijing strived to integrate cross-strait economies, advance social and cultural ties, and isolate Taiwan's political actors that took pro-independence positions. In December 2010, PRC state councilor Dai Bingguo stated, "The Taiwan question is related to the reunification and territorial integrity of China. It concerns the core interests of China."[20] Despite its desire for peaceful unification, the PLA enhanced its ability to implement complex joint operations by improving its planning and preparation.[21]

The PLA had developed measures to counter the United States' military intervention in any future cross-strait crisis. China's approach to dealing with this challenge was to develop the capability to attack military forces deployed within the Western Pacific, which the US military characterized as "anti-access" and "area denial" capabilities.[22]

Taiwan's defense capability. During the Obama administration, China's military modernization continued to advance. The cross-strait military balance had tilted in China's favor. Consequently, Taiwan took steps to build its war reserve stocks, improve its defense industrial base, enhance joint operations capability, and strengthen officer and noncommissioned officer corps. These improvements reinforced Taiwan's defense in the face of the Chinese military buildup. Following the release of its first Quadrennial Defense Review in March 2009, Taiwan focused on creating an all-volunteer military and reducing its active military strength from 275,000 to 215,000 personnel to create a "small but smart force."[23] China's defense budget was about ten times that of Taiwan's. Realizing that Taiwan could not match China's military spending, Taiwan integrated innovative and asymmetric measures into its defense planning to counter the PLA's growing capabilities.[24]

Cross-strait relations improved during the Obama administration. All advocates agreed, however, that to maintain the strategic balance it was necessary for the United States to continue arms sales to Taiwan. In January 2010, Obama approved an arms sales package to Taiwan despite China's strong opposition and retaliatory measures by summoning the US chargé d'affaires in Beijing, Kaye Lee, to protest and imposing sanctions on the US companies involved in arms sales to Taiwan. The decision to sell more defensive weapons to Taiwan revealed practical US support for Taiwan's democracy.[25]

The Individual Level:
Obama's Proactive Engagement with China

During Obama's presidential campaign, one of the criticisms was his lack of foreign policy experience. He would rely on his advisors, who were selected for their expertise. Obama had his view of US foreign policy, defined by growing cooperation on global issues. In a Democratic primary debate on April 26, 2007, Obama laid out his vision for Asian policy. He declared that the United States must take an active position in Asia Pacific in response to China's rise.[26]

The Obama-Hu Summits

Obama felt it was important for the United States to be able to work with China. On May 23, 2007, Obama gave a speech in the Senate to comment on his future policies toward China, stating: "It is critical the U.S. do all it can to ensure that China's rise is peaceful and its trade practices fair." To respond to a growing Chinese military, Obama suggested that the United States maintain a military presence in Asia Pacific and strengthen US alliances. In August 2008, Obama invited Joe Biden to serve as his running mate. Having served in the Senate since 1973, Biden was an experienced member of the Senate Foreign Relations Committee. He was chosen to fill a gap in Obama's foreign policy experience. Biden and Obama shared a similar view of foreign policy, emphasizing cooperation with allies and reserving force as a last resort.[27]

After assuming the presidency, Obama encountered the challenges of the Iranian and North Korean nuclear weapons development, and pressure from al-Qaeda in Afghanistan and Pakistan. In Obama's worldview, China's role in these issues was essential. His objective in the early months of his presidency was to prevent the decline in US-China relations that had occurred in previous administrations and to not undermine China's cooperation on global issues. Obama wanted to develop closer interactions with President Hu. He called Hu within days of the election, and later engaged in face-to-face meetings at several international conferences. Their first meeting occurred at the G-20 summit in London in April 2009. Both leaders agreed on establishing the Strategic and Economic Dialogue, which would bring together officials from both sides for annual meetings.[28] Obama and Hu agreed to hold US-China summits, to establish dialogues, and to resume military exchanges.[29] Regarding the Taiwan issues, Hu stressed the One China principle and requested that the United States stop arms sales to Taiwan. Beijing proposed issuing a joint statement or communiqué. The United States showed no interest in that because of earlier controversial experiences created by communiqués on the Taiwan issue.[30]

In 2010, Obama's strategy toward China rested on three principles. First, China should not be considered an inevitable adversary, but instead a potential partner in resolving global issues. In meeting this goal, Obama met with Hu four times in his first year in office and called him on the phone several times.[31] Second, China should accept the principles of freedom of navigation established by the UN Convention on the Law of the Sea. And it

262   Hedging the China Threat

should also work with the UN Security Council to halt the proliferation of nuclear weapons, particularly in North Korea and Iran. Third, the administration sought to ensure that China's rise served to stabilize Asia Pacific.[32]

Hu Jintao's Visit to the United States

In November 2009, Obama made a state visit to China. During the joint press statement on November 17, Hu said that the two sides had an in-depth exchange of views on furthering the relationship and major regional and international issues of shared interest. Both countries wanted to deepen cooperation in outer space, counterterrorism, military-to-military ties, science and technology, and high-speed railway infrastructure. They would work with other parties concerned to continue the denuclearization process of the Korean Peninsula and the six-party talks process to uphold peace in Northeast Asia. They also stressed that resolving the Iranian nuclear issue through dialogue was very important.[33] Regarding Taiwan issues, the United States applauded the steps that China and Taiwan had taken to relax tensions and build closer ties. The United States supported the further development of these ties.[34]

In 2010, China's assertive actions alienated most of its neighbors. US-China relations became complicated. In their meeting in June 2010 at the G-20 summit in Toronto, Obama invited Hu to the United States for a state visit, reciprocating Obama's visit to China in 2009. At the time, high-level visits with Chinese leaders were unpopular at home in the United States. Obama, however, believed the bilateral relationship was key to achieving his foreign policy goals. Although Obama recognized that a state visit would attract more criticism than a lower-profile visit, he decided this was necessary to advance the relationship.[35]

In early September 2010, the director of the National Economic Council, Lawrence Summers, and Deputy National Security Advisor (NSA) Thomas Donilon traveled to Beijing for three days of meetings with Chinese leaders. They discussed Hu's visit to the United States in 2011.[36] The Donilon-Summers trip aimed to convey to Beijing that Obama did not see US-China relations in zero-sum terms and was interested in cooperation. Hu's trip to the United States presented an opportunity to put the relationship on a solid track for the Obama presidency.[37] On January 19, 2011, Obama hosted Hu for a dinner at the White House. Obama pressed Hu hard about the North Korean uranium enrichment program. Hu finally agreed to a formulation under which China would express "concern" over the North Korean program, and oppose activities inconsistent with North Korea's international obligations.[38] Obama and Hu also went over economic issues. Hu released news of purchasing 200 Boeing aircraft.[39]

Obama's 2011 Trip to Asia

In 2011, Obama molded his Asia strategy into a unified diplomatic, military, and economic refocusing called the "pivot" or "rebalancing" to Asia. The team that crafted Obama's China policy underwent a significant personnel reshuffle. James Steinberg and Jeffrey Bader left the administration. The US ambassador to China, Jon Huntsman, also stepped down. Bader's replacement, Daniel Russel, had a background in Japanese affairs. Kurt Campbell, assistant secretary of state for East Asian affairs, gained influence in policymaking on China. The new teams shifted toward a "tougher line" toward China. In August 2011, Obama assigned Biden to visit China to forge a relationship with the president-in-waiting, Xi Jinping. According to Biden's NSA, Tony Blinken, Obama was investing in the future of the US-China relationship.[40]

The pivot to Asia was announced during Obama's 2011 trip to Asia. He spoke at the Asia-Pacific Economic Cooperation (APEC) summit in Hawaii before traveling to Australia and ending his trip in Indonesia, where he became the first US president to attend the East Asia Summit (EAS). Obama emphasized that "the U.S. is a Pacific power, and we are here to stay." In his opening remarks at the 2011 APEC summit, Obama emphasized that Asia Pacific was a top priority for the United States. To integrate the US economy into the region, his administration announced plans for the Trans-Pacific Partnership (TPP), a US-backed free-trade agreement.[41]

While at the APEC summit, Obama focused on the economic aspects of the pivot. In Australia, Obama's speech emphasized the security of the pivot. In 2010, he clarified that the United States was interested in peacefully resolving China's maritime disputes to preserve the freedom of navigation. His announcement that the United States would deploy 2,500 US Marines to Australia surprised Beijing. He explained that deploying the forces would allow the United States to respond faster to challenges, including humanitarian crises and disaster relief.[42] Obama's policy of the pivot would include troop deployments to Australia, new naval deployments to Singapore, and military cooperation with the Philippines. The military presence in East Asia would be expanded.[43] Tensions in East Asia became greater during Obama's first two years in office. The Obama administration used military assets to signal Beijing that it would counter assertive PRC actions in the East and South China Seas.[44]

The Sunnylands Summit

In 2012, Obama's China policy was influenced by criticism from his opponent during the presidential campaign. Republican candidate Mitt Romney challenged Obama's China policy, criticizing Obama's weakness toward

264 *Hedging the China Threat*

China. As a result, Obama responded with a tougher stance toward China. Since 2010, Obama had taken a firm diplomatic stance against perceived Chinese aggression in the East and South China Seas. The Obama administration was concerned about the new Chinese leadership's repeated emphasis on building a strong navy and standing firm over territorial issues.[45] Soon after Xi became president, Xi's staff began working with the Obama administration to arrange meetings between the two presidents.

From June 7 to 8, 2013, Obama and Xi held informal meetings, dubbed the "Sunnylands Summit," at the Annenberg Estate in California. A US cybersecurity firm released a report detailing the activities of Chinese hackers allegedly connected to the PLA. The report claimed that Chinese cyberattacks had stolen intellectual property from US companies and targeted US government agencies. The Pentagon also accused Beijing of sponsoring hacking operations.[46] China denied supporting cyberattacks and turned these accusations back on the United States. Obama used the summit to resolve the cybersecurity issue. Obama warned Xi that if the cyberattacks were not addressed, it would be "an inhibitor to the relationship."[47]

However, a contractor for the US National Security Agency (NSA), Edward Snowden, revealed information on extensive surveillance being done by the NSA, both within the United States and abroad. Snowden stated that the NSA had hacking programs targeting universities, businesses, and government officials within China. At a March 2014 press conference, a spokesman for PRC's Ministry of National Defense dismissed US complaints of Chinese hacking as "a thief yelling 'Stop, thief!'" In meetings with Xi, Obama pointed out that "the U.S. does not engage in intelligence gathering to gain a commercial advantage."[48]

The State Level: From Pivot to Rebalance

The Obama administration was wary of China's aggressive island building in the South China Sea. Beijing viewed territory as the central pillar of its national interest. Its claims over Taiwan, the Diaoyu Islands, and the islands in the South China Sea conflicted with US interests. At the July 2010 Association of Southeast Asian Nations (ASEAN) Regional Forum (ARF), Secretary of State Hillary Clinton stated that the United States took no stance on the sovereignty issue in the South China Sea, but that the United States wanted the claimants to deal with the disputes peacefully.[49]

Key Players of the Obama Administration in China's Policy

From 2009 to 2010, the Obama administration saw China's island reclamation in the South China Sea as aggressive. The administration responded by pivoting toward Asia Pacific and rebalancing the US military presence. The rebalance policy was declared on October 11, 2011, with Secretary Clinton's article "America's Pacific Century" in *Foreign Policy*. The article stated that in the twenty-first century, Asia would represent the major market. She described economics as a significant motivation for the pivot or rebalance. While tensions in Asia increased, the Obama administration used military assets to signal to Beijing that it would counter assertive PRC actions in the region.[50]

Obama asked Hillary Clinton to lead the State Department. She had a long history with China, tracing back to her time as the first lady. During the 1995 World Conference on Women in Beijing, she rebuked China for lacking the right of people to assemble and to debate openly, which infuriated Chinese leaders. During her first official trip to China in February 2009, Clinton stated that human rights issues should not interfere with progress on other concerns. While Clinton carried out Obama's China policy, she had less influence on Obama's China strategy than other advisors, especially James Steinberg.[51] Deputy Secretary of State Steinberg was the most important advisor to Obama on China policy. He was selected by Obama to improve the US ties with Asia in general, and China in particular. He remained influential in China policy until his departure in mid-2011.[52] Steinberg was replaced by William Burns, a Middle East expert. However, Burns did not take over Steinberg's role in Asia policy. This role was filled by Kurt Campbell, assistant secretary of state for East Asian and Pacific affairs. Campbell had close ties with Japan and Taiwan. Steinberg's departure, coupled with Campbell's rise, marked a change for the Obama administration, which took a tougher stance toward China. When Clinton stepped down in 2013, John Kerry, who replaced Clinton, had a closer relationship with Obama. Kerry focused on dealing with crises in Syria and Ukraine, limiting his ability to focus on Asia.[53]

At the Pentagon, the role of Defense Secretary Robert Gates offered continuity in US-China military relations. Having previously served as George W. Bush's defense secretary, Gates was familiar with the top Chinese leadership. However, this would not lead to a trouble-free US-China relationship. With China angry over a US arms sale to Taiwan, Gates was refused permission to visit China in 2010. When Gates stepped down in 2011, Obama chose Leon Panetta as the new secretary of defense. Panetta had little experience with China. The timing of his appointment would make it difficult for him to have good relations with China because one of his tasks was promoting the pivot to Asia policy.[54] Chuck Hagel was chosen as secretary of defense in 2013. Hagel had shown a special interest in foreign affairs, serving on the Foreign Relations Committee of the Senate, including the Subcommittee on East Asian and Pacific Affairs. Hagel had a good understanding of China. Beijing had high hopes that Hagel, with his moderate views, would be willing to work with China.[55]

As for the NSC, Obama's China advisor was Jeffrey Bader, senior director for Asian affairs on the council. Bader exerted influence on shaping and

266   *Hedging the China Threat*

implementing China policy. He argued that the United States and China should work together to solve global issues while continuing support for Taiwan.[56] In 2011, Obama handpicked Thomas Donilon to replace NSA James Jones. Donilon, a member of Obama's inner circle, gave daily briefings to Obama. Donilon was an influential advocate for "rebalancing" US foreign policy "to focus more on China, Iran, and other emerging challenges." After Bader and Steinberg left the administration in 2011, Donilon took the lion's share of the work in advising and implementing Obama's China policy.[57]

Engaging and Hedging in US-China Relations

In 2005, Deputy Secretary of State Robert Zoellick stated that China's rise was not harming US interests. The United States encouraged China to become a "responsible stakeholder," urging China to work with the United States in global affairs. While the United States fostered a pragmatic relationship, it would monitor China's military buildup.[58] The Obama administration continued this approach. The balance of engaging and hedging in US-China relations continued. China's rising power reoriented the US foreign policy priority from the Middle East to East Asia.[59]

During the presidential campaign, Obama's foreign policy team believed the US policy toward a rising China could not rely solely on military strength and pressure on human rights. They suggested that the US presence in Asia should be strengthened in the face of a rising China. The team's core beliefs centered on alliances with US partners, a forward deployment in Asia, and a better US-China relationship to expand cooperation.[60]

The Obama administration's strategic principles toward Asia Pacific included as follows: first, as Asia Pacific emerged as the world's center of gravity, the region deserved priority in US foreign policy. Second, China's rise became a constructive force rather than a threat to peace. A sound China strategy should rest on welcoming China's emergence, its rise being consistent with international norms. Third, the United States' relations with Japan, South Korea, and Australia were critical to maintaining a framework of peace and stability in the region. Fourth, North Korea was emerging as a nuclear weapons state. The United States needed to break the cycle of its provocation, extortion, accommodation, and reward. Finally, the United States must participate in and lead the most important multilateral organizations in the region.[61]

Deputy NSA Tom Donilon suggested that the United States needed to rebuild its presence in East Asia, suggesting early steps to show this approach. Assistant Secretary of State for East Asian and Pacific Affairs Kurt Campbell supported an early trip to Asia by Secretary Hillary Clinton to demonstrate Asia's centrality to US interests. She agreed. The trip, from February 15 to 22, 2009, included: Japan, South Korea, China, and Indonesia.[62] Beijing viewed Clinton with suspicion because she had criticized human rights and trade issues in China during the campaign. However, Clinton's interactions with the Chinese leaders were solid throughout her meetings. She said that the US side presented its points on human rights while the Chinese side presented its points about Taiwan, and this was all predictable and resulted in formalistic exchanges. It did not prevent the two sides from exchanging views on global issues.[63]

At the July 2010 ASEAN Regional Forum, Clinton stated that the United States took no stance on the sovereignty disagreements in the South China Sea, but wanted the claimants to deal with the territorial disputes peacefully.[64] The administration responded by pivoting toward Asia Pacific and rebalancing the US military presence. Clinton emphasized that the United States would maintain close diplomatic dialogues with its allies of Japan, South Korea, the Philippines, Australia, and Thailand.[65]

As mentioned above, the rise of China's power reoriented the foreign policy priority of the United States from the Middle East to East Asia, leading to a strategic repositioning effort focused on Asia Pacific in 2011 (the "pivot to Asia," subsequently called the "rebalance to Asia"). Strengthening relations between the United States' regional allies to better integrate alliances played an essential role and ensured diversification of the United States' strategic approach, reducing China's influence in the region.[66]

The Arms Sales Skirmish

In 2010, the Pentagon prepared a proposal for arms sales to Taiwan, including Patriot missiles, Blackhawk helicopters, Harpoon training missiles, minesweeping ships, and an option for diesel submarines. The proposal then proceeded to a Principals Committee meeting in January to make the decisions. The committee was chaired by NSA Jim Jones and included Secretary of State Clinton; Secretary of Defense Robert Gates; the chairman of the Joint Chiefs of Staff (JCS), Admiral Michael Mullen; and the director of the CIA, Leon Panetta. The committee endorsed the package except for the submarines, which the Pentagon said would be inconsistent with the defensive character.[67]

On January 30, Senior Director for East Asian Affairs on the National Security Council Jeffery Bader met with the PRC ambassador to the United States, Zhou Wenzhong. Zhou expressed Beijing's anger over the sale, suggesting several proposals to soften US-China relations. A visit by Deputy Secretary Steinberg and Bader to Beijing was an important first step. After that, the new Chinese ambassador would arrive in Washington, hoping to meet Obama. In the next few weeks, Beijing's rhetoric over the sale heated up noticeably. Beijing threatened retaliation against US companies whose technology or parts were in the Taiwan arms sale package. Bader warned Zhou that any Chinese retaliation against companies would trigger a trade war and major retaliatory actions by the United States.[68]

268 *Hedging the China Threat*

During their trip to Beijing, Steinberg and Bader assured Beijing that Obama had devoted effort to building positive US-China relations in the face of domestic criticism. In all meetings, including those with State Councilor Dai Bingguo and Foreign Minister Yang Jiechi, Steinberg and Bader were subjected to a verbal assault, especially on Taiwan issues. China demanded that the United States halt arms sales to Taiwan. Steinberg and Bader were pressured for assurances that the United States would not sell arms to Taiwan. The United States refused to give such assurances.[69]

Secretary Gates called the arms sales "an important component of maintaining peace and stability in cross-strait relations and throughout the region." As a result, China cut off military contact with the United States. China argued that arms sales were a dangerous way of emboldening Taiwan's independence movement. The US-China military contacts resumed with the January 2011 visit by Gates to China, aimed to smooth over tensions before Hu's state visit. The PRC officials stated that further arms sales would have similar consequences. Many US officials thought of China's objections to Taiwanese arms sales as "theatrical" and "ritualistic."[70]

In September 2011, another arms sale was announced: an advanced retrofit program for Taiwan's F-16 A/B fighter jets, training, and spare parts for Taiwan's air force.[71] Beijing persisted in warning of consequences for US-China relations if the Obama government sold weapons to Taiwan or took other measures that increased US support for Taiwan.[72] The Obama administration showed no signs of halting arms sales to Taiwan. Washington viewed Taiwanese arms sales as an obligation, especially considering China's increasing military buildup.[73]

Increasing US-China Military Contacts

The Obama administration tried to improve the US-China military relationship, but the efforts were limited. The barriers, especially disagreements over Taiwan and tensions in the South China Sea, remained intact. In October 2009, Secretary Gates met Xu Caihou, vice chairman of the Central Military Commission (CMC), at the Pentagon. Gates noted his determination to break the "on-again, off-again" pattern. Both agreed to prioritize areas in the relations, including high-level exchanges, officer exchanges, cooperation in humanitarian efforts, and revitalizing the diplomatic channels. These efforts were curbed in 2010 when China ended contact in retaliation for a US arms sale to Taiwan. Gates visited China in January 2011, restoring US-China military ties. In May, General Chen Bingde, chief of the General Staff, traveled to the United States and met with the chairman of the JCS, Admiral Mike Mullen. Both announced that their militaries had committed to conducting a humanitarian and disaster relief exercise in 2012.[74]

Despite increasing unease, military contacts continued in 2012. Defense Secretary Leon Panetta said he was committed to building a "healthy, stable, reliable, and continuous mil-to-mil relationship with China." General Liang visited the United States in May, a visit many thought might be canceled following a US arms sale to Taiwan. Panetta and Liang announced that the United States and China would conduct joint counterpiracy exercises in the Gulf of Aden in late 2012. In June, Admiral Samuel Locklear, commander in chief of the Pacific Command, visited China. Locklear mentioned that a major priority of his trip was to explain the United States' renewed presence in the Pacific.[75]

In mid-September 2012, Secretary Panetta visited China after a trip to Japan when China and Japan were having a tense dispute over the Diaoyu Islands. Vice President Xi Jinping and Defense Minister Liang Guanglie used Panetta's visit as an opportunity to express discontent with Japan. Panetta tried to lessen China's concerns about the US stance on the Diaoyu debate and the pivot to Asia. Panetta stated, "Our rebalance to the Asia-Pacific region is not an attempt to contain China."[76]

From 2013 to 2014, bilateral military high-ranking contacts became more frequent. For example, the Chinese defense minister, Chang Wanquan, visited the United States in 2013. In return, the new US defense secretary, Chuck Hagel, visited Beijing in 2014. General Martin Dempsey, chairman of the JCS, and General Fang Fenghui, chief of the PLA General Staff, would also exchange visits in 2013 and 2014. Each visit was marked by certain results, with promises of joint military drills and exchange programs. On April 7, 2014, Hagel was taken on a historic tour of China's first aircraft carrier, the *Liaoning*. He was the first foreign official to be brought on board for a tour.[77] Despite frequent military contacts, the meetings were tense, and suspicion of each other's intentions ran deep.

The International Level: China Seas Disputes and North Korean Nuclear Issues

The growing tensions around China's territorial claims in the South and East China Seas had raised questions about whether China's growing power would lead not just to more forceful assertions of historical claims, but to ever expanding demands. China labeled "core interest" to describe its South China Sea claims. The increasing toughness of China's rhetoric in support of the legitimacy of its claims, coupled with the increase in the defense budget, provided evidence to those who worried that, if unchecked, China would become more aggressive.[78]

The Diaoyu/Senkaku Islands Dispute

In June 2004, Japan protested that China incorporated the disputed Diaoyu/Senkaku Islands (Japan calls them Senkaku Islands and China calls them

270 *Hedging the China Threat*

Diaoyu Islands) into its territory under the territorial sea law. Neither side came up with an agreement.[79] These islands were a group of uninhabited rocky islets in the East China Sea. Japan, China, and Taiwan had laid claim to the islands. A crisis occurred when a right-wing Japanese group landed on one of the islands to renovate a lighthouse and demanded that the government recognize it. Tension followed Japan's detention of the captain of a Chinese vessel that collided with two Japanese coast guard ships near the Diaoyu Islands in September 2010.[80] Under the US-Japan Treaty of Mutual Security and Cooperation of 1960, the United States was obligated to defend all territories administered by Japan, which included the Diaoyu Islands. The United States, however, did not take a position on the respective territorial claims of Japan and China over islands.[81]

In 2012, Beijing reacted angrily to Tokyo's move to nationalize Diaoyus/ Senkakus by purchasing the islands from a private owner. Japan and China began sending more naval vessels and aircraft into the region on patrols. The United States responded to the tensions by trying to preserve its neutrality, but insisted that the US-Japan treaty covered Diaoyus/Senkakus. Panetta emphasized this message during his visit to China in September. In November, Japan and the United States conducted a joint military exercise to simulate recapturing an island held by an enemy force. Beijing was upset at the United States' support for Japan's claim.[82] Chairman of the JCS Mullen and Secretary Clinton spoke publicly, reaffirming the US obligation to defend areas administered by Japan, including Diaoyus/Senkakus. In response to a question about a possible war, Senior Director for East Asian Affairs on the National Security Council Bader described US obligations under the treaty,[83] saying that United States recognized that "they [Diaoyus/Senkakus] are under the administration of Japan and fall under our security treaty obligations." The PRC Foreign Ministry condemned these statements. After the Obama-Xi summit in June 2013, Obama stated that while the United States did not take a stance on the sovereignty of the contested islets, China and Japan should seek to discuss this through diplomatic channels.[84]

Tensions in the South China Sea

The official territorial claim of the PRC government extended to waters within the "nine-dash line" that covers most of the South China Sea.[85] The Obama administration took no position on territorial claims to islands in the South China Sea asserted by China, Vietnam, the Philippines, Malaysia, Taiwan, and Brunei.[86] PLA naval deployments in the South China Sea had increased since 2000, and incidents between China and other claimant states were on the rise.

Assistant Secretary of State for East Asian and Pacific Affairs Kurt Campbell and his staff drafted a statement for Secretary Clinton to deliver at the annual meeting of the ARF in Hanoi in July 2010. Her draft reiterated the US position of not taking sides on territorial claims. It asserted US interests such as freedom of navigation, free commerce without intimidation, support for a collaborative process to resolve competing territorial claims, and US willingness to facilitate negotiations.[87] Clinton delivered her statement containing these principles in Hanoi at a closed-door session of the ARF. A dozen other countries spoke at the meeting on the issue. China's foreign minister, Yang Jiechi, denied that there were any problems in the South China Sea and warned ASEAN countries not to become involved in a faction organized by the United States. He also told Singapore's Minister for Foreign Affairs, George Yeo, that "China is a big country. Bigger than any other countries here." The remark was meant to deter the ASEAN states from seeking outside help. By September, as Obama was preparing to meet with the ten leaders of the ASEAN countries, China indicated that it was willing to begin expert talks on a code of conduct in the South China Sea.[88]

In April 2012, the Philippines and China began a standoff over the Scarborough Shoal. The clash began when a Philippine warship confronted Chinese fishing vessels near the shoal. Chinese surveillance ships arrived to defend the fishing vessels. This dispute spilled over to cause US-China tension. The Obama administration did assert its right to freedom of navigation in the area. Chinese officials accused the United States of interfering by driving a wedge between China and its neighbors. This incident caused tension because of a joint US-Philippine naval exercise that took place soon after the stalemate began. The Obama administration said the exercise had nothing to do with the territorial dispute, but China believed the drills demonstrated US support for the Philippines' claim.[89] In fact, the United States brokered an agreement that both China and the Philippines would withdraw from the shoal. The Philippines did withdraw, but China did not.

The spring of 2014 was a tense time in the South China Sea, as confrontations between China and the Philippines, and China and Vietnam, aggravated into maritime clashes. The Philippines filed an international arbitration case against China in late March. The case questioned the legality of China's nine-dash line claim to the South China Sea under the UN Convention on the Law of the Sea. China denounced this move, insisting on handling territorial disputes in bilateral discussions, but the United States offered strong support for the move. In May, the deployment of a Chinese oil rig to a disputed area resulted in clashes with Vietnam. The rig was set up 120 nautical miles from Vietnam's coast, which Hanoi saw as violating its exclusive economic zone. China said the rig was within China's territorial waters. The United States denounced the placement of the oil rig.[90]

In the Senate in May 2015, David Shears, assistant secretary of defense for Asian and Pacific security affairs, stated that the administration was assessing the military implications of land reclamation and was committed to taking effective action.[91] The United States would consider sending ships and aircraft within twelve nautical miles of constructed reefs near the Philippines

272   *Hedging the China Threat*

and other islands. This action would show its dedication to the freedom of navigation. In a speech at the Shangri-La Dialogue in May, Defense Secretary Ash Carter remarked that the United States would fly, sail, and operate wherever international law allowed, as US forces did worldwide. Carter appealed for a halt on island reclamation by all claimants.[92] President Xi Jinping promised Obama that China would not construct military bases on the reclaimed islands, but then the military bases were constructed in violation of the promise. As a result, the Obama administration was operating on several fronts to restrain China's assertiveness in the region.

The North Korean Nuclear Issue

The Obama government entered office poised to use the six-party talks and bilateral discussions with North Korea in seeking progress in getting Pyongyang to fulfill its obligations under agreements reached in the talks during the previous US administration. North Korea's escalating provocations created a major crisis in 2009 that forced the Obama government to change priorities and give top-level attention to dealing with Pyongyang. The provocations included a long-range ballistic missile test, a nuclear weapons test, withdrawal from the six-party talks, and resumption of nuclear weapons development.[93]

Secretary Kerry had been in office for little over a week when North Korea conducted its third nuclear test and the first since 2009. The United States and South Korea urged North Korea not to escalate the situation and also put pressure on China to prevent the test. China reacted to the test as follows: Foreign Minister Yang Jiechi summoned North Korea's ambassador to China. Yang relayed to him China's "strong dissatisfaction and firm opposition" to the nuclear test and demanded an end to further provocations. In early March, the UN Security Council approved a new round of sanctions against North Korea, with assets frozen on firms with ties to the North Korean military and sanctions targeting the sale of luxury goods. During that time, China pushed for a return to the six-party talks, while the United States maintained that Pyongyang must give a concrete show of its good faith before negotiations could resume.[94]

The United States sought to negotiate a conclusion to North Korea's nuclear and missile advancement. By the end of Obama's second term, the administration's "strategic patience" approach was under pressure and deemed by many critics to fail in appeasement. During Obama's tenure in office, North Korea conducted four nuclear weapons tests: in 2006, 2009, 2013, and two notably advanced tests in 2016. The United States and China shared a mutual concern for stability on the Korean Peninsula, and, ultimately, attaining verifiable denuclearization of the peninsula.[95] China claimed that it wanted denuclearization, but never used its economic leverage over North Korea to achieve it. China has continued to offer North Korea an economic lifeline.

Conclusion

The Obama administration advocated a pivot and, later, a rebalancing policy in the Asia Pacific region. President Obama sought to establish a constructive engagement with China. His administration encouraged China to become a "responsible stakeholder," urging it to work with the United States in global affairs. Nevertheless, the growing tensions regarding China's territorial claims in the South and East China Seas were raising questions in the United States about whether China's growing power would lead not just to more forceful assertions of historical claims, but to ever expanding demands.

The Obama administration's China policy included three important new concepts: (1) China should not be considered an inevitable adversary, but a potential partner in resolving critical global issues; (2) China should accept the principles of freedom of navigation established by the UN Convention on the Law of the Sea; and (3) China should work with the UN Security Council to halt the proliferation of nuclear weapons, particularly in North Korea and Iran.

At the individual level, President Obama believed that Asia Pacific was emerging as the world's economic center of gravity, and that the region deserved priority in US foreign policy. He thought a comprehensive China strategy should rest on welcoming China's emergence, seeing its rise as being consistent with international norms. However, to respond to a growing Chinese military, Obama suggested that the United States maintain a military presence in the Asia Pacific region and strengthen US alliances there.

At the state level during the Obama administration, a rebalancing policy was initiated, which began with the focus of US foreign policy shifting from the Middle East to Asia. The National Security Council supported Obama's position that the United States should work with China to solve global issues, but the National Security Council advocated that the United States should also reestablish the US role in the region and continue its support for Taiwan. The Pentagon supported the continuation of a US military presence in the region to avoid potential military conflicts in the South China Sea area.

At the international level, China's increasing military aggressiveness in the South China Sea raised concerns in neighboring countries. The Philippines, Vietnam, and Taiwan sought close security relations with the US government to counter China's rising threat. North Korea's escalating military provocations created a major crisis in 2009 that forced the United States to redirect its priorities once again, and to give more attention to dealing with Pyongyang. The United States wanted China to encourage North Korea to give up its nuclear program.

During the Obama administration, cross-strait relations greatly improved. The US government sought economic and security developments

274 Hedging the China Threat

with China to advance mutual global interests. China's territorial claims in the East and South China Seas, however, became much more aggressive after Xi Jinping assumed power. Obama responded with a pivot to Asia policy that caused increased tension between the two countries. When Donald Trump took office in 2017, the rising trade deficit and China's economic policies would cause his administration to launch a trade war with China.

Notes

1. Aiden Warren and Adam Bartley, *U.S. Foreign Policy and China: Security Challenges During the Bush, Obama, and Trump Administrations* (Edinburgh: Edinburgh University Press, 2021), p. 81.

2. Robert Sutter, "The Obama Administration and China: Positive but Fragile Equilibrium," *Asian Perspectives* 33, no. 3 (2009): 83.

3. "Full Text of President Ma's Inaugural Address," *China Post,* May 21, 2008.

4. Albert Willner, "International Relations Taiwan Strait Security Challenges," International Relations Taiwan Strait Security Challenges 8, no. 2 (2009).

5. Yunguang Deng and Ding Xing, "A Milestone in Cross-Straits Relations," *Beijing Review,* July 19, 2010.

6. Alan Romberg, "Cross-Strait Relations: Setting the Stage for 2012," *China Leadership Monitor,* no. 34 (February 2011): 3.

7. Charles Snyder, "Staff Report in Washington Dialogue: In a Phone Conversation with George Bush," *Taipei Times,* March 28, 2008.

8. Shin-yuan Lai, "The Current Stage of Cross-Strait Relations and the ROC Government's China Policy," Mainland Affairs Council, July 14, 2009, http://www .mac.gov.tw.

9. "President Hu Offers Six Proposals for the Peaceful Development of the Cross-Strait Relationship," Consulate General of The People's Republic of China in Chicago, December 31, 2008, http://www.china-embassy.org.

10. Willner, "International Relations Taiwan Strait Security Challenges."

11. "China Holds Biggest Ever Search, Rescue Drill," *China Post,* September 17, 2010.

12. Chi Wang, *Obama's Challenge to China: The Pivot to Asia* (Abingdon: Routledge, 2017), p. 201.

13. Charles K. S. Wu, "How Public Opinion Shapes Taiwan's Sunflower Movement," *Journal of East Asian Studies* 19, no. 3 (2019): 299.

14. Ming-sho Ho, *Challenging Beijing's Mandate of Heaven: Taiwan's Sunflower Movement and Hong Kong's Umbrella Movement* (Philadelphia: Temple University Press, 2019), pp. 100–104.

15. Ibid., pp. 112–116.

16. US Department of Defense, *Annual Report to Congress: Military and Security Developments Involving the People's Republic of China 2011* (Washington, DC: Office of the Secretary of Defense, 2011), pp. 2–3.

17. Wang, *Obama's Challenge to China,* p. 199.

18. US Department of Defense, *Annual Report to Congress: Military and Security Developments Involving the People's Republic of China 2016* (Washington, DC: Office of the Secretary of Defense, 2016), p. 87.

19. US Department of Defense, *Annual Report to Congress: Military and Security Developments Involving the People's Republic of China 2015* (Washington, DC: Office of the Secretary of Defense, 2015), p. 57.

20. US Department of Defense, *Annual Report to Congress: Military and Security Developments Involving the People's Republic of China 2012* (Washington, DC: Office of the Secretary of Defense, 2012), p. 17.

21. US Department of Defense, *Annual Report to Congress: Military and Security Developments Involving the People's Republic of China 2018* (Washington, DC: Office of the Secretary of Defense, 2018), p. 96.

22. US Department of Defense, *Annual Report to Congress: 2011,* p. 29.

23. US Department of Defense, *Annual Report to Congress: Military and Security Developments Involving the People's Republic of China 2010* (Washington, DC: Office of the Secretary of Defense, 2010), p. 49.

24. US Department of Defense, *Annual Report to Congress: Military and Security Developments Involving the People's Republic of China 2013* (Washington, DC: Office of the Secretary of Defense, 2013), p. 58.

25. De-Yuan Kao, "China Policy," in *The Obama Presidency: A Preliminary Assessment,* edited by Robert P. Watson, Jack Covarrubias, Tom Lansford, and Douglas M. Brattebo (New York: SUNY Press, S2012), p. 269.

26. Wang, *Obama's Challenge to China,* p. 29.

27. Ibid., pp. 30–33.

28. Jeffery Bader, *Obama and China's Rise* (Washington, DC: Brooking Institution Press, 2012), pp. 21–22.

29. Sutter, "The Obama Administration and China," p. 83.

30. Bader, *Obama and China's Rise,* p. 24.

31. Ibid., p. 69.

32. Ibid., p. 70.

33. Office of the Press Secretary, "Joint Press Statement by President Obama and President Hu of China," White House, November 17, 2009, https:// obamawhitehouse.archives.gov.

34. Ibid.

35. Bader, *Obama and China's Rise,* pp. 109–110.

36. Gerhard Peters and John T. Woolley, "Trip by National Economic Council Director Lawrence H. Summers and Deputy National Security Advisor Thomas E. Donilon to China," Press release, American Presidency Project, September 2, 2010.

37. Bader, *Obama and China's Rise,* pp. 115–118.

38. Ibid., pp. 126–127.

39. Ibid., pp. 127–128.

40. Wang, *Obama's Challenge to China,* pp. 81–87.

41. Ibid., pp. 88–91.

42. Ibid., pp. 91–92.

43. Ibid., p. 98.

44. Warren and Bartley, *U.S. Foreign Policy and China,* p. 97.

45. Wang, *Obama's Challenge to China,* pp. 113–117.

46. Ibid., pp. 119–121.

47. Ibid., pp. 121–122.

48. Ibid., pp. 122–123.

49. Warren and Bartley, *U.S. Foreign Policy and China,* pp. 92–93.

50. Ibid., pp. 95–111.

51. Wang, *Obama's Challenge to China,* pp. 34–35.

52. Ibid., pp. 44–46.

53. Ibid., pp. 35–38.

54. Ibid., pp. 38–40.

55. Ibid., pp. 41–42.

56. Ibid., pp. 47–48.

57. Ibid., pp. 50–51.

58. Warren and Bartley, *U.S. Foreign Policy and China,* p. 83.

59. Anca Vasilache, "The Rebalance to Asia Policy of the Obama Administration (2011–2017): Diversifying the United States Security Design in Asia-Pacific," *Perspective Politice* 15, nos. 1–2 (2022): 87.

60. Bader, *Obama and China's Rise,* p. 6.

61. Ibid., pp. 6–7.

62. Bader, *Obama and China's Rise,* pp. 9–10.

63. Ibid., p. 15.

64. Warren and Bartley, *U.S. Foreign Policy and China,* pp. 92–93.

65. Ibid., p. 97.

66. Vasilache, "The Rebalance to Asia Policy of the Obama Administration (2011–2017)," p. 87.

67. Bader, *Obama and China's Rise,* pp. 72–73.

68. Ibid., p. 74.

69. Ibid., pp. 76–77.

70. Wang, *Obama's Challenge to China,* pp. 169–173.

71. Office of the Secretary of Defense, *Military and Security Developments Involving the People's Republic of China 2014* (Washington, DC: Office of the Secretary of Defense, 2014), p. 57.

72. Sutter, "The Obama Administration and China," p. 90.

73. Wang, *Obama's Challenge to China,* pp. 172–173.

74. Ibid., pp. 163–165.

75. Ibid., pp. 166–167.

76. Ibid., pp. 167–168.

77. Ibid., pp. 168–169.

78. James Steinberg and Michael E. O'Hanlon, *Strategic Reassurance and Resolve: U.S.-China Relations in the Twenty-first Century* (Princeton: Princeton University Press, 2014).

79. Chietigj Bajpaee, "China Fuels Energy Cold War," *Asia Times Online,* March 1, 2005, http://www.atimes.com.

80. Bhubhindar Singh, "China-Japan Dispute: Tokyo's Foreign Policy of Pragmatism," *Eurasia Review,* October 8, 2010.

81. Bader, *Obama and China's Rise,* p. 107.

82. Wang, *Obama's Challenge to China,* pp. 108–109.

83. Bader, *Obama and China's Rise,* pp. 107–108.

84. Warren and Bartley, *U.S. Foreign Policy and China,* p. 128.

85. Steinberg and O'Hanlon, *Strategic Reassurance and Resolve.*

86. Bader, *Obama and China's Rise,* p. 104.

87. Ibid., pp. 104–105.

88. Ibid., pp. 105–106.

89. Wang, *Obama's Challenge to China,* pp. 100–106.

90. Ibid., pp. 138–140.

91. Warren and Bartley, *U.S. Foreign Policy and China,* p. 130.

92. Ibid., p. 131.

93. Sutter, "The Obama Administration and China," p. 85.

94. Wang, *Obama's Challenge to China,* p. 118.

95. Warren and Bartley, *U.S. Foreign Policy and China,* pp. 142–143.

14

Confronting a
More Assertive China:
The Trump Administration

AS THE PEOPLE'S REPUBLIC OF CHINA (PRC) ENHANCED ITS ECONOMIC AND military strength, it sought Indo-Pacific influence in the near term and global preeminence in the long term. During the Trump administration, the 2017 National Security Strategy (NSS) and the 2018 National Defense Strategy (NDS) expressed a pessimistic view of China. The 2019 Pentagon's *Indo-Pacific Strategy Report* confirmed the negative approach to China. The Trump administration's Free and Open Indo-Pacific (FOIP) strategy took a zero-sum approach to China. As a result, the United States deepened its security relationship with Taiwan. The objective of US defense engagement with Taiwan was to ensure that Taiwan remains secure and able to engage China on its own terms.[1] In December 2019, the outbreak of Covid-19 began in China. At the outset of the epidemic, China failed to respond immediately to the international community. The virus spread and caused massive casualties worldwide, especially in the United States. Consequently, US-China relations further deteriorated.[2]

Historical Events:
The Deterioration of China-Taiwan Relations

Since the chairwoman of the Democratic Progressive Party (DPP), Tsai Ing-wen, won Taiwan's presidency in 2016, cross-strait relations have deteriorated. Tsai promised to maintain the status quo in her China policy, but refused to accept the 1992 Consensus. China responded by adopting an aggressive strategy against Taiwan.[3] The PRC media threatened Taiwan with an invasion by releasing a video of a drill featuring an amphibious attack. The People's Liberation Army (PLA) stated, "It would defeat Taiwan's

278 Hedging the China Threat

independence at all costs," and increased its military activities near Taiwan. Since 2020, the PLA has increasingly flown warplanes and sent warships close to Taiwan proper, breaching the median line in the Taiwan Strait.[4]

China's Coercion Against Taiwan

After the DPP became the ruling party, public opinion surveys in Taiwan continued to show a growing Taiwanese identity. In a 1994 survey, 26.2 percent of participants in Taiwan said they were Chinese, 20.2 percent said they were Taiwanese, and 44.6 percent said they were both. In 2018, only 4.1 percent of participants said they were Chinese, 56.4 percent said they were Taiwanese, and 34.1 percent said they were both. China feared that the younger generation in Taiwan had abandoned the One China principle.[5] Accordingly, China flexed its military muscle against Taiwan, including verbal intimidations and saber rattling. For example, Xi Jinping told US Defense Secretary Jim Mattis during his visit to Beijing in June 2018 that China would not give up an inch of its territory. Wei Fenghe, the PRC's defense minister, stated in November in Beijing: "If anyone tries to separate Taiwan from China, the PLA will take military action at all costs." In addition, PLA naval ships sailed through the Taiwan Strait, including sending the *Liaoning* aircraft carrier to the east coast of Taiwan. After demonstrating the largest display of naval forces in the South China Sea in April 2018, China announced that it would conduct live-fire drills in the Taiwan Strait. China also stepped up flights of bombers and fighter jets around Taiwan.[6]

The downturn in cross-strait relations. Regarding its China policy, Tsai vowed to protect democratic principles and Taiwan's sovereignty. Tsai delivered the 2019 New Year's Day address, proposing the "Four Musts" as the basis for moving cross-strait relations: China must face the existence of the Republic of China (ROC) regarding Taiwan; it must respect the commitment of the Taiwanese people to freedom and democracy; it must handle cross-strait differences peacefully; and it must be government or government-authorized agencies that engage in negotiations. Tsai said Taiwan would not accept a Hong Kong–style arrangement and called on Beijing to respect Taiwan's political sovereignty.[7] Taiwan's Mainland Affairs Council also said, "Any democratic negotiation under the precondition of One China is a negotiation that aims to divide Taiwan and terminate Taiwan's sovereignty."[8] The Tsai government emphasized that cross-strait disputes must be handled based on equality, transparency, and the will of the people in Taiwan.

On January 2, 2019, Xi Jinping spoke at the fortieth anniversary of United States and China diplomatic relations, established in 1979. His remarks on cross-strait relations became China's policy toward Taiwan. The first was promoting unification and rebuking independence. Xi stressed that unification was an inevitable requirement for the great rejuvenation of the Chinese people, advocating that Taiwan reject independence and embrace peaceful reunification with China under One Country, Two Systems.[9] The second was institutionalizing economic cooperation. Xi's speech suggested bolstering cross-strait trade relations, institutionalizing economic cooperation, and forging a common market.[10] Third, Xi did not set a deadline for unification, but he warned that the Taiwan issue "should not be passed down from generation to generation." China did not rule out using force if Taiwan pursued "de jure independence."[11]

China's perception of rising tensions. Beijing stated that the mounting cross-strait tension was attributed to Tsai's refusal to accept the 1992 Consensus and the increased US-Taiwan "collusion." The Chinese leaders believed that if the trend did not stop, Taiwan would move toward de jure independence. China's perception of rising tension included the following: first, Taiwan was moving toward independence. Beijing condemned Tsai's administration because it had moved toward separatism.[12] Moreover, the percentage of Taiwanese who identified as Taiwanese rose to historic heights. According to a 2020 survey conducted by the Taiwan think tank, only 2 percent of participants identified as Chinese, while 62.6 percent identified as Taiwanese.[13] This trend has been frustrating Beijing. The second perception was that Taiwan was seeking international recognition. During the Covid-19 pandemic, Taiwan donated millions of masks and medical supplies to its diplomatic allies, the United States and European countries. Taiwan's medical diplomacy compared favorably to the Chinese image of intervention in Hong Kong protests, the spread of Covid-19, and its territorial expansion in the South China Sea.[14] Beijing interpreted Taiwan's active seeking of international recognition as Taiwan's attempt to change the status quo of cross-strait relations. The third perception was that the United States continued to increase support for Taiwan. From August to October 2020, Secretary of Health and Human Services Alex Azar and Under Secretary of State Keith Krach visited Taiwan. The arrival of the US officials enraged Chinese leaders, who considered the United States was violating China's domestic affairs.[15] From May to October 2020, the United States approved almost $5 billion in arms sales, including submarine-launched wire-guided torpedoes, high-mobility artillery rocket system launchers, and Harpoon coastal defense systems.[16]

Beijing perceived Taiwan's international recognition seeking, and the US intervention in Taiwan's affairs, as a threat to China's goals. Beijing used diverse approaches of coercive rhetoric, harsh diplomacy, and aggressive military actions against the Tsai administration.

280 *Hedging the China Threat*

China's bolstering of a military threat. China announced on March 5, 2019, that defense spending would grow by 7.5 percent to 1.19 trillion yuan ($177.6 billion). The increase in the defense budget was mainly allocated to develop new weapons, improve training conditions, and guarantee military reform and benefits for military personnel.[17] The Trump government found that the PRC security-related apparatuses tried to steal high technology from the United States to support China's defense modernization.

Beijing advanced an agenda of military modernization while pursuing economic growth and improving its technological strength. China's strategy aimed at achieving the objective of the "great rejuvenation of the Chinese nation."[18] Its strategic objectives were: perpetuating the Chinese Communist Party (CCP) rule, maintaining domestic stability, sustaining economic growth, defending sovereignty, and securing China's status as a great power. These objectives have been revealed in Xi's "China Dream," which strives to restore China's status as a powerful nation.[19] Beijing viewed the Taiwan independence movement as the gravest threat to peace in the Taiwan Strait. The PLA thought it was essential to send a clear warning to Taiwan by sailing ships and flying aircraft around Taiwan.[20]

On May 22, 2020, Premier Li Keqiang delivered a speech at the National People's Congress and left out the word "peaceful," referring to China's desire to unify with Taiwan.[21] On September 21, after PLA warplanes made rounds over the Taiwan Strait, China's Foreign Ministry said: "Taiwan is an inalienable part of Chinese territory and the median line in the Taiwan Straits does not exist."[22] The PLA said it would defeat Taiwan's independence at all costs. China's Defense Ministry warned Taiwan, "Those who play with fire are bound to get burned." Since early September, China had been conducting a show of force in the Taiwan Strait. PLA warplanes and naval ships roamed the strait almost daily with many of them breaching the median line, a boundary that both sides had hitherto respected. The PLA released a video in September displaying bombers making a simulated strike on a runway like Anderson Air Force Base in Guam.[23] On October 10, China staged an island invasion military exercise during Taiwan's National Day. The simulated attack was the first time in this decade that Chinese media had disclosed the entire process of a staged military landing in Taiwan.[24]

The Individual Level:
President Trump's Trade War Against China

The Trump worldview was the promise of the "Make America Great Again" campaign to put "America First." From 1999 to 2011, the United States lost 2.4 million manufacturing jobs to Chinese competition. Foreign companies were subjected to demands to transfer their technology to China. Theft of intellectual property also became common.[25] By 2015, many US policy elites saw China as a threat, calling for a reassessment of the engagement policy. Americans voiced dissatisfaction with China's intellectual property theft, cyber intrusion into high-tech firms, and agents seeking to obtain sensitive assets. Trump brought in China threat hawk, Peter Navarro, as director of the White House Office of Trade and Manufacturing Policy. Navarro helped Trump conduct a trade war with China. Trump also invited Michael Pillsbury, who argued that China pursued a "secret strategy to replace America as the global superpower," into his security team. The Trump administration, under the influence of conservatives in charge of US security-related policy, such as National Security Advisor (NSA) John Bolton, National Security Council (NSC) senior director for Asian affairs Matthew Pottinger, Assistant Secretary of Defense for Asian and Pacific Security Affairs Randall Schriver, and Trade Representative Robert Lighthizer, showed sympathy toward Taiwan in opposition to China.[26] They guided Trump toward a hostile relationship with Beijing. While many disagreed with Trump's methods, others were happy to see Trump holding China accountable.[27]

Trump acknowledged that US power rested on a strong economy. The stronger the economy, the greater the capacity to sustain large defense budgets to protect US interests. His objective was to reduce the US trade deficit, bring jobs back to the United States, and end unfair Chinese trade practices and technology theft. According to Bolton, Trump's advisors were split in dealing with China. His administration had panda huggers, like the Treasury secretary, Steven Mnuchin, and China hawks, like the secretary of commerce, Wilbur Ross, and the US trade representative, Robert Lighthizer.[28]

Trump's Concern About China's Unfair Trade

Trump thought trade deficits meant the United States was losing, and trade surpluses meant the United States was winning. Decreases in US manufacturing jobs resulted from lower labor costs in China.[29] Trump decided to launch punitive tariffs against China. Economists were concerned about the impact of the trade war, predicting that the United States and China would experience economic slowdowns. The first to occur was a slow decline in Chinese exports. The share of goods exported to the United States, reflected in the Chinese gross domestic product (GDP), fell from 7.2 percent in 2006 to 3.4 percent in 2017.[30] The second was unlikely to improve the US trade deficit. Increased imports from Mexico, South Korea, and Taiwan reflected shifts in global value chains.

In April 2018, ZTE, a Chinese telecom company, committed violations of US sanctions on Iran and North Korea. Secretary of Commerce Wilbur Ross attempted to impose huge fines and cut ZTE off from the US market, but the State Department worried about offending China. Trump was upset

282 *Hedging the China Threat*

with Ross's decision and wanted to modify his proposed heavy penalties. Trump called Xi and complained about China's trade practices and said China needed to buy more US agricultural products. Concerning ZTE, Trump said he had told Ross to work something out for China. Xi replied that if that were done, he would owe Trump a favor and Trump responded that he was doing this because of Xi.[31] Trump tweeted, "Xi and I are working together to give the Chinese phone company, ZTE, a way to get back into business, fast. Too many jobs in China were lost. The Commerce Department has been instructed to get it done!"[32]

The US-China Trade War

US-China economic relations had expanded since China linked its economy to the world in 1978. Bilateral merchandise trade rose from $2 billion in 1979 to $660 billion in 2018. Tensions, however, surfaced over economic issues claimed by the Trump administration, including the trade deficit, cyber espionage, and violation of intellectual property rights (IPR).

Trump was dedicated to decreasing US trade deficits. On March 8, 2018, he announced imposing additional tariffs on steel (25 percent) and aluminum (10 percent) against China. Later, China raised tariffs (from 15 percent to 25 percent) on US products in retaliation. On May 5, 2019, Trump stated that the previous tariffs of 10 percent levied on $200 billion worth of Chinese goods would increase to 25 percent.[33] In response, China imposed a 25 percent tariff on $60 billion of US goods on June 1. During the Group of 20 (G-20) Osaka summit on June 29, Trump and Xi agreed to a truce in the trade war. Prior tariffs would remain in effect, but no future tariffs would be enacted. Trump delayed the proposed tariffs to encourage renewed trade talks with China.[34]

In 2019, China was the United States' largest import country ($540 billion) and the third-largest export market ($120 billion). In 2015, US exports to China and bilateral foreign direct investment (FDI) flows provided 2.6 million jobs for Americans. Chinese visitors spent $33 billion in the United States in 2016 (the largest visitor spending). Boeing Corporation delivered 202 planes to China in 2017 (26 percent of global deliveries). General Motors has sold more cars and trucks in China than in the United States since 2010.[35] Despite intertwined bilateral trade, several issues triggered the trade war with Trump.

The first was the US trade deficit which set a record in 2018, despite Trump's efforts to restrain Beijing's trade aggressiveness.[36] China had cheaper labor and US companies were unable to compete with them. In 2018, US goods and services trade with China totaled an estimated $737 billion. Exports were $179 billion, and imports were $558 billion. The deficit with China reached $379 billion.[37] Trump thought the trade deficit was harmful to

Confronting a More Assertive China   283

the US economy because the rising US deficit with China between 2001 and 2013 had eliminated or displaced 3.2 million US jobs[38] Reducing the growing deficit became Trump's priority to provide more jobs for Americans.

The second was intellectual property rights (IPR). US business and government representatives voiced concerns over economic losses suffered by China's IPR infringement. A May 2013 study by the Commission on the Theft of American Intellectual Property estimated that global IPR theft costs the US economy $300 billion per year, of which China accounted for 50 percent ($150 billion) to 80 percent ($240 billion) of those losses. The US Department of Homeland Security reported that in 2017, goods from China and Hong Kong accounted for 78 percent of seized counterfeit goods valued at $941 million.[39]

The third issue was cybersecurity. The US intelligence community believed Beijing was a major source of cyber economic espionage. On May 19, 2014, the US Department of Justice issued an indictment against five members of the PLA for cyber espionage.[40] According to the 2018 *Foreign Economic Espionage in Cyberspace* report by the National Counterintelligence and Security Center, China systematically stole US technology and trade secrets.[41]

The fourth issue was accessing critical US technologies. Chinese firms invested billions of dollars in the US technology industry, raising concerns that Beijing had gained access to critical US technologies.[42] Trump raised security concerns over global supply chains of advanced technology such as information, communications, and telecommunications (ICT) equipment. In 2018, US ICT imports from China totaled $157 billion (60 percent of US ICT imports). On May 15, 2019, Trump issued an Executive Order on Securing the Information and Communications Technology and Services Supply Chain, banning certain ICT transactions.[43] Trump believed that increased Chinese investment in US high-tech sectors could threaten the United States.

The Xi administration took a stricter approach in response to the United States raising tariffs. Initially, China offered concessions on purchasing an extra $1.2 trillion of US products and allowing US companies to access finance, automobiles, and energy sectors. Xi, however, presided over a high-level government meeting and called on officials to prepare for a trade war. After the United States increased tariffs on $50 billion of Chinese goods on June 15, 2018, Beijing announced its own tariffs of the same scale and intensity in return. On June 21, 2019, Xi met a foreign delegation and told them that China would fight back against the US trade tariffs.[44]

The Trump-Xi summit. Trump thought China tried to influence the 2018 congressional elections against Republicans, planning for his defeat in 2020 because of his increased defense spending and the trade war. With

284 *Hedging the China Threat*

November's elections looming, there was little progress on the trade front, and attention turned to the Buenos Aires G-20 meeting from November 30 to December 1, 2018, when Xi and Trump would meet. Trump saw this meeting as a good opportunity to discuss trade issues with Xi.[45] On December 1, dinner with Xi was the last event before Trump returned to the United States. In the afternoon, Trump's team met Trump for a final briefing. US Trade Representative Robert Lighthizer thought a free-trade agreement with China would be suicidal. Still, Mnuchin was pleased by his success in getting China to agree to purchase more agricultural products and minerals. Bolton suggested that the United States bar all Chinese goods and services from the United States if China continued to steal US intellectual property. "I like that idea," said Trump. During the dinner, Xi began flattering Trump by saying he wanted to work with Trump for six more years. Xi said the United States had too many elections. Trump nodded. In a subsequent telephone conversation on December 29, Xi said that China hoped Trump would have another term by amending the US Constitution so he could stay longer.[46]

Trump proposed that US tariffs would remain at 10 percent rather than rise to 25 percent, as he had threatened. In exchange, Trump asked for increases in farm product purchases. If that could be agreed on, all the tariffs would be reduced. There would be a ninety-day period of negotiations to get everything done. Trump asked Xi to reduce China's exports of fentanyl, a deadly opioid causing huge health damage to youth across the United States, to which Xi consented. On December 3, 2018, the Trump team gathered at the White House to assess the results. Mnuchin asked, "Who's in charge?" about the coming negotiations. Trump named Lighthizer as the lead. In May 2019, Lighthizer visited Beijing. The Chinese had reneged on specific commitments they had made. As a result, Trump had been tweeting threats of new tariffs. Lighthizer announced he was ready for the next round of tariff increases to go into effect, which Trump was prepared to impose.[47]

During the Trump and Xi meeting at the 2019 Osaka G-20 summit on June 29, Xi said that some political figures in the United States were making erroneous judgments by calling for a new cold war. Trump then turned the conversation to the upcoming US presidential election, pleading with Xi to ensure Trump would win. He stressed the importance of farmers and increased Chinese purchases of soybeans and wheat in the electoral outcome. Trump raised the issue of the collapse in negotiations in May, urging China to return to the negotiation table. Xi answered by comparing the impact of an unequal deal with the United States to the humiliation of the Treaty of Versailles, which had taken Shandong Province from Germany, but given it to Japan. Xi said that if China suffered humiliation in trade negotiations, there would be an upsurge of patriotic feelings in China, directed against the United States. Trump implied that China owed the United States a favor for defeating Japan during World War II.[48]

Concerning the trade issue, Trump proposed that for the remaining $350 billion of trade imbalances, the United States would not impose tariffs, but he pushed Xi to buy as many US farm products as China could. Then, they would see if a deal was possible. Xi agreed that both sides should restart the trade talks, welcoming Trump's concession that there would be no new tariffs and agreeing that the two negotiating teams should resume discussions on farm products. Trade talks with China resumed after Osaka, but progress was slow. Trump tweeted on July 30, "They should probably wait out our election to see if we get one of the Democrat stiffs like Sleepy Joe. . . . The problem with them waiting, however, is that if I win, the deal that they get will be much tougher than what we are negotiating now . . . or no deal at all."[49]

Trump decided to impose the next round of tariffs on Beijing via Twitter: "China agreed to . . . buy agricultural products from the U.S. in large quantities but did not do so. President Xi said that he would stop the sale of Fentanyl to the United States, but this never happened. Many Americans continue to die! The U.S. will start putting a small additional Tariff of 10% on the remaining 300 billion dollars of goods and products beginning September 1. This does not include the 250 billion dollars already tariffed at 25%."[50]

The Huawei controversy. On December 1, 2018, Canadian authorities in Vancouver arrested Meng Wanzhou, chief financial officer of Huawei, a Chinese telecom firm. When Meng, the daughter of Huawei's founder, landed in Canada, she was arrested for concealing violations of US sanctions against Iran. At the December 7 White House Christmas dinner, Trump told Bolton that the United States had arrested "the Ivanka Trump of China." Trump implied that Huawei could be another US bargaining chip in the trade negotiations.[51]

By early May 2019, Secretary of Commerce Wilbur Ross was prepared to put Huawei on the Commerce Department's restriction list: precluding US firms from selling to Huawei without specific licenses. Mnuchin said Ross's initial press statement on Huawei was extreme, so Ross asked if he could read it aloud and let others decide, which he did. Trump thought it was a great statement—even "beautiful!" Mnuchin told Trump, "I gave you my advice, and you followed the wrong person." In the June 18 Xi-Trump phone call, Xi pressed hard on Huawei. Trump repeated his point that Huawei could be part of the trade deal. Xi warned that, if not appropriately handled, Huawei would harm the bilateral relationship. Xi described Huawei as an outstanding private Chinese company, having important relations with Qualcomm and Intel.[52] Xi wanted the ban on Huawei lifted, saying he wanted to work jointly with Trump personally on the issue, and

286 *Hedging the China Threat*

Trump seemed willing. Trump reversed his earlier position, and said he would allow US companies to sell to Huawei, effectively reversing Ross.[53]

Trump's Cross-Strait Policy

On December 2, 2016, President Tsai called President-elect Trump, requesting US support for Taiwan's bid for more international participation. Trump's Twitter post of Tsai as the "president of Taiwan" broke from past practices. The Trump team defended receiving Tsai's congratulatory call because she was the elected leader with close ties within the United States. Trump questioned whether the United States should adhere to the One China policy if the PRC challenged US interests. After his inauguration, Trump affirmed that his administration would honor the One China policy in his phone call with Xi Jinping.[54] Trump's interactions with Beijing and Taipei implied that Taiwan could become a bargaining chip. Trump wanted Beijing to do more in pressuring Pyongyang to abandon its nuclear and missile programs, even tying his decision not to have another phone call with Tsai to Xi's willingness to cooperate on the North Korea issue.[55]

The Trump administration pushed back against Beijing's aggression targeting Taiwan. Vice President Mike Pence noted that the United States believed Taiwan's embrace of democracy showed a better path for all the Chinese people.[56] Journalist Bob Woodward recounted a January 19, 2018, meeting at the White House where Trump and his national security team discussed the rationale for the United States defending Taiwan. Trump asked, "What do we get from protecting Taiwan?"[57]

On August 14, 2018, when Tsai made her transit stop in the United States on her way to Belize and Paraguay, she delivered a speech at the Ronald Reagan Library in California. She emphasized that Taiwan was willing to work with other countries to improve regional stability and peace. The State Department said that the US policy on Taiwan remained the same. At the second US-China Diplomatic and Security Dialogue on November 9, Secretary Mike Pompeo emphasized the strong US ties with a democratic Taiwan. He called on Beijing to respect Taiwan's international space and opposed unilateral actions by any party to alter the status quo.[58]

At the Buenos Aires dinner on December 1, 2018, Xi urged Trump to be prudent on Taiwan. Trump agreed. At the June 2019 G-20 meeting in Osaka, Xi urged that the United States should not allow Tsai to travel to the United States or sell arms to Taiwan. Secretary Pompeo then held back a congressional notification on the F-16 sale. John Bolton and Mick Mulvaney, however, persuaded Trump to agree to arms sales to Taiwan. On August 13, in a conference call with Trump, Bolton explained the political backfire if the sale did not proceed. Taiwan would pay $8 billion for the F-16s and Boeing would get many jobs in South Carolina. Trump finally said, "Okay, but do it quietly. John, you're not going to give a speech about it, are you?" [59]

Trump had sought to maintain friendly relations with Xi in hopes that he could reach a good deal with him. After this attempt failed, Trump no longer had the same incentive to please Xi. With the upcoming 2020 election, Trump took a tougher stance when dealing with China, particularly with Covid-19 severely hitting the United States. Trump emphasized that the virus had come from China.[60] Angered by Trump's blame for China spreading the virus, Chinese officials responded with a disinformation campaign suggesting that the virus was introduced to Wuhan when members of the US Army visited the city in the fall of 2019.[61]

The State Level:
The United States' Indo-Pacific Strategy and Its Impact on Taiwan

The Indo-Pacific emerged as a regional strategic framework in 2010 when Secretary of State Hillary Clinton emphasized its importance to global trade. China's Belt and Road Initiative (BRI) was launched in 2013 by Xi Jinping to develop infrastructure overseas by using Chinese labor, infrastructure resources, and wealth to link regional and global networks for development. In December 2017, the NSS stated that China attempted to displace the United States in the Indo-Pacific region. At the Asia-Pacific Economic Cooperation summit, Vice President Pence spearheaded the United States' opposition to the BRI, by informing state leaders that the United States viewed the BRI as engaging in debt diplomacy.[62] Since 2016, the PLA has increased patrols around and near Taiwan, using aircraft to threaten it. With China's rising economic expansion and military threat, Trump's security team was more willing to challenge China. Taiwan's security relations with the United States made strides.[63]

The US Strategy in the Indo-Pacific

On June 1, 2019, the Pentagon released the Indo-Pacific Strategy Report (IPSR), outlining the US vision for the region, the regional strategic challenges, and the defense strategy. The IPSR had been labeled as the US military policy to contain a rising China. In the report, Acting Secretary of Defense Pat Shanahan underlined that the Indo-Pacific was the Department of Defense (DoD) priority theater. China militarized the South China Sea, violating a 2015 pledge by Xi not to pursue militarization of the Spratly Islands. Thus, the US military strengthened close ties with Japan and South Korea. The United States also built the free and open

288 Hedging the China Threat

Indo-Pacific architecture by establishing the Quad network, which included Australia, India, Japan, and the United States.

The objectives of the Indo-Pacific Strategy were to pursue preparedness and partnerships in the region. The Pentagon enhanced joint force preparedness. Initiatives included investments in advanced training facilities to present a realistic training environment, investments in the air force and naval aviation to achieve an 80 percent fighter readiness goal, and investments in missile defense systems interoperable with Japan and Australia. The preparation focused on realistic training to confront China's military buildup. Regarding US alliances and partnerships, the United States increased interoperability to ensure that US military hardware and software could integrate with allies (Japan, South Korea, Australia, the Philippines) and partners (Singapore, Taiwan).

The Trump administration criticized China's assertive actions in the South China Sea. The United States sought to maintain the US naval presence and freedom of navigation (FoN) activities in the South China Sea. Secretary Mattis remarked that the Pentagon had been working intensively to counter China's military assertiveness. The administration increased US security cooperation with Vietnam and Indonesia. In March 2019, Secretary Pompeo declared that any attack on Philippine forces, aircraft, or vessels in the South China Sea would trigger mutual defense obligations under Article 4 of our Mutual Defense Treaty with the Philippines.[64]

Taiwan's Role in the United States' Indo-Pacific Strategy

The US-China Economic and Security Commission's 2019 report to Congress noted that the cross-strait military balance had shifted in China's favor, threatening Taiwan's ability to defend itself and the United States' ability to intervene. While the PLA could not yet capture Taiwan, it could keep the United States from coming to its aid under its anti-access/area denial (A2/AD) blockade.[65] The United States pursued a strong partnership with Taiwan. The DoD would provide Taiwan with defense articles and services to enable Taiwan to maintain its self-defense capability. Shared security rested on a growing network of alliances and close partnerships.

Mike Pompeo and Taiwan's policy. Soon after becoming Secretary of State, Mike Pompeo realized that the US engagement with China had previously been based on not angering Beijing. There was no meeting or phone call with Chinese officials that did not begin with a statement regarding Taiwan as an internal matter. Pompeo directed his team to reevaluate the United States' Taiwan policy and think creatively about engaging with Taiwan within the existing policy framework.[66] Given the importance of Taiwan's semiconductor industry, Pompeo endeavored to develop the US-Taiwan economic relationship. He dispatched Under Secretary of State Keith Krach to Taiwan in September 2020 to attend the memorial service of the late president Lee Teng-hui. During that trip, Krach became the highest-ranking State Department official ever to visit Taiwan. The Chinese flew warplanes into the Taiwan Strait to protest his visit.[67]

In the State Department, the Taiwan Contact Guidelines regulated issues like which federal buildings Taiwanese officials could enter, which Taiwanese officials could shake hands with US officials, and which rank of officials could or could not visit Taiwan. Pompeo canceled the guidelines in January 2021. After Pompeo's announcement, Taiwan's top representative to the United States, Bi-khim Hsiao, tweeted: "Decades of discrimination, removed. A huge day in our bilateral relationship."[68] In his memoir, Pompeo stated that "the United States should grant full diplomatic recognition to Taiwan. The free people of that island deserve it."[69]

The creation of the Taiwan Travel Act. The Taiwan Travel Act has improved US-Taiwan security relations. For the past three decades, the Taiwan government has requested its US counterparts to elevate their high-ranking official contacts. For example, when I served at the Ministry of National Defense (MND) in Taiwan from 2000 to 2008, the MND proposed that the contacts of high-ranking military officers from both countries could visit either country. The requests, however, had turned on deaf ears due to the One China policy acknowledged by the US government. With persistent efforts of all parties in Taiwan and the United States, the Taiwan Travel Act was passed by the US Congress and was signed into law by Trump on March 16, 2018.

The act allowed the following activities: (1) officials at all levels of the US government could travel to Taiwan to meet their Taiwanese counterparts; (2) the United States would allow high-level Taiwanese officials to enter the United States under respectful conditions when they met with US officials; and (3) the United States encouraged the Taipei Economic and Cultural Representative Office to conduct business in the United States.[70] In May 2019, the ROC's security general of the National Security Council, David Lee, had a dialogue with US NSA John Bolton, which marked the highest-level security officials' meeting for the first time in four decades.[71] The Taiwan Travel Act improved bilateral strategic partnerships with high-ranking officials who work together.

Pompeo underscored Taiwan's economic development, democratic society, and high-tech powerhouse as fitting with the United States' pursuit of like-minded partnerships in the Indo-Pacific. In addition to the Taiwan Travel Act, Trump signed the National Defense Authorization Act of 2018 and 2019, respectively. The two acts urged the Pentagon to strengthen military relations with Taiwan, deepening personnel exchanges, training, and exercises.[72]

290 Hedging the China Threat

The US arms sales to Taiwan. The Trump administration increased the quantity and quality of arms sales to Taiwan, considering moving away from its previous "bundling" method toward a case-by-case approach to addressing Taiwan's security needs. US military industries also enhanced relationships with their Taiwanese counterparts in the annual US-Taiwan Defense Conference Forum.[73]

Secretary of Defense James Mattis stated that the US military was committed to working with Taiwan and providing it with defensive weapons, consistent with the obligations in the Taiwan Relations Act. In June 2017, the United States announced the arms sale of $1.42 billion, including heavy-weight torpedoes, joint standoff weapons, and high-speed antiradiation missiles. In October 2018, the United States approved the sale of spare parts for F-16 fighter planes and other military aircraft worth up to $330 million.[74] In April 2019, the State Department approved the third arms sale to Taiwan, including pilot training programs, maintenance, and logistic support for Taiwan F-16 fighters, at an estimated $500 million.[75] On August 18, when asked about the F-16 sales, Trump confirmed his approval of the deal, adding: "It is $8 billion. It's a lot of money. That's a lot of jobs."[76] In September, the State Department announced $2.2 billion in arms sales, including 108 Abram tanks and around 250 Stinger surface-to-air missiles.[77]

During the Trump administration, the United States provided $15 billion worth of arms to Taiwan, dwarfing the Obama administration's $14 billion in eight years. Much of this included the weapons that Taiwan would desperately need in the event of a Chinese invasion.[78]

The US response to China's rising threat. The PLA increased military pressure against Taiwan during the Trump administration. Beijing sent military aircraft and vessels circling Taiwan proper, as a warning to the Tsai administration. Accordingly, the Pentagon increased sending US military vessels and warplanes to patrol the Taiwan Strait to deter China's coercion.[79] In July 2019, Beijing warned that it was ready for war if Taiwan moved toward independence. In response, a US Navy warship sailed through the Taiwan Strait. A Seventh Fleet spokesperson stated, "The ship's transit through the Taiwan Strait demonstrates the U.S.'s commitment to a free and open Indo-Pacific."[80] The increased US military activities in the Taiwan Strait were a sign of the US backing for Taiwan to confront China's aggressive military approach.[81]

The US DoD's annual report, *Military and Security Developments Involving the People's Republic of China*, was released on May 2, 2019. The report stated that Chinese leaders emphasized developing a military through realistic combat training to fight and win the war.[82] Despite rising US-China security disputes and mistrust, the Pentagon valued the impor-

Confronting a More Assertive China   291

tance of bilateral military relations to prevent a crisis from happening. The DoD's plan for military-to-military contacts with China focused on three priorities: encouraging China to act in ways consistent with the international order, promoting risk reduction, and risk management efforts.[83]

The DoD's 2019 Indo-Pacific Strategy Report (IPSR) discussed the US position on Taiwan. The strategy introduced Taiwan, Singapore, New Zealand, and Mongolia as Indo-Pacific democracies that were considered "reliable, capable, and natural" partners of the United States.[84] The IPSR conveyed in these terms the importance of Taiwan to the Trump administration: that a "strong, prosperous, and democratic Taiwan" is part of the rules-based order that the United States has a vital interest in upholding. It continued that the United States is pursuing a strong partnership with Taiwan, particularly under Beijing's pressure campaign against Taiwan.[85]

The International Level:
Japan Countering China and the Trump-Kim Summit

During the Trump administration, the East Asian situation was tense. On September 3, 2017, North Korea launched an intercontinental ballistic missile (ICBM) that could reach the East Coast of the United States with a nuclear device. In its sixth nuclear test, North Korea claimed the device tested was a hydrogen bomb. North Korea and South Korea opened the pathway for the summits between Donald Trump and Kim Jong-un, held in Singapore and Hanoi, respectively.[86] Chinese and Japanese relationships had been strained by Japan's wartime past, China's military modernization, and the Diaoyutai Islands dispute. Though both governments have tried to reduce tensions due to trade interests, the historical animosity and rise of nationalism could break their fragile relationship. The Chinese intrusions of vessels into Japanese territorial waters, and militarization in the South China Sea, posed a grave security concern to Japan.[87] In response, Japanese and US carrier groups jointly held a naval exercise from June 10 to 12, 2019, in the South China Sea to support the US strategy.[88]

Tense Relations Between China and Japan

Since 2012, China's sea and air power routinely conducted its operation in areas close to Japan and the Diaoyutai Islands. China also increased its land reclamation of the Spratly Islands.[89] Japan viewed the PLA's activities as provocative.

Distrust between China and Japan. Japanese prime minister, Shinzo Abe, paid a visit to China in October 2018 in the hope of lessening the growing

292 Hedging the China Threat

tensions in its relations with China. While the visit was viewed as a success in thawing the frozen relationship, the bilateral relations remained unchanged.[90] Some China-Japan developments deserved attention. First on the agenda were the stagnant China-Japan relations. China wanted to improve its ties with Japan, but failed to succeed. In a gesture of goodwill, China lifted its embargo on Japanese agricultural products in November 2018 due to the nuclear leak in the Fukushima tsunami in 2011. Japanese mobile phone carriers (SoftBank Group, NTT Docomo, and KDDI), however, decided not to use Chinese equipment in their 5G networks due to rising cybertheft concerns. China's "goodwill" gesture was negated by Japan's sanctioning of electronic products.[91] The second was the US interference in China-Japan relations, which were restrained by the US-Japan alliance and the escalating US-China rivalry. In March 2019, the Abe administration delayed its plans to invite Xi on a state visit to appease the Trump administration. This came when a trade war and Huawei's controversies brought US-China relations to a low point.[92] As the US-China competition intensified, Japan's prioritization of the US alliance restricted the room for improving China-Japan relations.

Japan's security strategy. The Japan National Security Strategy laid out principles to achieve its own security grounded on international cooperation. The National Defense Program Guidelines (NDPG) specified deterrence and responses to various situations based on the NSS. According to the NDPG, Japan Self-Defense Force (SDF) should be able to react to an attack on remote islands, ballistic missile attacks, cyberspace attacks, and natural disasters. This would be accomplished by holding training exercises, promoting defense cooperation, ensuring maritime security, and implementing international cooperation.[93]

As the security environment surrounding Japan became severe, the United States enhancement of its engagement with the regional countries became critical to Japan's security. It was crucial to have the presence of the US Forces Japan (USFJ) to respond to emergencies. The Guidelines for US-Japan Defense Cooperation functioned as a deterrent by conducting joint training and exercises, as well as joint intelligence, surveillance, and reconnaissance (ISR) activities. Two US-Japan security policy consultative platforms, critical to Japan's security and US interests, were the US-Japan Security Consultative Committee and the US-Japan Defense Ministerial Meeting. These security platforms focused on North Korea's abandonment of nuclear weapons, monitoring China's increased activities in the East China Sea, and confronting China's militarization in the South China Sea.[94]

The Japanese defense strategy had been viewed as a response to China's military power. Japan's National Defense Program Guidelines included converting two helicopter carriers into aircraft carriers, upgrading

Confronting a More Assertive China   293

electronic warfare capabilities, purchasing land-based missile defense systems, and researching hypersonic weapons. In this NDPG, the most important change was shifting the Japanese security posture from reactive to proactive, and regarding China as an adversary.[95] Beijing also believed that the Quadrilateral Security Dialogue (a dialogue between the United States, Japan, Australia, and India) and Tokyo's Free and Open Indo-Pacific strategy were evidence of Japan and the West containing China.[96]

North Korea's Nuclear Issues

When Trump addressed the UN General Assembly in September 2017, he said that if the United States were compelled to defend itself or its allies, it would have no choice but to destroy North Korea. Describing Kim Jong-un as "Rocket Man," Trump said the North Korean leader was on a suicide mission for his regime. In response, Kim called Trump "mentally deranged" and warned that he would "pay dearly" for threatening to destroy North Korea. On September 3, North Korea successfully tested the ICBM that could reach the East Coast of the United States. In its sixth nuclear test, North Korea claimed that the device tested was a hydrogen bomb, and that the test was successful.[97]

North Korea and South Korea opened the pathway for the summits between Trump and Kim, held in Singapore and Hanoi, respectively. Since March 2018, Kim has visited China four times, and Xi has visited North Korea once, in June 2019. Beijing urged all parties to embark on a dual-track approach to a political resolution of issues on the Korean Peninsula, concentrating on denuclearization and instituting a peace process. After the Trump-Kim summit in Hanoi in February 2019, progress between the United States and North Korea failed at the negotiating table. Discussions ended in a stalemate over what the United States described as unreasonable and disproportionate North Korean requests for sanctions relief, in exchange for only a limited submission of its nuclear capabilities.[98]

Kim indicated in April 2019 that North Korea's attitude toward negotiations with Washington would falter if the United States did not embrace a more accommodating negotiating position by the end of the year. Despite a symbolic Trump and Kim meeting at the demarcation line between North and South Korea on June 30, 2019, both sides could not produce tangible steps to advance denuclearization and peacebuilding. On January 21, 2020, a counselor to Pyongyang's mission at the UN in Geneva announced that North Korea would no longer adhere to its self-imposed moratorium on nuclear and long-range missile testing.[99] Trump held three publicized meetings with Kim, attempting to persuade him to abandon his nuclear weapons program. Trump even acknowledged that early in his presidency he delayed trade negotiations with China because he wanted to concentrate on North

294   Hedging the China Threat

Korea. Trump's diplomacy, however, did not work because Kim viewed nuclear weapons as vital to his own survival.[100]

Conclusion

Under the Trump administration's Free and Open Indo-Pacific strategy, the United States deepened its security relationship with Taiwan. President Trump's worldview was his promise to Make America Great Again campaign and to put America First. He voiced deep dissatisfaction with China's intellectual property theft and cyber intrusions into high-tech firms. The State Department, under the leadership of Secretary Mike Pompeo, directed its team to reevaluate the US-Taiwan policy and to think more creatively about engaging with Taiwan within the existing policy framework. During this period, Japan became extremely concerned with the increase of Chinese naval activities in Japanese territorial waters.

Trump's cross-strait policy included several important highlights: (1) Trump affirmed that his administration would honor the One China policy; (2) the United States opposed any unilateral actions by either China or Taiwan that might alter the status quo; and (3) the Taiwan Travel Act greatly improved US-Taiwan relations.

Viewing the Trump years at the individual level, the president questioned whether the United States should adhere to the One China policy if the PRC were to challenge US interests. Trump's interactions with Beijing and Taipei implied that Taiwan could become a bargaining chip. Initially, Trump had sought to maintain friendly personal relations with Xi Jinping in the hope that he could reach a good deal with Xi. After this attempt at strategy failed, Trump no longer had the same incentives to please Xi.

At the state level, as the United States took more assertive actions against China's military provocations, Taiwan's role in the US Indo-Pacific strategy increased. National Security Advisor John Bolton persuaded Trump to increase arms sales to Taiwan to confront the rising China military threat against Taiwan. Given the importance of Taiwan's thriving semiconductor industry, the State Department also endeavored to develop a closer US-Taiwan economic relationship. The US Congress enacted the Taiwan Travel Act to improve US-Taiwan security relations.

At the international level, China's growing militarization in the South China Sea posed a serious security threat to Southeast Asian countries. Following the Trump-Kim summit in Hanoi in February 2019, negotiations between the United States and North Korea failed. The talks ended in a stalemate when North Korea requested sanctions relief in exchange for only a limited reduction of its nuclear capabilities.

Initially, Trump appeared to have believed that his own personal relationship with Xi would be the key factor in settling US-China disputes.

Confronting a More Assertive China   295

Trump, for a time, sought to build a personal relationship with Xi as a way of getting China to change course, but he found that many of China's policies had roots and support that extended well beyond the control of Xi himself. Trump began to acknowledge the limits of personalized diplomacy. "We're probably not as close now, . . . But I have to be for our country," Trump said of Xi at an event in 2019.[101]

As Xi became more authoritarian at home and increasingly assertive in China's foreign policy, the US-China disagreements over trade, military, technology, and espionage exacerbated what had become a contentious relationship. The widespread Covid-19 pandemic fueled their fiery animosities. Washington felt less constrained to boost better relations with Taiwan. Over the course of Trump's four years in office, US officials increasingly came to view China as an adversary. After Trump failed to get reelected in 2020, US relations with China became even more strained. Early in Joe Biden's presidency, US-China relations deteriorated further when House Speaker Nancy Pelosi visited Taiwan. In response to Pelosi's visit, China launched what became known as the 2022 Taiwan Strait Crisis. The day after Biden was sworn in, Wang Huiyao, an advisor to China's State Council, commented that despite the election of a new US president, the US-China contradictions will continue to exist.[102]

Notes

1. Richard Bush, "The Trump Administration's Policies Toward Taiwan," Brookings Institution, June 5, 2019, https://www.brookings.edu.
2. "Full Text: Fighting COVID-19: China in Action," Xinhua, June 7, 2020.
3. Shao-cheng Sun, "The Taiwan Security Under the Trump Administration," *Strategic Vision,* no. 2 (February 2019): 11.
4. James Griffiths, "When It Comes to International Recognition, Even When Taiwan Wins, It Loses," CNN, September 29, 2020.
5. Sun, "The Taiwan Security Under the Trump Administration," p. 11.
6. Ibid., p. 12.
7. Ing-wen Tsai, "Full Text of President Tsai Ing-wen's New Year's Day Speech," *Focus Taiwan,* January 1, 2019.
8. Peter Martin and Dandan Li, "China's Xi Jinping Says Taiwan Must Be Unified with Mainland," *Bloomberg News,* January 1, 2019.
9. Ibid.
10. "Xi Jinping Says Taiwan Must and Will Be, Reunited with China," *BBC News,* January 2, 2019.
11. Richard Bush, "8 Key Things to Notice from Xi Jinping's New Year Speech on Taiwan," Brookings Institution, January 7, 2019, https://www.brookings.edu.
12. Andrew Erickson, "Full Text of 2019 Defense White Paper: China's National Defense in the New Era," Andrewerickson.com, July 24, 2019.
13. Chun-hui Yang and Jake Chung, "Poll Finds 62.6% Identify as Taiwanese," *Taipei Times,* September 25, 2020.
14. Jared Ward, "Taiwan's Medical Diplomacy in the Caribbean: A Final Stand Against Beijing?" *The Diplomat,* May 11, 2020.

296 *Hedging the China Threat*

15. Edward Wong, "U.S. Tries to Bolster Taiwan's Status, Short of Recognizing Sovereignty," *New York Times,* August 17, 2020.

16. "Taipei Economic and Cultural Representative Office in the United States (Transmittal No: 20-68)." Defense Security Cooperation Agency, October 26, 2020, https://www.dsca.mil.

17. "China's Defense Budget," GlobalSecurity.org, May 19, 2019.

18. Office of the Secretary of Defense, *Annual Report to Congress: Military and Security Developments Involving the People's Republic of China 2019* (Washington, DC: Office of the Secretary of Defense, 2019), p. 1.

19. Ibid., p. 3.

20. Ibid., pp. 5–10.

21. Yew Lun Tian and Yimou Lee, "China Drops Word Peaceful in Latest Push for Taiwan Reunification," Reuters, May 22, 2020.

22. Riyaz Khaliq, "China Heightens Taiwan Rhetoric Amid US Interference," Anadolu Agency, September 21, 2020.

23. Samson Ellis, "Here's What Could Happen if China Invaded Taiwan," *Japan Times,* October 8, 2020.

24. John Xie, "Amid Tensions with Taiwan," Voice of America, October 11, 2020.

25. Julian E. Zelizer, *The Presidency of Donald J. Trump* (Princeton: Princeton University Press, 2022), pp. 262–263.

26. Dean Chen, "The Trump Administration's One-China Policy: Tilting Toward Taiwan in an Era of U.S.-PRC Rivalry?" *Asian Politics and Policy* 11, no. 2 (April 23, 2019): 264–265.

27. Aiden Warren and Adam Bartley, *U.S. Foreign Policy and China: Security Challenges During the Bush, Obama, and Trump Administrations* (Edinburgh: Edinburgh University Press, 2021), pp. 157–158.

28. John Bolton, *The Room Where It Happened: A White House Memoir* (New York: Simon and Schuster: 2020), pp. 289–290.

29. Ibid., p. 290.

30. Lawrence Lau, "If the US-China Trade War Escalates, How Will the Chinese Economy Respond? Here Are the Numbers," *South China Morning Post,* July 29, 2018.

31. Bolton, *Room Where It Happened,* pp. 290–291.

32. Ibid., pp. 291–292.

33. Wayne Morrison, "China-U.S. Trade Issues," Congressional Research Service, July 30, 2018, https://fas.org.

34. Keith Bradsher, "China Loosens Foreign Auto Rules, in Potential Peace Offering to Trump," *New York Times,* April 17, 2018.

35. Morrison, "China-U.S. Trade Issues."

36. Doug Palmer, "U.S. Trade Gap with China Reaches All-Time High Under Trump," Politico, March 6, 2019.

37. "The People's Republic of China: U.S.-China Trade Facts," Office of the United States Trade Representative, https://ustr.gov.

38. Morrison, "China-U.S. Trade Issues."

39. Ibid.

40. Ibid.

41. National Counterintelligence and Security Center, *Foreign Economic Espionage in Cyberspace* (Washington, DC: National Counterintelligence and Security Center, 2018), pp. 5–7.

42. CFR Workshop, *Chinese Investment in Critical U.S. Technology: Risks to U.S. Security Interests,* Council on Foreign Relations, October 16, 2017, https://www.cfr.org.

Confronting a More Assertive China **297**

43. Morrison, "China-U.S. Trade Issues."

44. Deng Yuwen, "The US Sees the Trade War as a Tactic to Contain China. So Does Beijing," *South China Morning Post,* July 4, 2018.

45. Bolton, *Room Where It Happened,* pp. 294–296.

46. Ibid., pp. 296–297.

47. Ibid., pp. 299–301.

48. Ibid., pp. 301–302.

49. Ibid., pp. 302–303.

50. Ibid., p. 304.

51. Ibid., pp. 305–306.

52. Ibid., p. 308.

53. Ibid., p. 309.

54. Chen, "Trump Administration's One-China Policy," pp. 262–263.

55. Ibid., p. 269.

56. Ibid., pp. 265–266.

57. Bush, "Trump Administration's Policies."

58. Chen, "Trump Administration's One-China Policy," pp. 267–268.

59. Bolton, *Room Where It Happened,* pp. 313–314.

60. Zelizer, *Presidency of Donald J. Trump,* p. 275.

61. Ibid., p. 276.

62. Warren and Bartley, *U.S. Foreign Policy and China,* pp. 184–186.

63. Chen, "Trump Administration's One-China Policy," p. 264.

64. Warren and Bartley, *U.S. Foreign Policy and China,* pp. 171–173.

65. Ibid., p. 167.

66. Mike Pompeo, *Never Give an Inch: Fighting for the America I Love* (New York: HarperCollins, 2023), pp. 255–256.

67. Ibid., p. 256.

68. Ibid., p. 256.

69. Ibid., p. 257.

70. George Will, "Time Is on Taiwan's Side, as Long as the U.S. Is, too," *Washington Post,* September 25, 2019.

71. Shirley Tay, "As US-China Relations Sour, Taiwan's Value as a 'Chess Piece' May Rise," CNBC, June 11, 2019.

72. Chen, "Trump Administration's One-China Policy," p. 264.

73. Ibid., p. 262.

74. Sun, "Taiwan Security Under the Trump Administration," p. 15.

75. "Factbox: U.S. Arms Sales to Taiwan in the Past Decade," Reuters, June 6, 2019.

76. Dean Chen, *US-China-Taiwan in the Age of Trump and Biden: Towards a Nationalist Strategy* (New York, Routledge, 2022), p. 58.

77. Alex Ward, "The Trump Administration Authorized Arms Sales to Taiwan. China Isn't Pleased," Vox, July 9, 2019.

78. Pompeo, *Never Give an Inch,* p. 257.

79. Chen, *US-China-Taiwan in the Age of Trump and Biden,* pp. 265–266.

80. Idrees Ali and Huizhong Wu, "U.S. Warship Sails Through Taiwan Strait, Stirs Tensions with China," Reuters, July 24, 2019.

81. Tay, "As US-China Relations Sour, Taiwan's Value as a 'Chess Piece' May Rise."

82. Office of the Secretary of Defense, *Annual Report to Congress,* p. 44.

83. Ibid., p. 107.

84. Warren and Bartley, *U.S. Foreign Policy and China,* p. 198.

85. Ibid., pp. 200–201.

86. Ibid., pp. 191–194.

87. Japan Ministry of Defense, *Defense of Japan 2018,* October 22, 2018, https://www.mod.go.jp.

88. Franz-Stefan Gady, "US, Japan Aircraft Carriers Conduct Naval Exercise in South China Sea," *The Diplomat,* June 12, 2019.

89. Japan Ministry of Defense, *Defense of Japan 2018.*

90. Leo Lin, "Will the China-Japan Reset Continue in 2019?" *The Diplomat,* January 31, 2019.

91. Minoru Satake, "Japan's 4 Carriers to Shun Chinese 5G Tech," *Nikkei Asian Review,* December 10, 2018.

92. Andrea Fischetti and Antoine Roth, "A Structural Constraint to China-Japan Relations," *Tokyo Review,* April 12, 2019.

93. Japan Ministry of Defense, *Defense of Japan 2018.*

94. Ibid.

95. Lin, "Will the China-Japan Reset Continue in 2019?"

96. Stephen Nagy, "It's Too Early to Write Off the Indo-Pacific Strategy," *Japan Times,* July 24, 2018.

97. Warren and Bartley, *U.S. Foreign Policy and China,* pp. 191–192.

98. Ibid., p. 194.

99. Ibid., pp. 194–195.

100. Zelizer, *Presidency of Donald J. Trump,* p. 268.

101. Ibid., p. 268.

102. Zelizer, *Presidency of Donald J. Trump,* p. 277.

15

The Taiwan Straight Crisis of 2022–2023: The Biden Administration

ON JANUARY 19, 2021, ANTONY BLINKEN, WHO WAS GOING TO BECOME THE secretary of state for President Joe Biden, testified at his confirmation hearing that he had fundamentally agreed with the direction of President Donald Trump's China policy by taking a tougher approach to China.[1] During his campaign, Biden mentioned core principles in his China policy: work with US allies to make an effective China policy, persuade China to accept the world order, and cooperate with China to deal with world problems.[2]

In April, Biden sent a delegation to Taiwan led by former senator Chris Dodd, a close friend of Biden's. The White House called this visit a personal signal of Biden's commitment to Taiwan. In response, China dispatched twenty-five warplanes to intrude on Taiwan's air defense identification zone (ADIZ). The Taiwan Affairs Office of the People's Republic of China (PRC) commented that the response of the People's Liberation Army (PLA) was an "actual combat" exercise to curb "Taiwan-U.S. collusion."[3]

Historical Events: The Taiwan Strait Crises of 2022 and 2023

Since 2016, when Tsai Ing-wen won the presidential election, Taiwan's policy under Xi Jinping has become more aggressive. In 2019, President Xi stated that China did not promise to renounce the use of force.[4] The Xi administration has framed reunification with Taiwan as a requirement for achieving the China Dream. Since the PLA warplanes' intrusions have become more frequent, Taiwan's Ministry of Defense said jet pilots would no longer scramble to encounter the PLA aircraft each time, and would instead track them with ground-to-air missiles.[5] With the rising cross-strait

300 Hedging the China Threat

tension, *The Economist* labeled Taiwan "the most dangerous place on Earth."[6] With the strong rhetoric and increased military activities, the PLA has taken steps to enhance its capabilities to take Taiwan by force.

China's Strong Rhetoric and Increased Military Activities

Since President Tsai was reelected in 2020, Beijing has intensified its rhetoric against her administration. It asserts that the escalating cross-strait tension was attributed to Tsai's refusal to accept the 1992 Consensus and her collusion with the US government.

Strong rhetoric against Taiwan's leader. In March 2021, the PRC premier, Li Keqiang, said that China would deter any separatist act seeking Taiwan's independence. The PRC's Ministry of Defense claimed that Taiwan's separatists remained the gravest threat to peace in the Taiwan Strait. Their first criticism was Taiwan's move toward independence. The PLA threatened, "Taiwan independence means war."[7] China claimed that Taiwan's ruling party, the Democratic Progressive Party (DPP), was pushing for independence in every possible area. For example, a high school history curriculum in Taiwan made Chinese history part of East Asian history. China warned that pushing for independence in education would poison the younger generation in Taiwan.[8] Its second criticism was Taiwan's collusion with the United States. After Tsai took office, US-Taiwan relations improved. US cabinet and Congress members increasingly visited Taiwan, which enraged Chinese leaders, who viewed the United States as violating China's domestic affairs.[9] Chinese leaders and media threatened Taiwan, saying it would pay a heavy price for seeking independence—they would take Taiwan by force.[10]

The military threat. As China prepared to use military means against Taiwan, PLA warplanes started to intrude on Taiwan's ADIZ. Since September 2020, warplanes have been flying across the median line of the Taiwan Strait and flying around Taiwan almost daily. The purposes of this harassment were to intimidate Tsai's government, test Taiwan's military response, and prepare for a future invasion. China also took steps to prevent US intervention. As the PLA deployed missiles along the southeast coastal areas of China, their pilots conducted long-distance flight training. The PLA released a video displaying bombers making a simulated strike against Anderson Air Force Base in Guam.[11] The PLA also conducted exercises simulating the invasion of Taiwan on October 10, 2020, the Republic of China (ROC) National Day. On April 5, 2021, the navy announced that the *Liaoning* aircraft carrier was conducting exercises near Taiwan.[12] China believed that an effective way to prevent Taiwan from separating from China was to use military coercion.

To show the resolution of defending its homeland, ROC foreign minister Joseph Wu stated that Taiwan's defense was its people's responsibility. They would defend themselves to the very end. In March 2021, ROC defense minister Chiu Kuo-cheng said, "I always tell my peers to stop asking, how many days do we need to hold out? The question is, how many days does China want to fight? We'll keep them company for as long as they want to fight."[13] In 2021, Tsai's administration increased its military budget by 10 percent, to about $15 billion annually.[14] Tsai has sought to bolster Taiwan's defense by reforming the reserves and purchasing weapons. Her administration has pushed to revive Taiwan's domestic weapons manufacturing, including submarines, armored vehicles, and aircraft.[15]

The Taiwan Strait Crisis of 2022

On July 19, 2022, the *Financial Times* reported that House Speaker Nancy Pelosi would visit Taiwan in August. The PLA warned that it would not stand idly by. In a phone conversation with Biden, Xi Jinping asked Biden to prevent Pelosi from visiting Taiwan. Biden responded that Congress was an independent branch of government and that he would not intervene. Biden advised Xi not to take provocative actions should the visit happen.[16] On August 2, Pelosi's delegation arrived in Taiwan. In response, China conducted several large-scale military exercises beginning on August 3, ushering in the 2022 Taiwan Strait Crisis.[17]

Before the crisis. As US-Taiwan relations became more robust, Beijing reacted with stronger rhetoric. The chairman of the Joint Chiefs of Staff (JCS), General Mark Milley, and his PRC counterpart, General Li Zuocheng, held a video conference on July 7, 2022. Milley underlined the importance of dialogue in improving crisis communications and reducing risk between the two militaries. Li said that China has no room for compromise with Taiwan and warned, "If anyone provokes China, he will surely meet the firm countermeasures of the Chinese people." National Security Advisor (NSA) Jake Sullivan held a meeting with the director of the office of the PRC Foreign Affairs Commission, Yang Jiechi, on May 18 and June 13, respectively. Yang criticized Biden's Taiwan policies, including "erroneous words and deeds" that interfered with China's internal affairs. Yang opposed the United States playing the "Taiwan card." On July 28, Biden and Xi held their virtual conference. Xi reiterated the warning that "those who play with fire will get burned." Biden restated that the United States opposed unilateral efforts to change the status quo.[18]

The first phase of the military exercise (August 3 to 10): Retaliation for Pelosi's visit. On August 3, 2022, Tsai met with a Pelosi-led delegation and presented her with an award to thank her for enhancing US-Taiwan relations. Tsai said that facing China's military threats, Taiwan would work with the Biden administration to strengthen security cooperation.[19] Pelosi's visit infuriated China, and it canceled planned exchanges with the United States. Economic sanctions were levied against Taiwan. More than 2,000 of Taiwan's food products were suspended from being imported to China.[20] Several civilian flights in Fujian Province were canceled, clearing the airspace in the Taiwan Strait to engage in military operations. PLA missiles splashed down around Taiwan's territorial waters, flying over Taiwan's cities for the first time.[21]

The first phase of the PLA's military operations lasted from August 4 to 7. On August 4, the PLA launched ballistic missiles into multiple exercise zones around Taiwan. The following day, the East Theater Command (ETC) of the PLA conducted air and sea combat drills around Taiwan to test their joint combat capabilities. On August 6, the ETC focused on land attack and sea assault capabilities with joint air and naval operations in the sea and airspace around Taiwan, clearing paths for amphibious forces to launch beach assaults against Taiwan. On August 7, on the scheduled final day of exercises, the ETC conducted live-fire drills in the waters and airspace around Taiwan.[22]

China announced new military exercises to engage in joint antisubmarine and sea assault operations on August 8. In the next two days, China engaged in multiple cyberattacks against Taiwan's political and military targets. The PLA continued exercises focusing on joint support operations such as aerial refueling and sea support. On August 10, the ETC announced that operations around Taiwan had concluded. It, however, would continue to monitor the region, conduct military training, and regularly organize combat patrols in the Taiwan Strait.[23]

The Tsai government was on high alert. After the PLA launched ballistic missiles over Taiwan, Tsai vowed to "firmly defend their sovereignty and national security, and stick to the line of defense of democracy and freedom." Those missiles also got the attention of Japan's government. Five of them landed inside Japan's exclusive economic zone (EEZ). Japanese prime minister Fumio Kishida called for a halt to them and said Japan would work with the United States to maintain stability in the Taiwan Strait.[24] Secretary Blinken, in a virtual joint press conference with the foreign secretary of the Philippines, Enrique Manalo, in Manila on August 6, said the United States was determined to de-escalate tensions over the Taiwan Strait. Blinken pointed out that China's launching of missiles impeded the passage of ships to the Taiwan Strait, and accused China of using Pelosi's trip as a "pretext" to change the status quo in Taiwan.[25]

The second phase of military pressure (August 11 to August 31): Reactions to the US official visit. During the second phase, many US leaders began visiting Taiwan, which angered Chinese leaders by responding with mili-

The Taiwan Straight Crisis of 2022–2023   303

tary coercion. Despite China's official conclusion of the exercises, six navy vessels and twenty-two aircraft intruded into areas around Taiwan from August 11 to 14. On August 15, a US congressional delegation led by Senator Ed Markey arrived in Taipei. The next day, the ETC announced that it would begin joint combat readiness patrols and real-combat drills in the waters and airspace around Taiwan. On August 21, Governor Eric Holcomb of Indiana arrived for an economic development trip, making him the first Indiana governor to travel to Taiwan in seventeen years. Beijing expressed strong discontent.[26]

Senator Marsha Blackburn visited Taiwan and met with Tsai on August 26. The PLA responded by conducting joint patrols and combat exercises in air and sea areas near Taiwan. The PRC's embassy in Washington issued a statement that China would take resolute countermeasures to Blackburn's visit. On August 28, the US Navy sent two cruisers through the Taiwan Strait. US officials said transits would continue. The ETC monitored the two ships and maintained a high alert.[27] On August 30, Arizona governor Doug Ducey arrived in Taiwan, beginning a three-day trip. PRC's Ministry of Foreign Affairs responded to this visit by stating that China rejected any US-Taiwan official interaction. The following day, seven Chinese vessels and sixty-two aircraft were reported in areas around Taiwan.[28]

During the crisis, the PLA staged its largest military exercises around Taiwan. Chinese warplanes and warships swarmed across the Taiwan Strait and the PLA launched missiles over Taiwan, creating a new normal of a closer presence against Taiwan.[29] These exercises showcased the PLA's increased confidence in its capabilities. Its objectives included the following: first, it intended to impose political costs on Taipei and undermine support for Tsai among Taiwan's public.[30] Tsai would bear the responsibility of closer relations with the United States. Second, the military exercises were part of Chinese deterrence and signaled efforts toward the United States, Taiwan, and US allies. They demonstrated how determined China was to exert control over Taiwan and to intimidate the United States and Japan for intervention. Third, these exercises allowed the PLA to prepare various military operations against Taiwan and the United States.[31] Fourth, this gave the Chinese an opportunity to test the Taiwan and US responses to these incursions.

The United States had two different reactions to the crisis. Media and scholars were critical of the Pelosi visit for endangering US security. The Biden administration and Congress targeted China for overreacting. The debate highlighted differences among Americans over US policy toward China and Taiwan. On the one hand, the Biden administration and Congress suggested hardening US policy to counter Beijing. This supported Taiwan as an important partner in dealing with these challenges. On the other hand, many US specialists on China, along with large business firms in partnership with China, opposed Washington hardening its policy toward China.[32]

304 *Hedging the China Threat*

China's white paper on Taiwan. The PRC's Taiwan Affairs Office published a white paper titled, "The Taiwan Question and China's Reunification in the New Era" on August 10, 2022. Released during the PLA's military exercises against Taiwan,[33] the white paper stated that the actions of the Democratic Progressive Party (DPP) resulted in tension in China-Taiwan relations. They claimed it undermined peaceful reunification and encouraged the separatist forces in Taiwan.[34]

The white paper clarified in what circumstances China would use force. It stated, "We will only be forced to take drastic measures to respond to the provocation of separatist elements or external forces, should they ever cross our red lines."[35] Although it suggested that China would be less willing to use military force, the document urged China to have the courage and skill "to mobilize all factors to fight."[36] It reflected Beijing's toughened positions against Taiwan: it would not guarantee that Taiwan could maintain its democracy after reunification. The white paper emphasized China's goal to complete reunification. Beijing believed that increasing people-to-people contacts and economic and cultural exchanges were no longer sufficient to drive cross-strait relations in the direction Beijing wanted. China would rely on its growing political, economic, and military power to push Taiwan.[37] Although releasing the white paper was an important part of implementing the strategy of the Chinese Communist Party (CCP) toward Taiwan during the Xi administration, it was also a tough response to the Taiwan Strait Crisis.[38]

Taiwan's Response

Tsai signaled that Taiwan would not flinch, but also would not provoke. Most Taiwanese scholars suggested that the United States and Taiwan strengthen bilateral relations and solidify Taiwan's international support. The Taiwanese partisan policy was divergent from China's policy. Both major political parties, the DPP and the Kuomintang (KMT), presented themselves as safekeepers of Taiwan. The opposition KMT argued it could deal with Beijing to lower risk and preserve stability. Since Beijing refused to deal directly with the DPP, the ruling party's response had been to bolster Taiwan's relations with the United States against Chinese pressure.[39]

Taiwan's military was monitoring the situation on high alert. During China's exercises, Taiwan's Ministry of National Defense announced that its missile defense capabilities had been activated.[40] The armed forces kept repeating that the military had everything under control, emphasizing that the situation was being monitored and that Taiwan was prepared. The Ministry of Foreign Affairs of Taiwan was messaging the international community. It painted the events as China's attempt to bully Taiwan and appealed to the global community to stand with Taiwan.[41] The military leaders agreed with the urgent need for more training for conscripts and reservists. They knew Taiwan must defend itself, but they also hoped the United States would do more to deter Beijing from trying to take Taiwan by force.[42]

The US-China Chip War

Since 2022, the Biden administration has increased its competition with China in the semiconductor industry. In August 2022, Biden signed the Creating Helpful Incentives to Produce Semiconductors (CHIPS) and Science Act, a $52.7 billion industrial policy to bolster research, enhance the supply chain, and revitalize production.[43] In October, the administration enacted restrictions on China's chip manufacturing industry, curbing the sale of advanced chips to China and making it difficult to transfer advanced chip and supercomputer technology to China.[44] To Beijing's leadership, the sanctions showed that the United States was launching a chip war against China.[45]

The Taiwan Semiconductor Manufacturing Company (TSMC) produces 90 percent of the world's most advanced processor chips. The Biden administration pushed TSMC to build a manufacturing facility in Arizona, and allocated billions of dollars to incentivize companies to establish manufacturing facilities in the United States.[46] China's official mouthpiece, the *Global Times*, stated that Washington would not hesitate to hijack Taiwan's semiconductor manufacturing sectors. Beijing said that the conspiracy between the United States and the Taiwan secessionists might threaten Taiwan's semiconductor sector.[47]

On January 31, 2023, Xi Jinping noted that it was imperative to move faster toward self-reliance in science and technology to relieve the stranglehold that some countries had on China's development of core technologies. In response to the latest export controls, the Beijing government only went as far as initiating a dispute with the World Trade Organization (WTO). The United States is aiming to prevent China from becoming an artificial intelligence (AI)–advanced military power.[48]

The 2023 Taiwan Strait Crisis

President Tsai traveled through the United States in late March and early April 2023. Tsai landed in Los Angeles on April 4, after visits to Belize and Guatemala, marking the final leg of her seventh trip to the United States since becoming president in 2016. House Speaker Kevin McCarthy met Tsai in California. Before the meeting, Beijing warned that it would respond with resolute actions. Biden's officials emphasized Tsai's visit, calling it a "transit" rather than an "official" trip.[49]

Tsai's 2023 US transit. In the warning against the Tsai-McCarthy meeting, the PRC Foreign Ministry labeled Tsai "the head of Taiwan's independence

306   Hedging the China Threat

secessionist forces." China's Taiwan Affairs Office warned that such contact would be a provocation that could destroy the cross-strait peace.[50]

During the Tsai-McCarthy meeting, McCarthy said the US-Taiwan bond "is stronger now than at any time or point in my lifetime." He committed to more timely arms sales to Taiwan.[51] In her speech, Tsai emphasized that freedom must be fought for. Initiatives in enhancing Taiwan's self-defense capabilities, fostering economic ties, and supporting Taiwan's meaningful participation in the international community have safeguarded shared interests.[52]

On April 7, the PLA said it would hold "combat readiness patrols," focusing on "testing the ability to seize sea, air, and information control." The ROC's Defense Ministry said it would respond calmly and with a serious attitude. PRC maritime authorities announced an inspection patrol operation in the Taiwan Strait. Chief of the European Union, Ursula von der Leyen, was in China to meet Xi and said stability in the Taiwan Strait was paramount. Xi responded that expecting China to compromise with Taiwan was "wishful thinking."[53]

On April 8, China began three days of military exercises around Taiwan. China held combat readiness patrols until April 10. The drills involved exercises in the Taiwan Strait to the north and south of Taiwan and in the sea and airspace to its east. The PLA said, "This is a serious warning to the Taiwan independence separatist forces and external forces' collusion and provocation. This is a necessary action to defend national sovereignty and territorial integrity." At the time of the first PLA exercise, the ROC's Defense Ministry said that forty-two PLA planes and eight ships crossed the strait's median line. A delegation of US legislators, led by Michael McCaul, chairman of the House Foreign Affairs Committee, visited Taiwan. McCaul said the delegation was in Taipei to show its support for a democratic Taiwan.[54]

On April 10, the PLA drills involved fighters, navy destroyers, aircraft carriers, and missile speedboats. During the exercise, the *USS Milius,* a guided missile destroyer, monitored China's actions. The United States said it had the resources and capabilities to ensure peace and stability in the region. On April 11, the PLA declared it was ready to fight after completing three days of combat drills simulating a blockade to seal off Taiwan.[55] Taiwan's foreign minister, Joseph Wu, condemned Beijing's actions in an interview with CNN. He warned that the PRC seemed to be trying to get ready to launch a war against Taiwan. While Wu emphasized that "defending Taiwan is our own responsibility," he noted that the United States seemed more determined than ever to create a situation so that China would know that its military attack against Taiwan would incur a heavy cost.[56]

The Individual Level:
Biden's "Defending Taiwan" Against China's Threat?

President-elect Biden said he would not make immediate changes in policies toward China, but planned to review the US-China relations with allies to develop a comprehensive and coherent strategy. He believed the best China strategy was to get US allies on the same page.[57] Antony Blinken, who was to be secretary of state in the administration, indicated that Biden planned to take a multilateral approach by joining the support of allies to increase the United States' leverage on China.[58]

Biden's China Policy

Biden has argued that the US response to China's rise should be to enhance US education and infrastructure. On April 16, 2021, Biden met with Japanese prime minister Yoshihide Suga in Washington. Concerning China issues, Biden and Suga committed to strengthening their alliance to counter China. Biden supported Japan's defense under the US-Japan Security Treaty, which included using nuclear weapons. Both leaders reaffirmed that Article V of the treaty applied to the Diaoyutai Islands/Senkaku Islands. They also reiterated objections to China's unlawful maritime activities in the South China Sea. Biden and Suga encouraged a peaceful resolution between China and Taiwan.[59]

Defending Taiwan. Under Biden, US-Taiwan relations substantially improved. On January 20, 2021, the State Department invited Hsiao Bi-khim, the ROC's representative to the United States, to attend Biden's inauguration. In March, Biden vowed to honor US commitments to Taiwan, while stating that Taiwan was a "critical economic and security partner."[60]

A succession of US presidents had made it clear that they would respond militarily to unprovoked attacks by China. In an interview broadcast by *ABC News* on August 20, Biden was asked why Chinese media ridiculed Taiwan leaders. They said that the United States could not be trusted because of the US withdrawal from Afghanistan. Biden replied that Taiwan, South Korea, and NATO were in different situations than Afghanistan. He appeared to lump Taiwan together with countries to which the United States had defense commitments.[61] At a CNN town hall event on October 22, a participant asked Biden if he would vow to protect Taiwan. Biden said that he would. A White House spokesman later said that Biden's remarks did not signify a change in policy. A CNN anchor then asked Biden a second time if the United States would come to Taiwan's defense in the event of an attack by China. Biden replied, "Yes, we have the commitment to do that."[62]

308 Hedging the China Threat

On May 23, 2022, Biden had a summit with Prime Minister Fumio Kishida. After the meeting, the leaders held a joint press conference in Tokyo. When asked "Are you willing to get involved militarily to defend Taiwan, if it comes to that?" Biden said, "Yes. That's the commitment we made."[63] In response to Biden's remarks, the PRC's Foreign Ministry spokesman, Wang Wenbin, stated that "China expresses strong dissatisfaction and firm opposition to the remarks by the U.S. side."[64] US defense secretary Lloyd Austin said Biden had restated the US commitment under the Taiwan Relations Act "to help provide Taiwan the means to defend itself."[65]

On September 18, Biden was asked in a CBS *60 Minutes* interview whether US forces would defend Taiwan, Biden replied, "Yes." Asked to clarify if he meant that unlike in Ukraine, US forces would defend Taiwan in the event of a Chinese invasion, Biden replied, "Yes." China responded that Biden's comments sent a wrong signal to separatist forces. Taiwan's Foreign Ministry expressed its thanks to Biden for reaffirming the US government's rock-solid security commitment. It said that Taiwan would strengthen its self-defense capabilities and deepen the close US-Taiwan security partnership.[66]

The Biden-Xi summit. On the eve of the Lunar New Year on February 10, 2021, Xi and Biden held their first phone call since Biden took office. Biden emphasized the US concerns about China's aggressive economic practices and its increasing military threat against Taiwan, while Xi focused on mutual respect, cooperation, and dialogue. To build a better working relationship, Biden avoided sensitive topics such as China's repression of the Uyghurs in Xinjiang and its crushing of democracy in Hong Kong.[67]

On March 18, 2022, Xi and Biden held their first conference call since Russia invaded Ukraine. Their talk focused on Russia's invasion. Biden described the consequences if China provided material support to Russia. Biden reiterated that the US policy on Taiwan had not changed. He underlined that the United States continued to oppose any unilateral changes to the status quo.[68] Biden reiterated that the United States and its allies were not targeting China and did not support Taiwan's independence.[69]

On July 28, Biden and Xi had another call, discussing US-China cooperation and issues surrounding Taiwan and Ukraine. The White House stated that the call was a part of Biden's efforts to manage differences and work together where mutual interests align. Regarding Taiwan, Xi said that the United States should not "play with fire," and that the United States should abide by the One China policy and implement the three US-China joint communiqués. The White House readout stated that Biden underscored that the US policy had not changed and that the United States strongly opposed unilateral efforts to change the status quo or undermine peace across the Taiwan Strait.[70]

On November 14, Biden and Xi held their first face-to-face meeting since Biden had become president. The meeting was in the run-up to the Group of 20 (G-20) summit in Bali, Indonesia. Biden stated that both countries could manage differences, prevent competition from becoming conflict, and find ways to work together on urgent global issues. Xi stated, "We need to find the right direction for the bilateral relationship going forward and elevate the relationship." The meeting touched on key issues relating to US-China bilateral relations, including China's economic development, Taiwan, and regional security. The PRC's meeting readout stated that China took Biden's Five No's statement seriously. The United States did not "seek to change China's system, start a new cold war, strengthen alliances against China, support Taiwan's independence, or break off ties with China." China stated that the Taiwan question was the first redline that must not be crossed. The White House readout stated that the US stance on the One China policy had not changed, but that the United States opposed any unilateral changes to the status quo by either side.[71]

The National Security Strategy under Biden. On October 12, 2022, Biden declared that the challenge for the United States would be "outcompeting China and restraining Russia." In his National Security Strategy (NSS), Biden stated that he was more worried about China's moves toward authoritarian governance with a revisionist foreign policy than about a declining Russia.[72] The NSS stated that the PRC used its economic, diplomatic, military, and technological power to create more permissive conditions for its own authoritarian model. The PRC also invested in its military to erode US alliances in the Indo-Pacific. To counter this, Biden's strategy toward China focused on three initiatives. The first was to invest in the foundations of US strength at home: competitiveness, innovation, resilience, and democracy. The second initiative was to align US efforts with its network of allies and partners. The third was to compete with the PRC to defend US interests.[73] Biden committed to standing up to China with a speedier US military modernization.[74]

The Chinese Balloon Incident

When a Chinese spy balloon floated across the United States in early February 2023, the incident caused an uproar in the United States. The Pentagon said it was tracking the balloon and, on February 4, a US fighter jet shot it down off the coast of South Carolina. On February 9, Assistant Secretary of Defense Melissa Dalton told senators during a hearing that the United States had collected pod equipment from the balloon, including high-tech devices that could receive communication signals and other sensitive information.[75] On February 10, the United States downed a

310   Hedging the China Threat

"high-altitude object" off the coast of Alaska. The US military shot down another object spotted over the Great Lakes region on February 12. The spy balloon incident prompted Secretary Blinken to postpone a planned visit to Beijing and has further strained US-China relations.[76]

After the United States announced the balloon's existence, Chinese officials admitted that the object belonged to China, but added it was a civilian airship used for research purposes that had been blown off course. They regretted the unintended entry of the airship into US airspace. When the United States shot the balloon down, the PRC called it a "clear overreaction . . . unacceptable and irresponsible."[77] On February 16, Biden stated, "I gave the order to take down these three objects due to hazards to civilian commercial air traffic and because we could not rule out the surveillance risk of sensitive facilities."[78] On April 3, *NBC News* reported that according to senior US officials, the Chinese spy balloon was able to gather intelligence from several sensitive US military sites. They said China could control the balloon to transmit the information it collected back to Beijing in real time.[79]

Biden planned to speak with Xi and noted, "I think the last thing that Xi wants is to fundamentally rip the relationship with the U.S. and with me." On the same day, China put Lockheed and Raytheon on an "unreliable entities list" over arms sales to Taiwan, banning them from imports and exports related to China in its latest sanctions against the US companies. Lockheed made the F-22 Raptor fighter jet that flew the mission to shoot down the Chinese balloon and Raytheon made the AIM-9X Sidewinder missile that blew it out of the sky.[80]

Biden directed his team to develop rules for addressing unidentified objects in the future. He asked NSA Sullivan to do the following: establish an inventory of unmanned airborne objects; develop measures to better detect these objects in US airspace; update rules for launching these into the skies; and designate Secretary Blinken to lead in establishing norms in space.[81]

The State Level:
The Biden Administration's China and Taiwan Policies

Biden's China team earned his confidence through their years of service. Secretary of State Antony Blinken thought that China could resist pressure from the United States, which represented a quarter of the global gross domestic product (GDP). China, however, could not ignore a US-led alliance comprising 50–60 percent of the global GDP. Secretary of Defense Lloyd Austin called for forging coalitions in Asia.[82] NSA Jake Sullivan believed China to be a much more challenging competitor than the Soviet Union, yet that cooperation with China on transnational issues was essential.

Through working with allies, the United States could deter Chinese security threats. William Burns, director of the Central Intelligence Agency (CIA), emphasized that nothing mattered more for the United States than dealing with China. Kurt Campbell, coordinator for the Indo-Pacific at the National Security Council (NSC), thought the United States needed to be more realistic in dealing with China and the focus should be strengthening the United States and rebuilding its alliances.[83]

The Biden Team's Growing Support for Taiwan

Arms sales and high-level officials' visits to Taiwan have continued under the Biden administration. The growing US-China rivalry has increased Taiwan's attraction to the US government to confront China. The State Department has urged China to cease military pressure by affirming that the US commitment to Taiwan is rock solid.[84] Kathleen Hicks, deputy secretary of defense, commented that the US commitment to Taiwan must be "crystal clear" under the rising China threat.[85] Maintaining China-Taiwan peace has been the priority for the Biden administration. NSA Jake Sullivan called for the United States to invest in capabilities that would bolster deterrence in the Taiwan Strait. Secretary Blinken ensured that the United States would equip Taiwan with the necessary capabilities to defend itself.[86]

As China's aircraft and warships harassed Taiwan, Secretary Austin responded that he would "ensure that the U.S. is living up to its commitments to support Taiwan's ability to defend itself."[87] The Biden administration has maintained its commitments outlined in the Taiwan Relations Act (TRA) and the Six Assurances by providing arms sales, carrying out freedom of navigation exercises in the Taiwan Strait, advocating for Taiwan's international participation, and sending US officials to Taiwan.[88]

The State Department: Rising US-China Tensions

The State Department, under Blinken's leadership, sought a results-oriented relationship with China. The United States ensured China's support for exerting pressure on North Korea to end its nuclear program, reducing the US trade deficit with China, stopping the flow of illegal opioids from China to the United States, and seeking progress on the South China Sea disputes.[89] Secretary Blinken charged that China had become more repressive. The United States would align with allies and partners to defend US interests.[90]

The face-off between Blinken and Chinese top diplomats. On March 18–20, 2021, the United States and China held the first high-level meeting in Alaska, with Secretary Blinken and NSA Sullivan and their Chinese counterparts, Yang Jiechi and Wang Yi, in attendance. Each side rebuked

312   *Hedging the China Threat*

the other's policies. Blinken criticized China for hostile actions in the South China Sea, military intimidation of Taiwan, aggressive trade policies, and human rights abuses. Yang singled out the US efforts to contain China by pressuring other nations to join the United States in confronting China. Yang responded for sixteen minutes, over the agreed-on two-minute limit protocol.[91] For an astonished press, witnessing the exchange of heated arguments was like being present at the dawn of a new cold war. The *New York Times* warned that these harsh exchanges could result in a dangerous decay in US-China relations.[92]

On June 11, Blinken and Yang had a phone conversation. Blinken underscored US concerns over issues in Hong Kong, Xinjiang, and Taiwan, and stressed the need to investigate Covid-19. In turn, Yang criticized the United States for interfering in China's internal affairs, slandering China over Covid-19, and forming anti-China factions. He urged the United States to abide by the One China principle. Despite disagreements, Blinken put forward an expanded list of areas for US-China cooperation, including the denuclearization of the Korean Peninsula, "shared global challenges" brought by Iran and Burma, and the climate crisis.[93]

On September 23, 2022, Wang Yi met with Blinken at the UN General Assembly in New York. Wang called for "steering bilateral relations back on the track of steady development," while Blinken discussed the need to maintain open lines of communication and manage the US-PRC relationship. Wang warned that the Biden administration should stop hollowing out the One China policy, interfering in China's internal affairs, and stopping the sanctions on Chinese businesses. Blinken stated that the Biden administration was committed to maintaining peace and stability across the Taiwan Strait.[94]

On February 18, 2023, Blinken met with Wang in Munich, Germany, while both attended the security conference. Blinken emphasized the violation of US sovereignty by the presence of the PRC surveillance balloon in US territorial airspace. Wang responded that the shooting down of the balloon by the United States was an abuse of the use of force and a violation of international practice. On the Ukraine crisis, Blinken discouraged China from supporting Russia in its war with Ukraine. He warned China about the consequences if China provided material support to Russia.[95] Wang said Beijing would propose a political settlement. He stated that "The China-Russia comprehensive strategic partnership of coordination is built based on non-alliance, non-confrontation, and non-targeting of third countries."[96]

The State Department's China policy under Blinken. On May 26, 2022, Blinken spoke at George Washington University. His speech focused on the State Department's policy toward China. Blinken stated that the United States was not seeking a new cold war. The Biden administration's strategy could be summed up in three key words: invest, align, and compete. The administration was investing in the United States, starting with a modern industrial strategy to expand US technological influence and also reenergizing its network of alliances and partnerships. In addition, the United States was protecting US technological competitiveness to defend companies and countries against China's efforts to gain access to sensitive technologies.[97] On security issues, Blinken stated that Biden instructed the Pentagon to stay ahead of China. The United States would employ an "integrated deterrence" approach, by bringing together US allies and partners. They would work across the conventional, nuclear, space, and informational domains to counter US rivals. On Taiwan issues, the State Department opposed any unilateral changes to the status quo from either side. The United States expected cross-strait differences to be resolved by peaceful means. It would assist Taiwan in maintaining its self-defense capability. The State Department supported Taiwan's meaningful participation in the international community.[98]

The Pentagon's and National Security Council's engagement with China. On April 21, 2022, US defense secretary Lloyd Austin spoke to the PRC's defense minister, General Wei Fenghe, in Cambodia. Austin and Wei discussed defense relations and regional and global security issues. Austin emphasized the need to responsibly manage competition and maintain open lines of communication. The secretary also discussed the importance of dialogue on reducing strategic risk, improving crisis communications, and enhancing operational safety. He raised concerns about the increasingly dangerous behavior demonstrated by PLA aircraft in the region. He affirmed that the United States would continue to fly, sail, and operate wherever international law allows.[99] The PRC State Council's readout stated that China hoped to establish stable relations with the United States, but that the United States should not underestimate China's determination and capability. Regarding Taiwan, it said that the PLA would resolutely safeguard national sovereignty and territorial integrity.[100]

Biden's security team showed strong support for Taiwan. NSA Sullivan called for the United States to invest in capabilities that would bolster deterrence in the Taiwan Strait.[101] On June 13, 2022, during the Sullivan-Yang meeting in Luxembourg, Yang pointed out that Biden had assured China that the United States did not support Taiwan's independence and was not seeking to start a new cold war with China. In response, Sullivan underscored the importance of maintaining open lines of communication to manage competition between the two countries.[102] On January 5, 2023, NPR host Steve Inskeep interviewed Sullivan. Responding to the question of potential military conflict across the Taiwan Strait, Sullivan said, "There is a risk of conflict with respect to Taiwan, but I believe that with responsible stewardship,

314   *Hedging the China Threat*

we can ensure that this contingency never comes to pass. And that is our responsibility." Sullivan, however, acknowledged that achieving this objective would require coordination with allies.[103]

The International Level: The Russian Invasion of Ukraine

On February 24, 2022, Russia invaded Ukraine. At the outset, Russian forces were successful in their military operation, but they encountered strong Ukrainian resistance. The Russian military was hindered by poor logistics and ineffective communications. The Ukrainian Armed Forces (UAF) have proven more resilient than Russia expected. Many observers are skeptical that either Russia or Ukraine will be able to achieve a decisive battlefield victory soon.[104] Despite heavy casualties, neither side will back down soon. The US hopes that the continuing Russian military failure in Ukraine, and the mounting economic costs of sanctions, will persuade Russia to quit. However, there is no evidence that Russia's military forces are about to collapse. Neither is there evidence of an imminent economic crisis in Russia.[105]

The US Response

Biden once called Vladimir Putin a "killer" who "had no soul." The Putin administration has pursued an aggressive foreign policy, culminating in an all-out invasion of Ukraine. After Russia attacked Ukraine, the United States rallied the world to support the Ukrainian people. With a broad coalition, Ukraine has the resources to defend itself.[106]

Alongside allies and partners, the United States is helping to make Russia's war on Ukraine a failure. Across Europe, NATO is united in standing up against Russia. The United States will continue to assist Ukraine in the following ways: (1) the United States will support Ukraine in its fight for its freedom; (2) the United States will defend NATO territory and deepen a coalition with allies and partners to prevent Russia from causing further harm to European security; (3) the United States will not allow Russia to achieve its objectives through using or threatening to use nuclear weapons[107]; and (4) the United States will conduct collective training of the UAF at the battalion level in Western-style tactics and UAF brigade-level leadership to coordinate, integrate, and sustain combined arms operations. The supplies of US and Western weapons have improved Ukraine's firepower capability.[108]

The United States and its allies and partners are united in support of Ukraine in response to Russia's invasion. From January 2021 to April 2023, the United States invested over $35.8 billion in security assistance to Ukraine, which included over 1,600 Stinger antiaircraft systems, 10,000

Javelin antiarmor systems, 58,000 other antiarmor systems and munitions, and more.[109] Under US leadership, more than fifty allies and partner countries have provided security assistance to Ukraine, with over \$13 billion.[110]

China's Views

On February 22, 2022, PRC foreign minister Wang Yi attended the Munich Security Conference. Wang stated that China supported the sovereignty of all countries, including Ukraine. He emphasized that all countries' sovereignty, independence, and territorial integrity must be safeguarded because these are the basic principles of the UN Charter. Wang, however, criticized NATO, asking, "If NATO keeps expanding eastward, is it conducive to maintaining peace and stability in Europe?" He stated that all parties should work for a resolution of the Ukraine crisis through dialogue.[111]

On February 24, 2023, the PRC Ministry of Foreign Affairs commented on "China's Position on the Political Settlement of the Ukraine Crisis." Its key points were as follows. (1) Respect the sovereignty of all countries. The sovereignty, independence, and territorial integrity of all countries must be effectively upheld. (2) Abandon the Cold War mentality. The security of a region should not be achieved by strengthening or expanding its military allies. (3) Cease hostilities and resume peace talks. All parties should support Russia and Ukraine in resuming direct dialogue as quickly as possible, to reach a comprehensive cease-fire. (4) Resolve the humanitarian crisis. The UN should be supported in coordinating and channeling humanitarian aid to conflict zones. (5) Reduce strategic risks. The threat or use of nuclear weapons should be opposed. And (6) Promote postconflict reconstruction. The international community needs to take measures to support reconstruction.[112]

A Lesson Learned for Taiwan

Ukraine is suffering a violent struggle for its survival. Unfortunately, Taiwan could experience a similar fate. Applying lessons from the Ukraine crisis could be important for defending Taiwan in the future.[113] For Putin, if the United States entered into a military conflict with China because of Taiwan, the United States could shift its attention away from the Ukrainian theater, which would grant Russia an opportunity to avoid defeat.[114] Xi Jinping has expressed that he wants to see the unification of Taiwan, which could include the use of force. Most people in Taiwan see themselves as Taiwanese, which could motivate them to fight. Taiwan has announced the resumption of conscription to replace four-month training with one-year military service. According to a Taiwanese poll released in August 2022, 65.5 percent of participants supported a year-long compulsory military service.[115]

316 *Hedging the China Threat*

There are some lessons for Taiwan to learn from the war in Ukraine. Ukraine is an internationally recognized state, but Taiwan is not. China boasts an economy ten times the size of Russia's. China makes no secret of its intention to take over Taiwan. Besides its political will, China has been upgrading its military capabilities. Taiwan has revised its military doctrine to embrace asymmetric defense, upgrade its military capacities, and engage in a whole-of-society push toward full defense. In confronting China, Taiwan needs strong backing from the international community.[116]

If China chooses to invade Taiwan, it will prepare on a large scale that will be impossible to conceal. Maintaining a close watch on military movements will be critical. Real-time intelligence sharing could be the critical factor in alerting the world to a possible invasion. The more allies that monitor PLA movements during future exercises, the better Taiwan can prepare for China's invasion. Taiwan should devote its satellites and other advanced intelligence collection capabilities to this effort. Knowing that an invasion would come largely by sea, Taiwan and the United States should focus on stockpiling large numbers of asymmetric capabilities such as cruise missiles, short-range mobile air defenses, naval mines, and drones.[117]

The Biden administration is strengthening Taiwan's defense to deter a move by the PRC leaders. The United States is concerned that a shifting military balance of power in China's favor will make a military invasion of Taiwan more likely.[118] The Ukraine crisis incentivized the Taiwan government to actively coordinate with Washington. However, with the billions of dollars of aid given to the Ukrainians, will the United States even have the resources available to defend Taiwan? This issue has become a grave concern for US strategic watchers.

Conclusion

During the Biden administration, China launched two large-scale military exercises against Taiwan in response to House Speaker Nancy Pelosi's visit to Taiwan in 2022 and House Speaker Kevin McCarthy's meeting with Taiwan's president Tsai in California in 2023. President Biden stated at least four times from 2020 to 2023 that the United States would come to Taiwan's defense in the event of an attack by China. The Biden national security team has regarded China as the most serious competitor to the United States and, consequently, has taken a hard-line approach toward China.

From 2021 to 2023, the Biden administration's cross-strait policy focused on three initiatives. The first initiative was to invest in the foundations of US strength at home: competitiveness, innovation, resilience, and democracy. The second initiative was to align US efforts with the United

States' network of allies and partners. The third initiative was to compete militarily and economically with the PRC in defense of US interests. Regarding the Taiwan issues, the United States has made it clear that it would uphold its commitments under the Taiwan Relations Act to support Taiwan's self-defense and to maintain the US military capacity to resist any force against Taiwan.

In analyzing US policies and strategies under Biden at the individual level, the president has believed that the best strategy to confront the rise of China's threat is to get US allies to work together. During the first three years of Biden's presidency, the US-Taiwan security relations greatly improved. At the state level, the growing US-China rivalry has increased Taiwan's attraction to the US government to confront China. The State Department has urged China to cease military pressure by affirming that the US commitment to Taiwan continues to be rock solid. The State Department has also assisted Taiwan in participating in international organizations such as the World Health Organization. At the international level, Russia's invasion of Ukraine in 2022 caused the United States to shift its major attention away from the China-Taiwan problem. By providing weapons to Ukraine and imposing economic sanctions against Russia, the United States hoped that the continuing Russian military failure in Ukraine and the mounting economic costs of sanctions would persuade Russia to abandon its conquest. Almost two years into Russia's invasion, however, there is no evidence that Russia's military forces are about to collapse, nor is there evidence of an imminent economic crisis in Russia. Ukraine is suffering a violent struggle for its survival. Taiwan, surely, recognizes that it could experience a similar fate and should carefully consider the Russian-Ukrainian conflict as a cautionary tale. Learning from the war in Ukraine could be an important lesson for the Taiwan government.

During the Biden administration, Beijing has seen Washington moving away from its One China policy. In Beijing's view, Biden's repeated security commitments to Taiwan and changing the language on State Department web pages have provided ample evidence of this shift. An essential goal for Beijing in the ongoing crisis is to deter the US government from moving away from the One China policy. Domestic factors in the United States, China, and Taiwan have played a key role in this seemingly never-ending crisis. In the United States, maintaining a confrontational approach toward China has had bipartisan backing. China's social media has grumbled about Beijing's weak response to the US policy toward Taiwan. With the rise of Taiwanese identity among the youth, who see themselves not as Chinese but as Taiwanese only, cross-strait relations are likely to further deteriorate.[119] All of these factors have created a complex and dangerous world situation. To avoid war, the world needs level-headed and wise leaders rather than powermongers.

Notes

1. Julian E. Zelizer, *The Presidency of Donald J. Trump* (Princeton: Princeton University Press, 2022), pp. 259–260.

2. John Cooper, "The Biden Administration's China and Taiwan Policies: Connecting the Dots," *East Asian Policy* 13, no. 3 (2021): 104.

3. Yimou Lee and Ben Blanchard, "Taiwan Says China Bolstering Ability to Attack, Blockade Island," Reuters, March 19, 2021.

4. Alex Ward, "How China Could Force Biden's Hand on Defending Taiwan," Vox, May 5, 2021.

5. Erin Hale, "Is China Really About to Invade Taiwan?" Al Jazeera, April 14, 2021.

6. Justin Metz, "The Most Dangerous Place on Earth," *The Economist,* May 1, 2021.

7. Joshua Keating, "How Long Can the Biden Administration Stall a Crisis in Taiwan?" *Slate,* February 2, 2021.

8. "Beijing Criticizes Taiwan's De-Sinicization Act," CGTN, April 15, 2018.

9. Gabriel Crossley and Ben Blanchard, "China Threatens Retaliation over New U.S. Arms Sales to Taiwan," Reuters, October 22, 2020.

10. "Tsai's Soft Rhetoric Cannot Fool World on 'One China,'" *Global Times,* October 11, 2020.

11. Lee and Blanchard, "Taiwan Says China Bolstering Ability to Attack, Blockade Island."

12. Zhang Han and Liu Xuanzun, "1st Reported Taiwan Arms Sales Under Biden Admin Come Early, Further Strain Situation," *Global Times,* April 20, 2021.

13. Ryan Pickrell, "Taiwan Warns It Will Fight to 'the Very Last Day' if Attacked as China Steps Up Its Military Activity Nearby," *Insider,* April 7, 2021.

14. Michael E. O'Hanlon, "An Asymmetric Defense of Taiwan," Brookings Institution, April 28, 2021, https://www.brookings.edu.

15. Hale, "Is China Really About to Invade Taiwan?"

16. Bonnie Glaser, "US-China Relations Sink Further Amid Another Taiwan Strait Crisis," *Comparative Connections* 24, no. 2 (September 2022): 29–42.

17. Christopher Twomey, "The Fourth Taiwan Strait Crisis Is Just Starting," War on the Rocks, August 22, 2022.

18. Glaser, "US-China Relations Sink."

19. "President Tsai Meets US delegation Led by House of Representatives Speaker Nancy Pelosi," Office of the President Republic of China (Taiwan), August 3, 2022, https://english.president.gov.tw.

20. Glaser, "US-China Relations Sink."

21. Bonny Lin, ed., *The Military Dimensions of the Fourth Taiwan Strait Crisis,* Center for Strategic and International Studies (CSIS), August 23, 2022, https://www.csis.org.

22. Bonny Lin, Brian Hart, Matthew P. Funaiole, Samantha Lu, Hannah Price, and Nicholas Kaufman, "Tracking the Fourth Taiwan Strait Crisis," CSIS, August 5, 2022, https://www.csis.org.

23. Ibid.

24. Brad Lendon, "Military Drills Drum Home China's Relentless Message in the Taiwan Strait," CNN, August 5, 2022.

25. Michaela Del Caller, "US Vows to De-escalate Tensions in Taiwan Strait to Keep the Philippines, Region Safe," GMA News Online, August 6, 2022.

26. Bonny Lin et al., "Tracking the Fourth Taiwan Strait Crisis."

The Taiwan Straight Crisis of 2022–2023   319

27. Brad Lendon, "Why China's Response to US Warships in Taiwan Strait Surprised Analysts," CNN, August 29, 2022.

28. Lin et al., "Tracking the Fourth Taiwan Strait Crisis."

29. Lendon, "Why China's Response."

30. Lendon, "Military Drills Drum Home China's Relentless Message in the Taiwan Strait."

31. Lin et al., "Tracking the Fourth Taiwan Strait Crisis."

32. Robert Sutter, "Taiwan Strait Crisis Strengthens US Resolve to Support Taiwan, Counter China," *The Diplomat,* September 10, 2022.

33. Wang Qi, Yang Sheng, and Bai Yunyi, "China Releases White Paper on Taiwan Question and Reunification, Outlines the Irreversible Historical Process, Stronger Capability and Rock-Solid Resolution in the New Era," *Global Times,* August 10, 2022.

34. "China Releases White Paper on Taiwan Question, Reunification in the New Era," State Council of the People's Republic of China, Xinhua, August 10, 2022.

35. Qi, Sheng, and Yunyi, "China Releases White Paper on Taiwan Question and Reunification."

36. Lin et al., "Tracking the Fourth Taiwan Strait Crisis."

37. Ibid.

38. Qi, Sheng, and Yunyi, "China Releases White Paper on Taiwan Question and Reunification."

39. Ryan Hass, "What Is Taiwan's Plan to Protect Itself Against Chinese Pressure?" Brookings Institution, August 19, 2022.

40. Twomey, "The Fourth Taiwan Strait Crisis Is Just Starting."

41. Lin, *The Military Dimensions of the Fourth Taiwan Strait Crisis.*

42. Hass, "What Is Taiwan's Plan to Protect Itself Against Chinese Pressure?"

43. Zhuoran Li, "The Future of the China-US Chip War," *The Diplomat,* March 2, 2023.

44. Tatsuhito Tokuchi, "China Determined Not to Be Slowed by U.S. Chip Controls," *Japan Times,* March 23, 2023.

45. Li, "The Future of the China-US Chip War."

46. Ibid.

47. Hu Weijia, "US 'Chip War' Puts Taiwan's Semiconductor Sector in a Tough Position," *Global Times,* March 16, 2023.

48. Tokuchi, "China Determined Not to Be Slowed by U.S. Chip Controls."

49. Bochen Han and Robert Delaney, "US House Speaker Kevin McCarthy Meets Taiwanese President Tsai Ing-wen in California," *South China Morning Post,* April 6, 2023.

50. Bonny Lin, Brian Hart, Samantha Lu, Hannah Price, and Matthew Slade, "Putting Taiwan President Tsai Ing-wen's U.S. Transit in Context," CSIS, April 5, 2023, https://www.csis.org.

51. Han and Delaney, "US House Speaker Kevin McCarthy Meets Taiwanese President Tsai Ing-wen in California."

52. "President Tsai Meets US House Speaker Kevin McCarthy and Bipartisan Group of Congress Members in California," Office of the President Republic of China (Taiwan), April 6, 2023, https://english.president.gov.tw.

53. Helen Davidson, "China Begins Military Drills Around Taiwan After US Speaker Meeting," *The Guardian,* April 7, 2023.

54. "China Begins Three Days of Military Drills in Taiwan Strait," Al Jazeera, April 8, 2023.

320 Hedging the China Threat

55. Britt Clennett and Joyce Huang, "China 'Ready to Fight' After 3 Days of Large-Scale Military Drills Around Taiwan," *ABC News,* April 11, 2023.

56. Jim Sciutto, "Military Exercises Suggest China Is Getting 'Ready to Launch a War Against Taiwan,' Island's Foreign Minister Tells CNN," CNN, April 11, 2023.

57. "Biden's China Team," USC US-China Institute, January 14, 2021, https://china.usc.edu.

58. China Briefing Team, "US-China Relations in the Biden Era: A Timeline," March 6, 2023, China Briefing.

59. "U.S.-Japan Joint Leaders' Statement: U.S.-Japan Global Partnership for a New Era," White House, April 16, 2021, https://www.whitehouse.gov.

60. Cooper, "The Biden Administration's China and Taiwan Policies," pp. 109−112.

61. Tyrone Siu, "U.S. Position on Taiwan Remains Unchanged Despite Biden Comment," Reuters, August 20, 2021.

62. Stephen McDonell, "Biden Says US Will Defend Taiwan if China Attacks," BBC, October 22, 2021.

63. "Remarks by President Biden and Prime Minister Kishida Fumio of Japan in Joint Press Conference," White House, May 23, 2022, https://www.whitehouse.gov.

64. China Briefing Team, "US-China Relations."

65. Trevor Hunnicutt and Sakura Murakami, "Biden Says He Would Be Willing to Use Force to Defend Taiwan against China," Reuters, May 23, 2022.

66. David Brunnstrom and Trevor Hunnicutt, "Biden Says U.S. Forces Would Defend Taiwan in the Event of a Chinese Invasion," Reuters, September 18, 2022.

67. China Briefing Team, "US-China Relations."

68. "Readout of President Joseph R. Biden Jr. Call with President Xi Jinping of the People's Republic of China," White House, March 18, 2022, https://www.whitehouse.gov.

69. China Briefing Team, "US-China Relations."

70. Ibid.

71. Ibid.

72. David Sanger, "Biden's National Security Strategy Focuses on China, Russia and Democracy at Home," *New York Times,* October 12, 2022.

73. "National Security Strategy," (Washington DC: White House, October 12, 2022), pp. 1–2, 23–24, www.whitehouse.gov/wp-content/uploads/2022/10/Biden-Harris-Administrations-National-Security-Strategy-10.2022.pdf.

74. David Sanger, "Biden's National Security Strategy Focuses on China, Russia and Democracy at Home," *New York Times,* October 12, 2022.

75. Eleanor Watson, "What We Know so Far About the Chinese Spy Balloon and the Other Objects the U.S. Shot Down," *CBS News,* February 20, 2023.

76. Phil Stewart, "U.S. Completes Chinese Balloon Recovery, Object Searches Called Off," Reuters, February 17, 2023.

77. Tessa Wong and Fan Wang, "How Has China Reacted to the Balloon Saga?" BBC, February 16, 2023.

78. Peter Alexander and Rebecca Shabad, "Biden Says Chinese President Xi Doesn't Want to Damage Relations with U.S. After Spy Balloon, in an Exclusive Interview," *NBC News,* February 16, 2023.

79. Courtney Kube and Carol Lee, "Chinese Spy Balloon Gathered Intelligence from Sensitive U.S. Military Sites, Despite U.S. Efforts to Block It," *NBC News,* April 3, 2023.

80. "Biden Says He Will Speak to China's Xi About Balloon Incident," *Arab News,* February 17, 2023.

The Taiwan Straight Crisis of 2022–2023   321

81. Alexander and Shabad, "Biden Says Chinese President Xi Doesn't Want to Damage Relations with U.S. After Spy Balloon."

82. "Biden's China Team."

83. Ibid.

84. Keating, "How Long Can the Biden Administration Stall a Crisis in Taiwan?"

85. Derek Grossman, "Biden Doubles-Down on Trump's Taiwan Policy, but Will It Last?" *Nikkei Asia,* February 6, 2021.

86. David Sacks, "Biden Administration Sends Important Signals for the Future of U.S.-Taiwan Ties," Council on the Foreign Relations, January 28, 2021, https://www.cfr.org.

87. Ibid.

88. Bonnie Glaser, "Biden to Adopt Policy of 'Doing No Harm' to Taiwan: Bonnie Glaser," *Focus Taiwan,* January 22, 2021.

89. US Department of State, "U.S.-China Relations," https://www.state.gov.

90. Glaser, "US-China Relations Sink Further Amid Another Taiwan Strait Crisis," pp. 29–42.

91. Cooper, "The Biden Administration's China and Taiwan Policies," pp. 105–106.

92. Thomas Wright, "The US and China Finally Get Real with Each Other," Brookings Institution, March 22, 2021, https://www.brookings.edu.

93. China Briefing Team, "US-China Relations."

94. Ibid.

95. Giulia Heyward and John Ruwitch, "Blinken Meets with China's Top Diplomat in First Meeting Since Balloon Controversy," NPR, February 18, 2023.

96. China Briefing Team, "US-China Relations."

97. Antony Blinken, "The Administration's Approach to the People's Republic of China," US Department of State, May 26, 2022, https://www.state.gov.

98. Ibid.

99. "Readout of Secretary of Defense Lloyd J. Austin III's Meeting with People's Republic of China (PRC) Minister of National Defense General Wei Fenghe," US Department of Defense, November. 22, 2022, https://www.defense.gov.

100. "Readout of National Security Advisor Jake Sullivan's Phone Call with Politburo Member Yang Jiechi," White House, May 18, 2022, https://www.whitehouse.gov.

101. Sacks, "Biden Administration."

102. China Briefing Team, "US-China Relations."

103. H. J. Mai and Steve Inskeep, "Biden's National Security Adviser Is Hopeful War over Taiwan Can Be Prevented," NPR, January 6, 2023, https://www.npr.org.

104. Andrew S. Bowen, "Russia's War in Ukraine: Military and Intelligence Aspects," Congressional Research Service, February 13, 2023, https://www.documentcloud.org.

105. Brian Michael Jenkins, "Consequences of the War in Ukraine: The End and Beyond," RAND, March 8, 2023, https://www.rand.org.

106. "National Security Strategy," Washington DC: White House, October 12, 2022), pp. 25–26, https://www.whitehouse.gov/wp-content/uploads/2022/10/Biden-Harris-Administrations-National-Security-Strategy-10.2022.pdf.

107. Ibid., p. 26.

108. Bowen, "Russia's War in Ukraine," p. 27.

109. "U.S. Security Cooperation with Ukraine," US Department of State, April 4, 2023, https://www.state.gov.

110. Ibid.

111. China Briefing Team, "US-China Relations."

322 *Hedging the China Threat*

112. "China's Position on the Political Settlement of the Ukraine Crisis," Ministry of Foreign Affairs of the People's Republic of China, February 24, 2023, https://www.fmprc.gov.cn.

113. Jeffrey Hornung, "Ukraine's Lessons for Taiwan," War on the Rocks, March 17, 2022, https://warontherocks.com.

114. Pavel Baev, "Taiwan Is Feeling the Pressure from Russian and Chinese Autocracy," Brookings Institution, March 16, 2023, https://www.brookings.edu.

115. Tzu-yun Su, "8 Lessons for Taiwan from Russia's War in Ukraine," Russia Matters, January 18, 2023, https://www.russiamatters.org.

116. Nathalie Tocci, "Taiwan Has Learned a Lot from the War in Ukraine—It's Time Europe Caught Up," Politico, December 20, 2022, https://www.politico.eu.

117. Hornung, "Ukraine's Lessons for Taiwan."

118. Amanda Hsiao, "Pelosi's Visit Makes Clear the Dangers of an Incoherent US Policy on Taiwan," International Crisis Group, August 2, 2022, https://www.crisisgroup.org.

119. Twomey, "The Fourth Taiwan Strait Crisis Is Just Starting."

16

The Future of
US-China-Taiwan Relations

As a leading democracy and a technological powerhouse, Taiwan is a key partner of the United States in East Asia. Even though they do not have formal diplomatic relations, both countries share similar democratic values and robust economic links. Taiwan has become an important US partner in trade, semiconductors, science, and technology. With the Taiwan Relations Act (TRA), the US government established an unofficial relationship with Taiwan. The United States has a long-standing One China policy, which is guided by the TRA, the three US-China Joint Communiqués, and the Six Assurances. The United States opposes unilateral changes to the status quo from either side and expects cross-strait differences to be resolved peacefully.[1]

China views the improved US-Taiwan relationship as having altered the status quo, by enhancing Taiwan's claims to become a de facto sovereignty and blocking China's goals for unification. Though the United States has made clear that its policy is not to support Taiwan's independence, China accuses the United States of hollowing out its One China policy. Wanting to appear strong before his domestic audience, President Xi Jinping sent a clear message to deter incremental departures from the One China policy when his administration increased military coercion against Taiwan. With slowing economic growth, the leadership of the People's Republic of China (PRC) can ill afford to look weak in the face of what is viewed by nationalists as US bullying.[2]

The Biden administration has named China as the country's largest long-term threat. The Pentagon regards China as the top "pacing challenge." China has been threatening Taiwan and attempting to erode US alliances in East Asia. The Pentagon began to closely monitor the military activity of the People's Liberation Army (PLA), such as the PLA exercises

323

324 *Hedging the China Threat*

in April 2023 around Taiwan, after President Tsai Ing-wen met with House Speaker Kevin McCarthy on April 6 in the United States. The military exercises mirrored those that occurred after previous House Speaker Nancy Pelosi visited Taiwan in August 2022. Biden has stated that the United States would defend Taiwan if China were to attempt an invasion.[3]

In this book, I used three levels of analysis (individual, state, and international) to analyze the US-Taiwan security relations regarding China's threat, from the Harry Truman to the Joe Biden administrations. The United States' hedging against China's threat toward Taiwan was influenced by decisions of the US presidents since Truman, by policymaking of key US political institutions, and by changes in the international system. At the individual level of analysis, I emphasized the interests and worldviews of the presidents. At the state level, I explored the issues of how and why institutions and policies have changed. And at the international level, I highlighted the influence and impact of important global events on triangular relations between China, Taiwan, and the United States.

President Abraham Lincoln once said to his cabinet: "Gentlemen, the vote is 11 to 1 and the 1 has it." Only Lincoln's vote mattered.[4] In the United States, as commander in chief, the president is in charge of all national security and foreign affairs. It is the president who, ultimately, must make decisions concerning the use of force. As the commander of the military, the president is bound by law to protect national interests and to maintain credibility.[5] On the other hand, the president cannot make all decisions. He needs the help of various governmental organizations to make and implement decisions. The State Department, the National Security Council (NSC), the Pentagon, Congress, and the Central Intelligence Agency (CIA) are the major branches of government that are involved in foreign and security policy toward China and Taiwan. Their policies are influenced by organizational standard operating procedures (SOPs) and culture. The changing international environment also has had a significant impact on US policy toward China and Taiwan. The perceptions of a Chinese threat, as well as considerations of US interests throughout Asia, have influenced US cross-strait policy.

The Trajectory of Triangular Relations: Three Levels of Analyses

Since the government of the Republic of China (ROC) retreated to Taiwan in 1949, the US government has played a vital role in hedging China's threat against Taiwan throughout the past seven decades. There are important lessons to be learned from the trajectory of US-China-Taiwan relations at the three levels of analysis.

The Harry Truman to Lyndon Johnson Administrations:
From Hands off Taiwan to Becoming Allies

After mainland China fell into the hands of the Chinese Communists, President Truman had no desire to defend Taiwan. His hands-off policy lasted only until the outbreak of the Korean War. The US military believed that if the PRC took over Taiwan, it would pose a threat to the US interests in East Asia. During the Dwight Eisenhower administration, the United States and the ROC signed a Mutual Defense Treaty. In dealing with the Offshore Islands Crises in the 1950s, US allies urged for US-PRC dialogues to diminish the military conflicts. After becoming president, John F. Kennedy was committed to preventing PRC expansion. His advisors believed that the PRC was a threat that had to be contained. In the years following Kennedy's assassination, President Lyndon Johnson did not make significant changes in US policy because his administration was preoccupied with the Vietnam War.

At the individual level, President Truman was prepared to establish diplomatic relations with China after the ROC government lost the Chinese Civil War. He believed that continuing to support the ROC could hinder future US-PRC relations and would waste US resources by placing them in the hands of Chiang Kai-shek's incompetent government. At the state level, the US military strengthened its security ties with Taiwan after the Chinese military fought against US armed forces in the Korean Peninsula. The Pentagon believed that by cooperating with Taiwan, further communist expansion could be prevented. At the international level, the United States believed that North Korea's attack on South Korea was part of a larger plan by Communist China and the Soviet Union to increase their dominance in East Asia. The Korean War significantly influenced President Truman and his administration to change their Taiwan policy from abandonment to support of Taiwan.

President Eisenhower's goals in resolving the two Offshore Islands Crises in the 1950s were to avoid military conflicts with the PRC and to keep the crises from escalating. Eisenhower was averse to sending the US military to intervene in the 1954–1955 crisis because he thought these islands did not have strategic value. However, he did threaten China with nuclear weapons as a deterrent to defend these islands. Eisenhower became more cautious in dealing with the 1958 Quemoy Crisis because he did not have a strong desire to defend Quemoy. At the state level, as China escalated the 1954–1955 crisis, the Eisenhower administration decided to help with the evacuation of ROC military and civilian personnel from the Dachen islands. During the Quemoy Crisis, military vessels from the United States convoyed ROC supply ships to Quemoy while strictly adhering to a three-mile limit. The policies of the Eisenhower security team were not only to keep Quemoy from falling, but also to avoid a direct conflict with China. At the international level, relations between the United States and its allies were strained due to allies' fears that the crises would escalate into a world war. Most US allies urged the Eisenhower administration to engage in negotiations with China. Eisenhower's views on preventing the escalation of a crisis had a significant impact on the State Department, the NSC, and military leaders.

The Kennedy administration maintained the status quo of cross-strait policy. At the individual level, President Kennedy was constrained by his narrow presidential victory, which prevented him from pursuing a more flexible China policy. He believed that any change in China's policy would be met with fierce domestic opposition. Kennedy remained convinced that Mao Tse-tung's regime was a disrupter of international order. At the state level, despite increasing demands in the State Department for a more flexible US foreign policy toward the PRC, most of Kennedy's senior advisors believed that the Chinese Communists posed a grave threat to the United States and its allies and that China's ambitions had to be contained. During the 1962 Taiwan Strait Crisis, the CIA and the Pentagon engaged in considerable infighting and competition. The military criticized the CIA's poor performance in intelligence gathering. At the international level, Nikita Khrushchev sought peaceful coexistence with the United States. Mao was critical of Khrushchev's "revisionism." During the 1962 Sino-Indian border conflict, Kennedy responded to Jawaharlal Nehru's request for military assistance to India. The conflict influenced Kennedy's assessment of China's expansionist intentions. Kennedy's fear of domestic political repercussions continued to prevent him from incorporating new elements into his US-China policy.

During the Johnson administration, Johnson's cross-strait policy was similar to that of the Kennedy and Eisenhower administrations. The Johnson administration supported the ROC's possession of China's seat in the United Nations. At the individual level of analysis, while President Johnson thought that the United States could no longer avoid recognizing the PRC indefinitely, Beijing's lack of reciprocity hampered bilateral relations. Johnson saw little chance of success unless the PRC's attitude toward the United States shifted. At the state level of analysis, the Johnson administration proposed travel exchanges with China, but China rejected the US proposals. In 1962, when President Chiang Kai-shek pressed for US support of ROC operations on the mainland, the State Department thought that the concept was impractical, and therefore rejected it. At the international level of analysis, the division between Beijing and Moscow widened after the Cuban Missile Crisis in 1962. At the height of the Cultural Revolution, Chiang Kai-shek requested US assistance in retaking China. He sent Johnson a message urging him to use the Beijing-Moscow split and social unrest on the mainland to remove the Mao regime, eliminate the PRC nuclear threat, and end the Vietnam War. Taipei felt that the ROC would require only US approval and logistical support. Concerned that such a plan could easily escalate into greater US involvement, Johnson was against this action.

The Future of US-China-Taiwan Relations   327

From the Truman through the Johnson administrations, the overall goals of US policymaking in hedging China's threat against Taiwan were aimed at avoiding military conflicts with the PRC, preventing a crisis from further escalating, and maintaining the US status as a world leader.

The Richard Nixon to Jimmy Carter Administrations: From Rapprochement to Normalization

As the split between Moscow and Beijing intensified, the Richard Nixon administration sought rapprochement with China to confront the rising threat of the USSR. The Gerald Ford administration started to move slowly toward normalization. President Jimmy Carter then committed to establishing diplomatic relations with China by accepting China's three preconditions: the One China principle, abrogation of the US-ROC defense treaty, and the withdrawal of US forces.

During the Nixon administration, Nixon's historic trip to China marked a significant shift in US cross-strait policy. At the individual level, Nixon acknowledged that with the PRC being a rising power, the United States should not try to keep it isolated from the global community. Since his presidency began in 1969, Nixon had been interested in changing relations with China to capitalize on the antagonistic USSR-PRC relationship. Nixon directed Henry Kissinger to make efforts to engage China. At the state level, the NSC's growing influence over Chinese policy strained relations with the State Department and the Pentagon. As the United States improved its relations with China, US-Taiwan tensions began to surface. Following a raid by ROC forces on China, the State Department requested assurances from Taipei that prior notice would be given for any future military action on the mainland. However, the ROC complained to the United States that its request for F-4s remained unfilled. At the international level, a Sino-Soviet border military conflict in March 1969 provided the impetus for a thaw between the United States and the PRC. Chinese concerns over the Soviet threat had motivated China to improve relations with the United States.

The Ford administration moved toward normalization with China. At the individual level of analysis, Ford assumed the presidency during the gravest constitutional crisis in US history. The new president faced public discontent with the Watergate scandal and the defeat of the Vietnam War. While Ford was in office, the key player forming the US policy toward China was Kissinger. Ford continued to improve US-China relations on Kissinger's advice, hoping for a peaceful resolution to cross-strait relations. At the state level, after Kissinger was appointed secretary of state, the State Department increased its influence in shaping China's policy. The NSC's influence on China's policy began to wane, but National Security Advisor (NSA) Brent Scowcroft and Secretary Kissinger began to develop friendly

328 Hedging the China Threat

working relationships at the NSC and the State Department. As US-China relations improved, the Ford administration reduced arms sales to Taiwan and withdrew US forces from Taiwan. At the international level of analysis, Ford continued Nixon's détente policy with the Soviet Union. China feared that these developments would lead to its isolation and to a strengthening of the Soviet Union. Leaders in Washington and Beijing acknowledged that their improved relations served as an effective counterbalance to Moscow. They also viewed Taiwan as a secondary issue in the US-PRC relationship, subordinate to the strategic US-Soviet-China triangle.

The Carter administration established diplomatic relations with the PRC. At the individual level, Carter's top priority on assuming office was to complete the transition of US diplomatic recognition from Taiwan to China. Carter decided to comply with China's demands regarding Taiwan, including the repeal of the defense treaty, the withdrawal of all troops, and the acceptance of the One China principle. At the state level of analysis, the NSC supported accepting China's conditions for normalizing relations with Taiwan. The State Department, on the other hand, remained neutral. The military was cautious, urging normalization while not jeopardizing Taiwan's security. Many members of Congress were outraged by Carter's decision to end official relations with Taiwan. As a result, Congress passed the Taiwan Relations Act. At the international level, Beijing continued to regard Moscow as the most serious external threat. The deterioration of relations between Moscow and Beijing strengthened US-China ties.

From the Nixon to the Carter administrations, there were several normalization patterns with China. The NSC and the State Department were more favorable toward normalization, but the military was more cautious in approaching China. However, the three apparatuses believed that cross-strait relations could be resolved peacefully.

The Ronald Reagan to George W. Bush Administrations: From a Competitor to a Partner

The Ronald Reagan administration believed that while China could be useful in leveraging US efforts to reduce Soviet power, the United States did not need to make concessions to China. China cracked down on pro-democracy student protests during the George H. W. Bush administration. The US Congress demanded a harsh response to the PLA's massacre of peaceful protestors in the Tiananmen Square incident. During the Bill Clinton administration, the 1995–1996 Taiwan Strait Crisis demonstrated that a cross-strait confrontation could lead to US-China military conflict. Soon after taking office, George W. Bush set out to counter China's rise. However, building a global coalition to combat terrorism in the aftermath of the September 11 terrorist attacks facilitated closer ties with China.

The Future of US-China-Taiwan Relations   329

Reagan's China policy shifted from the right to the center during his presidency. At the individual level of analysis, Reagan was regarded as one of the most ardent supporters of Taiwan in US politics during the 1970s, but because of the further split between Moscow and Beijing he was forced to develop a closer relationship with China. At the state level, Reagan's first secretary of state, Alexander Haig, pushed for a close relationship with China. However, Haig's successor, George Shultz, believed that the United States did not need to make fundamental concessions to China to work with it. At the international level, the Reagan administration promoted several initiatives that heightened tensions with Moscow. The United States increased defense spending to modernize its forces and achieve technological advances. The CIA armed and trained the Afghan resistance following the Soviet invasion of Afghanistan in 1979. China also participated in these covert operations against Russia. President Reagan was a vocal opponent of communism and a staunch supporter of Taiwan, but his China policy had shifted from confrontation to engagement to counter the Soviet Union. Balance-of-power considerations had a significant impact on Reagan's decisionmaking.

The Tiananmen Square incident in 1989 harmed US-China relations during the George H. W. Bush administration. At the individual level of analysis, President Bush had a good relationship with Chinese leaders and saw China as having geostrategic value to the United States. He did not want the crisis to sever bilateral ties. To appease critics of his poor economic performance and to show disapproval for China's crackdown on peaceful protesters, Bush chose to sell 150 fighter jets to Taiwan to boost the US economy. At the state level, the US Congress was outraged by Beijing's violence and demanded harsh penalties for the PLA's massacre of protesters. Following the crisis, the Pentagon halted military relations with China. At the international level, the fall of communist regimes and the US military victory in the Gulf War stunned the PLA. The United States possessed vast technological superiority over Iraq's Chinese-made weapons. It raised serious concerns among China's senior military leaders about their military technology.

The PRC launched military exercises against Taiwan during the Clinton administration, ushering in the 1995–1996 Taiwan Strait Crisis. At the individual level of analysis, Clinton had a favorable impression of Taiwan. Before taking office, he visited Taiwan and praised its economic development. Clinton's interactions with China's top leaders, on the other hand, had been tense. During Clinton's first meeting with President Jiang Zemin, Jiang lectured him on the hegemonic nature of US meddling in Chinese domestic affairs. At the state level, following the November 1995 PLA exercises against Taiwan, the CIA established a special task force to monitor PLA activities in the Taiwan Strait. The military, the State Department, and the NSC decided to send two carriers near Taiwan's waters in March 1996. Clinton supported the decision to deter further military aggression by China. At

330   *Hedging the China Threat*

the international level, following the crisis, regional countries, particularly Japan and Australia, reacted negatively to the PRC's military coercion against the Taiwan presidential election. The crisis began to ease after a series of US-China talks and a US show of force to deter China's military escalation.

The George W. Bush administration gradually improved its relations with China because the US government needed China's assistance in fighting terrorists after 9/11. At the individual level of analysis, before assuming office, Bush condemned Beijing as an opponent of religious freedom. He referred to Chinese leaders as "the butchers of Beijing," claiming that China was a competitor, not a partner. He emphasized Taiwan's significance to US national interests. Following the EP-3 incident, the US Congress condemned China's detention of US military personnel. Many Americans perceived China to be a threat. In response to negative public and congressional perceptions of China, the George W. Bush administration took a tougher stance toward China. At the international level, the US formation of a global coalition to combat terrorism after 9/11 facilitated closer ties with China. As a result, Bush's policy shifted to prioritizing relations with China over those with Taiwan. The United States desired more stable relations across the Taiwan Strait. The Bush administration welcomed Chinese assistance in the antiterrorism campaign as US-China relations improved.

The patterns of each administration began to show toughness toward China from the Reagan to the George W. Bush administrations. However, as China's global influence grew and other international challenges took precedence, the United States began to shift from a strategic competitor to a strategic partner with China. If a strategic alliance with China against the Soviet Union were possible, the United States might have considered its relationship with Taiwan. But as the strategic values of relations with China deteriorated, so did the US incentives to make concessions regarding Taiwan. The international balance of power had a significant impact on US-Taiwan relations. From the Reagan to George W. Bush administrations, the United States pursued a balanced dual-track policy of friendly official relations with China and friendly unofficial relations with Taiwan.

The Barack Obama to Joe Biden Administrations: Rising Tension Between Two Superpowers

With China becoming more assertive in the South China Sea and with Taiwan, its growing power has aroused grave concern to the United States and Taiwan. The Barack Obama administration advocated a "rebalanced" policy to Asia. The United States responded to China's rise by increasing US military presence and strengthening US alliances in the region. The Donald Trump administration expressed a pessimistic view of China. Trump believed that stopping China's unfair economic growth was the best way to

The Future of US-China-Taiwan Relations   331

deal with China. The Taiwan Strait Crises of 2022–2023 under the Biden administration became very dangerous. Asked by the media if the United States would come to Taiwan's defense in the event of an attack by China, Biden responded in the affirmative.

At the individual level, President Obama believed that the Asia Pacific region had emerged as the world's center of gravity and that it deserved priority in US foreign policy. He attempted to build a positive relationship with China. At the state level, the Obama administration proposed that the United States maintain a military presence in the Asia Pacific region and strengthen its alliances. The Pentagon ensured the continuity of US-China military engagement. The NSC proposed that the United States and China work together to solve global problems while reestablishing the US role in the region and maintaining support for Taiwan. The United States urged China to become a "responsible stakeholder," and to work with the United States in global affairs. At the international level, regional countries expressed concern about China's expanding territorial claims and military activities in the East and South China Seas.

The Trump administration strengthened its security relationship with Taiwan. At the individual level, Trump's worldview embodied the Make America Great Again campaign's promise to prioritize America First. He expressed his dissatisfaction with China's unfair trade practices. Trump questioned whether the United States should maintain the One China policy if the PRC posed a threat to US interests. Trump had hoped to strike a favorable deal with Xi Jinping by maintaining friendly relations with him. Trump's interactions with Beijing and Taipei raised the possibility of Taiwan being used as a bargaining chip. At the state level, given the significance of Taiwan's semiconductor industry, the Trump administration established a close US-Taiwan economic relationship. The US military responded forcefully to China's military provocations against Taiwan as Taiwan's role in the Indo-Pacific strategy grew. At the international level, China's incursions of vessels into Japanese territorial waters, as well as militarization in the South China Sea, posed a security threat to Japan and regional countries.

During the Biden administration, China launched two military exercises in response to Nancy Pelosi's visit to Taiwan in 2022, and Kevin McCarthy's meeting with Tsai in California in 2023. The US government stated that it would honor its TRA commitments to support Taiwan's self-defense and to maintain the United States' ability to resist any force directed at Taiwan. At the individual level, Biden believed that gaining the support of the US allies was the best strategy for dealing with the rise of China's threat. Under Biden's leadership, US-Taiwan security relations have improved. In the event of a Chinese attack, Biden has stated that the United States would assist Taiwan. At the state level, the growing US-China rivalry increased Taiwan's appeal to the Biden administration in its efforts to confront China.

332 *Hedging the China Threat*

By reiterating the United States' unwavering support for Taiwan, the State Department urged China to cease military pressure. At the international level, the United States hopes that Russia's continued military failure in Ukraine will persuade it to withdraw. Ukraine has endured a bloody survival struggle, and lessons from the war in Ukraine could help Taiwan defend itself in the future. As China became more assertive toward Taiwan, the Trump and Biden administrations became more supportive of Taiwan's defense to prevent a military invasion by China.

In Beijing's view, Biden's repeated statements about sending US military forces to defend Taiwan, as well as his administration's constant engagement with its Taiwan counterpart, demonstrate that the US government has significantly changed its One China policy. During the 2022–2023 Taiwan Strait Crises, Beijing's primary goal was to deter the slow erosion of the US One China policy. Domestic factors in the United States, China, and Taiwan have all played a significant role in this crisis. Maintaining a confrontational posture toward China has bipartisan support in the United States. China's social media has been critical of Beijing's lackluster response. With the rise of Taiwanese identity among Taiwan's youth, cross-strait relations will further deteriorate.[6]

The Future Trend: The Dangerous Strait

Since the ROC government's retreat to Taiwan in 1949, the US government has played a critical role in mitigating China's threat in the Taiwan Strait. The prevention of any Chinese military invasion is a critical component of the US security commitments to Taiwan.

During the Cold War, the Truman administration sent the Seventh Fleet into the Taiwan Strait to prevent the PRC from attacking Taiwan when the Korean War broke out in 1950. The PRC attempted to achieve unification through military means. The United States responded with diplomatic or military means to de-escalate tensions because the United States and Taiwan were allies under the Mutual Defense Treaty. As the United States sought a better relationship with China to counter the rising threat of the Soviet Union, Nixon sought rapprochement with China. Taiwan's importance to the United States declined throughout the 1970s. The Carter administration established diplomatic relations with the PRC, ended formal diplomatic recognition of the ROC, and terminated the Mutual Defense Treaty in 1979. However, the Taiwan Relations Act was passed by the US Congress and has become the US foreign policy guide for its unofficial relations with Taipei. From the end of diplomatic relations between Washington and Taipei in 1979 until the end of the Cold War in 1991, the United States maintained resilient but unofficial ties with Taiwan.

At the end of the Cold War, China's rise as an economic and military power was viewed as a threat to the United States. As a result of China's growing security threat, the United States became more willing to provide military assistance to Taiwan. Prior to the 1990s, the ROC government committed Taiwan to eventual unification with China. Leaders in Taipei promoted Taiwan's identity from the 1990s to the 2000s to gain international recognition. Their commitment to the One China policy gave way to a separate political identity for Taiwan. As a result, the Chinese government has become more aggressive toward Taiwan.

The US policy in cross-strait relations is based on China's nonuse of force and Taiwan's refusal to declare independence. The United States opposes any changes in the Taiwan Strait status quo made by either side. Relations between Washington and Beijing have deteriorated since 2020. To counter China's coercion, the US government has become more assertive.

This analysis explores the future of triangular relations after examining the Cold War and post-Cold War US policies regarding triangular relations. It is unclear whether the United States would defend Taiwan if China attacked. Since the Carter administration terminated the Taiwan defense treaty in 1980, US cross-strait relations have been governed by a policy of strategic ambiguity. The disadvantage of strategic ambiguity is that Washington cannot send Chinese leaders a clear message of deterrence. As a result, after becoming president, Biden stated several times that he would defend Taiwan. Taiwan is important to the United States because the two countries share common interests and values. The following subsections forecast the future trajectory of US-China-Taiwan relations in light of historical lessons.

Risky Tensions

According to Beijing, Taiwan is an inalienable part of Chinese territory. Xi Jinping has tried to persuade the Chinese people that unification with Taiwan is a "sacred mission" to realize the China Dream. If Xi Jinping abandons his stated commitment to achieving unification, he will likely lose his claim to ultimate power. He cannot take this risk. Taiwan is strategically important due to its location at the center of the First Island Chain. If the PLA gains control of Taiwan, it will be able to project military power all the way to the Pacific Ocean. This would severely limit the United States' ability to freely navigate the region and would jeopardize its security.

With the rise in the intensity of the China menace, Taiwan has developed a closer relationship with the United States, particularly after President Tsai Ing-wen took office. For example, the US Congress passed several legislative acts (Taiwan Travel Act in 2018, Taipei Act in 2020, Taiwan Policy Act of 2022, etc.), which committed the US government to help Taiwan improve its international standing. Biden has dispatched cabinet members and ranking

334 Hedging the China Threat

officials to Taiwan, so as to strengthen bilateral relations. The visits angered the Chinese leaders and public, who viewed the US government as violating China's domestic affairs. US arms sales to Taiwan have also increased. Beijing has warned the Biden administration not to back Taiwan's "separatist forces."

Since World War II, the United States has been the leading power in Asia Pacific. Today, the United States has military forces stationed in Japan, South Korea, Australia, and the Philippines. The US military presence is an essential component in maintaining peace and stability in Asia Pacific. If the United States failed to defend Taiwan, regional security would be impacted.[7] Many military analysts warn that an invasion by China appears imminent. Therefore, the military presence of the United States in the Taiwan Strait has become apparent. Small teams of US troops, including the US Marines and Army Special Forces, have trained with the ROC military in Taiwan. If there is to be a war between the United States and China, Taiwan will almost certainly be the spark.

Achieving reunification with Taiwan would be Xi Jinping's crowning achievement. Beijing has vowed that Taiwan's declaration of independence would immediately trigger war. After winning the presidency of the Republic of China in 2016, Tsai Ing-wen rejected the 1992 Consensus embraced by her predecessor, former president Ma Ying-jeou. If Xi Jinping believes that Taiwan's peaceful unification cannot be achieved, he will likely resort to force. To this end, the PLA is intensifying its preparations for an invasion of Taiwan.

Taiwan is a global leader in high technology, as it dominates the outsourcing of semiconductor manufacturing. The Taiwan Semiconductor Manufacturing Company (TSMC) makes 90 percent of the most advanced processors in iPhones, supercomputers, and artificial intelligence applications. TSMC also makes chips for US fighter jets, Mars probes, and the highest-end processes. If Taiwan becomes a province of China, Beijing will gain control over Taiwan's high-tech industry and disrupt the US supply chain for advanced chips.

The loss of Taiwan to the Beijing regime would also shatter global democracy and would only embolden Xi's hard-line policies. On taking office, Xi consolidated his power and began to tighten social control in China. First, his regime began abusing the human rights of its ethnic minorities, particularly the Uighurs in Xinjiang. More than 1 million Uighurs are imprisoned in so-called re-education camps. Second, Beijing's involvement in Hong Kong's political affairs has been controversial. Beijing's control in Hong Kong triggered a historic record of student protests and police crackdowns. Third, Beijing routinely bans anything reflecting Western democratic values, including reality TV shows, boy bands, and foreign computer games. Finally, studying "Xi Jinping Thought" has been made compulsory in China's primary schools. The educational control of the PRC has become aggressive. If a democratic Taiwan is taken over by China, the democratic values in the world that the United States helped establish will be seriously diminished.[8]

The Future of US-China-Taiwan Relations 335

With annual increases in military spending in double digits, the PLA has acquired both quality and quantity of innovative weapons. China has deployed thousands of ballistic missiles against Taiwan along its coast. The US military is extremely concerned about China's cyber, space, and information technology; joint operations; precision strike capability; and nuclear arsenal expansion. Additionally, the PLA has expanded its military training and exercises.

The PLA's buildup also seeks to deter the United States from intervening in a cross-strait conflict. Chinese leaders believe that their biggest obstacle to unification is US intervention. In the face of intervention from US forces, the PLA is focused on an anti-access/area denial (A2/AD) strategy. It seeks to prevent US forces from using overseas bases while denying US assets the freedom to maneuver within striking distance of Chinese territory. China is developing some of the world's most advanced weapons systems, including space-based weapons, laser weaponry, drones, and hypersonic missiles. China's increased military buildup has pushed the United States to increase its military activity in the Taiwan Strait. In response, US warships have sailed monthly through the Taiwan Strait.

US-China friction is increasing, and a new cold war is looming large. With their heavy-handed assertiveness in the South China Sea, Taiwan, Xinjiang, and Hong Kong, Chinese leaders have tarnished China's image. With Covid-19 resulting in a worldwide pandemic, anti-Chinese sentiment is rising. An alliance was announced between the United States, Australia, and the United Kingdom to counter China's assertiveness in the Pacific. Far from backing down, Chinese foreign and security policies have become more hostile. Xi Jinping has also claimed that "anyone who dares to bully us will have their heads bashed bloody against a Great Wall of Steel."

The PLA has actively conducted activities in the East China Sea, the South China Sea, and especially the Taiwan Strait. The United States has increased its presence above these waters.[9] The United States expressed concern about the lack of communication regarding the PLA's aggressive actions. In a November 2022 meeting with Xi, Biden underscored the importance of avoiding conflict and maintaining open lines of communication. Later that month, Secretary Austin met his Chinese counterpart, Wei Fenghe, in Cambodia. Since then, attempts to contact high-level officials from the PLA, after the United States shot down the Chinese spy balloon, have been rebuffed. China claimed that the United States was seeking to change the status quo in Taiwan through arms sales and congressional engagements with Taiwan's leaders.[10]

The PLA has been more forceful in its activities around Taiwan since Nancy Pelosi visited in August 2022 and President Tsai met with Kevin McCarthy in the United States in April 2023. These increased Chinese military activities around Taiwan have become the new normal.[11] On April 18, 2023, Admiral John Aquilino, commander of the Indo-Pacific Command, told Congress that the Chinese threat to Taiwan had increased, but declined

336 *Hedging the China Threat*

to endorse other top military brass who have suggested timelines for a possible conflict. When asked about warnings, Aquilino and his predecessor, Admiral Philip Davidson, told a House Armed Services Committee hearing that China could move before 2027. Admiral Mike Gilday, chief of naval operations, said the United States must prepare for possible action before 2024. Aquilino stressed that the US Defense Department and defense industry needed to move more quickly to reduce the odds of a conflict.[12]

US Commitment

The US resolve against China is also increasing. When asked by reporters if the United States would come to Taiwan's defense in the event of an attack by China, President Biden has repeatedly replied that he would defend Taiwan.[13] However, the United States has become aware of the possibility of experiencing potential armed conflict with China should it fail to handle the Taiwan issue. Managing stable bilateral relations, without escalating conflict with Beijing, has become the top mission. The security commitment from Washington has become a double-edged sword. If the commitment is strong enough for the Taiwanese people, it may embolden the supporters of independence, pushing Taiwan to cross the redline. However, if the commitment is too weak, Beijing may not be deterred from military aggression against Taiwan.[14]

On April 19, 2023, a US congressional war game led by Republican representative Mike Gallagher that simulated a Chinese invasion of Taiwan showed the need to arm Taiwan "to the teeth." The results showed that the United States' resupplying of Taiwan would be impossible after a conflict begins. The United States must boost the production of long-range missiles. Anxiety about a possible conflict over Taiwan has become a rare bipartisan issue in Washington.[15] On April 20, Admiral Aquilino told the Senate Armed Services Committee that support for Ukraine had not depleted munitions needed for the potential defense of Taiwan nor degraded any capabilities.[16] He supported using presidential drawdown authority, which rapidly transfers weapons directly from US stocks and foreign military financing for weapons, to surge capabilities to defend Taiwan. The United States is working to clear an $18 billion foreign military sales backlog with Taiwan.[17] Some scholars have also suggested that the United States and Taiwan should increase cooperation on cybersecurity, information warfare, and countering Chinese propaganda. They should also conduct regular intelligence consultations on Chinese strategic intentions and joint analysis of PLA exercises to identify potential attack indicators.[18]

Faced with imminent Chinese threats, Taipei has anticipated increased security assistance from Washington. It is important that Taiwan also seek risk-averse policy options. Hedging, a strategic approach, does not mean choosing between Washington and Beijing, but adopting risk management.

As US-China relations are characterized by deeper hostility, it has become more urgent for Taiwan not to fan the flames, thereby minimizing the risk of an intensifying cross-strait security dilemma.[19]

Curbing the Conflicts

According to some military observers, if the United States intervenes in a cross-strait military conflict, this might result in a war between the United States and China. Since a war across the Taiwan Strait would be extremely costly, all parties should de-escalate and prevent armed conflict from happening. When written in Chinese, the word "crisis" comprises two characters: one represents danger, and the other represents opportunity. Now is the time for strategic planners to devise creative ideas to diminish the crisis.[20]

Political scientist Stefan Wolff's TEDTalks on Nov 9, 2010, on curbing the tension of military conflicts extracts lessons from Northern Ireland, Liberia, and Timor to show that leadership, diplomacy, and institutional design are effective tools in forging peace. Leadership needs to be determined and visionary in its commitment to peace. Diplomacy must apply the right incentives and pressures to help the sides reach an equitable compromise. Institutional design requires innovative thinking and flexible implementation.[21]

If these three tools have worked in war-torn countries, the ROC government might consider learning these lessons and taking the initiative.

Taiwan-China relations. Taiwanese and Chinese political leaders should share a commitment to preventing war across the Taiwan Strait. Taiwan's government has several options available to it.

1. The Taiwanese leaders must strive for peace across the Taiwan Strait. They should do everything possible to avoid war. Taiwan's response to China's provocation must be vigilant—otherwise, China will use Taiwan's response as an excuse to launch military attacks. Even though the current cross-strait relations face obstacles, both governments should seek any means possible to overcome them.

2. Governments, academics, and even militaries of China and Taiwan should engage in dialogue and contact. Engagement is an effective way to resolve disputes because only the Taiwanese and Chinese can reach an understanding. Future presidents of Taiwan could publicly express their strong desire to build peace across the Taiwan Strait. Based on the principle of "seeking common ground while reserving differences," they could propose a summit with the Chinese president to pursue a solution for peace between the two countries.

3. The governments of the ROC and the PRC have set up the Mainland Affairs Council and the Taiwan Affairs Office of the State Council, respectively, for handling cross-strait issues. These two organizations should develop creative ideas and flexible policies for implementation. Taiwan could

338   Hedging the China Threat

suggest a "no independence" proposal and seek cross-strait confidence-building measures in exchange for a PRC promise to forsake the use of force.

US-Taiwan relations. Taiwan's relationship with the United States remains critical to Taiwan's security because in the past seven decades, the US government played the role of Taiwan's security guarantor. The US government has several options available to ensure Taiwan's security.

1. *Encourage dialogues across the strait.* The Taiwanese government could request that the US government or a third party (Japan, South Korea, Australia, or the European Union) establish a diplomatic mechanism to facilitate dialogue and conflict resolution between Taiwan and China. Other nations in the region could also facilitate a constructive platform to help Taiwan and China find ways to coexist peacefully.

2. *Bolster US-Taiwan security relations.* In keeping with the spirit of the TRA, the United States and Taiwan could strengthen their bilateral security relations. Taiwan should upgrade its military capability with US assistance, including the purchase of advanced drones, the expansion of military training, the modernization of weapon systems, and the enhancement of its military fighting capacity to deter China. However, while building up close relations, Taiwan should keep a low profile and demeanor to avoid retaliation from China.

3. *Support Taiwan's posture of deterrence.* Since the Pentagon's software and hardware are seeking integration with allies and partners, Taiwan's security and military apparatuses should engage actively with their US counterparts. Taiwan could also request the United States to support Taiwan's deterrence posture. This assistance could include bolstering Taiwan's reserve forces and developing an innovative defense strategy to assist Taiwan in minimizing its vulnerabilities.

Taiwan security approaches. China has posed a grave security threat to Taiwan. Taiwanese leaders must inform the public that the likelihood of a military conflict across the Taiwan Strait has increased. Citizens of Taiwan must prepare for the worst-case scenario. In the face of escalating Chinese military threats, Taiwan should bolster its military capabilities in the following ways.

1. *Reach a consensus on its policy on China.* The polarization of Taiwanese politics, as well as the inability to reach a consensus on key issues, has exacerbated societal mistrust. Taiwan's two major political parties have opposing views on China. They have attacked each other, weakening Taiwan. To protect Taiwan from China's military coercion, the ruling party should reach an agreement on its China policy to serve Taiwan's national interests and mend Taiwan's divisive society.

2. *Show determination to defend its homeland.* Taiwan's government should constantly emphasize that Taiwanese people are responsible for its

The Future of US-China-Taiwan Relations   339

defense. They should prepare to fight until the bitter end. With China's increasing military aggression, Taiwan's military exercises should be designed to simulate all possible scenarios of an enemy invasion of Taiwan. Taiwan should send a clear message to the international community that its military is committed to defending Taiwan and will not take advantage of the United States' security commitment.

3. *Enhance domestic weapons research and production.* Taiwan's limited defense budget makes acquiring desired weapons systems difficult. In contrast, China's growing economic power and increased defense budget have dramatically shifted the military balance across the Taiwan Strait in its favor. Considering China's vehement opposition to Taiwan's acquisition of foreign-made weapons, the Taiwanese government should actively promote the revival of domestic weapons production, especially focusing on submarines, unmanned aerial vehicles, and military aircraft.

4. *Prepare for war.* Taiwan must fight for its own survival in the face of China's imminent military threat. Thus, military training and defense education are important and necessary for Taiwanese citizens. In preparation for future potential military conflicts, Taiwan's military should increase its military training, develop more creative asymmetrical tactics, and strengthen its fighting will.

The US government. The United States could also play a significant role in lowering tensions in the Taiwan Strait. As a result, the US government could do the following.

1. *Enhance Taiwan's capacity for self-defense.* Taiwan should pursue security cooperation with allies and partners of the United States. In the event of a military conflict breaking out in the Taiwan Strait, these nations could be indispensable pillars of Taiwan's support. The United States could facilitate Taiwan's efforts to deepen security relations with US allies to garner more international support. If China attacks Taiwan, the United States should continue to work with allies and partners to increase the diplomatic, military, and economic costs for Beijing.

2. *Increase crisis communications with China.* Even though China has a history of ignoring hotlines during crises involving the United States and China, the US government should continue to pursue flexible crisis communications with China. The United States and China should maintain open channels of communication so that the two countries can discuss their differences in an open manner and reduce the risk of conflict.

3. *Push Taipei and Beijing to engage in dialogues.* The US government has refused to act as a mediator between China and Taiwan. However, it could encourage Taipei and Beijing to improve their communication channels to maintain the status quo and avoid miscalculations that could lead to military conflict.

340 *Hedging the China Threat*

According to Stefan Wolff, the process of dealing with conflict is full of setbacks. It might take a generation to accomplish, but it requires today's leaders to take responsibility and to learn the right lessons. Taiwan and China must be prepared to return to the negotiating table if an agreement stalls. As the saying goes, "There is no bad peace, but there is no good war."

Notes

1. "U.S. Relations with Taiwan: Fact Sheet," Bureau of East Asian and Pacific Affairs, May 28, 2022, https://www.state.gov.
2. Amanda Hsiao, "Avoiding the Next Taiwan Strait Crisis," International Crisis Group, July 29, 2022, https://www.crisisgroup.org.
3. Ellen Mitchell, "How the Pentagon's Point Man in the Indo-Pacific Is Keeping China in Check," *The Hill,* April 18, 2023.
4. Margaret G. Hermann, Thomas Preston, Baghat Korany, and Timothy M. Shaw, "Who Leads Matters: The Effects of Powerful Individuals," *International Studies Review* 3, no. 2 (Summer 2001): 84.
5. Paul E. Peterson, "The President's Dominance in Foreign Policy Making," *Political Science Quarterly* 109, no. 2 (Summer 1994): 215–234.
6. Christopher Twomey, "The Fourth Taiwan Strait Crisis Is Just Starting," War on the Rocks, August 22, 2022.
7. Shao-cheng Sun, "Back to the Table: Negotiations Needed to Reduce Rising Tensions Across the Taiwan Strait," *Strategic Vision* 10, no. 51 (December 2021): 24.
8. Ibid., p. 25.
9. Mitchell, "How the Pentagon's Point Man in the Indo-Pacific Is Keeping China in Check."
10. Chris Gordon, "China Shows 'Concerning Lack of Interest' in Talks, DOD Says," *Air & Space Forces Magazine,* April 18, 2023.
11. Ibid.
12. Demetri Sevastopulo, "US Commander Pushes Back Against Colleagues 'Guessing' Taiwan Invasion Date," *Financial Times,* April 18, 2023.
13. Sun, "Back to the Table," p. 26.
14. Charles Chong-Han Wu, "The Taiwan Policy Act and the Future of U.S.-Taiwan Relations," Stimson Center, December 13, 2022, https://www.stimson.org.
15. Michael Martina, "U.S. War Game on Taiwan Shows Need for 'Decisive Action' to Boost Arms," Reuters, April 20, 2023.
16. Svetlana Shkolnikova, "'We Can Do Both': Indo-Pacific Commanders Rebuke Republicans Who Say Ukraine Aid Harms Readiness for Chinese Threat," *Stars and Stripes,* April 20, 2023.
17. Nick Wilson, "Aquilino Signals Support for Taiwan-Focused Weapons Transfers," *Inside Defense,* April 20, 2023.
18. Kristen Gunness and Phillip C. Saunders, *Averting Escalation and Avoiding War: Lessons from the 1995–1996 Taiwan Strait Crisis* (Washington, DC: National Defense University Press, December 2022).
19. Wu, "The Taiwan Policy Act and the Future of U.S.-Taiwan Relations."
20. Sun, "Back to the Table," p. 27.
21. Stefan, Wolff, "Stefan Wolff: The path to ending ethnic conflicts | TED Talk," TED, Nov 9, 2010.

Acronyms

ADIZ	air defense identification zone
AI	artificial intelligence
AIT	American Institute in Taiwan
APEC	Asia-Pacific Economic Cooperation
ARATS	Association for Relations Across the Taiwan Strait
ARF	ASEAN Regional Forum
ASEAN	Association of Southeast Asian Nations
A2/AD	anti-access/area denial
BRI	Belt and Road Initiative
CBGs	carrier battle groups
CBMs	confidence-building measures
CCP	Chinese Communist Party
CHIPS	Creating Helpful Incentives to Produce Semiconductors
CIA	Central Intelligence Agency
CINCPAC	commander in chief, Pacific
CMC	Central Military Commission
CSSTA	Cross Strait Service Trade Agreement
DIA	Defense Intelligence Agency
DoD	Department of Defense
DPP	Democratic Progressive Party
DPRK	Democratic People's Republic of Korea
EAS	East Asia Summit
ECFA	Economic Cooperation Framework Agreement
EEZ	exclusive economic zone
ETC	East Theater Command
ETIM	East Turkistan Islamic Movement
FBI	Federal Bureau of Investigation

342   *Acronyms*

FDI	foreign direct investment
FECOM	Far East Command
FOIP	Free and Open Indo-Pacific
FoN	freedom of navigation
FTAs	free-trade agreements
GDP	gross domestic product
G-20	Group of 20
ICBM	intercontinental ballistic missile
ICT	information, communications, and telecommunications
IDF	Indigenous Defense Fighter
INER	Institute of Nuclear Energy Research
IPR	intellectual property rights
IPSR	Indo-Pacific Strategy Report
ISR	intelligence, surveillance, and reconnaissance
JCS	Joint Chiefs of Staff
JUSMAG ROC	Joint US Military Advisory Group to the Republic of China
KMT	Kuomintang
LSTs	Landing Ship, Tanks
MAAG	Military Assistance Advisory Group
MAC	Mainland Affairs Council
MAP	Military Aid Program
MFN	Most-Favored Nation
MND	Ministry of National Defense
MOFA	Ministry of Foreign Affairs
MoU	Memorandum of Understanding
MRBM	medium-range ballistic missile
NAC	National Affairs Conference
NDPG	National Defense Program Guidelines
NDS	National Defense Strategy
NIE	National Intelligence Estimate
NPC	National People's Congress
NPT	Nuclear Non-Proliferation Treaty
NSA	national security advisor
NSB	National Security Bureau
NSC	National Security Council
NSDM	National Security Decision Memoranda
NSS	National Security Strategy
NSSM	National Security Study Memoranda
PD	Presidential Directives
PLA	People's Liberation Army
PRC	People's Republic of China
PRM	Presidential Review Memoranda

ROC	Republic of China
ROK	Republic of Korea
SALT	Strategic Arms Limitation Talks
SCC	Special Coordination Committee
SDF	Self-Defense Force
SEF	Straits Exchange Foundation
SOPs	standard operating procedures
SRG	Senior Review Group
START	Strategic Arms Reduction Treaty
TECRO	Taipei Economic and Cultural Representative Office
TPP	Trans-Pacific Partnership
TRA	Taiwan Relations Act
TSMC	Taiwan Semiconductor Manufacturing Company
TSU	Taiwan Solidarity Union
UAF	Ukrainian Armed Forces
USFJ	US Forces Japan
USPACOM	US Pacific Command
WHO	World Health Organization
WSAG	Washington Special Actions Group
WTO	World Trade Organization

Bibliography

"Alexander Haig's Fall from Grace." Association for Diplomatic Studies and Training, June 13, 2016. https://adst.org.

Ali, Idrees, and Huizhong Wu. "U.S. Warship Sails Through Taiwan Strait, Stirs Tensions with China." Reuters, July 24, 2019.

"Artillery Combat of the August 23 Quemoy Bombardment." Republic of China (ROC) Ministry of National Defense. CD, no. 000267140001003 (Top Secret).

"Backgrounder: Chronology of Meetings Between Chinese President Jiang and US Presidents." China.org.cn, February 21, 2002.

Bader, Jeffery. *Obama and China's Rise*. Washington, DC: Brooking Institution Press, 2012.

Bajpaee, Chietigj. "China Fuels Energy Cold War." *Asia Times Online,* March 1, 2005. http://www.atimes.com.

Blackwill, Robert D., and Philip Zelikow. *The United States, China, and Taiwan: A Strategy to Prevent War*. Council Special Report. Washington, DC: Council on Foreign Relations, 2021.

Blanton, Shannon L., and Charles W. Kegley. *World Politics: Trend and Transformation*. Boston: Cengage, 2020.

Bose, Meena, and Paul Fritz, eds. *The George W. Bush Presidency*. Washington, DC: Nova Science, 2016.

Bradsher, Keith. "China Loosens Foreign Auto Rules, in Potential Peace Offering to Trump." *New York Times,* April 17, 2018.

Brzezinski, Zbigniew. *Power and Principles: Memoirs of the National Security Adviser 1977–1981*. New York: Farrar, Straus, Giroux, 1985.

Brookes, Peter. *U.S.-Taiwan Defense Relations in the Bush Administration*. Heritage Foundation, November 14, 2003. https://www.heritage.org.

Broomfield, Emma. "Perceptions of Danger: The China Threat Theory." *Journal of Contemporary China* 12, no. 5 (2003): 265–284.

Burr, William. "The Beijing-Washington Back-Channel and Henry Kissinger's Secret Trip to China: September 1970–July 1971." *National Security Archive Electronic Briefing Book,* no. 66 (February 27, 2002). https://nsarchive2.gwu.edu.

Bush, George H. W., and Jeffrey A. Engel. *The China Diary of George H. W. Bush: The Making of a Global President*. Princeton: Princeton University Press, 2008.

346   Bibliography

Bush, Richard. "8 Key Things to Notice from Xi Jinping's New Year Speech on Taiwan." Brookings Institution, January 7, 2019.

Bush, Richard. *At Cross Purposes: U.S.-Taiwan Relations Since 1942*. London: Taylor and Francis Group, 2004.

Bush, Richard. "Order from Chaos: What the Historic Ma-Xi Meeting Could Mean for Cross-Strait Relations." Brookings Institution, November 9, 2015.

Bush, Richard. "The Trump Administration's Policies Toward Taiwan." Brookings Institution, June 5, 2019.

Bush, Richard. *Uncharted Strait: The Future of China-Taiwan Relations*. Washington, DC: Brookings Institution Press, 2013.

Campbell, Kurt M., Nirav Patel, and Richard Weitz, *The Ripple Effect: China's Responses to the Iraq War*. Washington, DC: Center for a New American Security, October 2008.

Carpenter, Ted Galen. *America's Coming War with China: A Collision Course over Taiwan*. New York: Palgrave Macmillan, 2005.

CFR Workshop. *Chinese Investment in Critical U.S. Technology: Risks to U.S. Security Interests*. Council of Foreign Relations, October 16, 2017. https://www.cfr.org.

"The Chairman of the U.S. Joint Chiefs of Staff." UPI Archives, January 19, 1985. https://www.upi.com.

Chang, Gordon H. "JFK, China, and the Bomb." *Journal of American History* 74, no. 4 (March 1988): 1287–1310.

Chang, Gordon H. "To the Nuclear Brink: Eisenhower, Dulles, and the Quemoy-Matsu Crisis." *International Security* 12, no. 4 (Spring 1988): 96–123.

Chang, Jaw-ling Joanne. "Negotiation of the 17 August 1982 U.S.-PRC Arms Communique: Beijing's Negotiating Tactics." *China Quarterly,* no. 125 (1991): 35–54.

Chang, Jaw-Ling, ed. *R.O.C.-U.S.A. Relations, 1979–1989*. Taipei: Institute of American Culture Studies, Academia Sinica, 1991.

Chang, Jaw-ling Joanne. *United States–China Normalization: An Evaluation of Foreign Policy Decision Making*. Baltimore: University of Maryland, 1986.

Chen, Dean. "The Trump Administration's One-China Policy: Tilting Toward Taiwan in an Era of U.S.-PRC Rivalry?" *Asian Politics and Policy* 11, no. 2 (April 2019): 250–278.

Chen, Dean. *US-China-Taiwan in the Age of Trump and Biden: Towards a Nationalist Strategy*. New York: Routledge, 2022.

"China Begins Three Days of Military Drills in Taiwan Strait." Al Jazeera, April 8, 2023.

"China's Defense Budget." GlobalSecurity.org, May 19, 2019.

"China Holds Biggest Ever Search, Rescue Drill." *China Post,* September 17, 2010.

"Chinese President Jiang Zemin Attends Seattle Summit." China.org.cn, July 12, 2011.

"The Chinese Revolution of 1949." Office of the Historian. https://history.state.gov.

Chiu, Hungdah, ed. *China and the Taiwan Issue*. New York: Taylor and Francis, 1979.

Chou, David. "U.S. Roles in the 1995–1996 Taiwan Strait Crisis." In *Security Relationship Between the U.S. and Taiwan: After the 1996 Mini-Crisis,* edited by David Chou. Taipei: Mei-de, 1997. 1–28.

"Chronology of U.S.-China Relations, 1784–2000." Office of the Historian. https://history.state.gov.

Chu, Shin, and Yong Wang. "The Beginning and End of the Three Taiwan Strait Crises." *Literary Circles of CPC History* 3 (1997), 44–47.

Clinton, David W. *The Two Facts of National Interest*. Baton Rouge: Louisiana State University, 1994.

Clough, Rough N. *Island China*. Cambridge: Harvard University Press, 1978.

Colman, Jonathan. *The Foreign Policy of Lyndon B. Johnson: The United States and the World, 1963–1969*. Edinburgh: Edinburgh University Press, 2010.

Compilation of Documents in China-US Relations, vol. 2. Beijing: World Knowledge Press.

Condit, Kenneth W. *The Joint Chiefs of Staff and National Policy*, vol. 2: *1947–1949*. Washington, DC: Office of the Chairman of the Joint Chiefs of Staff, 1996.

Condit, Kenneth W. *History of the Joint Chiefs of Staff*, vol. 6: *The Joint Chiefs of Staff and National Policy, 1955–1956*. Washington, DC: Office of the Chairman of the Joint Chiefs of Staff, 1998.

Cooper, John. *A Quiet Revolution: Political Development in the Republic of China*. Lanham, MD: University Press of America, 1988.

Cooper, John. "United States Taiwan Policy: How the 2004 (Taiwan) Presidential Election Put It to the Test." In *Sources of Conflict and Cooperation in the Taiwan Strait*, edited by Yongnian Zheng and Raymond Ray-Kuo Wu, 149–167. Hackensack, NJ: World Scientific, 2006.

"Dean Acheson: United States Position on China." August 5, 1949. USC US-China Institute. https://china.usc.edu.

Deng, Ben Lian. "US Taiwan Policy During the George W. Bush Administration (2001−2009)." *Cadernos Argentina Brasil* 7, no. 1 (2018).

Deng, Yunguang, and Ding Xing. "A Milestone in Cross-Straits Relations." *Beijing Review*, July 19, 2010.

Doak, Barnett. *US Arms Sales: The China-Taiwan Tangle*. Washington, DC: Brookings Institution, 1982.

Dobbs, Charles. *Triangles, Symbols, and Constraints: The United States, the Soviet Union, and the People's Republic of China, 1963–1969*. Lanham, MD: University Press of America, 2010.

Dowen, Robert. "Reagan Policy of Strategic Cooperation with China: Implication for Asian-Pacific Stability." *Journal of East Asian Affairs* 2, no. 1 (Spring−Summer 1982): 43–69.

Dowen, Robert. *The Taiwan Pawn in the China Game*. Washington, DC: Georgetown University Press, 1979.

Driver, Nick. "Clinton holds summit meeting with Jiang," UPI Archives, November 20, 1993. https://www.upi.com.

Easton, Ian. "The Korean War Saved Taiwan from the Clutches of Chairman Mao." *The National Interest*, April 10, 2020.

Eisenhower, Dwight D. *The White House Years: Mandate for Change, 1953−1956*. Garden City, NY: Doubleday1963.

Ellis, Samson. "Here's What Could Happen if China Invaded Taiwan." *Japan Times*, October 8, 2020.

Erickson, Andrew. "Full Text of 2019 Defense White Paper: China's National Defense in the New Era." Andrewerickson.com, July 24, 2019.

"Factbox: U.S. Arms Sales to Taiwan in the Past Decade." Reuters, June 6, 2019.

Fairchild, Byron, and Walter Poole. *History of the Joint Chiefs of Staff*, vol. 7: *The Joint Chiefs of Staff and National Policy, 1957–1960*. Washington, DC: Office of the Chairman of the Joint Chiefs of Staff, 2000.

Feldman, Harvey. "A New Kind of Relationship." In *A Unique Relationship: The United States and the Republic of China Under the Taiwan Relations Act*, edited by Ramon H. Myers, 25–48. Stanford: Hoover Institution Press, 1989.

348 *Bibliography*

Feldman, Harvey. "President Reagan's Six Assurances to Taiwan and Their Meaning Today." Heritage Foundation, October 2, 2007. https://www.heritage.org.

Feldman, Harvey. "Taiwan, Arms Sales, and the Reagan Assurances." *American Asian Review* 19, no. 3 (Fall 2001).

Fetzer, James. "Clinging to Containment: China Policy." In *Kennedy's Quest for Victory,* edited by Thomas G. Paterson, 178–197. Oxford: Oxford University Press, 1989.

Fischetti, Andrea, and Antoine Roth. "A Structural Constraint to China-Japan Relations." *Tokyo Review,* April 12, 2019.

Foreign Economic Espionage in Cyberspace. Washington, DC: National Counterintelligence and Security Center, 2018.

Fu, Jen-ken. *Taiwan and the Geopolitics of the Asian-American Dilemma.* New York: Praeger, 1992.

"Full Text: Fighting COVID-19: China in Action." Xinhua, June 7, 2020.

"Full Text of President Ma's Inaugural Address." *China Post,* May 21, 2008.

Gady, Franz-Stefan. "US, Japan Aircraft Carriers Conduct Naval Exercise in South China Sea." *The Diplomat,* June 12, 2019.

Garson, Robert. "Lyndon B. Johnson and the China Enigma." *Journal of Contemporary History* 32, no. 1 (January 1997): 63–80.

Garver, John W. *Face Off: China, the United States, and Taiwan's Democratization.* Seattle: University of Washington Press, 1997.

Gawthorpe, Andrew. "Ford, Kissinger and US Asia-Pacific Policy." *The Diplomat,* August 15, 2014.

Gellman, Barton. "U.S. and China Nearly Came to Blows in 1996." *Washington Post,* June 21, 1998.

"Gerald R. Ford: The 38th President of the United States." White House. https://www.whitehouse.gov.

"Gerald R. Ford Biography." Gerald Ford Foundation. https://geraldrfordfoundation.org.

Gerson, Michael S. *The Sino-Soviet Border Conflict: Deterrence, Escalation, and the Threat of Nuclear War in 1969.* Alexandria, VA: Center for Naval Analyses, November 2010.

Goh, Evelyn. *Constructing the U.S. Rapprochement with China, 1961–1974: From "Red Menace" to "Tacit Ally."* Cambridge: Cambridge University Press, 2004.

Goh, Evelyn. "Nixon, Kissinger, and the 'Soviet Card' in the U.S. Opening to China, 1971–1974." *Diplomatic History* 29, no. 3 (June 2005): 475–501.

Goldstein, Lyle J. "When China Was a 'Rogue State': The Impact of China's Nuclear Weapons Program on US–China Relations During the 1960s." *Journal of Contemporary China* 12, no. 37 (November 2003): 739–764.

Gordon, Leonard H. D. "United States Opposition to Use of Force in the Taiwan Strait, 1954–1962." *Journal of American History* 72, no. 3 (December 1985): 637–660.

Greene, John Robert. "Gerald Ford: Foreign Affairs." University of Virginia Miller Center, September 30, 2023. https://millercenter.org.

Griffiths, James. "When It Comes to International Recognition, Even When Taiwan Wins, It Loses." CNN, September 29, 2020.

Grossman, Derek. "Is the '1992 Consensus' Fading Away in the Taiwan Strait?" RAND, June 3, 2020.

Gunness, Kristen, and Phillip C. Saunders. *Averting Escalation and Avoiding War: Lessons from the 1995–1996 Taiwan Strait Crisis.* Washington, DC: National Defense University Press, December 2022.

Bibliography   349

Guo, Baogang, and Chung-Chian Teng, eds. *Taiwan and the Rise of China: Cross-Strait Relations in the Twenty-first Century.* Lanham, MD: Lexington Books, 2012.

Gurtov, Melvin. "The Taiwan Strait Crisis Revisited: Politics and Foreign Policy in Chinese Motives." *Modern China* 2, no. 1 (January 1976): 49–103.

Haig, Alexander M., Jr. *Caveat: Realism, Reagan, and Foreign Policy.* New York: Macmillan, 1984.

Halperin, Morton. *The 1958 Taiwan Strait Crisis: A Documented History.* Santa Monica: RAND, 1966.

Han, Huai-chi. *Contemporary Chinese Army's Military Work.* Beijing: China Social Sciences, 1989.

Harding, Harry, and Yuan Ming, eds. *Sino-American Relations 1945–1955: A Joint Reassessment of a Critical Decade.* Washington, DC: Scholarly Resources, 1989.

Harris, John F. "Clinton, Jiang Confer." *Washington Post*, October 25, 1995.

Hayes, Jarrod. *Constructing National Security: U.S. Relations with India and China.* London: Cambridge University Press, 2013.

"Henry Kissinger." Gerald R. Ford Foundation, September 30, 2023. https://geraldrfordfoundation.org.

Herkert, Alex. "U.S. Intelligence and Cross-Strait Relations: Intelligence Failures and U.S. Policy Toward the Two Chinas." *American Intelligence Journal* 34, no. 1 (January 2017): 102–110.

Hickey, Dennis Van Vranken. "Continuity and Change: The Administration of George W. Bush and US Policy Toward Taiwan." *Journal of Contemporary China* 13, no. 40 (August 2004): 461–478.

Hickey, Dennis Van Vranken. "Parallel Progress: US-Taiwan Relations During an Era of Cross-Strait Rapprochement." *Journal of Chinese Political Science* 20, no. 4 (December 2015): 369–384.

Hickey, Dennis Van Vranken. *United States–Taiwan Security Ties: From Cold War to Beyond Containment.* Westport, CT: Praeger, 1994.

Hickey, Dennis Van Vranken, and Yitan Li. "Cross-Strait Relations in the Aftermath of the Election of Chen Shui-bian." *Asian Affairs: An American Review* 28, no. 4 (2002): 201–216.

Hinton, Harold C. *The Republic of China on Taiwan Since 1949 in America and Island China.* New York: University Press of America, 1989.

"History." Government of Portal the Republic of China (Taiwan), https://www.taiwan.gov.tw.

"History of the National Security Council, 1947–1997," White House. https://georgewbush-whitehouse.archives.gov.

Ho, Ming-sho. *Challenging Beijing's Mandate of Heaven: Taiwan's Sunflower Movement and Hong Kong's Umbrella Movement.* Philadelphia: Temple University Press, 2019.

"Hu Jinto: The Cross-Strait Resume Dialogue Under the 1992 Consensus," Xinhua, March 26, 2008.

Hu, Xiaobo. "A Milestone as Well as a Milestone: The Jiang-Clinton Summit." *Issues and Studies* 33, no. 12 (December 1997): 1–18.

Huntington, Samuel P. *Political Order in Changing Societies.* New Haven: Yale University Press, 1968.

Ijiri, Hidenori. "The China-Taiwan Problem in Lieu of U.S.-Japan Leadership Sharing." *Issues and Studies* 33, no. 5 (May 1997): 51–79.

Japan Ministry of Defense. *Defense of Japan 2018.* October 22, 2018. https://www.mod.go.jp.

350 Bibliography

Jennings, Ralph. "Wary of Beijing, Taiwan Doubles Down on South China Sea Island." Voice of America, March 29, 2021.

Jie, Dalei. "The Rise and Fall of the Taiwan Independence Policy: Power Shift, Domestic Constraints, and Sovereignty Assertiveness (1988–2010)." Philadelphia: University of Pennsylvania Dissertations, 2012.

Jon, Pevehouse, and Goldstein Joshua. *International Relations*. London: Pearson, 2020.

Jordan, Amos A., William Taylor Jr., and Lawrence J. Korb. *American National Security: Policy and Process*. Baltimore: Johns Hopkins University Press, 1989.

Kan, Shirley. *China/Taiwan: Evolution of the "One China" Policy—Key Statements from Washington, Beijing, and Taipei*. Report for Congress. Washington, DC: Congressional Research Service, June 1, 2004.

Kan, Shirley. *Democratic Reforms in Taiwan: Issues for Congress*. Washington, DC: Congressional Research Service, May 26, 2010.

Kan, Shirley, et al. *China-U.S. Aircraft Collision Incident of April 2001: Assessments and Policy Implications*. Washington, DC: Congressional Research Service, October 10, 2001.

Kang, Jean. "Firmness and Flexibility: Initiations for Change in U.S. Policy, Toward Communist China, 1961–1963." *American Asian Review* 21, no. 1 (Spring 2003).

Kao, De-Yuan. "China Policy," in *The Obama Presidency: A Preliminary Assessment,* edited by Robert P. Watson, Jack Covarrubias, Tom Lansford, and Douglas M. Brattebo (New York: SUNY Press, 2012).

Kesselman, Mark, Joel Krieger, and William A. Joseph. *Introduction to Comparative Politics: Political Challenges and Changing Agendas*. Boston: Cengage, 2019.

Khaliq, Riyaz. "China Heightens Taiwan Rhetoric Amid US Interference." Anadolu Agency, September 21, 2020.

Kim, Hong, and Jack Hammersmith. "U.S.-China Relations in the Post-Normalization Era, 1979–1985." *Pacific Affairs* 59, no. 1 (Spring 1986): 69–91.

Kissinger, Henry. *The White House Years*. Boston: Little, Brown, 1979.

"Kissinger's Second Visit to China in October 1971." Translated by Gao Bei. In *Xin Zhongguo waijiao feng yun* [Winds and Clouds in New China's Diplomacy], vol. 3, edited by Pei Jianzhang, 59–70. Beijing: Shijie zhishi, 1994.

Klintworth, Gary. "Crisis Management: China, Taiwan, and the United States—The 1995–96 Crisis and Its Aftermath." Parliament of Australia. https://www.aph .gov.au/.

Knott, Stephen. "George H. W. Bush: Foreign Affairs." University of Virginia Miller Center, September 30, 2023. https://millercenter.org.

Kochavi, Noam. *A Conflict Perpetuated: China Policy During the Kennedy Years*. Westport, CT: Greenwood, 2002.

Komine, Yukinori. *Secrecy in US Foreign Policy: Nixon, Kissinger and the Rapprochement with China*. Milton Park: Taylor and Francis Group, 2008.

Kraft, Victoria Marie. *The U.S. Constitution and Foreign Policy: Terminating the Taiwan Treaty*. New York: Green Press, 1991.

Kraus, Charles. "Nixon's 1972 Visit to China at 50." Wilson Center, February 21, 2022. https://www.wilsoncenter.org.

Kulacki, Gregory. "Nuclear Weapons in the Taiwan Strait Part I." *Journal for Peace and Nuclear Disarmament*, no. 2 (October 2020): 310–341.

Lai, Shin-yuan, "The Current Stage of Cross-Strait Relations and the ROC Government's China Policy." Mainland Affairs Council, July 14, 2009. http://www.ma .gov.tw.

Lamy, Steven L., John S. Masker, and John Baylis. *Introduction to Global Politics.* New York: Oxford University Press, 2019.

Lasater, Martin. *The Changing of the Guard: President Clinton and the Security of Taiwan.* Oxford: Westview, 1993.

Lasater, Martin. *Policy in Evolution: The US Role in China's Reunification.* Boulder: Westview, 1989.

Lasater, Martin. *U.S. Interests in the New Taiwan.* Boulder: Westview, 1993.

Lau, Lawrence. "If the US-China Trade War Escalates, How Will the Chinese Economy Respond? Here Are the Numbers." *South China Morning Post,* July 29, 2018.

Leng, Tse-Kang, and Nien-chung Chang Liao. "Hedging, Strategic Partnership, and Taiwan's Relations with Japan Under the Ma Ying-jeou Administration." *Pacific Focus* 31, no. 3 (December 2016): 357–382.

Lerche, Charles O. *Foreign Policy of the American People.* Englewood Cliffs, NJ: Prentice Hall, 1967.

Li, Xiaobing, Xiabo Hu, and Yang Zhong, eds. *Interpreting U.S.-China-Taiwan Relations: China in the Post–Cold War Era.* Lanham, MD: University Press of America, 2008.

Lilley, James R., and Jeffrey Lilley. *China Hands Nine Decades of Adventure, Espionage, and Diplomacy in Asia.* New York: Public Affairs, 2005.

Lin, Gang. "The Changing Relations Across the Taiwan Strait." In *Interpreting U.S.-China-Taiwan Relations: China in the Post–Cold War Era,* edited by Xiaobing Li, Xiabo Hu, and Yang Zhong, 127–150. Lanham, MD: University Press of America, 2008.

Lin, Hsiao-ting. "U.S.-Taiwan Military Diplomacy Revisited: Chiang Kai-shek, Baituan, and the 1954 Mutual Defense Pact." *Diplomatic History* 37, no. 5 (November 2013): 971–994.

Lin, Leo. "Will the China-Japan Reset Continue in 2019?" *The Diplomat,* January 31, 2019.

Lin, Mao. "China and the Escalation of the Vietnam War: The First Years of the Johnson Administration." *Journal of Cold War Studies* 11, no. 2 (Spring 2009): 35–69.

Liu, Ta-Jen, *A History of Sino-American Diplomatic Relations, 1840–1974.* Taipei: China Academy, 1978.

"Mainland Policy and Work." Mainland Affairs Council. https://www.mac.gov.tw/en.

Mann, James. *About Face: A History of America's Curious Relationship with China from Nixon to Clinton.* New York: Knopf, 1999.

Mann, Jim. "U.S. Considered 64 Bombing to Keep China Nuclear-Free." *Los Angeles Times,* September 27, 1998.

Mann, Jim, and Charles Wallace. "Clinton, Chinese President Meet Before Summit." *Los Angeles Times,* November 14, 1994.

Mao, Zedong. *A Collection of Mao Zedong's Military Papers.* Beijing: Military Science Press, 1993.

Mao, Zedong. *Selected Works of Mao Zedong on Diplomacy.* Beijing: Central Historical Literature Press and World Knowledge Press, 1994.

Martin, Peter, and Dandan Li. "China's Xi Jinping Says Taiwan Must Be Unified with Mainland." *Bloomberg News,* January 1, 2019.

Matray, James Irving, ed. *Northeast Asia and the Legacy of Harry S. Truman: Japan, China, and the Two Koreas.* Kirksville, MO: Truman State University Press, 2012.

352 Bibliography

Matthews, Mark. "Clinton OKs Visit by Taiwan President." *Baltimore Sun,* May 23, 1995.

McClelland, Charles A. "Action Structures and Communication in Two International Crises: Quemoy and Berlin." *Background* 7, no. 4 (February 1964): 201–215.

McDowall, Roy Campbell. *Howard's Long March: The Strategic Depiction of China in Howard Government Policy 1996–2006.* Canberra: ANU Press, 2009.

Military Affair Bureau of the Ministry of National Defense. *August 23 Taiwan Strait Battle.* Taipei: Military Affair Bureau of the Ministry of National Defense, 1998.

Morgan, Iwan. "Richard Nixon's Opening to China and Closing the Gold Window." *History Today,* June 15, 2018.

Morrison, Wayne. "China-U.S. Trade Issues." Congressional Research Service, July 30, 2018. https://fas.org .

"The Most Dangerous Place on Earth." *The Economist,* May 1, 2021.

Murray, Douglas J., and Paul R. Viotti. *The Defense of Policies of Nations: A Comparative Study.* Baltimore: Johns Hopkins University Press, 1994.

Nagy, Stephen. "It's Too Early to Write Off the Indo-Pacific Strategy." *Japan Times,* July 24, 2018.

Nakatsuji, Keiji. "How Did or Did Not Japan Respond to 1995–1996 Taiwan Strait Crisis." Kyoto: Ritsumeikan University, December 2018.

"National Security Study Memoranda (NSSM)." National Archives. https://www.nixonlibrary.gov.

Newmann, William. "Kennedy, Johnson, and Policy Toward China: Testing the Importance of the President in Foreign Policy Decision Making." *Presidential Studies Quarterly* 44, no. 4 (December 2014): 640–672.

Niu, Jun. "A Further Discussion of Decision-making in the 1958 Shelling of Jinmen," *Journal of Modern Chinese History* 3, no. 2 (2009): 147–164.

Nixon, Richard. *Public Papers of the Presidents of the United States: Richard Nixon,* vol. 1: *1969.* Washington, DC: Government Printing Office, 1971.

Nixon, Richard. *RN: The Memoirs of Richard Nixon.* New York: Warner Books, 1978.

Noble, George Bernard, and E. Taylor Parks. *American Foreign Policy, 1950–1955: Basic Documents.* Washington, DC: Government Printing Office, 1957.

Office of the Press Secretary. "Joint Press Statement by President Obama and President Hu of China." White House, November 17, 2009. https://obamawhitehouse.archives.gov.

Office of the Secretary of Defense. *Annual Report to Congress: Military and Security Developments Involving the People's Republic of China 2020.* Washington, DC: Office of the Secretary of Defense, 2020.

Ostrom, Charles, Jr., and Brian L. Job. "The President and the Political Use of Force." *American Political Science Review* 80, no. 2 (June 1986): 541–566.

Palmer, Doug. "U.S. Trade Gap with China Reaches All-Time High Under Trump." Politico, March 6, 2019.

Pasquale, Charles D. "Pivotal Deterrence and United States Security Policy in the Taiwan Strait," Norfolk, VA: Old Dominion University Dissertation, 2007.

Pellegrin, Charles J. "There Are Bigger Issues at Stake: The Administration of John F. Kennedy and United States–Republic of China Relations, 1961–63." In *John F. Kennedy History, Memory, Legacy: An Interdisciplinary Inquiry,* edited by John Delane Williams, Robert G. Waite, and Gregory S. Gordon, 100–115. Grand Forks: University of North Dakota, 2010.

"The People's Republic of China: U.S.-China Trade Facts." Office of the United States Trade Representative. https://ustr.gov.

Bibliography   353

Perlez, Jane, and Grace Tatter. "Plots and Private Planes: How Henry Kissinger Pulled Off a Secret Trip to China." WBUR, February 18, 2022.

Peters, Gerhard, and John T. Woolley. "Trip by National Economic Council Director Lawrence H. Summers and Deputy National Security Advisor Thomas E. Donilon to China." Press release, American Presidency Project, September 2, 2010.

"Policy of Containment and Policy of Liberation." *Taiwan Today,* June 1, 1953.

Pompeo, Mike. *Never Give an Inch: Fighting for the America I Love.* New York: HarperCollins, 2023.

Poole, Walter S. *The Joint Chiefs of Staff and National Policy,* vol. 8: *1961–1964.* Washington, DC: Office of the Chairman of the Joint Chiefs of Staff, 2011.

Poole, Walter S. *The Joint Chiefs of Staff and National Policy 1973–1976.* Washington, DC: Office of Joint History, Office of the Chairman of the Joint Chiefs of Staff, 2015.

"President Bush and Secretary Baker." In *A Short History of the Department of State.* US Department of State. https://history.state.gov.

"President Clinton and President Jiang Zemin Joint Press Conference, 1997." USC US-China Institute, October 29, 1997. https://china.usc.edu.

"President Hu Offers Six Proposals for the Peaceful Development of the Cross-Strait Relationship." Consulate General of the People's Republic of China in Chicago, December 31, 2008. http://www.china-embassy.org.

"President Johnson Halts Bombing in Vietnam." NYPR Archive, October 31, 1968. https://www.wnyc.org.

"President Reagan's Six Assurances to Taiwan." Congressional Research Service. June 13, 2023, https://sgp.fas.org.

"Presidential Review Memoranda (PRM)." Jimmy Carter Library. https://www.jimmycarterlibrary.gov.

Rearden, Steven, and Kenneth R. Foulks Jr. *The Joint Chiefs of Staff and National Policy 1977–1980.* Washington, DC: Office of the Chairman of the Joint Chiefs of Staff, 2015.

Rigger, Shelley. *Politics in Taiwan: Voting for Democracy.* London: Routledge, 2002.

Romberg, Alan D. "Cross-Strait Relations: Setting the Stage for 2012." *China Leadership Monitor,* no. 3 (2021): 1–24.

Romberg, Alan. *Rein In at the Brink of the Precipice: American Policy Toward Taiwan and U.S.-PRC Relations.* Washington, DC: Henry L. Stimson Center, 2003.

Romm, Joseph. *Defining National Security: The Nonmilitary Aspects.* New York: Council of Foreign Affairs, 1993.

Ross, Robert. "The 1995–96 Taiwan Strait Confrontation: Coercion, Credibility, and the Use of Force." *International Security* 25, no. 2 (Fall 2000): 87–123.

Rushkoff, Bennett. "Eisenhower, Dulles and the Quemoy-Matsu Crisis, 1954–1955." *Political Science Quarterly* 96, no. 3 (Autumn 1981): 465–480.

Sacks, David, and Chris Miller. "The War over the World's Most Critical Technology: A Conversation with Chris Miller." Council on Foreign Relations, January 3, 2023. https://www.cfr.org.

Satake, Minoru. "Japan's 4 Carriers to Shun Chinese 5G Tech." *Nikkei Asian Review,* December 10, 2018.

Santayana, George. *Life of Reason, Reason in Common Sense* (New York: Charles Scribner's Sons, 1905).

Schaller, Michael. "Ronald Reagan and the Puzzles of 'So-Called Communist China' and Vietnam." In *Reagan and the World: Leadership and National Security,*

1981–1989, edited by Bradley Lynn Coleman and Kyle Longley, 191–210. Lexington: University Press of Kentucky, 2017.

Schnabel, James F., and Robert J. Watson. *The Joint Chiefs of Staff and National Policy,* vol. 3: *1950–1951 The Korean War Part One.* Washington, DC: Office of the Chairman of the Joint Chiefs of Staff, 1998.

Schuman, Michael. "Keep an Eye on Taiwan." *The Atlantic,* October 10, 2020.

Shaheen, Therese. "Why Taiwan Matters." *National Review,* July 15, 2021.

Shambaugh, David. *Tangled Titans: The United States and China.* Lanham, MD: Rowman and Littlefield, 2012.

Sheng, Lijun. "Chen Shui-bian and Cross-Strait Relations." *Contemporary Southeast Asia: A Journal of International and Strategic Affairs* 23, no. 1 (April 2001): 122–148.

Sheng, Lijun. *China and Taiwan.* Singapore: ISEAS, 2002.

Shih, Gerry. "China Launches Combat Drills in Taiwan Strait, Warns U.S. Not to 'Play with Fire.'" *Washington Post,* September 18, 2020.

Singer, J. David. "Review: International Conflict: Three Levels of Analysis." *World Politics* 12, no. 3 (April 1960): 453–461.

Singh, Bhubhindar. "China-Japan Dispute: Tokyo's Foreign Policy of Pragmatism." *Eurasia Review,* October 8, 2010.

Snyder, Charles. "Staff Report in Washington Dialogue: In a Phone Conversation with George Bush." *Taipei Times,* March 28, 2008.

Soman, Kuttan. *Double-Edged Sword: Nuclear Diplomacy in Unequal Conflicts— The United States and China, 1950–1958.* Westport, CT: Greenwood, 2000.

Stashwick, Steven. "China's South China Sea Militarization Has Peaked." *Foreign Policy,* August 19, 2019.

Steinberg, James, and Michael O'Hanlon. *Strategic Reassurance and Resolve: U.S.-China Relations in the Twenty-first Century.* Princeton: Princeton University Press, 2014.

Straaveren, Jacob Van. *Air Operation in the Taiwan Crisis of 1958.* Washington, DC: US Air Force Historical Division Liaison Office, 1962.

Suettinger, Robert L. *Beyond Tiananmen: The Politics of U.S.-China Relations 1989–2000.* Washington, DC: Brookings Institution Press, 2003.

Sun, Shao-cheng. "A Study on the United States Military Security Commitments to the Republic of China (1949–1998)." Master's thesis, National Defense University, Taipei, 1998.

Sun, Shao-cheng. "The Taiwan Security Under the Trump Administration." *Strategic Vision,* no. 2 (February 2019): 11–17.

Sutter, Robert G. "Bush Administration Policy Toward Beijing and Taipei." *Journal of Contemporary China* 12, no. 36 (August 2003): 477–492.

Sutter, Robert G. "The Obama Administration and China: Positive but Fragile Equilibrium." *Asian Perspectives* 33, no. 3 (2009): 81–106.

Sutter, Robert G. "The Taiwan Problem in the Second George W. Bush Administration—US Officials' Views and Their Implications for US Policy." *Journal of Contemporary China* 15, no. 48 (August 2006): 417–441.

Sutter, Robert G. "The TRA and the United States' China Policy." In *A Unique Relationship: The United States and the Republic of China Under the Taiwan Relations Act,* edited by Ramon H. Myers, 49–78. Stanford: Hoover Institution Press, 1989.

Swanson, Eric P. "Seventh Fleet Standoff: A Two-Cut Analysis of the Decision to Neutralize Taiwan in June 1950." *Concept,* no. 38 (2015).

"Taipei Economic and Cultural Representative Office in the United States (Transmittal No: 20-68)." Defense Security Cooperation Agency. https://www.dsca.mil.

"Taiwan Education and Training Services Industry Snapshot." International Trade Administration, March 24, 2023. https://www.trade.gov.

"Taiwan-China Relations over 40 Years: Policies Which Changed the Landscape." Special Broadcasting Service. https://www.sbs.com.au.

 "Taiwan-U.S. Relations." Taipei Economic and Cultural Representative Office in the United States, March 18, 2021. https://www.roc-taiwan.org.

"Taiwanese/Chinese Identity (1992/06~2022/12)." Election Study Center of the National Chengchi University, January 13, 2023. https://esc.nccu.edu.tw.

Tay, Shirley. "As US-China Relations Sour, Taiwan's Value as a 'Chess Piece' May Rise." CNBC, June 11, 2019.

Teng, Emma J. "Taiwan and Modern China." *Oxford Research Encyclopedias,* May 23, 2019. https://oxfordre.com.

Tian, Yew Lun, and Yimou Lee. "China Drops Word Peaceful in Latest Push for Taiwan Reunification." Reuters, May 22, 2020.

Truman, Harry S. "Statement on Formosa, January 5, 1950." USC US-China Institute, February 25, 2014. https://china.usc.edu.

Tsai, George. "The Taiwan Strait Crises: Analysis of China, Taiwan and United States Relationship." PhD diss., Northern Arizona University, 1985.

Tsai, Ing-wen. "Full Text of President Tsai Ing-wen's New Year's Day Speech." *Focus Taiwan,* January 1, 2019.

Turnbull, Jim. "Lt. Shane Osborn: Looking at a Miracle." *Naval Aviation News,* September 27, 2011.

Twomey, Christopher. "The Fourth Taiwan Strait Crisis Is Just Starting." War on the Rocks, August 22, 2022.

US Department of Defense. *Annual Report to Congress: Military and Security Developments Involving the People's Republic of China 2010*. Washington, DC: Office of the Secretary of Defense, 2010.

US Department of Defense. *Annual Report to Congress: Military and Security Developments Involving the People's Republic of China 2011*. Washington, DC: Office of the Secretary of Defense, 2011.

US Department of Defense. *Annual Report to Congress: Military and Security Developments Involving the People's Republic of China 2012*. Washington, DC: Office of the Secretary of Defense, 2012.

US Department of Defense. *Annual Report to Congress: Military and Security Developments Involving the People's Republic of China 2013*. Washington, DC: Office of the Secretary of Defense, 2013.

US Department of Defense. *Annual Report to Congress: Military and Security Developments Involving the People's Republic of China 2014*. Washington, DC: Office of the Secretary of Defense, 2014.

US Department of Defense. *Annual Report to Congress: Military and Security Developments Involving the People's Republic of China 2015*. Washington, DC: Office of the Secretary of Defense, 2015.

US Department of Defense. *Annual Report to Congress: Military and Security Developments Involving the People's Republic of China 2016*. Washington, DC: Office of the Secretary of Defense, 2016.

US Department of Defense. *Annual Report to Congress: Military and Security Developments Involving the People's Republic of China 2018*. Washington, DC: Office of the Secretary of Defense, 2018.

US Department of Defense. *Annual Report to Congress: Military and Security Developments Involving the People's Republic of China 2019*. Washington. DC: Office of the Secretary of Defense, 2019.

356   Bibliography

US Department of State. "2. Memorandum of Conversation." January 8, 1977. *Foreign Relations of the United States (FRUS), 1977–1980*, vol. 3, *China*. https:// history.state.gov.

US Department of State. "3. Memorandum from Michel Oksenberg of the National Security Council Staff to the President's Assistant for National Security Affairs (Brzezinski)." January 25, 1977. *FRUS, 1977–1980*, vol. 13, *China*.

US Department of State. "4. Intelligence Report Prepared in the Office of Economic Research, Central Intelligence Agency." February 1977. ER 77-10049. *FRUS, 1977–1980*, vol. 13, *China*.

US Department of State. "5. Memorandum of Conversation." February 8, 1977. *FRUS, 1977–1980*, vol. 13, *China*.

US Department of State. "7. Telegram from the Department of State to the Embassy in the Republic of China." February 10, 1977. *FRUS, 1977–1980*, vol. 13, *China*.

US Department of State. "10. Telegram from the Department of State to the Embassy in the Republic of China." February 16, 1977. *FRUS, 1977–1980*, vol. 13, *China*.

US Department of State. "10. Telegram from the Embassy in Poland to the Department of State." January 29, 1964. *FRUS, 1977–1980*, vol. 18, *China*.

US Department of State. "12. Memorandum from Michel Oksenberg of the National Security Council Staff to the President's Assistant for National Security Affairs (Brzezinski)." February 16, 1977. *FRUS, 1977–1980*, vol. 13, *China*.

US Department of State. "14. Intelligence Memorandum Prepared in the Central Intelligence Agency." March 1977. *FRUS, 1977–1980*, vol. 13, *China*.

US Department of State. "16. Memorandum from the President's Assistant for National Security Affairs (Brzezinski) to President Carter." March 8, 1977. *FRUS, 1977–1980*, vol. 13, *China*.

US Department of State. "22. Telegram from the Department of State to the Embassy in Poland." April 2, 1964. *FRUS, 1977–1980*, vol. 13, *China*.

US Department of State. "22. Telegram from the Department of State to the Embassy in the Republic of China." March 26, 1977. *FRUS, 1977–1980*, vol. 13, *China*.

US Department of State. "23. Editorial Note." *FRUS, 1977–1980*, vol. 13, *China*.

US Department of State. "24. Editorial Note." August 8, 1962. *FRUS, 1961–1963*, vol. 22, *Northeast Asia*.

US Department of State. "25. Paper Prepared in the Policy Planning Council." April 14, 1964. *FRUS, 1977–1980*, vol. 13, *China*.

US Department of State. "29. Editorial Note." *FRUS, 1969–1976*, vol. 1, *Foundations of Foreign Policy, 1969–1972*.

US Department of State. "29. Editorial Note." *FRUS, 1961–1963*, vol. 22, *Northeast Asia*.

US Department of State. "30. Paper Prepared in the Policy Planning Council." *FRUS, 1964–1968*, vol. 30, *China*.

US Department of State. "31. Memorandum from the President's Assistant for National Security Affairs (Brzezinski) to President Carter." June 14, 1977. *FRUS, 1977–1980*, vol. 13, *China*.

US Department of State. "34. Summary of Conclusions of a Policy Review Committee Meeting." June 27, 1977. *FRUS, 1977–1980*, vol. 13, *China*.

US Department of State. "38. National Intelligence Analytical Memorandum." *FRUS, 1977–1980*, vol. 13, *China*.

US Department of State. "41. Memorandum of Conversation." July 30, 1977. *FRUS, 1977–1980*, vol. 13, *China*.

US Department of State. "43. Memorandum of Meeting: Summary Meeting at the White House on Taiwan Straits Situation." August 25, 1958. *FRUS, 1958–1960*, vol. 19, *China*.

Bibliography   357

US Department of State. "43. Letter from President Carter to Secretary of State Vance." August 18, 1977. *FRUS, 1977–1980*, vol. 13, *China*.

US Department of State. "44. Address by President Ford." September 18, 1974. *FRUS, 1969–1976*, vol. 38, part 1, *Foundations of Foreign Policy, 1973–1976*.

US Department of State. "44. Telegram from the Department of State to the Embassy in the ROC." August 18, 1977. *FRUS, 1977–1980*, vol. 13, *China*.

US Department of State. "48. Memorandum of Conversation." August 23, 1977. *FRUS, 1977–1980*, vol. 13, *China*.

US Department of State. "49. Memorandum of Conversation." August 24, 1977. *FRUS, 1977–1980*, vol. 13, *China*.

US Department of State. "49. Memorandum for the Record." September 15, 1964. *FRUS*. 1964–1968, vol. 30, China.

US Department of State. "50. Memorandum of Conversation." August 24, 1977. *FRUS, 1977–1980*, vol. 13, *China*.

US Department of State. "52. Telegram from Secretary of State Vance to the Department of State and the White House." August 25, 1977. *FRUS, 1977–1980*, vol. 13, *China*.

US Department of State. "52. Memorandum of Meeting, Subject: Summary of Meeting at the White House on the Taiwan Strait Situation." August 29, 1958. *FRUS, 1958–1960*, vol. 19, *China*.

US Department of State. "60. Memorandum for the Record." October 19, 1964. *FRUS, 1964–1968*, vol. 30, *China*.

US Department of State. "62. Report of Meetings." October 23–24, 1964. *FRUS, 1964–1968*, vol. 30, *China*.

US Department of State. "66. Memorandum of Conference with President Eisenhower." September 4, 1958. *FRUS, 1958–1960*, vol. 19, *China*.

US Department of State. "67. Memorandum Prepared by Secretary of State Dulles." September 4, 1958. *FRUS, 1958–1960*, vol. 19, *China*.

US Department of State. "68. White House press release." September 4, 1958. *FRUS, 1958–1960*, vol. 19. *China*.

US Department of State. "74. Telegram from the Department of State to the Embassy in the Republic of China." December 21, 1964. FRUS, 1964–1968, vol. 30, *China*.

US Department of State. "75. Memorandum from the President's Special Adviser for Science and Technology (Press) to President Carter." January 23, 1978. *FRUS, 1977–1980*, vol. 13, *China*.

US Department of State. "76. Memorandum from the Joint Chiefs of Staff to Secretary of Defense McNamara." January 16, 1965. *FRUS, 1964–1968*, vol. 30, *China*.

US Department of State. "77. National Intelligence Estimate." February 10, 1965. NIE 13–2–65. *FRUS, 1964–1968*, vol. 30, *China*.

US Department of State. "80. National Intelligence Estimate." March 10, 1965. NIE 13–3–65. *FRUS, 1964–1968*, vol. 30, *China*.

US Department of State. "81. Telegram from the Embassy in the Republic of China to the Department of State." March 23, 1965. *FRUS, 1964–1968*, vol. 30, *China*. https://history.state.gov.

US Department of State. "82. Airgram from the Embassy in the Republic of China to the Department of State." April 14, 1965. *FRUS, 1964–1968*, vol. 30, *China*.

US Department of State. "84. Memorandum from the Secretary of Defense (McNamara) to the President." March 16, 1964. *FRUS, 1964–1968*, vol. 1, *Vietnam*.

US Department of State. "86. Memorandum of Conversation, by the Ambassador at Large (Jessup)." June 25, 1950. *FRUS, 1950*, vol. 7, *Korea*.

358   Bibliography

US Department of State. "86. Memorandum on Formosa, by General of the Army Douglas MacArthur." June 14, 1950. *FRUS, 1950,* vol. 7, *Korea.*

US Department of State. "88. National Security Study Memorandum 2121." October 8, 1974. *FRUS, 1973–1976,* vol. 18, *China.*

US Department of State. "89. Paper Prepared in the Central Intelligence Agency." October 1974. *FRUS, 1969–1976,* vol. 18, *China.*

US Department of State. "89. Action Memorandum from the Assistant Secretary of State for Far Eastern Affairs (Bundy) to Secretary of State Rusk." June 16, 1965. *FRUS, 1973–1976,* vol. 18, *China.*

US Department of State. "89. Telegram from the Secretary of State John Dulles to the Embassy in Poland." September 14, 1958. *FRUS, 1958–1960,* vol. 19, *China.*

US Department of State. "90. Study Prepared by the Ad Hoc Interdepartmental Regional Group for East Asia and the Pacific." November 12, 1974. *FRUS, 1973–1976,* vol. 18, *China.*

US Department of State. "94. Editorial Note." *FRUS, 1969–1976,* vol. 17, *China.*

US Department of State. "94. Memorandum of Conversation." November 26, 1974. *FRUS, 1973–1976,* vol. 17 *China.*

US Department of State. "95. Memorandum from James C. Thomson, Jr., of the National Security Council Staff and the President's Special Assistant for National Security Affairs (Bundy) to President Johnson." August 5, 1965. *FRUS, 1964–1968,* vol. 30, *China.*

US Department of State. "100. Letter from President Ford to Republic of China Premier Jiang Jingguo." January 8, 1975. *FRUS, 1973–1976,* vol. 18, *China.*

US Department of State. "101. Memorandum from Richard H. Solomon and W. Richard Smyser of the National Security Council Staff to Secretary of State Kissinger." January 15, 1975. *FRUS, 1973–1976,* vol. 18, *China.*

US Department of State. "102. Memorandum from the Assistant Secretary of State for East Asian and Pacific Affairs (Habib), the Deputy Assistant Secretary of State for East Asian and Pacific Affairs (Gleysteen), the Director of the Policy Planning Staff (Lord), and Richard H. Solomon of the NSC Staff to Secretary of State Kissinger." July 3, 1975. *FRUS, 1973–1976,* vol. 18, *China.*

US Department of State. "103. Memorandum of Conversation." September 20, 1965. *FRUS, 1964–1968,* vol. 30, *China.*

US Department of State. "104. Address by President Carter to the Nation." December 15, 1978. *FRUS, 1977–1980,* vol. 1, *Foundations of Foreign Policy.*

US Department of State. "104. Memorandum of Conversation." September 22, 1965. *FRUS, 1964–1968,* vol. 30, *China.*

US Department of State. "105. Draft Response to National Security Study Memorandum 1061." February 16, 1971. *FRUS.* 1969–1976, vol. 17, *China.*

US Department of State. "105. Message from the President's Special Assistant for National Security Affairs (Bundy) to the Chief of the Central Intelligence Agency Station in Taipei (Cline)." April 17, 1962. *FRUS, 1961–1963,* vol. 22, *Northeast Asia.*

US Department of State. "106. Memorandum from W. Richard Smyser and Richard H. Solomon of the National Security Council Staff to Secretary of State Kissinger." April 11, 1975. *FRUS, 1973–1976,* vol. 18, *China.*

US Department of State. "107. Memorandum of Conversation." September 26, 1965. *FRUS, 1964–1968,* vol. 30, *China.*

US Department of State. "108. Memorandum of Conversation." May 20, 1978. *FRUS, 1977–1980,* vol. 13, *China.* https://history.state.gov.

Bibliography 359

US Department of State. "108. Memorandum from the Assistant Secretary of State for East Asian and Pacific Affairs (Habib), the Deputy Assistant Secretary of State for East Asian and Pacific Affairs (Gleysteen), the Director of the Policy Planning Staff (Lord), and Richard H. Solomon of the National Security Council Staff to Secretary of State Kissinger." May 8, 1975. *FRUS, 1973–1976*, vol. 18, *China*.

US Department of State. "110. Memorandum of Conversation." May 21, 1978. *FRUS, 1977–1980*, vol. 13, *China*.

US Department of State. "111. Memorandum of Conversation." May 22, 1978. *FRUS, 1977–1980*, vol. 13, *China*.

US Department of State. "113. Memorandum from the Director of the Bureau of Intelligence and Research (Hilsman) to Secretary of State Rusk." May 29, 1962. *FRUS, 1961–1963*, vol. 22, *Northeast Asia*.

US Department of State. "113. Memorandum from the President's Assistant for National Security Affairs (Brzezinski) to President Carter." May 25, 1978. *FRUS, 1977–1980*, vol. 13, *China*.

US Department of State. "115. Memorandum of Conversation." December 29, 1965. *FRUS, 1964–1968*, vol. 30.

US Department of State. "116. Telegram from the Central Intelligence Agency Station in Saigon to Director of Central Intelligence McCone, Saigon." June 7, 1962. *FRUS, 1961–1963*, vol. 22, *Northeast Asia*.

US Department of State. "118. Message from the Premier of the People's Republic of China Chou En-lai to President Nixon." April 21, 1971. *FRUS, 1969–1976*, vol. 17, *China*.

US Department of State. "118. Memorandum for the Record." June 18, 1962. *FRUS, 1961–1963*, vol. 22, *Northeast Asia*.

US Department of State. "119. Memorandum from the Director of the Bureau of Intelligence and Research (Hilsman) to Secretary of State Rusk." June 18, 1962. *FRUS, 1961–1963*, vol. 22, *Northeast Asia*.

US Department of State. "119. Memorandum From Secretary of State Vance to President Carter." June 13, 1978. *FRUS, 1977–1980*, vol. 13, *China*.

US Department of State. "120. Memorandum of Conversation." October 17, 1975. *FRUS, 1973–1976*, vol. 18, *China*.

US Department of State. "122. Record of Meeting." June 20, 1962. *FRUS, 1961–1963*, vol. 22, *Northeast Asia*.

US Department of State. "123. Memorandum for the Record, Gettysburg." June 21, 1962. *FRUS, 1961–1963*, vol. 22, *Northeast Asia*.

US Department of State. "124. Memorandum of Conversation." October 21, 1975. *FRUS, 1973–1976*, vol. 18, *China*.

US Department of State. "124. Memorandum from Acting Secretary of State George W. Ball to President Kennedy." June 21, 1962. *FRUS, 1961–1963*, vol. 22, *Northeast Asia*.

US Department of State. "125. Memorandum of Conversation." October 22, 1975. *FRUS, 1973–1976*, vol. 18, *China*.

US Department of State. "126. Letter from the Assistant Secretary of Defense for International Security Affairs (Nitze) to the Under Secretary of State for Political Affairs (McGhee)." June 21, 1962. Department of State, Central Files, 611.93/6-2162 (Secret). *FRUS, 1961–1963*, vol. 22, *Northeast Asia*.

US Department of State. "126. Memorandum of Conversation." October 23, 1975, *FRUS, 1973–1976*, vol. 18, *China*.

360   *Bibliography*

US Department of State. "126. Telegram from the Embassy in the Republic of China to the Department of State." February 22, 1966. *FRUS, 1964–1968,* vol. 30, *China.*

US Department of State. "127. Memorandum from Secretary of State Kissinger to President Ford." October 24, 1975. *FRUS, 1973–1976,* vol. 18, *China.*

US Department of State. "129. Memorandum of Conversation." October 25, 1975. *FRUS, 1973–1976,* vol. 18, *China.*

US Department of State. "129. Response to National Security Study Memorandum 1241." May 27, 1971. *FRUS, 1969–1976,* vol. 17, *China.*

US Department of State. "130. Memorandum of Conversation." October 31, 1975. *FRUS, 1973–1976,* vol. 18, *China.*

US Department of State. "130. Message from the Premier of the People's Republic of China Chou En-lai to President Nixon." May 29, 1971. *FRUS, 1969–1976,* vol. 18, *China.*

US Department of State. "131. Backchannel Message from the Chief of the Liaison Office in China (Bush) to Secretary of State Kissinger." November 6, 1975. *FRUS, 1973–1976,* vol. 18, *China.*

US Department of State. "131. Telegram from the Embassy in Poland to the Department of State." June 23, 1962. *FRUS, 1961–1963,* vol. 22, *Northeast Asia.*

US Department of State. "132. Memorandum of Conversation." June 24, 1962. *FRUS, 1961–1963,* vol. 22, *Northeast Asia.*

US Department of State. "132. Memorandum from Secretary of State Kissinger to President Ford." November 20, 1975. *FRUS, 1973–1976,* vol. 18, *China.*

US Department of State. "132. Message from the Government of the United States to the Government of the People's Republic of China." June 4, 1971. *FRUS, 1969–1976,* vol. 17, *China.*

US Department of State. "133. Editorial Note." *FRUS, 1973–1976,* vol. 18, *China.*

US Department of State. "133. Memorandum of Conversation." June 25, 1962. *FRUS, 1961–1963,* vol. 22, *Northeast Asia.*

US Department of State. "134. Memorandum from Secretary of Defense McNamara to President Kennedy." June 25, 1962. *FRUS, 1961–1963,* vol. 22, *Northeast Asia.*

US Department of State. "134. Memorandum of Conversation." December 2, 1975. *FRUS, 1973–1976,* vol. 18, *China.*

US Department of State. "135. Memorandum for the Record." June 26, 1962. *FRUS, 1961–1963,* vol. 22, *Northeast Asia.*

US Department of State. "137. Editorial Note." June 27, 1962. *FRUS, 1961–1963,* vol. 22, *Northeast Asia.*

US Department of State. "137. Memorandum of Conversation." December 4, 1975. *FRUS, 1973–1976,* vol. 18, *China.*

US Department of State. "138. Editorial Note." *FRUS, 1973–1976,* vol. 18, *China.*

US Department of State. "139. Memorandum of Conversation." July 9, 1971. *FRUS, 1969–1976,* vol. 17, *China.*

US Department of State. "141. Memorandum from the President's Assistant for National Security Affairs (Brzezinski) to President Carter." October 11, 1978. *FRUS, 1977–1980,* vol. 13, *China.*

US Department of State. "141. Special National Intelligence Estimate." July 5, 1962. *FRUS, 1961–1963,* vol. 22, *Northeast Asia.*

US Department of State. "142. Memorandum for the Files." April 25, 1966. *FRUS, 1964–1968,* vol. 30, *China.*

US Department of State. "144. Memorandum from the President's Assistant for National Security Affairs (Kissinger) to President Nixon." July 14, 1971. *FRUS, 1969–1976,* vol. 17, *China.*

Bibliography 361

US Department of State. "145. Memorandum from the President's Special Assistant (Rostow) to President Johnson." April 30, 1966. *FRUS, 1964–1968,* vol. 30, *China.*

US Department of State. "145. Telegram from the Department of State to the Embassy in the Republic of China." July 16, 1971. *FRUS, 1969–1976,* vol. 17, *China.*

US Department of State. "147. Memorandum from President Nixon to His Assistant for National Security Affairs (Kissinger)." July 19, 1971. *FRUS, 1969–1976,* vol. 17, *China.*

US Department of State. "148. Message from the Assistant Secretary of State for Far Eastern Affairs (Harriman) to the Ambassador to the Republic of China (Kirk)." August 8, 1962. *FRUS, 1961–1963,* vol. 22, *Northeast Asia.*

US Department of State. "148. Paper Prepared in the Central Intelligence Agency." June 1976. *FRUS, 1973–1976,* vol. 18, *China.*

US Department of State. "149. Memorandum from Secretary of State Rusk to President Johnson." May 14, 1966. *FRUS, 1964–1968,* vol. 30, *China.*

US Department of State. "150. Presidential Directive/NSC 431." November 3, 1978. *FRUS, 1977–1980,* vol. 13, *China.*

US Department of State. "152. Interagency Intelligence Memorandum." November 14, 1978. NI IIM 78-10024. *FRUS, 1977–1980,* vol. 13, *China.*

US Department of State. "154. Memorandum from the Joint Chiefs of Staff to Secretary of Defense Brown." November 20, 1978. JCSM-335-78. *FRUS, 1977–1980,* vol. 13, *China.*

US Department of State. "156. Memorandum of Conversation, Suspension of US Convoy Escorting During Chicom Ceasefire." October 7, 1958. *FRUS, 1958–1960,* vol. 19, *China.*

US Department of State. "159. Backchannel Message from the Chief of the Liaison Office in China (Woodcock) to Secretary of State Vance and the President's Assistant for National Security Affairs (Brzezinski)." December 4, 1978. 1330Z. *FRUS, 1977–1980,* vol. 13, *China.*

US Department of State. "159. Letter from Secretary of Defense McNamara to Defense Minister of the Republic of China Chiang Ching-kuo." June 16, 1966. *FRUS, 1964–1968,* vol. 30, *China.*

US Department of State. "159. Memorandum of Conversation." October 15, 1971. *FRUS, 1969–1976,* vol. 17, *China.*

US Department of State. "162. Memorandum from the President's Assistant for National Security Affairs (Brzezinski) to President Carter." December 5, 1978. *FRUS, 1977–1980,* vol. 13, *China.*

US Department of State. "165. Memorandum from the President's Assistant for National Security Affairs (Kissinger) to President Nixon." *FRUS, 1969–1976,* vol. 17, China.

US Department of State. "166. Backchannel Message from the Chief of the Liaison Office in China (Woodcock) to Secretary of State Vance and the President's Assistant for National Security Affairs (Brzezinski)." December 13, 1978. *FRUS, 1977–1980,* vol. 13, *China.*

US Department of State. "166. Memorandum From President Eisenhower to Secretary of State Dulles," October 7, 1958. *FRUS, 1958–1960,* vol. 19, *China.*

US Department of State. "167. Backchannel Message from the Chief of the Liaison Office in China (Woodcock) to Secretary of State Vance and the President's Assistant for National Security Affairs (Brzezinski)." December 13, 1978. *FRUS, 1977–1980,* vol. 13, *China.*

US Department of State. "167. Editorial Note," *FRUS, 1969–1976,* vol. 17, *China.*

362 *Bibliography*

US Department of State. "169. Memorandum of Conversation." October 29, 1971. *FRUS, 1969–1976,* vol. 17, *China.*

US Department of State. "170. Backchannel Message from the Chief of the Liaison Office in China (Woodcock) to Secretary of State Vance and the President's Assistant for National Security Affairs (Brzezinski)." December 15, 1978. 1024Z. *FRUS, 1977–1980,* vol. 13, *China.*

US Department of State. "171. Backchannel Message from Secretary of State Vance and the President's Assistant for National Security Affairs (Brzezinski) to the Ambassador to the Republic of China (Unger)." December 15, 1978. *FRUS, 1977–1980,* vol. 13, *China.*

US Department of State. "172. Backchannel Message from the President's Assistant for National Security Affairs (Brzezinski) to the Chief of the Liaison Office in China (Woodcock)." December 15, 1978. 1551Z. *FRUS, 1977–1980,* vol. 13, *China.*

US Department of State. "173. Backchannel Message from the Ambassador to the Republic of China (Unger) to Secretary of State Vance and the President's Assistant for National Security Affairs (Brzezinski)." December 15, 1978. *FRUS, 1977–1980,* vol. 13, *China.*

US Department of State. "179. Memorandum from Secretary of Defense Brown to the President's Assistant for National Security Affairs (Brzezinski)." December 23, 1978. *FRUS, 1977–1980,* vol. 13, *China.*

US Department of State. "181. Memorandum from the President's Assistant for National Security Affairs (Brzezinski) to the Deputy Secretary of State (Christopher)." December 26, 1978. *FRUS, 1977–1980,* vol. 13, *China.*

US Department of State. "183. Telegram from the U.S. Pacific Command to the Department of State and the White House." December 30, 1978. *FRUS, 1977–1980,* vol. 13, *China.*

US Department of State. "194. Memorandum of Conversation." February 21, 1972. *FRUS, 1969–1976,* vol. 17, *China.*

US Department of State. "195. Memorandum of Conversation." February 21, 1972. *FRUS, 1969–1976,* vol. 17, *China.*

US Department of State. "198. Memorandum of Conversation." February 23, 1972. *FRUS.*

US Department of State. "198. Special National Intelligence Estimate." November 3, 1966. SNIE 13–8–66. *FRUS, 1964–1968,* vol. 30, *China.*

US Department of State. "200. Memorandum from Secretary of State Rusk to President Johnson." November 5, 1966. *FRUS, 1964–1968,* vol. 30, *China.*

US Department of State. "203. Joint Statement Following Discussions with Leaders of the People's Republic of China." February 27, 1972. *FRUS, 1969–1976,* vol. 17, *China.*

US Department of State. "205. Memorandum of Conversation." January 29, 1979. *FRUS, 1977–1980,* vol. 13, *China.*

US Department of State. "206. Oral Presentation by President Carter to Chinese Vice Premier Deng Xiaoping." January 30, 1979. *FRUS, 1977–1980,* vol. 13, *China.*

US Department of State. "207. Memorandum of Conversation." January 30, 1979, *FRUS, 1977–1980,* vol. 13, *China.*

US Department of State. "208. Memorandum of Conversation." January 30, 1979. *FRUS, 1977–1980,* vol. 13, *China.*

US Department of State. "212. Oral Message from Chinese Vice Premier Deng Xiaoping to President Carter." *FRUS, 1977–1980,* vol. 13, *China.*

Bibliography 363

US Department of State. "219. Summary of Conclusions of a Special Coordination Committee Meeting." February 19, 1979. *FRUS, 1977–1980*, vol. 13, *China*.

US Department of State. "224. Memorandum from the Secretary of Defense (McNamara) to the President." June 25, 1964. *FRUS, 1964–1968*, vol. 1, *Vietnam*.

US Department of State. "226. Research Paper Prepared in the National Foreign Assessment Center, Central Intelligence Agency." March 1979. *FRUS, 1977–1980*, vol. 13, *China*.

US Department of State. "232. Memorandum from Secretary of the Treasury Blumenthal to President Carter." March 22, 1979. *FRUS, 1977–1980*, vol. 13, *China*.

US Department of State. "233. Memorandum from Secretary of Defense Brown to the President's Assistant for National Security Affairs (Brzezinski)." March 23, 1979. *FRUS, 1977–1980*, vol. 13, *China*.

US Department of State. "235. Editorial Note." *FRUS, 1977–1980*, vol. 13, *China*.

US Department of State. "272. Memorandum from Secretary of State Vance to President Carter." September 18, 1979. *FRUS, 1977–1980*, vol. 13, *China*.

US Department of State. "273. Memorandum from the President's Assistant for National Security Affairs (Brzezinski) to President Carter." September 18, 1979. *FRUS, 1977–1980*, vol. 13, *China*.

US Department of State. "274. Letter from President Carter to Secretary of State Vance, Secretary of Defense Brown, and the President's Assistant for National Security Affairs (Brzezinski)." September 19, 1979. *FRUS, 1977–1980*, vol. 13, *China*.

US Department of State. "283. Memorandum from Secretary of Defense Brown to President Carter." December 13, 1979. *FRUS, 1977–1980*, vol. 13, *China*.

US Department of State. "312. National Intelligence Estimate." June 5, 1980. NIE 11/13–80. *FRUS, 1977–1980*, vol. 13, *China*.

US Department of State. "327. Memorandum from Michel Oksenberg to the President's Assistant for National Security Affairs (Brzezinski)." December 19, 1980. *FRUS, 1977–1980*, vol. 13, *China*.

US Department of State. "337. Memorandum of Conversation, by the Director of the Office of Chinese Affairs (McConaughy)." November 2, 1954, *FRUS, 1952–1954*, vol. 14, part 1, *China and Japan*.

US Department of State. "449. Letter from the President to Senator Mike Mansfield." December 17, 1964. *FRUS*, 1964–1968, vol. 1, *Vietnam*.

US Department of State. "1945–1952: NSC-68, 1950." *Milestones in the History of U.S. Foreign Relations: 1945–1952*.

US Department of State. "1945–1952: The Truman Doctrine, 1947." *Milestones in the History of U.S. Foreign Relations: 1945–1952*.

US Department of State. "1953–1960: The Taiwan Straits Crises: 1954–55 and 1958." *Milestones in the History of U.S. Foreign Relations: 1953–1960*.

US Department of State. "1969–1976: The Presidencies of Richard M. Nixon and Gerald R. Ford." *Milestones in the History of U.S. Foreign Relations: 1969–1976*.

US Department of State. "1977–1980: China Policy." *Milestones in the History of U.S. Foreign Relations: 1977–1980*.

US Department of State. "1977–1980: The Presidency of Jimmy Carter." *Milestones in the History of U.S. Foreign Relations: 1977–1980*.

US Department of State. "1981–1988: The Presidency of Ronald W. Reagan." *Milestones in the History of U.S. Foreign Relations: 1981–1988*.

US Department of State. "1981–1991: U.S.-Soviet Relations." *Milestones in the History of U.S. Foreign Relations: 1981–1988*.

364   Bibliography

US Department of State. "The August 17, 1982, US-China Communiqué on Arms Sales to Taiwan." *Milestones in the History of U.S. Foreign Relations: 1981–1988.*

US Department of State. "Biographies of the Secretaries of State: Henry A. (Heinz Alfred) Kissinger (1923–)." Office of Historian of the State Department.

US Department of State. "Bush's Foreign Policy." Office of Historian of the State Department. https://history.state.gov.

US Department of State. "Foreword." *FRUS, 1964–1968,* vol. 30, *China.* https://history.state.gov.

US Department of State. "History of the National Security Council, 1947–1997." White House. https://georgewbush-whitehouse.archives.gov.

US Department of State. "Letter from President Ford to People's Republic of China Premier Zhou Enlai." January 23, 1975. *FRUS, 1973–1976,* vol. 18, *China.* https://history.state.gov.

US Department of State. "Memorandum for the Record: White House Briefing on China." May 17, 1962. Central Intelligence Agency, DCI (McCone) Files, Job 80-B01285A.

US Department of State. "Memorandum of a Conversation Between the President and the Secretary of State." April 4, 1955." *FRUS, 1955–1957,* vol. 2, *China.*

US Department of State. "52. Memorandum of Meeting, Subject: Summary of Meeting at the White House on the Taiwan Strait Situation." August 29, 1958. *FRUS, 1958–1960,* no. 52. US Department of State. "Statement by the President on the First Chinese Nuclear Device." October 16, 1964. *The American Presidency Project.* https://www.presidency.ucsb.edu.

US Department of State. "Summary." *FRUS, 1969–1976,* vol. E-13, *Documents on China.*

US Department of State. "Telegram from the Embassy in Poland to the Department of State." April 5, 1962. *FRUS, 1961–1963,* vol. 22, *China, Korea, Japan.* Department of State, Warsaw, Central Files, 611.93/4-562.

US Department of State. "United States Relations with China: Boxer Uprising to Cold War (1900–1949)." US Department of State Archive. https://2001-2009.state.gov.

US Department of State. "US Enters the Korean Conflict." National Archives. https://www.archives.gov.

Vasilache, Anca. "The Rebalance to Asia Policy of the Obama Administration (2011–2017): Diversifying the United States Security Design in Asia-Pacific." *Perspective Politice* 15, nos. 1–2 (2022): 87–96.

Wang, Bing-Nan. *Memoirs of Nine Years' Sino-US Ambassador Talks.* Beijing: World Knowledge Press, 1985.

Wang, Chi. *George W. Bush and China: Policies, Problems, and Partnerships.* Lanham, MD: Lexington Books, 2009.

Wang, Chi. *Obama's Challenge to China: The Pivot to Asia.* Abingdon: Routledge, 2017.

Wang, Dinglie, et al., *Contemporary Chinese Air Force.* Beijing: Chinese Social Science Press, 1989.

Wang, Qinfxin Ken. "Japan's Balancing Act in the Taiwan Strait." *Security Dialogue* 31, no. 3 (September 2000): 337–342.

Ward, Alex. "The Trump Administration Authorized Arms Sales to Taiwan. China Isn't Pleased," Vox, July 9, 2019.

Ward, Jared "Taiwan's Medical Diplomacy in the Caribbean: A Final Stand Against Beijing?" *The Diplomat,* May 11, 2020.

Warren, Aiden, and Bartley, Adam. *U.S. Foreign Policy and China: Security Challenges During the Bush, Obama, and Trump Administrations.* Edinburgh: Edinburgh University Press, 2021.

Watson, Robert J. *History of the Joint Chiefs of Staff,* vol. 5: *The Joint Chiefs of Staff and National Policy, 1953–1954.* Washington, DC.: Office of the Chairman of the Joint Chiefs of Staff, 1998.

Weber, Nathaniel R. "United States Military Advisory Assistance During the Cold War, 1945–1965." PhD diss., Texas A&M University, 2016.

"What's Behind the China-Taiwan Divide?" BBC, May 26, 2021.

White House. "History of the National Security Council, 1947–1997." White House Archives. https://georgewbush-whitehouse.archives.gov.

Whiting, Allen S. "China's Use of Force, 1950–96, and Taiwan." *International Security* 26, no. 2 (Fall 2001): 103–131.

Whitman, Alden. "The Life of Chiang Kai-shek: A Leader Who Was Thrust Aside by Revolution." *New York Times,* April 6, 1975.

Why Taiwan Matters: Hearing Before the House Committee on Foreign Affairs. 112th Congress, Serial No. 112-42, June 16, 2011. https://www.govinfo.gov.

Wiggins, Don. "History of U.S. Military Assistance to Taiwan: 1950–1959, Part 1." *US Taiwan Defense Command Blog,* September 20, 2010. http://ustdc.blogspot .com.

Will, George. "Time Is on Taiwan's Side, as Long as the U.S. Is, too." *Washington Post*, September 25, 2019.

Willner, Albert. "International Relations Taiwan Strait Security Challenges." *International Relations Taiwan Strait Security Challenges* 8, no. 2 (2009): Taiwan Strait Security Challenges. Chinacurrents.com.

Wolff, Stefan. "Stefan Wolff: The Path to Ending Ethnic Conflicts." TED Talk, Nov 9, 2010.

Wong, Edward. "U.S. Tries to Bolster Taiwan's Status, Short of Recognizing Sovereignty." *New York Times,* August 17, 2020.

Wu, Charles K. S. "How Public Opinion Shapes Taiwan's Sunflower Movement." *Journal of East Asian Studies* 19 no. 3 (2019): 289–307.

"Xi Jinping Says Taiwan 'Must and Will Be, Reunited with China." *BBC News,* January 2, 2019.

Xia, Yafeng. "The Cold War and Chinese Foreign Policy." E-International Relations, July 16, 2008. https://www.e-ir.info.

Xie, John. "Amid Tensions with Taiwan." Voice of America, October 11, 2020.

Yang, Chun-hui, and Jake Chung. "Poll Finds 62.6% Identify as Taiwanese." *Taipei Times,* September 25, 2020.

Yang, Hengjun. "Chiang Ching-kuo, China's Democratic Pioneer." *The Diplomat,* December 10, 2014.

"Ye Jianying on Taiwan's Return to Motherland and Peaceful Reunification." China.org.cn, September 30, 1981.

Yuwen, Deng. "The US Sees the Trade War as a Tactic to Contain China. So Does Beijing." *South China Morning Post,* July 4, 2018.

Zelikow, Philip. "The Statesman in Winter: Kissinger on the Ford Years," *Foreign Affairs* 78, no. 3 (May–June 1999): 123–128.

Zelizer, Julian E. *The Presidency of Donald J. Trump.* Princeton: Princeton University Press, 2022.

Zetter, Kim. "Burn After Reading." *The Intercept,* April 10, 2017.

Zhang, Baijia, and Qingguo Jia. "Steering Wheel, Shock Absorber, and Diplomatic Probe in Confrontation Sino-American Ambassadorial Talks Seen from the

Chinese Perspective." In *Re-examining the Cold War: U.S.-China Diplomacy, 1954–1973,* edited by Robert S. Ross and Changbin Jiang, 173–199. Cambridge: Harvard University Asia Center, 2001.

Zhang, Qingminy. "The Bureaucratic Politics of US Arms Sales to Taiwan." *Chinese Journal of International Politics* 1, no. 2 (Winter 2006): 231–265.

Zhou, Michael. "For China, the History that Matters Is Still the Century of Humiliation." *South China Morning Post,* September 28, 2021.

Zubok, Vladislav, and Constantine Pleshakov. *Inside the Kremlin's Cold War: From Stalin to Khrushchev.* Cambridge: Harvard University Press, 1996.

Index

Abe, Shinzo, 291–292
Acheson, Dean, 26–37
ADIZ. *See* Air defense identification zone
AI. *See* Artificial intelligence
Air defense identification zone (ADIZ), 299–300
AIT. *See* American Institute in Taiwan
Allies, 78–79, 89–91, 95, 97, 110, 112, 133, 137, 145, 162, 171–172, 177, 187, 195, 237, 244, 261, 267, 279, 288, 293, 299, 303, 307–317, 325–326, 331–332, 338–339
America First, 280, 294, 331
American Institute in Taiwan (AIT), 178, 183, 217, 239
Anti-access/area denial (A2/AD), 260, 288
Anti-Secession Law, 8, 10, 242
APEC. *See* Asia-Pacific Economic Cooperation
ARATS. *See* Association for Relations Across the Taiwan Strait
ARF. See ASEAN Regional Forum
Arms procurement: Aegis system, 238–239; F-16, 159, 203–211, 224, 239, 247, 268, 286, 290; FX aircraft, 149, 172–174, 178, 182–183
Artificial intelligence (AI), 305, 334
Asia Pacific, 131, 187, 223, 226, 231–232, 245, 257, 261, 262–269, 273, 287, 331, 334

Asia-Pacific Economic Cooperation (APEC), 226, 263, 287
Association for Relations Across the Taiwan Strait (ARATS), 6, 198, 216
Association of Southeast Asian Nations (ASEAN), 264, 271
ASEAN Regional Forum (ARF), 264

Back channel, 75, 111, 115, 134
Baker, James, 193, 196–197, 200, 202–210, 218
Balance of power, 12, 17, 33, 37, 86, 109, 111, 120, 162, 316, 329–330
Bandung Conference, 45, 55, 77
Beijing, 4–7, 9, 11–14, 26–28, 37, 46–47, 55–57, 64, 70, 74–79, 86–94, 97–100, 105–121, 125–139, 146–153, 156, 160–161, 172–211, 216, 218–238, 242–253, 257–270, 278–281, 283–294, 300–305, 310, 317, 326–339
Belt and Road Initiative (BRI), 287
Berger, Sandy, 223, 230
Biden, Joe, 1, 11, 15, 19, 171, 261, 263, 295, 299, 301–317, 323–324, 330–336
Blinken, Antony, 263, 299, 302, 307, 310–313
Bolton, John, 281, 284–286, 289, 294
Bowles, Chester A., 64, 72–73
Bradley, Omar, 29–31
Brezhnev, Leonid, 98, 136
BRI. *See* Belt and Road Initiative

368 *Index*

Brzezinski, Zbigniew, 18, 143–146, 150–154, 157, 159–164, 172, 186
Bundy, McGeorge, 63, 72, 75, 89, 93–94, 99
Bush, George H. W., 13, 19, 108–130, 134, 172–177, 183, 193–211, 226–329
Bush, George W., 19, 234, 237–253, 265, 328, 330

Carrier battle groups, 7, 52, 215, 220–223, 227–232, 269, 278, 291, 300
Carter, Jimmy, 13–14, 18–19, 139–140, 143–165, 171–178, 187, 193, 228, 239, 327–328, 332–333
CCP. *See* Chinese Communist Party
Cease-fire, 26, 42, 45–57, 78, 119–120, 137, 209, 315
Central Intelligence Agency (CIA), 27, 35–37, 53, 56, 66, 70–72, 75–80, 85–86, 91, 94–95, 98, 114–115, 128–129, 133–134, 144, 161, 163, 188–189, 193, 199, 222, 224, 229, 233, 267, 311, 324–329,
Chen, Shui-bian, 7–8, 238–242, 246–247, 252
Cheney, Dick, 193, 204, 206, 241, 248
Chiang, Ching-kuo, 5, 67, 85–88, 96–97, 128, 154–157, 160, 174, 178–179, 197
Chiang, Kai-shek, 4–5, 19, 25–37, 41–49, 53–54, 58, 64–70, 75, 79, 86–91, 96–97, 116–117, 135, 177, 325–326
China Dream, 280, 299, 333
CIA. See Central Intelligence Agency
China-Vietnam border dispute, 162–163
Chinese Civil War, 3, 36, 27, 97, 325
Chinese Communist Party (CCP), 25, 164, 194, 208, 211, 242, 280, 304; Central Military Commission (CMC), 4, 44, 194, 201, 219, 229, 268; Politburo Standing Committee, 46, 194, 218–219
CINCPAC. *See* Commander in chief, Pacific
Clinton, Bill, 7, 19, 204–205, 208, 211, 215–229, 231, 233, 237–238, 243–244, 328–329
Clinton, Hillary, 257, 264–267, 270–271, 287

Cold War, 4, 12–16, 34–35, 113, 118, 187–189, 199, 208–211, 231–233, 284, 309–315, 332–335
CMC. *See* Central Military Commission
Commander in chief, Pacific (CINCPAC), 43, 158
Communiqué: 1972 Shanghai Communiqué, 107–110, 115, 129–135, 140, 145; 1979 Joint Communiqué, 146–148, 152–158, 173–174; 1982 US-PRC Communiqué, 175–185, 203, 238
Counterterrorism, 250–251, 262
Covid-19, 11, 277, 279, 287, 295, 312, 335
Cross-strait relations, 1–2, 7–14, 197–198, 238–239, 242, 250, 253, 257–260, 268, 273, 277–279, 304, 317, 327, 337; 1992 Consensus, 6–9, 216, 242, 257, 277, 279, 300, 334; Confidence-building measures (CBMs), 258, 338; Economic Cooperation Framework Agreement, 9; Cross Strait Service Trade Agreement (CSSTA), 258–259; Economic Cooperation Framework Agreement (ECFA), 258–259
Cuban Missile Crisis, 67, 76, 98, 100, 326
Cultural Revolution, 18, 85–86, 105, 126, 195, 326
Cybersecurity, 264, 282–283, 302, 336, 292

Defense Intelligence Agency (DIA), 158, 183
Democratic Progressive Party (DPP), 9, 11, 197, 238, 240–241, 246, 258–259, 277–278, 300, 304
Deng Xiaoping, 5, 126–131, 137–138, 145–157, 162–165, 171–175, 180–186, 194–210, 227, 238
Department of Defense (DoD), 10, 30, 53–54, 64–65, 70–75, 80, 97, 114, 116, 120, 128, 161, 164, 173, 178, 182–188, 195, 204, 211, 220–230, 233, 241–245, 249, 264–268, 273, 287–290, 299. 313–331
De-Sinicization, 11, 12
Détente, 19, 76, 80, 92, 98–99, 129, 135–139, 187, 257, 328

Index **369**

DIA. *See* Defense Intelligence Agency
Diaoyus/Senkakus Islands, 269–270
DoD. *See* Department of Defense
DPP. *See* Democratic Progressive Party
Dulles, John Foster, 36, 41–45, 48, 50–57

Eagleburger, Lawrence, 193–194, 201–202, 207
Eisenhower, Dwight, 19, 36, 41–58, 68, 75, 80, 85, 99, 325–326
EP-3 incident, 237, 248–253, 330

Federal Bureau of Investigation (FBI), 106, 250
First Island Chain, 16, 333
Ford, Gerald, 19, 125–139, 143, 154, 158, 175–177, 206, 327–328
Formosa Resolution, 4, 41–49, 71, 117
Freedom of navigation, 261–263, 271–273, 288, 311

G-20. See Group of 20
Gorbachev, Mikhail, 18, 189, 195, 199, 208
Great Leap Forward, 277
Group of 20 (G-20), 257, 261–262, 282–286, 309
Guidelines for National Unification, 6–7, 238
Gulf War, 208–210, 329

Haig, Alexander, 172–178, 180–189, 329
Hands-off policy, 31, 37, 325
Harriman, W. Averell, 64, 67, 70–74, 99
Hu Jintao, 8, 247, 257–258, 262

ICBM. *See* Intercontinental ballistic missile
Indo-Pacific, 15, 277, 287–294, 309–311, 331, 335
Intellectual property rights (IPR), 282–283
Intercontinental ballistic missile (ICBM), 96, 291
Intermediate-Range Nuclear Forces Treaty, 188–189
IPR. *See* Intellectual property rights

JCS. *See* Joint Chiefs of Staff
Johnson, Lyndon, 19, 85–100, 325–327

Joint Chiefs of Staff (JCS), 29–30, 42, 85, 115–117, 121, 132, 145, 158, 176, 229, 267, 301

Kelly, James, 241, 245
Kennan, George, 34–35
Kennedy, John F., 19, 58, 63–80, 85, 88–89, 99, 111, 325–326
Kerry, John, 244, 265, 272
Khrushchev, Nikita, 77–80, 97–100, 138, 326
Kim Il Sung, 36–37
Kim, Jong-un, 291
Kissinger, Henry, 13, 106–120, 125–134, 140, 153, 186, 206, 228, 327
KMT. See Kuomintang
Korean War, 12, 25–37, 42, 64, 70, 77, 94–95, 325, 332
Kuomintang (KMT), 197–199, 241–242, 257–259, 304

Lee, Teng-hui, 6–8, 13–14, 197–198, 215–233, 238–239

MAAG. *See* Military Assistance Advisory Group
Ma Ying-jeou, 8–9, 257–259, 334
MacArthur, Douglas, 29–32, 36
Macmillan, Harold, 79
Mao Tse-tung, 4, 26–28, 33, 36–37, 41–47, 56, 64, 68, 70, 73, 76–80, 85, 88, 94, 97–100, 107, 109, 113, 126–127, 131–134, 137–138, 153, 161, 326
MAP. *See* Military Aid Program
Matsu, 4, 7, 41–42, 44–52, 54–55, 68, 71, 75, 117, 121
McCarthy, Joseph, 11, 305–306, 316, 324, 331, 335
McCarthy, Kevin, 28–31, 72
MFN. *See* Most-Favored Nation
McNamara, Robert, 63, 71, 75–76, 85–88, 91–97
Military Aid Program (MAP), 31, 33, 87
Military Assistance Advisory Group (MAAG), 32–33, 116, 158, 160
Most-Favored Nation (MFN), 147, 207–208
Mutual Defense Treaty, US-ROC, 4, 12–13, 19, 41–43, 67, 108, 110, 128,

370 *Index*

148, 157, 160, 164, 244, 288, 325, 332

National Security Council (NSC), 26–35, 42–47, 50–52, 58, 71–72, 75, 79, 89, 93, 98–99, 108–120, 125–135, 144–147, 151–156, 163, 182–185, 196, 204–206, 211, 217, 222–223, 227–233, 240, 244, 265, 281, 304, 311, 315, 324–328, 331; China Desk, 36, 73, 207, 210; NSC-68, 34–35

National Security Strategy (NSS), 35, 245, 277, 292, 309

NATO. See North Atlantic Treaty Organization

Nehru, Jawaharlal, 78, 80, 326

Nine-Point Proposal, 173–174

Nixon, Richard, 13, 19, 51, 68, 100, 105–120, 125–131, 135–139, 144, 153, 177, 200, 206, 327–328, 332

Nixon Doctrine, 112, 118

North Atlantic Treaty Organization (NATO), 55, 162, 183, 187, 245, 307, 314–315

North Korea, 28, 31, 36–37, 118, 196, 226, 229, 237, 247, 250–253, 261–262, 266, 269, 272–273, 281, 286, 291–294, 311, 325

NSC. See National Security Council

Nuclear weapons, 35, 41, 47–54, 57–58, 70, 74, 76, 80, 86, 91–98, 119, 136, 138, 188–189, 229, 251, 261–262, 266, 272–273, 292–294, 307, 315, 325; Denuclearization, 251, 262, 272, 293, 312; Strategic Arms Limitation Talks (SALT), 129, 136; Strategic Arms Reduction Treaty (START), 188

Obama, Barack, 19, 253, 257–274, 290, 330–231

One China policy, 7–8, 14, 219, 226–227, 239–240, 244–247, 252, 286, 289, 294, 308–312, 317, 323, 331–333

One China, One Taiwan, 90, 106, 127, 228, 233

One Country, Two Systems, 5, 186, 227, 279

Operation Desert Storm, 209–210

Outer Mongolia, 69–70

Pelosi, Nancy, 10, 206–208, 295, 301–303, 316, 324, 331, 335

Pence, Mike, 286–287

People's Liberation Army (PLA), 4, 6, 11, 14, 16, 25, 30, 32, 36–37, 41–58, 64–65, 70–71, 75–78, 85, 88, 91–92, 95, 97, 108, 158, 185–186, 193, 195, 200, 202, 210–211, 219–224, 229–234, 248–249, 252, 260, 264, 269–270, 277–280, 283, 291, 299–206, 313, 316, 323, 328–329, 333–336.

People's Republic of China (PRC), 1, 4, 6, 10, 25–27, 41, 63, 85, 105, 143, 171, 193, 216–217, 238, 257, 277, 290, 299, 323

PRC government organizations: Ministry of Foreign Affairs, 248, 303, 315; Ministry of National Defense, 264; Taiwan Affairs Office, 11, 238, 242, 299, 304, 306, 337; National People's Congress, 5, 8, 173, 195, 242, 280

Perry, William, 224, 227–231

Pivot to Asia, 263–269, 274

Pompeo, Mike, 286–289, 294

Powell, Colin, 245–248, 251

Putin, Vladimir, 314–315

Reagan, Ronald, 13, 19, 137, 171–189, 193, 206, 286, 328–330

Rebalance to Asia, 267

Redline, 8, 309, 336

Rice, Condoleezza, 244–248, 259

ROC constitution, 13, 216, 241

ROC government organizations: Executive Yuan, 198, 222, 259; Legislative Yuan, 9, 259; Ministry of National Defense, 8, 15, 289, 299, 304; Ministry of Foreign Affairs, 110, 222, 304; Mainland Affairs Council, 198, 240, 258–259, 278, 337; National Security Bureau, 222; National Unification Council, 6–7, 238, 247; Straits Exchange Foundation, 6, 198, 216, 224, 258

Rumsfeld, Donald, 129, 133, 245, 248

Rusk, Dean, 33, 35, 63–64, 66, 68, 71–72, 75, 79, 87–91, 94–95, 99

Scowcroft, Brent, 125, 129, 133, 135, 139, 193–194, 200–203, 206, 210–211, 327

Semiconductor, 16, 288, 294, 305, 323, 331, 334; Taiwan Semiconductor Manufacturing Company (TSMC), 305, 334

Senate, 44, 64, 68, 93, 147, 196, 201, 206–208, 218, 227, 261, 265, 271, 336

Senior Review Group (SRG), 118, 133

Seventh Fleet, 12, 25, 28, 31, 33, 36–37, 43, 52–53, 290, 232

Shultz, George, 179–180, 184–189, 329

Sino-Indian border conflict, 28, 80, 98, 100, 326; China-India War, 76, 98, 100; Aksai Chin, 78

Six Assurances, 178–179, 186, 189, 239, 245, 252, 311, 323

Six-party talks, 262–272

South China Sea tension, 11, 16, 237, 248–249, 263–274, 278–279, 288–295, 307, 311–312, 330–331, 335; Nine-dash line, 270–271

Southwest provinces, 85, 88

Soviet Union, 12, 18, 22–37, 70–80, 95–99, 112–113, 120–121, 126–130, 133–139, 144, 151–154, 158, 160–164, 172, 180–191, 185–188, 199–202, 208–211, 228, 310, 325, 328–332

Spy balloon, 309–310, 335

Stalin, Joseph, 37, 76–77, 97–99

Stevenson, Adlai, 64, 69, 72, 79, 89–90

Sunflower Movement, 9, 258–259

Sunnylands Summit, 263–264

Taipei Economic and Cultural Representative Office (TECRO), 217–218, 222–223, 289

Taiwan, 1–19, 25–37, 41–58, 63–76, 79–80, 85–93, 96–100, 105–112, 116–120, 126–129, 131–135, 139–164, 171–186, 189, 193, 197–198, 203–206, 210–211, 215–234, 237–252, 257–273, 277–281, 286–295, 299–317, 323–339

TECRO. See Taipei Economic and Cultural Representative Office

Taiwan independence movement, 8, 10, 153, 280

Taiwan Relations Act (TRA), 13, 143, 147, 164, 172, 178, 222, 239, 244, 247, 290, 308, 311, 317, 328, 332

Taiwan Strait crises: 1954-1955 Taiwan Strait Crisis, 4, 43–57; 1958 Taiwan Strait Crisis, 5, 45–47, 52–58, 73, 325; 1962 Taiwan Strait Crisis, 63, 67, 75, 326; 1995-1996 Taiwan Strait crisis, 19, 215–234; 2022–2023 Taiwan Strait Crises, 10–11, 299–306, 316–317

Tiananmen Square incident, 13, 19, 193–211, 328–329

TRA. See Taiwan Relations Act

Trade war, 267, 274, 281–283, 292

Truman, Harry S., 1, 12, 19, 25–37, 46, 63, 324–327, 332; Truman Doctrine, 34

Trump, Donald, 19, 274, 277–295, 330–331

Tsai Ing-wen, 9–12, 240, 277–279, 286, 290, 299–306, 316, 324, 331, 334

Two Chinas policy, 46–47, 58, 63–65, 90, 106, 110, 127, 150, 172, 225, 228

United Kingdom, 46, 55, 64, 79, 162, 186–187, 335

United Nations, 5, 28, 31, 44, 55, 64, 68–70, 79–80, 85, 108, 177, 193, 197, 217, 228, 244, 261, 271, 273, 293, 312, 326; Successor states plan, policy, 69

US Congress, 4, 6, 26, 30–35, 41, 44, 50, 54, 80, 86, 88, 93–94, 96, 110–112, 117, 125, 137, 143, 147, 151, 160, 164, 173, 178, 183–184, 193–211, 217–218, 225–230, 244, 249, 283, 286–289, 294, 300–303, 324, 328–336

US Forces Japan (USFJ), 293; US-Japan Alliance, 231–232, 292

US Policy of Containment, 33–37, 42, 63, 71–72, 85–86, 93–96, 117, 237

USSR, 98–100, 106–114, 118–121, 132–135, 138, 187, 327

Vance, Cyrus, 18, 139–140, 144–146, 150–161

Vietnam War, 19, 65, 85–86, 88–95, 100, 105–113, 116, 119, 129, 131, 137, 149, 325–327

372 *Index*

Wang Ping-nan, 56, 67, 71–74, 86–87
War on terror, 237, 247, 250–251
Warsaw talks, 4, 56–57, 73–74, 78, 86
Watergate scandal, 111, 125, 129, 327
Weinberger, Caspar, 176, 180–182, 185, 189
World War II, 3, 15, 25, 27–28, 33–36, 136–38, 285, 334
World War III, 27–28

Xi Jinping, 9, 259, 263, 269, 272, 274, 278, 286–287, 294, 299, 301, 305, 315, 323, 331–335

Zhou Enlai, 36, 42, 45, 51–55, 64, 69, 78, 86, 89, 92, 106, 109–113, 119, 126, 128, 131, 153, 267

About the Book

THE UNITED STATES HAS NEVER FORMALLY RECOGNIZED TAIWAN AS A SOVEREIGN state, yet it has provided the country with security assistance since the establishment of the Republic of China (ROC) government there in 1949. What accounts for this equivocal stance? And how is the US leveraging Taiwan against China?

To unpack this complex triangular relationship, Shao-cheng Sun explores the history of US commitments to the ROC since the presidency of Harry S. Truman. His analysis of each successive administration's policymaking reveals the interplay of personal, domestic, and global interests in what has become one of the most precarious situations in world politics today.

Shao-cheng Sun is associate professor of political science at The Citadel.